MAFIA POLITICS

A Riccardo

MAFIA POLITICS

Marco Santoro

polity

First published in 2022 by Polity Press

Polity Press
65 Bridge Street
Cambridge CB2 1UR, UK

Polity Press
101 Station Landing
Suite 300
Medford, MA 02155, USA

ISBN-13: 978-0-7456-7067-6
ISBN-13: 978-0-7456-7068-3(pb)

A catalogue record for this book is available from the British Library.

Library of Congress Control Number: 2021938677

Typeset in 10 on 12pt Sabon
by Fakenham Prepress Solutions, Fakenham, Norfolk NR21 8NL
Printed and bound in Great Britain by CPI Group (UK) Ltd, Croydon

The publisher has used its best endeavours to ensure that the URLs for external websites referred to in this book are correct and active at the time of going to press. However, the publisher has no responsibility for the websites and can make no guarantee that a site will remain live or that the content is or will remain appropriate.

Every effort has been made to trace all copyright holders, but if any have been overlooked the publisher will be pleased to include any necessary credits in any subsequent reprint or edition.

For further information on Polity, visit our website:
politybooks.com

Contents

Acknowledgements

This book has been long in the making. In some form, it started in the late 1980s as an undergraduate thesis (*tesi di laurea*) under the guidance of Lorenzo Ornaghi and the late Gianfranco Miglio at the Catholic University of Milan. My ideas on mafia politics began with their teachings and provocative ideas regarding politics and theory. Moving from political theory to sociology by way of political and institutional history gave me many opportunities to encounter other approaches and meet many people. I would like to remember here the late Cesare Mozzarelli for giving me a sense of what the *métier d'historien* can be, and Marzio Barbagli for showing me what good empirical sociology should be, and what it cannot be.

A book published in Italian in 2007 (*La voce del padrino*, a title which plays with 'His Master's Voice' formula in ways that can work only in Italian) was a first major step in my research on mafia politics, to which this book is indebted for Chapter 6. I would like to thank Gianfranco Morosato and Sandro Mazzadra for making that publication possible.

In the years since then, many colleagues and friends have contributed to further shaping and refining my ideas, as well as offering venues for me to present and discuss them. Obviously, I cannot mention everyone, but here I would like to thank a few of the many who have helped pave the way to the publication of this book.

Thanks to Jeff Alexander for inviting me to the Yale Center for Cultural Sociology in 2008 to present my early ruminations on mafia culture structures, and to Philip Smith for reading and commenting on an early paper presented at a seminar on culture and power organized by Fredrik Engelstadt and Wendy Griswold in a wonderful place on a fiord near Oslo in December 2007. Thanks to Harrison C. White for our discussion with his students on the mafia while briefly visiting

Columbia's Department of Sociology and attending his lessons on language and society in 2008. Thanks to Randall Collins for inviting me to Las Vegas in 2011 to present an early version of the argument developed in this book (under the title of Chapter 7) at the annual Congress of the American Sociological Association, and to George Derluguian for organizing the Presidential Panel on mafias where I tried it out. Thanks to Christian Frankel and Paul du Gay for inviting me to the Copenhagen Business School in that same year to present and discuss an early version of Chapter 6.

Thank you, Cristiana Olcese and Mike Savage, for inviting me to the London School of Economics in 2013 to present my ideas on mafia and aesthetics (to be developed in my next book, hopefully) at a conference and then as a guest in the Sociology Department. Thanks to Nando dalla Chiesa for inviting me many times to the Summer School on organized crime and mafias that he has been directing at the University of Milan, offering a venue to discuss my ideas with colleagues and people from the antimafia movement (who usually disliked them). Last, but not least, thanks to Gisèle Sapiro for welcoming me to the EHESS in Paris in 2015 to present my research on the mafia as an invited scholar, and to Deborah Puccio-Den for discussing it in a dedicated seminar during my stay.

My colleagues at the former Department of Communication, University of Bologna, also deserve thanks for their discussion of a very early presentation of Chapter 5. Thanks to Claudio Paolucci for his support in that early phase. Fabio Dei has been supporting me more recently, also contributing anthropological references and criticism of my argument about the place of the gift in mafia politics.

Among colleagues and friends who read and commented on early versions of my argument from a scholarly perspective alien to mafia studies, I recall with pleasure Peter Bearman, Johan Heilbron, George Steinmetz and Alessandro Duranti. The late Alessandro Pizzorno was an insightful commentator of some early writings and an inspiring presence while writing this whole book.

Roberta Sassatelli, Monica Sassatelli and Jasper Chalcraft helped develop the book proposal and put it into good English. Thank you for your help.

Umberto Santino and Anna Puglisi of the Centro Siciliano di Documentazione Giuseppe Impastato made my Palermo trips stimulating and productive. Researchers on the mafia will be ever grateful to you. Cirus Rinaldi and Giovanni Frazzica also contributed to my enjoyment of that strange city during my time there. Thanks to Barbara Grüning for helping with any German translations that came up and for giving me a sense of Italian and even mafia life in comparison with

German social life, especially in the DDR. Federica Cabras made me aware of the Nigerian mafia and what young scholars can do while studying young victims of that kind of mafia. Federica Timeto helped me to better understand Sicily and Sicilians, while generously hosting me in Palermo with her cats, showing me films, books, pictures, places and much else. Marco Solaroli and Matteo Gerli helped as research assistants in many professional and friendly ways.

The list of colleagues deserving mention would be too long, but I want to specifically recall here the following: Raimondo Catanzaro, Umberto Santino, Nando dalla Chiesa, Alberto Vannucci, Monica Massari, Maurizio Catino, Federico Varese (who also read and commented on Chapter 3: thank you, Federico!), Felia Allum, Filippo Sabetti, Rocco Sciarrone, Alessandra Dino, Lucia Michelutti, Damiano Palano, Filippo Barbera. Barbara Carnevali deserves a special mention for reading and supporting an early statement of Chapter 2's ontological argument. I haven't been so generous with her symmetrical requests of reading, and for this I'm still apologizing.

I would thank Diego Gambetta whose work on the mafia I discovered while writing my undergraduate thesis and attending a seminar he gave in Milan in 1987. His harsh reaction to a critical note of mine published a few years later indirectly fostered my research on the mafia to this day (an exemplary case of unintentional effects of intentional actions, I would say).

Thanks to Richard Burket for your precious and professional help in making my English correct and more readable and much shorter, and to Jonathan Skerrett at Polity for patiently awaiting my chapters over all these years, offering suggestions and encouragement: I'm sure I would never have finished without your gentle but determined spurs.

In the many years I have been working on this book (very slowly at the beginning and then quickly in the last two years), my personal life has been animated by many changes and challenges. Thank you, Roberta, with whom this book project started (as did many other projects, including the biggest one): without you I doubt I would ever have thought about it. Thank you, Federica, for giving me the pathos, flavour, generosity and love of your detested Sicily, as well as a clear idea of what feminism and anti-speciesism may be in sentimental affairs. The Minotaur is still with me! Thank you, Federica, for your critical but passionate approach to mafia studies, your very special antimafia militancy, and your attitude towards life. Battiato has gone, but I always remember you with deep affection. Thank you, Barbara: you have been so close to me so many times and in so many ways in all these years that no words can do justice. Finally, thank you, Chiara: your grace and love is a wonderful 'free' gift (it does exist, indeed!). Time will tell us where *le vent nous portera*.

My son has been a source of joy and personal growth in all these years. I dedicate this book to you, Riccardo. *Grazie per sopportare un padre che ti tormenta da quando avevi nove anni per farti vedere* Salvatore Giuliano. *Ancora non sono riuscito a convincerti. Un giorno lo guarderemo insieme, ne sono certo.*

Opening epigraph from: *Becoming Deviant*, David Matza, Copyright 1969, Prentice-Hall. Reproduced by permission of Taylor & Francis Group.

Epigraph to chapter 3, reproduced with permission, is © 2008 by the University of Klagenfurt, Karl Popper Library.

Epigraph to chapter 5 is reproduced, with permission, from *The British Journal of Sociology* © 1957 London School of Economics.

Among their most notable accomplishments, the criminological positivists succeeded in what would seem the impossible. They separated the study of crime from the workings and theory of the state.

Matza 1969, 143

Crime is a political phenomenon and must be analyzed accordingly.

Chambliss 1989, 204

Preface

The political philosophers who taught me a generation ago were quite clear that whatever was to be called 'political' must have something to do with the State: if phrases like 'University politics' or 'Church politics' were used, then they meant that these institutions were playing a part in State politics: otherwise the phrases were simply metaphors. But political structures can be recognized at all levels and in all kinds of activities and can, when appropriate, be compared with one another.

Bailey 2001 [1969], 12

Unlike Frederick Bailey, the political theorists who taught me (in the early 1980s in Italy) were well aware that politics can have a life of its own, quite distinct from the 'state'. Moving from ideas originally proposed by scholars such as Gaetano Mosca, Vilfredo Pareto, Max Weber and Carl Schmitt, and apparently, though not often explicitly, backed by scientists operating in the life sciences (e.g., Wilson 1975; de Waal 2007 [1982]), they were not afraid to recognize 'political structures ... at all levels and in all kinds of activities' (to follow the words of Bailey). The so-called 'mafia' could easily fit these ideas. In the case of Mosca, this fitness was probably not incidental. As a Sicilian, Mosca was well aware of the limits of the state in monopolizing politics, even though, as a liberal scholar educated in law and committed to national unity, this awareness was not something he could so explicitly and publicly extend to the mafia. In fact, Mosca wrote intensively about the mafia, but never explicitly about it being a 'political structure'. Weber came closer to this vision, referring to the camorra and the mafia as cases of 'intermittent financing of political groups' (1978 [1922], 195) – but it is far from clear whether he considered camorra and mafia as political groups in themselves or as channels for financing more established and acknowledged political groups. Schmitt never wrote a line about the mafia, but his seminal and much debated 'concept of the political' is capable of accommodating almost anything that might generate a certain degree of intensity in the relations among friends and enemies – a suggestion that could inspire a whole research programme about all those 'social unities' that are commonly labelled as 'criminal organizations', including not only mafias but also terrorist groups and even hybrid formations claiming to be states, such as ISIS.

None of these research lines has been systematically pursued in mafia studies – a few attempts moving along these lines notwithstanding (e.g., Sabetti 1984; Calise 1988; Catanzaro 1992 [1988]; Santino 1994; Schneider and Schneider 2004; Collins 2011). In mafia studies, the assumption of an almost perfect and normatively backed equivalence between 'state' and politics has been dominant, and only rarely called into question. It is as if social scientists, when studying mafias, tend to believe in states and their claims much more than when they are studying states as such. In some way, this may be considered an indication of the success of criminology, the discipline that, in the words of an influential sociologist of deviance, 'has managed the astonishing feat of separating the study of crime from the contemplation of the state' (Cohen 1996, 4). Suspended between the mafia and the state, mafia scholars have little doubt about where to go. If mafia has to do with politics, says the common wisdom, this is only because it also has to do with the state – as an object of law enforcement and a potentially disruptive force within the state (with mafia being responsible for criminal activities such as corruption, collusion and even violence against representatives of the state). Mafias may at best have 'policies', but not 'politics' – because 'politics' is another thing. Or better: *should be* another thing.

The sense in which politics is intended in this book is rather different. Following a few established, albeit marginalized in mafia studies, traditions in political philosophy and anthropology (e.g., Leach 1954; Bailey 1971, 2001 [1969]; Geertz 1963; Freund 1965; Swartz et al. 1966; Swartz 1969; Thompson 1975; Scott 1985; Derrida 1988; Masters 1989; Rancière 1998), politics is here conceived of as different from the 'state'. The concept of politics is wider than the concept of the state, and politics as a sphere of human action is larger than what the state, as a historically grounded institution, comprises. Politics exists before, besides and beyond the state. It is probably true that the state is the main protagonist in the political life of modern times, even though there are clues that this is not always the case and that states are losing their authority, and that other forms of political organization do exist beside, behind and sometimes within the state (e.g., Skalnik 2004). But the state has never, in fact, managed to exhaust the sphere of politics. Thinking of 'mafia politics', both meanings of politics suggested by Bailey should therefore be included: that is, we should consider mafia as both an institution playing a part in state politics and as a political structure on its own, independently from any assumptions we may have about the 'state'. As the first meaning is better known, the main focus of this book is on the second meaning.

There are a few expressions in contemporary research that resonate with 'mafia politics', the term I have chosen for the title of this book. The first that comes to mind is possibly Achille Mbembe's (2003) notion of 'necropolitics'. For Mbembe, the creation of the state's Other as a permanent enemy to be killed, and the consequent management and disposition of dead (and disappeared) bodies under state auspices, illustrates the 'necropolitics' at the heart of contemporary governance. Mbembe (2003, 13) explicitly opposes this politics to mainstream political theorists' notions of liberal democracies based on the collective agreements of self-aware, autonomous citizens. This approach could help us get at what Veena Das and Deborah Poole (2004, 6) have referred to as 'the secret life of the state' existing behind the official rhetoric of centralized bureaucratic rationality and the rule of law. Undoubtedly, mafia pertains to a zone of social life where the dead are very present – and not only mass media but also art photography on the mafia has directed their focus precisely to this area.

However, for all its fascination and cognitive appeal, the notion of 'necropolitics' covers only one region, and probably not the largest, of what I mean by 'mafia politics', lacking not only any precise institutional reference, but missing the specific link to the protection of life that is at the core of mafia politics – and not bare life (as Agamben would call it, the simple life of those who are struggling for survival) but political life, as *bios* (Agamben 1998). In this sense, 'mafia politics' could be closer to another proposed term, 'gastro-politics' (Appadurai 1981), insofar as it would direct our attention to the ways in which politics works as a vital resource, grounded in human appetites and longing for a safe existence. 'By gastro-politics', wrote Appadurai, 'I mean conflict or competition over specific cultural or economic resources as it emerges in social transactions around food. In this sense, gastro-politics is a common feature of many cultures' (1981, 495). Clearly, also in this case, the focus is more on materiality, albeit semiotically dense, than on social relationships and their management. Mafia politics is radically about the latter.[1]

Research on the mafia is very insidious – because 'mafia' is an insidious reality. It is something that exists, so it is a reality: this book never claims the contrary. But the reality of this 'reality' is a complex one: it is multilayered, multivocal, with blurred boundaries with respect to other social realities. This is not uncommon in research on 'social things' (e.g., Lemert 1997). In the case of the mafia, however, this is the absolutely normal situation: everything can be read differently, everything could be an object of discussion, everything seems to change according to the perspective from which it is seen. Not surprisingly, the mafia may be as difficult to study as the state – and I would like to recall here the words of Philip Abrams:

> We have come to take the state for granted as an object of political practice and political analysis while remaining quite spectacularly unclear as to what the state is ... the state, conceived of as a substantial entity separate from society has proved a remarkably elusive object of analysis ... the difficulty of studying the state can be seen as in part a result of the nature of the state, but in an equally large part must be seen as a result of the predispositions of its students. (1988, 59, 61–2)

The difficulties in studying the state are nowhere more evident than when dealing with crime. The nexus of state and crime is far from exceptional. The very existence of crime and criminals is obviously a matter of state authority and state laws (e.g., Briquet and Favarel–Garrigues 2010). But the links between crime and state are not limited to official penalties, courts, police, prisons and the like. It seems there are strong tendencies for states to engage directly in criminal activities or to enter the world of crime *in spite* of itself, or at least of its official claims. You do not need to look to the distant past or very far away to see these tendencies at work. In the Middle East, organizations such as Hezbollah in Lebanon and the Islamic State in Syria and Iraq provide local governance while participating in a range of offshore illicit activities and organizing terrorist activities (e.g., Haidar 2019). Armed groups in Afghanistan, Colombia and Mali have been engaged in drug trafficking, often with the connivance, if not outright participation, of state agencies (e.g., McCoy 2003). In Somalia, organized piracy emerged a decade ago as a central factor in the country's political economy – and its complex politics and long-running civil war (Shortland and Varese 2016). In the Sahel and North Africa, militant, terrorist and militia fortunes have been tied to dynamics in organized hostage markets and in drug, oil and cigarette smuggling. In Central Africa, the traffic in diamonds and wildlife is well established (Bayart et al. 1999). In the Balkans and Turkey, cigarette smuggling, organ trafficking, human trafficking and trade in stolen cars have all been factors in the region's recent past and post-war politics (cf. Cockayne 2016; see also Chambliss 1989; Heyman 1999; Nordstrom 2007; Wilson 2009; Chambliss et al. 2010).

To investigate the political nature of mafias is strategic to answering a question many people are asking nowadays: how is the convergence between mafias and states, which is happening in every corner of the world right before our eyes, possible? How can it be that risks of 'mafia states' are emerging worldwide? The answer given in this book is simple: because mafias and states share exactly the same nature, because they are two institutional forms of political life, because even if they are almost opposites, they are arranged in such a way as to make one the perfect counterpart of the other. Like *yin* and *yang*, they are mutually reinforcing and complementary.

This book has been a long time in the making. In a way, it started as a *tesi di laurea* (Master's thesis) in 1988 in political science, which developed into a book twenty years later (Santoro 2007). In the meantime, I have worked on many other topics – such as the social history of legal professions, the sociology of artistic production and cultural consecration, the social theory of Pierre Bourdieu, the Chicago School of sociology, the international circulation of ideas – all of which have helped me to refine my vision of the mafia by exposing me to literature that is not typically used by mafia scholars. The 2007 book is the most immediate antecedent to this one – the latter sharing some arguments of the former but adding many new insights mainly drawn from research programmes I was not aware of back then (in part because they were not yet available), such as the debate on Southern Theory and alternative traditions in social theory (Reed-Danahay 1995; Alatas 2006a, 2014; Connell 2007; Patel 2010; Comaroff and Comaroff 2012) and the new historiography of the state (Ruggie 1993; Spruyt 1994; Thompson 1994; see also van der Pijl 2007).

In its main thesis, this book joins a series of other books that are contributing from different perspectives and intellectual traditions to develop what I would call a *political theory of the mafia* – something nobody yet seems ready to openly propose as such, but whose seeds have been sown in the past few decades by many scholars, including two giants in the historical social sciences: Eric Hobsbawm (1959) and Charles Tilly (1985). What a (sociologically grounded and historically sensitive) political theory of the mafia might look like is the question that inspired and drove the writing of this book.

1
Mafia, Politics and Social Theory: An Introduction

Throughout the history of the human race no land and no people have suffered so terribly from slavery, from foreign conquests and oppressions, and none have struggled so irrepressibly for emancipation as Sicily and the Sicilians. Almost from the time when Polyphemus promenaded around Etna, or when Ceres taught the Siculi the culture of grain, to our day, Sicily has been the theater of uninterrupted invasions and wars, and of unflinching resistance. The Sicilians are a mixture of almost all southern and northern races; first, of the aboriginal Sicanians, with Phoenicians, Carthaginians, Greeks, and slaves from all regions under heaven, imported into the island by traffic or war; and then of Arabs, Normans, and Italians. The Sicilians, in all these transformations and modifications, have battled, and still battle, for their freedom.

Marx 1860

The Argument

This book aims to offer a fresh perspective on mafias which, in many ways, is an alternative to what nowadays constitutes the mainstream in this research field. Taking the Sicilian case as its main reference point, the book develops the idea that what mafiosi do is better understood if framed not as '(organized) crime', nor as 'business' or 'economy', as a widespread scholarly wisdom maintains,[1] but as 'politics'. Like feudalism, the city-state or the empire, what we call 'mafia' identifies first and foremost a way of organizing and managing human relationships among people who mutually recognize themselves as participants in the same collective identity: political relationships, in other words. This view resonates with, and qualifies, the description of mafia set forth by a renowned insider, Bill Bonanno, the son of Cosa Nostra godfather Joseph 'Joe' Bonanno: '[Mafia] is in the way one person connects to another. Mafioso is, first and last, about the nature of relationships' (Bonanno 1999, xv).

That mafiosi *also* perform some politically relevant functions – e.g., they provide votes to politicians – is well known, but this book goes well beyond this simple and well-documented fact. It argues that the mafia *is inherently a political institution, which may perform a number of different functions (as political parties do, for instance), but is especially well suited to performing political ones because the nature of social relationships in mafia life is eminently political.*

To be sure, the mafia may be even more than politics: as this book maintains from the start, what we call 'mafia' is really a total social fact (as Marcel Mauss would say) wherein politics, economics, religion, sexuality, morality and many other social things converge and coexist. The book acknowledges this complexity but chooses to analytically emphasize the political side of this totality because of its centrality to the whole architecture. Politics is the pillar of that 'total social fact' called mafia. Seen from the vantage point of politics, it is argued, the mafia may be better captured in its genesis, its inner working mechanisms and its reproductive/expansive power.

Of course, how we conceive of 'politics' is essential to consider. If we narrowly define politics as the sphere of the (liberal, constitutional, maybe also democratic) state, the mafia falls out of this realm, by definition. It can thus be easily relegated to other – presumably less noble and less legitimate – institutional fields, such as economics, business and, obviously, crime. But if we adopt a wider and more historically sound concept of politics, and accept that there have been, and still are, various ways of organizing political life, including ways that have been and still are framed as 'crime' by the (liberal, constitutional, maybe also democratic) state, then a whole research field opens itself up to our investigations. That is the move made by this book, which could also be read as a book on politics and the ways of conceiving it in contemporary sociological terms.

But mafia is not simply 'politics' at large (as it is not simply 'business', even for those observers and scholars who adopt an economic perspective). If politics is, indeed, a very general category, mafia exhibits the features of only a *certain kind* of politics: more precisely, it accounts for a certain *mode of political organization*. The latter is at the centre of the book, which develops what I would call *a political theory of the mafia*, modelling the political aspect of mafia's social totality, and putting it centre stage. A major claim of the book is that this political mode is deeply rooted in a popular reinterpretation of an ancient and diffused aristocratic culture[2] and should be conceived as a mode of political expression of historically subaltern groups in their quest for status and power.

Put in other terms: I suggest that what we call 'mafia' could be conceived of as a sort of popular or folk politics that has gained some degree of local and even translocal hegemony by innovatively drawing on cultural models which are firmly opposed to bourgeois ones – ranging from aristocratic to subaltern modes of cultural expression. 'Mafia' is what may happen to 'hidden transcripts', James C. Scott's (1990) famous formula for capturing subaltern *infrapolitics*,[3] when their bearers become locally dominant while refusing to culturally transform into a fully-fledged dominant class imbued with bourgeois, middle-class values, i.e. the values at the core of the contemporary global social world. The warrior ethos of the old aristocratic classes (in Sicily, the baronial culture; in Japan, the samurai ethos) is the cultural horizon of mafiosi – not the spirit of capitalism, not a bourgeois civic culture (see Elias 1982 [1969]; on the samurai ethos, see Ikegami 1997; on the Sicilian *baroni*, see Pontieri 1943; Marino 1964). Instead of challenging the old hierarchies and eventually creating new ones – which is the aim of 'progressive' subaltern groups, according to modernist and socialist visions of politics – mafiosi have worked, and still work, hard in order to 'achieve a superior rank while making no objection to the persistence of a hierarchical order' (Gould 2003, 164). Out of utopia, and in purely analytical terms, there is no special reason to prefer the first ('progressive') option to the second (call it 'conservative'). This analytical distinction is a crucial point for understanding the mafia in sociological terms – a distinction this book maintains in order to develop a non-normative, non-statist, and alternative understanding of the mafia as a global form.

At risk of being repetitive, a warning is necessary at this point in order to prevent possible objections and even misunderstandings – and the book elaborates on this, as it is a crucial theoretical element of the whole argument. Contrary to what our received wisdom might suggest, to say that *mafia is of a political nature* is not the same as advancing an equation between the mafia and the state – a common stance in the past, especially among lawyers and jurists. Indeed, this book argues that the mafia is very different from the state, even if they can both be placed in the sphere of politics. But the state, as a historical institution, has not monopolized politics, and politics may be organized in many other ways (see Masters 1989; Poggi 1991; Schmitt 1996 [1932]). To be sure, the equation of mafia with the state has been strongly criticized by many scholars in recent decades, including the promoters and supporters of an economic theory of the mafia who conceive of it as an industry for private protection. This book maintains that they are right in saying that the mafia is different from the state, but that they go too far when they infer from this that the mafia is 'a specific economic enterprise' (Gambetta 1993, 1).

Mafia may be an enterprise, but it is far from patently obvious that it is an *economic* enterprise. It is one thing to say that mafiosi 'produce and promote' something like protection, but it is quite another to say that they also *sell* what they produce and promote. Production is such a general category of social life that anything humans do can be subsumed under this rubric: from culture to deviance to space. Promotion is a communicative function that can work in any setting, from industry to social movements to family. On the contrary, selling is a much more specific activity, which presumes the existence of a market and the working of a commoditization process – something that has only occurred in certain places and times, and with reference to certain goods (e.g., Sassatelli 2007). As I will show, mafiosi do not sell; they simply give their 'help', they offer their 'support', while ritually emphasizing their disinterest; characteristically, they make gifts. And a gift is a totally different thing from a commodity (Mauss 1990 [1925]; Bourdieu 1980, 1996 [1992], 2017; Gregory 1982; Godbout and Caillé 1998; Godelier 1999; Silber 2009; Liebersohn 2011; Caillé 2020).

To insist that 'mafia' is not to be mistaken for the state does not mean that the state is irrelevant for the understanding of mafia. As the currently dominant, most legitimate mode of political organization worldwide, the (modern, originally European) state is clearly the necessary reference point for any understanding of the mafia – be this framed in political terms, as suggested here, or in criminological and/or economic terms, as maintained by current scholarship. What is crime and what belongs to economics instead of politics is contingent upon the state and its workings. A close look at the state as a historically grounded political institution should therefore be pivotal in any serious analysis of the mafia. However, this is an intellectual gambit that current scholarship on mafia rarely makes, preferring to move from implicit and normative ideas of the state. The consequence is that, even in the best literature, a *sociology of the mafia* is contrasted with a *philosophy of the state* – leaving the state, as it were, in the heaven of pure ideals and forms while firmly locating the mafia in the dirty, material ground. The absence of the state was normal in the social sciences in the 1950s to 1970s – the same period in which mafia studies developed (e.g., Hobsbawm 1959; Hess 1970; Schneider and Schneider 1976; Arlacchi 1983a; for partial exceptions, see Blok 1974; Sabetti 1984). It is less acceptable in current scholarship, after the 'return of the state' occurred in the 1980s (e.g., Almond 1988; Spruyt 2002). We could say that, in mafia studies, the state still needs to be brought back in (Evans et al. 2010 [1985]).

This book aims to facilitate this move, and argues for the adoption of a heuristic symmetry in the study of the mafia.[4] What new light could be shed on the mafia if we put aside the normative claims of the (European, liberal, modern) state and look at both the mafia *and* the state in truly sociological, i.e. empirically disenchanted, terms? What new light could be shed on the mafia if we put the state, with its normative claims, in brackets and problematize our hopes for the advent of a never fully gained 'modernity'? What light could we shed on the mafia if we consider the idea that politics includes the voices and actions of subalterns (Guha 1999 [1983]; Rancière 1998; Scott 1985, 1990), and accept that people coming from the subaltern classes may become dominant in certain conditions – not necessarily backed by the state's laws and codes – while remaining faithful to their social and cultural background?

These are the questions from which this book springs. In replying, it argues that what we name 'mafia' may be conceived of as a special mode of political organization whose institutional logic can be identified through a comparison with other (equally historical) modes – such as the (territorial, sovereign, and originally European) state, the city-state, the city-league, various patrimonial forms of administration, and more primitive forms of political organization such as the chiefdom. While identifiable with none of those, the mafia draws elements, techniques and mechanisms from many of them, in an institutional synthesis that may really be considered as a masterwork of (collective and individual) social engineering.

The words 'mafia' and 'mafiosi'

The origins of the name 'mafia' remain rather obscure. A number of hypotheses exist, some of them more persuasive than others. The confusion started in the very early days after Italian unification (1861), when suggestions about the original meaning and the linguistic roots of the word made their first appearance. Strange as it may seem, no written evidence of the word exists before Italian unification; indeed, dictionaries of the time did not hesitate to attribute the matrix of the name to northern Italian dialect – be it the Piedmontese or the Tuscan vernacular. At least on this point some agreement has been reached relatively quickly: no one would object anymore to the fact that 'mafia' is a Sicilian word that existed well before Italian unification – even if how much before is far from clear, given that the etymological roots of the word are not clear. The first documented occurrence of the term dates back to 1865, when the word was evoked in an official, but not public, report by a Piedmontese officer to account for everything against the new government that could be said to exist in Sicily – including anarchists and socialists. The first authoritative testimony about the word and its social uses in common speech dates back to 1889. According to the influential Sicilian folklorist Giuseppe Pitrè (1841–1916), the adjective *mafiusu* (in Italian translated as 'mafioso') was in use in his Palermo neighbourhood when he was a child, with the meaning of 'cute', 'smart', 'well done' (Pitrè 1889, 2008). No immediate connection with crime existed at the time, according to this authoritative source. In fact, the source of the association with the criminal world of what was previously a word with aesthetic and maybe ethical connotations was a literary invention. In the early 1860s, a drama was written and performed in Palermo with the title of *I mafiusi di la Vicaria*, set in a prison (Vicaria was the traditional name of the prison building in Palermo) with a few prisoners as characters. This was a story of prison life and eventual redemption, in which a sort of local boss, after years spent in prison acting as the 'provider of social order', found a new civic consciousness once free. Originally staged in 1863 and performed in Sicilian theatres throughout that decade, the drama had some relevant success in the 1880s, even being represented in theatres in Rome. In sum, an event in the ongoing national public sphere was at the origin of an association – that of the name 'mafia' with a certain social phenomenology linked to the world of prisons and gangs – which would know further success in subsequent decades. With the massive Italian migration to the US, the word 'mafia' reached the other shores of the Atlantic, thereby starting its international circulation – a phenomenon we are still witnessing today.

Two points need some further clarification. First, if not the name, then the social reality to which the name refers pre-existed the arrival of the Piedmontese army. References to a social phenomenology appearing similar to what was subsequently intended with the term 'mafia' without being named as such date back to at least 1838: not exactly prisons and gangs, but 'fraternities' and 'sects' operating as 'small Governments inside the Government' (see Pontieri 1945, 190–1). Second, regarding the etymology, the most accredited argument among an array of many is that mafia's roots are in the Arabic language – Arabic being the idiom of the conquerors of the island in the High Middle Ages – and Arabic is a strong matrix of many Sicilian dialectal words still current today (Arab influences are still visible today in other cultural forms, such as regional Sicilian cuisine and some local artistic expressions, like folk music). Possibly, the most sociologically interesting hypothesis about etymology sees the name 'mafia' derived from the Arabic *mu'afa* which means 'safety and protection'. Certainly, it is the most acceptable also because of the theoretical understanding of protection as one crucial objective of mafiosi activities, if not their core activity. What mafiosi do, says the sociological current common wisdom, is provide protection to people and things. While made famous and analytically elaborated by Gambetta (1993), this association with protection is widespread in the literature on the mafia, at least since the beginning of the twentieth century. Interestingly, protection is far from a special activity of mafiosi: indeed, protection is exactly what any political institution and leader would claim to provide, according to a well-established line of thought dating back to Greek political theory, and with Thomas Hobbes as its modern champion. As 'protection' is what mafia deals with, it is worth investigating what protection is and what its provision entails – something we will do in the next chapter.

There is a last hypothesis, authoritatively advanced by the Italian linguist Mario Alinei, a major scholar of Indo-European languages, who sees in the word 'mafia' a derivation from the Osco-Umbrian (ancient pre-Latin italic language) *(a)mafla*, whose meaning is 'comparable' to the Latin *amicitia* (friendship) with an immediate reference to the meaning of 'political friendship', i.e. alliance, which for Alinei may account for the positive meanings attached to the word 'mafia' in Sicily and in the *Mezzogiorno*.

Source: Novacco 1959; Hess 1970; Lo Monaco 1990; Patella 2002; Alinei 2007.

The Setting (The Case Study)

The Sicilian mafia is the main empirical focus of this book, on the assumption that, while not exhausting the phenomenon, this regional and historical case has a sort of ontological primacy – at the very least for giving the name to the category. However, in developing and testing its arguments, the book makes comparative references to other mafias as well, especially the American *Cosa Nostra* (strongly linked to the Sicilian mafia), the Neapolitan *camorra*, the Calabria-based *'ndrangheta*, the Russian *mafiya*, the Japanese *yakuza* and the Chinese *triads*. An unusual comparative attention is also devoted to a still relatively understudied instance of mafia, the Indian mafia (Ghosh 1991; Michelutti et al. 2018). It is one of the strategic moves of the book to compare cases of mafia life in geographically and culturally distant locations that may have some commonalities in their political histories. What makes India an interesting comparative case for a study of mafia focused on the Sicilian case is its colonial past under the British.

Suffice it to say that, over ten centuries, Sicily was conquered and ruled by such different peoples as Muslim Saracens, Normans, the French, Aragones, the Spanish and, finally, (northern) Italians. After unification, Sicily accounted for a large portion of the Italian emigration towards the United States, Latin America and Africa. Emigration means not only exit and loss, but also gaining new ideas and institutions through transnational circuits, mimicry and imitation. The American experience is an integral part of the Sicilian mafia's current repertoire – a pattern that works also for other Italian mafias. But the same could be said for other experiences of contact and interchange as well. Muslim domination lasted two centuries, leaving a deep cultural heritage that is still visible in folklore, language, art and gastronomy (Britt 2007; Dalli 2008). In the twelfth century, Sicily was the site of one of the very first experiments in state-building in the world (under the Normans, who introduced feudalism to the island), before becoming a sought-after colony of grand foreign powers like the rising French monarchy, the Habsburg Empire and then the Bourbons, who dominated in Spain and Italy from the sixteenth century well into the nineteenth. Sicily's status changed many times; sometimes it was a totally dependent colony (not only under foreign powers in Paris or Madrid, but also under Italian continental cities like Naples), at other times it was a semi-autonomous regional state. When the mafia was first 'discovered' – something which occurred in the 1830s – Sicily was still a dominated country in the Mediterranean Sea, at the extreme southern periphery of Europe, very close to Africa, and longing for its independence, or at least some degree of political autonomy (Abulafia 1977, 1987; Bresc and Bresc-Bautier 1993; Takayama 2019).

While never formally a colony, for centuries Sicily had been under the dominion of some other, often foreign, political centre. The famous Sicilian Vespers (1282) epitomises the strong tensions this situation of subjection could generate. After Spanish domination, which lasted for more than two centuries (see Benigno 2007), a British protectorate was established in 1806 continuing until 1816 – a short period, but also a very productive one (Simon 2021). In those few years, in fact, a series of reforms changed the political and institutional structure of the island – including the definitive demise of feudalism and experimentation with a liberal constitution and parliamentary monarchy (Mack Smith 1968). The first half of the nineteenth century was a period of intense mobilization, and insurgences occurred in 1820, 1838, 1848 and 1866 (Nicotri 1934). Even after Italian unification (1861), Sicily was periodically the site and target of political projects of separation from the Italian national state, seen by many Sicilians as a colonial power. In 1943, the Sicilian separatist movement gained new force and, with the aid, it seems, of organized banditry (for the occasion promoted to the status of a newly formed Sicilian army) and the mafia, produced the most impressive moment of crisis in national identity since unification (Marino 1979). The granting of regional autonomy to Sicily after the Second World War was mainly an institutional response from the national centre to this deep and dangerous local quest for independence. In brief, we could say that the Sicilian mafia evolved in a context of semi-colonial dependence periodically marked by violent popular insurgencies against foreign dominators. The aforementioned alliance of mafia with political separatism was hardly occasional. We can say that no event of political mobilization in the modern history of Sicily, at least since the 1830s, has taken place without the active presence of the mafia and mafiosi. This presence is just the tip of the iceberg of the political role played by the mafia in Sicily, and, from this basis, in other parts of the globe.

The decades that predated the discovery of the (Sicilian) mafia were the same in which a relatively new institutional form, the sovereign territorial state, was expanding its hegemony from specific regions of central Europe, such as England and France (and to a lesser degree Prussia), where it was first elaborated, to the rest of Europe, including Sicily. Historically, both France and England had important vested interests in the Mediterranean island: France in the thirteenth century (the period of the Vespers), England (the other island where the Normans dominated and had started the institutional experiments which strongly contributed to the early emergence of the state: see Strayer 1970) until the early nineteenth century, during and after the Napoleonic wars, when Sicily was under the protection of the United Kingdom.

The multilayered political and social history of Sicily, from the Middle Ages to national unification under the Kingdom of Italy (1861) and beyond, accounts for the institutional synthesis that the name 'mafia' has the power to evoke. It is a claim of this book that understanding the Sicilian mafia means accounting for its social and institutional genesis in this complex and long-lasting web of influences and interests impinging upon Sicily since the Middle Ages (see Greif 2006 for a discussion about the lasting influence of medieval institutions). The rise of the mafia is just another aspect of the history of the conflict between the state and other political forms – such as city-states, empires, city-empires, as well as more primordial but effective organizations such as clans, families, warrior-leagues and so on – and it is within this history that it has to be embedded. Some elements suggest that the mafia's institutional history may also be embedded in the history of political ideas, including utopian (e.g., socialist and, especially, anarchist) ones. In this respect, even though they are probably exceptional, the stories of Vito Cascio Ferro and Bernardino Verro – respectively, an influential godfather who was a leading local socialist and anarchist in his youth, and a renowned Sicilian trade unionist who was a mafioso in his youth – are enlightening. As a minor point of the book, I emphasize the anarchist moment as the plea for an understanding of the mafia's structure and functions independently from any concession to the state as a political ideal and an institutional model; as I will never be tired of repeating, I want to analyse and assess 'the mafia' from a radically nonstate-centric and, possibly, non-Westernized point of view. This emphasis on anarchism is not only a theoretical move but a return to what I see as one major historical spur to the development of mafias all over the world, including Italy. Contrary to an entrenched belief – including Francis Marion Crawford's claim, which I will cite in the next section – anarchism and the mafia, at least in Sicily and the US, ran parallel for a while. The book also capitalizes on this historical connection to derive a few theoretical implications.

However, the Mediterranean region is a cultural formation on its own (Cassano 2001; Piterberg et al. 2010), and in this historical and geographical juncture we have to locate the historical experience that gave 'mafia' its name, i.e. the Sicilian mafia. This was actually the great insight of Fernand Braudel's 1949 study, *The Mediterranean World*: the idea that it was possible to have a society maintaining itself through the active exchange of goods, people and ideas without a unified 'administrated territory' as we know it in our statist times. This book further develops the idea that Sicily – i.e. the place where something like 'a mafia' was first identified in the 1860s and from which every analysis of the mafia as a social type should start – is located in this Mediterranean world between Europe (i.e. a dominant region of the global North) and Africa, or better, the African shores of the Mediterranean Sea (i.e. an important piece of the global South). It occupies an interstitial location between Europe/civilization and Africa/barbarism (see, e.g., Niceforo 1899). It is worth recalling that, just after political unification, many functionaries and soldiers coming from the northern Italian regions labelled Sicily as 'Africa' (see Schneider 1998; Moe 2002). Indeed, there are also documented connections between mafiosi and Africa at least since the end of the nineteenth century – and in some periods, there was a mafia family based in Tunis. But the relation between the mafia and Muslim Africa goes deeper than this, and has to do with the common roots in the medieval Arab and Muslim domination that produced the word 'mafia' itself – a local popular derivation from Arab terms meaning, not by chance, 'protection, shelter' (see Patella 2002; see also pp. 5–7).

This 'zone of contact' has a culture of its own. Honour is a well-known element of this Mediterranean cultural world (Peristiany 1965; Herzfeld 1987; Peristiany and Pitt-Rivers 1992; Blok 2001; Giordano 2012), on which even Pierre Bourdieu (1977) focused attention in his early experiences as an ethnologist working in Algeria among the Berbers (it must be recalled that the Berbers were among Sicily's rulers in the Middle Ages). Other common features can be listed as well – for instance, a certain conception of justice and of personal loyalties (e.g., Rosen 2002; Cornell 2005). Indeed, we should remember that Sicily was also heavily influenced by Greek culture, as its eastern shores were colonized by the Greeks in the eighth century BC. As shown by van Wees (2001), archaic ancient Greek society and politics had many similarities with the contemporary mafia's culture of violent competition. However, it is a matter of fact that although the Greek influence was strong in the eastern provinces of Sicily, that was not the case in the western provinces, where the mafia developed. In the western provinces of the island, it is the Arabs who left a legacy. Rather than conceiving them just as mere evidence of deeply rooted traditions, I suggest that the similarities between the Sicilian mafia and ancient Greek politics have to do with what, in the last chapter of the book, will be called the 'elementary forms of political life' (see also Posner 1979).

What the Arab, Greek and African elements remind us is that Sicily, and the Sicilian mafia as well, developed in an area where the globalizing world about which we so intensively talk today was already somehow in place (Abu-Lughod 1989). Sicily existed midway between North and South, influenced by European history but geographically, and even ethnologically, closer to the Mediterranean world, to that southern part of Europe which borders on the northern part of Africa. Using concepts elaborated in northern Europe, at the historical core of the global North, or in the US to understand other parts of the world is an example of what a few years ago Susanne Rudolph (2005) termed 'the imperialism of categories' (see also Rudolph and Rudolph 2010). This is also what sociological research on the mafia has typically done, exporting concepts and methods typically rooted in Anglo-American Lockean universal liberalism (sometimes in German neo-Kantian ethical universalism) and applying them to make sense of the mafia's patterns of social life, that is, a totally different historical, geographical and cultural experience. This alternative, southern location and identification is what this book wants to privilege, grounding our understanding of the Sicilian mafia in situated, local knowledge, and connecting the sociological understanding of the mafia to alternative conceptual repertoires, on the one hand, and to contemporary pleas for the rethinking of the social sciences as a world scale affair, on the other (e.g., Chakrabarty 2000; Alatas 2006a; Connell 2007; Patel 2010; Comaroff and Comaroff 2012, 2016). This is the object of the Chapters 4–6 of this book, which offers what I would label a *political anatomy of the (Sicilian) mafia*.

To limit the history of mafia – even of the Sicilian mafia – to the adventures of a single country would in any case mean to surreptitiously accept what has been called methodological nationalism – the methodological assumption that 'a particular nation would provide the constant unit of observation through all historical transformations, the "thing" whose change history was supposed to describe' (Wimmer and Glick Schiller 2002, 305). Problematic in all cases, this assumption is especially troubling in the study of mafias. Wherever and whenever they developed – in the first half of the nineteenth century in southern Italy, at the beginning of the twentieth century in the eastern US, in the eighteenth century in Japan and China, after the collapse of communism in Russia – mafias are indeed part and parcel of a series of overlapping transnational, sociospatial networks of power which embrace large and largely unpredictable areas of the world (Mann 1986a, 1986b; Castells 2000; Collins 2011).

The scope of mafia groups has always been larger than the individual regions from which they take their various names and to which they extend their jurisdiction. In these overlapping networks comprising entire national societies and their borders, imperialistic projects of political control launched from some centre have had to come to terms with locally grounded instances of mobilization and resistance. In many senses, especially when seen from the southern regions of Italy, the same political mobilization that produced Italy as a national state was one of those imperialistic projects launched by a northern centre. The history of the Sicilian mafia runs parallel to that of the national state at least since 1865 – when the term was used for the first time in an official document to identify the troubling local social conditions of resistance to the new government met by functionaries coming from the north of the peninsula. Emerging mafiosi specialized in mediation between local communities and the representatives of the central state. In Sicily, as in other cases, the mafia emerged as a structure of intermediation and communication between variously identifiable centres and their peripheries (Blok 1974; Schneider and Schneider 1976). But mafias inter-acted and communicated also among themselves. While there is good evidence that mafias developed autonomously in more than one centre of diffusion (Sicily, Calabria, Naples, New York, Hong Kong, etc.), there are also clues that imitation and exchanges of items and practices have been common among the various instances. This is particularly clear in the case of the Russian mafia, whose adepts have often imitated Sicilian mafiosi to legitimize their identities and acquire an effective technology of the self (see Varese 2001; Volkov 2002; Gambetta 2009).

At the same time, we should notice that even though mafias have developed in many different parts of the globe, they do not exist every-where, and even in the same country (e.g., the US) not every ethnic group has produced its own mafia. Why mafia develops in some places or among some people and not in others – under the same structural conditions, of course – is something only a culturally sensitive analysis could hope to explain. Using a well-known metaphor (Swidler 1986; see also Tilly 1978, 1995), we could say that the cultural repertoire used by would-be mafiosi has to show some consistency to be recognized as such, and the ingredients for the formation of a mafia-like repertoire of collective and individual practice may not be available everywhere.

This original and constitutive transnational, global scope of mafias explains the subtitle originally imagined for this book: 'a southern view'. It claims that we gain in both sociological understanding and political effectiveness (that is, in our fight against organized crime) if we recognize the mafia as a culturally based expression/form of political organization, variously developed in its plural instances far from the established centres but always in some relationship with them. This form may have run parallel to the development of the state (and the diffusion of capitalism as well), but it is fundamentally different from the modern state (and capitalism) as institutional mode(s) of organizing political (and, respectively, economic) life.

To describe the mafia as 'a state inside the state', a 'shadow state', a 'counterstate', or as 'the dark side of capitalism', a 'deviant form of capitalist entrepreneurship' and, last but not least, as an 'industry' (if this concept is used in its now common economic sense), misses the point, and loses the possibility of capturing the intimate constitution of a phenomenon that normally overcomes the established boundaries of the individual state and does not necessarily follow those of the (transna-tional) capitalist system. *The mafia has an institutional autonomy which is irreducible to both the state and capitalism, two originally European institutions that have largely monopolized the minds of social scientists – including scholars of mafia – since the nineteenth century, and only in the last two decades have they been subjected to detailed criticism with respect to their usefulness and soundness as universal categories of social analysis*. From this angle, the book tries to go beyond the 'imperialism of categories' – the academic practice of imposing concepts on the others, in other words, 'the export of concepts as part of a hegemonic relationship' (Rudolph 2005, 6) – situating knowledge of and on the mafia in a globalizing world and, above all, in a globalizing social theory (Burawoy 2005; Connell 2007; Patel 2010; Comaroff and Comaroff 2012). In this move, the established intellectual centres are resisted and other centres are reclaimed. It is a southern theory of the mafia that this book aims to develop. Figure 1.1 represents the subversive intellectual move the book attempts in a map-like form (from early modern times).

Where Is the 'Politics' in Mafia Politics?

As stated previously, this book argues that in looking for core characteristics of mafia(s), we are better placed if we focus our research on the political sphere, on the realm of political institutions and political

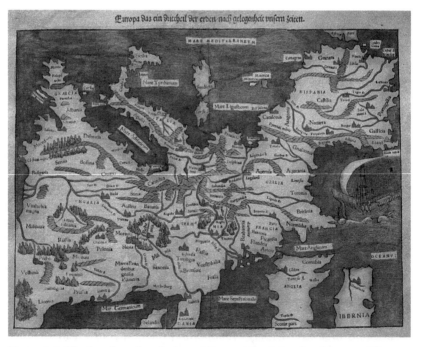

Figure 1.1: The 'modern description of Europe', by Sebastian Münster ('Europa das ein Drittheil der Erden nach Gelegenheit unsern Zeiten', 1578).

life. The main tenet of the book is that 'the political', as a relatively autonomous sphere of action (e.g., Schmitt 1996 [1932]; Freund 1965; Pizzorno 1986; Meier 1990; Mouffe 2005) that is different from 'the economic' or 'the criminal' (whatever this means) as such, is at the heart of the mafia. As *protection* is generally recognized to be one of the central activities – if not *the* central activity – of the political sphere, and the typical object of political obligation (Tilly 1985; Miglio 2011; see also White 2009; Ferris 2011), we may expect to find mafiosi dealing, like active political actors, mostly (albeit not exclusively) with protection. The historical evidence, in fact, says that mafiosi – in Sicily as elsewhere – typically present themselves as protectors, and that protection is possibly the central, though not unique, function they perform, together with mediation and enforcement, functions that in any case are implicated in the provision of protection.

How they deal with this general activity/object is far from clear, however. It is the main task of this book to throw light on this issue, which lies at the core of mafia studies, restoring to *the political meaning of protection* its fullness as both a social function and the content of human obligations (see also Ferris 2011). An emphasis on the political nature of the mafia is not totally unprecedented. We can find seeds and fragments of this vision, albeit often hidden between the lines, in authors as diverse as Max Weber (1978 [1922]), Eric Hobsbawm (1959), Charles Tilly (1974, 1985), Anton Blok (1974), Filippo Sabetti (1984), Raimondo Catanzaro (1992 [1988]), Umberto Santino (1994), Vadim Volkov (2002), Jane and Peter Schneider (2004) and, more recently, Randall Collins (2011). Never either explicitly or openly discussed, the equation between mafia and politics (or political rule) was already apparent in Gaetano Mosca's foundational text on political science (originally published in 1896), as the following excerpt attests:

Psychological and intellectual isolation on the part of the lower classes, as well as too noticeable differences in beliefs and education between the various social classes, give rise to social phenomena that are very interesting to the student of the political sciences, dangerous as they may be to the societies in which they occur. In the first place, as a consequence of their isolation *within the lower classes, another ruling class, or directing minority, necessarily forms,* and often this new class is antagonistic to the class that holds possession of the legal government. When this *class of plebeian leaders is well organized* it may seriously embarrass an Official government. In many Catholic countries the clergy is still the only authority that exerts any moral influence over the peasantry, and the peasants extend to the parish priest all the confidence that they withhold from the government official. In other countries, where the people look upon the public functionary and the nobleman if not exactly as enemies certainly as utter strangers, *the more resolute and aggressive of the plebeians sometimes succeed in organizing widespread and fairly permanent associations, which levy assessments, administer a special justice of their own and have their own hierarchies of officials, their own leaders, their own recognized institutions.* So a real State within the State comes into being, *a government that is clandestine but often more feared, better obeyed, and if not better loved certainly better understood, than the legal government.* (1939 [1896], 116–17; emphasis added)

Never named, the mafia's phenomenology was clearly in the author's mind and local knowledge, having been born in Palermo and politically engaged as a deputy representative of a mandate near Palermo, and well known in mafia chronicles. We can easily infer from this excerpt that Mosca believed the 'social phenomenon' of the mafia was as 'dangerous to the society in which it occurs' as it was 'very interesting to the student of the political sciences'. Indeed, it was a real, true government – 'clandestine' but often 'better obeyed' and even 'better understood': this is how the political sociologist Mosca conceptualized the mafia. However, these intellectual concerns and sociological insights never developed into a comprehensive research programme in his writings (see, e.g., Mosca 1980 [1900]; 1933). Indeed, to find the first clear assertion about the political nature of a mafia-like social phenomenon (called by its name, this time), you have to look not to a strictly academic work, but to an article written and published in the *Political Science Quarterly* (official journal of the the Academy of Political Science founded in 1880) by the Neapolitan anarchist lawyer Francesco Saverio Merlino, who, for political motives, had emigrated to the US in 1891. After having presented the character of 'the Camorrist', a figure he admits he had 'frequent opportunities, professional and other, to become acquainted with', Merlino continues, asking 'Who, then, was the Camorrist? And who gave him the authority for his acts?' What follows is enlightening:

The answer is that he was a member of a secret association, and that the power he wielded was conferred by nobody, but was merely assumed. Yet he was not necessarily a criminal. He might, strictly speaking, commit no action for which he would be amenable to punishment; and whatever illegality there was in the fact itself of the existence of the Camorra, was practically obviated by custom and by the acquiescence of the government. The Camorra was, indeed, almost a branch of the government. Yet the government at times persecuted it, and ultimately has nearly destroyed it. At the height of its glory, the Camorra acted quite independently of the government, and rather as its rival. The society then was, in fact, a lesser government established on the margin of the greater. (1894, 466–7)

To find something along these lines with respect to the Sicilian mafia, you probably have to go to a now-forgotten semi-historical essay by the American writer Francis Marion Crawford, who, in his two-volume book *The Rulers of the South. Sicily, Calabria, Malta*, offers this enlightening, if pessimistic, assessment:

> [*Mafia*] *is a complete and highly efficient form of self-government*, which exists, and will continue to exist, in defiance of the constitutional monarchy under which it is supposed to live. An ancient tyrant would have destroyed it by the brutal process of massacring half the population and transplanting the rest to the mainland, but no civilized method of producing the same result seems to have occurred to statesmen. The Bourbons employed the Mafia to keep order, the present government tolerates it because it cannot be crushed; when the Mafia joined Garibaldi, the Bourbons fell, and it remains to be seen what will happen in the south when the Mafia turns against the monarchy it has called in. It is to be hoped that such a catastrophe is far removed from present possibility, and it is at least a somewhat reassuring fact that the Mafia is the very reverse of anarchic, or even socialist; it is, indeed, one of the most highly conservative systems in the world. (1901, *ii*, 373; emphasis added)

Interestingly, Crawford set forth this 'political' definition of the mafia as a counterpart to the reading of the phenomenon advanced by Antonino Cutrera in his *La mafia e i mafiosi* (1900), a study in criminal sociology considered a landmark text in mafia studies to this day (see Chapter 2 of that book). Cutrera was a policeman, however, and his point of view was necessarily that of the (Italian, national, constitutional and monarchical) state he was serving. From *this point of view*, the mafia could never be a 'complete and highly efficient form of self-government', because it could only be crime, albeit a particularly complex and puzzling form of crime. In a sense, I would suggest Crawford's outsider perspective – grounded as it was on his personal experience as an American writer living in southern Italy after a few years spent as a young man in colonial India studying Sanskrit and editing a journal on local (i.e. Indian) affairs – anticipates the perspective this book tries to develop in a more radical and consistent form, that is, a non-statist, non-Eurocentric, non-nationalist view of mafia as a different ruling class and form of government. Crawford, of course, was not alien to Eurocentric prejudice, and inevitably perceived the south of Italy – as he had colonial India – with Anglo-Saxon eyes (incidentally, there is a wide British literature on Indian criminality, which presents many analogies with Italian commentaries on the Sicilian mafia of the same period: for two enlightening contemporary studies, see the now classic Guha 1999 [1983], and Mayaram 2003). But his decentred vision as an observer with no vested interests in his object of study had potentialities worthy of further development. The scholars he makes reference to – all Euro-American social scientists, indeed, with the important exception of Mosca, whose situated knowledge of Sicilian social life had to come to terms with his rooted national and liberal attitudes, an issue surely less urgent for the anarchist Merlino – are certainly helpful in this endeavour. Think of Weber's description of mafias (and camorras) as financial channels for political groups (it is not clear which groups he had in mind, however), of Tilly's astute discussion of the analogy between the early state and organized crime, and more recently of Collins's reading of mafias as patrimonial alliances that survived the state's penetration of the modern world, and indeed contributed to its failure as a monopolistic agency.

This work builds on all these previous scholarly contributions which have shed light on the political side of the mafia. None of these scholars, however, has systematically tried to develop a comprehensive analysis of the mafia as a political institution or form, modelling it as such and analytically contrasting it to other models seemingly more convincing and acceptable, such as those typically developed in the fields of criminology and economics, or even economic sociology – which in fact are still the dominant perspectives in the literature (e.g., Cressey 1969; Arlacchi 1983a; Reuter 1983; Schneider and Schneider 1976; Catanzaro 1992 [1988]; Gambetta 1993, 2009; Sciarrone 2009 [1998]; Paoli 2003; Varese 2001, 2010). This is what this book aims to do, furthering the knowledge we have of the *political dimension of the mafia*, while embedding it in a critical theory of the political conditions of knowledge production in the social sciences. This makes the book a useful critical review of current scholarship, too. It is not a textbook, but rather a comprehensive critical guide to the available literature that advances a fresh interpretation of old and new evidence (for a first step in this direction, see Santoro 2007, 2011).

In this endeavour, political anthropology can offer powerful tools – such as Elman Service's (1962) bands/tribes/chiefdoms/states taxonomy and its developments, or Abner Cohen's (1981) dramaturgical model of elite politics in Africa (see also Carneiro 1981; Claessen and Skalnik 1979, 1981; Runciman 1982) – and some use will be made of them. The category of the chiefdom looks especially enlightening for classifying and making sense of mafia political structures. Equally promising for a re-reading of the available evidence is the analysis of political strategies developed by Frederick Bailey (2001 [1969]) after he watched the famous televised US congressional hearings of Joe Valachi on the criminal organization of Cosa Nostra. This analysis shows how a large part of the strategies elaborated and employed by mafiosi – which exhibit surprising similarities to those used by the Swat Pathans in Pakistan (Barth 1969) – already make sense in the context of political competition and leadership selection, and that a purely economic reading (as economic strategies of businessmen) does not add much to their understanding. But to capture mafia political architecture as it exists and works in institutional environments that also include the state, we need models permitting us to relativize, historicize and criticize the state's claims as well as its imagery. Anthropological models are, unfortunately, too naive with respect to the history of political institutions and accept an idea of the state that is too general and transhistorical for our interests (see Spruyt 1994, 195n2). We need more specific, and historically determinate, conceptual instruments. This is what Tilly's (1985) reading of early war-making states as organized crime, or Scott's (1998) deconstruction of the liberal state's imagination and cognitive claims, can offer us. Carl Schmitt's (1966 [1932]) theory of the political – and work on political conflict and political friendship grounded on it (e.g., Kelly 2003; Mouffe 2005; Slomp 2007) – could also offer important ideas and suggestions even for an empirically based social theory like that pursued in this book. Through these studies, it is possible to put in brackets the modern, territorial, sovereign, rational, European state's claims of objectivity, universality and equity, and look at the political game as it is practised in real life, even from within the historically specific form of the Western state, and against its supposed universality, equity and rationality.

While useful in analytical terms, these works are not enough by themselves. We need additional tools if we want to grasp the mafia's identity and specificity. I suggest it is possible to find these tools in such different and seemingly at odds sources as Marcel Mauss's theory of the gift (1990 [1925]), especially as revised by Bourdieu (e.g., 1996 [1992], 1997, 2017; see also Silber 2009); German formal sociological theory based on both historical research on ancient European peoples and ethnographic research on colonial societies (e.g., Schurtz 1902; Simmel 2009 [1908]; Schmalenbach 1977 [1922]; Vierkandt 1931); and recent work in cultural sociology focused on the deepest foundations of social life in symbolic codes and structures (e.g., Alexander 2003, 2013; Smith 2005; Alexander et al. 2011). Indeed, a secondary contribution of this book is the attempt to merge different and usually non-communicating strains of theoretical work in a compact analysis. I will discuss these intellectual resources in the following chapters when useful.

Contesting Eurocentric Social Theory

If these (European and North American) works provide the toolkit for attempting an overall anatomy of the mafia as a mode of political organization, the crucial metatheoretical background of the book is located in three related streams of contemporary thought: (1) the rise of alternative, i.e. non-Western and Southern, discourses in the social and historical sciences, including subaltern studies (Ludden 2001; Chakrabarty 2000; Alatas 2006a; Connell 2007; Patel 2010; Comaroff and Comaroff 2012); (2) the current revision in political science of the theory of the state in light of a more globalized – i.e. non-Eurocentric – understanding of political life (e.g., Spruyt 1994; Thompson 1994; Scott 1998; Steinmetz 1999; Rudolph and Jacobsen 2006; Rudolph and Rudolph 2010); (3) the resurgence of anarchism as a theoretical structure and cognitive device in the social sciences (see Clastres 1988 [1974]; Graeber 2004; Scott 2010, 2012; for an earlier contribution directly relevant to our topic, see Reclus 1891). In the following, I will elaborate briefly on these points.

As for the first point, besides the notion of subaltern politics, I would underline what can be gained in mafia studies from the rediscovery of Ibn Khaldūn's social theory of solidarity, what the medieval Arab scholar called 'asabiyya (Khaldūn 1967). The name of Ibn Khaldūn has been much discussed recently as an early pioneer of sociology and a great source for those alternative discourses in the social sciences that current globalization is reclaiming (see especially Ahmed 2003; Rosen 2005; Alatas 2006b). To be sure, Ibn Khaldūn was well known long before this recent resurgence of interest spurred by global thinking, as a forerunner, together with Vico, of Comte's idea of sociology, even among Italian scholars (e.g., Barnes and Becker 1938). His great work, *The Muqaddimah*, was (in its French translation) a source for nineteenth-century scholars of politics and ethnicity, such as Ludwig Gumplowicz, himself a source for Mosca's political sociology. This early and now classical contribution can be profitably used in mafia studies as well – not surprising, considering the Mediterranean location of Sicily, the medieval Arab colonisation and the Arab roots of the very word 'mafia.'

A brief description of the concept will suffice.[5] 'Asabiyya is, for Ibn Khaldūn, the fundamental bond of human society and the basic moving force of historical dynamics. The first basis of this force is undoubtedly in nature, in the sense that 'asabiyya, in its most common form, is derived from tribal (male) consanguinity. The inconvenience of this 'racial' conception was already overcome in Arab antiquity by the inclusion of the institutions of affiliation and spiritual kinship, to which Ibn Khaldūn accords great importance in the formation of an effective 'asabiyya. Most important, 'asabiyya is grounded on personal leadership and loyalty more than impersonal, objective institutions – a point contemporary scholars tend to undervalue even though it is crucial for understanding Ibn Khaldūn's theory as embedded in its time and culture (Rosen 2005).

Whether based on blood ties or on some other feeling, '*asabiyya* is, for Ibn Khaldūn, the force which impels groups of human beings to assert themselves, to struggle for primacy, to establish hegemonies, dynasties and empires. It is a main tenet of Khaldūn's theory that, once power has been seized, the dominant group tends to lose the '*asabiyya* on which it was originally based and substitute other forces for it, which sets the ground for a relaxation of customs and a general weakening of moral life. This makes room for the rise to power of a newly emerging social group endowed with a stronger, more genuine and sanguine '*asabiyya*. We can suggest that something very similar to '*asabiyya* is what empowers mafia groups, providing them with that social cohesion and strong inner solidarity that is the main resource of mafiosi and that mafia institutions are supposed to cultivate and reproduce. In a sense, we could even suggest that 'mafia' *is* a manifestation of '*asabiyya*, that the latter is what the term really means. How this principle of solidarity works inside the mafia and what consequences this has for both mafiosi and the wider social life constitute a central topic of this book.

As mentioned above, this book also capitalizes on recent scholarship on the European state. As many scholars of international relations argue these days, the sovereign state has always been far from that omnipotent, omniscient and norm-inspired institution that political theorists, politicians and even sociologists have argued and still claim it to be (Ruggie 1993; Spruyt 1994; Thompson 1994). If the practice of the state is very different from the image of the state transmitted by its theory, the theory of the mafia has often been predicated on a fallacious and highly ideological view of the state as a true monopolist of legitimate force. This book tries to restore the balance, moving from a realistic understanding of the state as a limited, ambivalent and contradictory qua historical institutional form.

The persistence and global spread of mafia-like arrangements is indeed living proof of how the state has historically encountered serious problems in establishing itself as an autonomous system of rules faithful to its formally enacted charters and its ideal, if not ideological, claims of purely legal rule (e.g., Mitchell 1988, 1991; Scott 1998; Migdal 2001). What makes a modern state is the principle of territorial sovereignty, i.e. territorial exclusivity and centralization. The adoption of this principle was the critical turn in the political organization of Western history (e.g., Strayer 1970; Poggi 1978, 1991; Mann 1986a, 1986b; Ruggie 1993). We often take the present system of sovereign states for granted and move from the assumption that this development was inevitable. But it was not, and the history of mafias is there to confirm this. There would be no mafia if the state did not exist – because we would not be able to see mafia without the spectacles, and the alternative model, of the state. But we should also add that there would be no mafia if the state were such a powerful institution as political philosophers and their sociologist followers usually maintain. In a sense, we could say that, while the sovereign state has won against the city-state, the city-league and the empire (Spruyt 1994), it has still yet to win against the mafia. And there are many signs suggesting the victory is not as close as we would hope.

Finally, I would like to emphasize the anarchist moment – the third point of my list – given that one major point of the book is the plea for an understanding of mafia structures and functions independently from any concession to the state as a political ideal and an institutional model. I want to examine and assess the mafia from a radically nonstate-centric, and non-Westernized, point of view – a move that follows recent suggestions coming from anthropological theory (Graeber 2004; Scott 2012) but whose roots date back at least to the now classic *Mutual Aid* by the Russian anarchist prince Piotr Kropotkin (1902; see also Kinna 1995), who possibly knew nothing about the mafia and other outlaw societies in southern Italy, but whose ideas about cooperation and communal associations resonate subtly and strongly with the core of mafia ideology and social structure. This emphasis on anarchism is not only a theoretical move, but a return to what I see as a major historical spur to mafia development all over the world, including Italy. Contrary to Crawford's claim (which lacked the historical knowledge we have today), anarchism and the mafia – at least in Sicily and the US – ran parallel for a while (see Lupo 2009), and this book tries to capitalize on this historical connection as well.

We are again getting close to the central thrust of the book: the mafia is a historically grounded and culturally informed manifestation of a way of organizing political relationships and political life that is different, and alternative, to the modern European state as grounded on the rule of law. This may be apparent in the case of Asian mafias, like yakuza and triads, but it has to be recognized in Western cases like the Italian mafias as well. As a Mediterranean institution focused on personal ties and obliga-tions among selected males, *the Sicilian mafia asks to be understood not as a failure of the modern Western state (and its companion, 'civil society'), nor as an industry (whose conditions of existence are rooted in the failure of the state to provide generalized trust), but as a different, typically Southern, institutional arrangement of social life with strong political implications.*

As a long, though not mainstream, tradition of scholarship – call it the political-realist tradition, not by chance strongly embedded in Italian intellectual life at least since Machiavelli (see Levine 1995), and in modern times advanced and promoted by a Sicilian scholar like Mosca

(1939 [1896]) – holds, politics as human activity occurs in every situation where a group of people organizes itself and works for improving their well-being by trying to persuade others of their legitimacy and justification as power-holders, even in spite of their arbitrariness and violent enforcement of their rule (Mouffe 2005; see also Miglio 2011). There is nothing intrinsically good in the political field, apart from the desired well-being of its most powerful and successful agents, especially when seen from their particular point of view. Like many effective political actors, mafia groups usually succeed in presenting themselves – not only to their members, but to other constituencies as well – as legitimate guarantors of social order and efficacious providers of collective opportunities. This is what makes mafia associations different from common criminal groups or gangs, and makes them potentially relevant actors in the same political field in which the state (with its many elements and fragments) acts as the legitimate and legal provider of order, while being only one of the main actors in concrete situations. This grassroots legitimacy – which is empirically documented in many instances of mafia history – has to be accounted for in any sociological understanding of the mafia. This asks for a culturally sensitive approach to mafia, open to accepting the 'natives' point of view' as well as the effectiveness of its working as a social organization in local conditions. Only from this standpoint can we hope to grasp the meaningful structures through which mafiosi interact and really construct their social world, making it understandable and meaningful to both them and their social constituencies – including interested partners.

Culture is indeed a crucial aspect of the mafia, as of every other social thing, as a focus on its articulated symbolism and its communicative features immediately shows. This has long been recognized, of course, but has been incredibly forgotten or minimized in the most recent literature – probably because of an awareness of the traps that the concept of culture may convey.[6] But the discussion of culture, the concept of culture and cultural analysis has not stopped with Talcott Parsons and 1950s American functionalism, as many mafia scholars seem to believe. Fortunately, recent developments in cultural sociology (e.g., Alexander et al. 2011; Inglis and Almila 2016) offer tools and concepts useful for penetrating the symbolism and cultural structures of the mafia way of life without falling either into the reductionism of rational action theory (RAT) and the ethological model of communication analysis (such as signalling theory: see Gambetta 2009), or into the weaknesses and tautologies of traditional cultural theory grounded on functionalism (strongly and rightly rejected by Gambetta and others, who, however, err in considering this tradition as *the* cultural approach, without realizing that it is just one, and among the weakest, possible approach to cultural analysis; e.g., Alexander 2003; see also Swidler 1986; Sewell 2005; Santoro and Solaroli 2016).

A Final Note on Sources and Method

This book is not based on new ethnographic or statistical or historical evidence. Even if it makes use of some undervalued and neglected sources, it is an exercise in metatheorizing. At the same time, it is an attempt to reflect, utilizing new theoretical resources, on a relationship that has often been studied by scholars of mafia, including scholars of so-called 'organized crime' (an expression I would always put in quotation marks for reasons I will explain in the next chapter): namely, the relationship between social reality and imagination – sociological imagination, but also literary imagination, and any other kind of imagination through which representations are generated and transmitted. In this exercise, I have relied upon an array of different kinds of sources:

- sociological, anthropological and historical studies on the Sicilian mafia, since its inception in post-unification Italy to current studies of various kinds of mafias all over the world;
- literary sources, with all the caveats suggested by the rich tradition of literary sociology (for praises of literature as strategic sources for sociohistorical research, especially on crime, see Benigno 2015 and Boltanski 2014);
- investigations by journalists and reporters, recalling that journalism is a field with its own rules (Benson and Neveu 2005) and, no different from criminology, history or sociology, which means journalistic sources have to be weighed against these rules;
- autobiographies and memories of mafiosi or people close to them;
- judicial and police sources, and other institutional (state) sources, such as parliamentary inquiries and committee hearings.[7]

Whenever possible, I have privileged sources coming directly from mafiosi voices or writings, beyond the state officers' mediation (as in police reports or trial proceedings) and possibly even scholars' mediation (e.g., Arlacchi's edited interviews, or even ghost writers or co-authors, albeit in the latter cases we can assume mafiosi viewed and accepted the text). This means that I have privileged sources such as letters, verbatim witness accounts, taped conversations and the like. In reading these sources, I have used every available critical methodology useful for deciphering or better discovering and extracting 'hidden voices' between the lines, and capable of keeping any bias coming from state-mediated representations under control (from Bourdieu's field analysis to Carlo Ginzburg's evidential paradigm, from critical discourse analysis to deconstruction).

2

The 'Mafia' in 'Mafia Studies': (Re)constructing a Sociological Object

The Mafia is an organized crime formation with Sicilian roots; branches in France, Tunisia, and the Americas; and a recent presence in Russia and Eastern Europe. Its historical successes vis-à-vis other criminal groups, particularly in the United States, have made the word mafia (whose origin has never been convincingly traced) a brand name for organized crime. Recently repressed on both sides of the Atlantic, the Mafia, as such, may be on the wane, although reduced vigilance could allow a resurgence.

Schneider 2008, 550

What is 'mafia'? Encyclopaedic entries nowadays repeat something like a mantra, well represented by the epigraph of this chapter: the mafia is a form of organized crime, possibly the most successful organized crime formation to have ever existed, so much so as to give its name to the whole genre. Cinema and novels have greatly contributed to this characterization of mafia in recent decades (e.g., Renga 2019 [2011]). But this general definition is far from exhaustive. Indeed, there is no shortage of alternative conceptions in the academic literature: it is a primitive, popular, 'prepolitical' movement, according to the influential Marxist historian Eric Hobsbawm (1959); a way of acting according to a shared set of *sub*cultural norms and values for the German sociologist/criminologist Henner Hess (1970); a 'power syndicate' for the American crime historian Alan Block (1983) – who worked not on the Sicilian mafia but on its branch in the US; a structure of mediation historically developed to fill the gaps between local society and a loose and weak national state, according to the Dutch anthropologist Anton Blok (1974); an aspect of the development of a 'capitalism of mediation' in the global economy for the American anthropologists Jane and Peter Schneider (1976). We could continue for some time with definitions like these, apparently lacking in consistency and disorienting to even the most patient student.

In order to move beyond such a simple list of definitions and to look for some conceptual patterns, in this chapter I provide an overview of the social research that has been done on the mafia, mapping the main currents and approaches that have developed since the early studies on the Sicilian mafia (and still earlier on the camorra) published in the 1860s up to recent works, authored by sociologists, anthropologists, economists, criminologists and political scientists. Since Hobsbawm's pioneering contribution, historians too have devoted growing attention to mafia(s) – especially since the 1990s – and I will consider their works as well insofar as they have seriously built upon the social sciences or have improved on the contribution of the social sciences in some way. A distinction between theoretical approaches and theorized identities is then proposed, which permits us to distinguish, inter alia, between economic theories of the mafia as a political institution and economic theories of the mafia as an economic institution. After this narrative, I will try to reorganize the historical materials – at least the most recent ones, published since the 1970s, which comprise what we may call the modern scholarship on mafia – locating authors and works in a socio-intellectual space, or 'field' (Bourdieu), illuminating the main dimensions according to which mafia research (especially sociological mafia research, which is probably the leading discipline in the field) is currently produced, evaluated and reused.

In a sense, this chapter is a contribution to the *sociology of mafia studies,* or what we could call *mafiology.* A caveat is necessary at this point: I am not interested here in providing a history of ideas about mafias so as to reconstruct how something labelled as *mafia* or 'the mafia' has been constructed as an object of (social) research, in particular, as a sociological object. One of the main troubles of social research on the mafia is a sort of epistemological *naïveté* – not so different from what may happen in other research areas, to be sure, though with potentially more pernicious consequences. We can extend to mafia studies what Bourdieu noticed about social research in general:

> [M]ost of the time, researchers take as objects of research the problems of social order and domestication posed by more or less arbitrarily defined populations, produced through the successive partitioning of an initial category that is itself pre-constructed: the 'elderly', the 'young', 'immigrants' … The first and most pressing scientific priority, in all such cases, would be to take as one's object the social work of construction of the pre-constructed object. (Bourdieu and Wacquant 1992, 229)

In the case of the 'mafia', moving from 'the problems of social order and domestication' could be reasonable if the objective were to provide instructions useful for agents of social order (police forces and policy-makers) in their law enforcement activities against supposed criminals. But it is much less so when the objective is knowledge and understanding, first and foremost – including knowledge of the social conditions that make it possible to identify something like the 'mafia'.

'Mafia' is clearly a pre-constructed notion, a vernacular label, a folk-concept variously employed and manipulated by social agents that has not always been transferred into scholarly discourse with the necessary epistemological vigilance. The 'construction of the object' is 'no doubt the most crucial research operation and yet the most completely ignored' (Bourdieu and Wacquant 1992, 225). There is no such ready thing as 'the mafia' in the world. Mafia exists if, when and where we are able to see it because of our mental maps. The problem is twofold: first, there are many ideas of mafia – and people debate about which is the sounder or more plausible, or at least the less fantastic, concept. Indeed, what mafia really is, is part and parcel of the now century-and-a-half-long debate on the mafia, in academia as well as the public sphere. Second, what the 'other' of mafia might be is far from clear. Is it 'the state' as such? Or is it a certain historical form of the state? Or is it an ideal state – a representation of what we would like the state to be but which we can never really see? 'Seeing like a state' is far from an easy accomplishment, and failure is a common outcome of grand utopian schemes, as James C. Scott (2010) has persuasively shown. So, what about 'the mafia'? What does it mean to be 'mafia-like'? What does 'seeing something like a mafia' – paraphrasing but also reversing Scott's influential formula – mean, if indeed it has any meaning at all? This is what I will try to assess in this chapter.

An Archaeology of 'Mafia Studies', 1860–1900

It is a fact that the academic literature on mafia has been dominated by the social sciences and by sociology in particular. Also, for an almost perfect coincidence in timing – sociology as a positivist discipline started its rise in the same decades that the 'mafia' was discovered, if not 'invented', in Italy – sociology has been a hegemonic force of knowledge in the study of mafia since its inception. Of course, you do not find the names of Marx, Durkheim, Weber and the like in the list of authors directly contributing to what we would call 'mafia studies'. Marx wrote on many things, including Native Americans and even mysterious tribunals of the Middle Ages such as the Vehmic courts (*Feme*), but he never wrote on mafia or camorra. Even though *L'Année sociologique* reviewed a few Italian texts on mafia and camorra in its early volumes (all authored by the jurist-sociologist Richard Gaston), it does not seem that Durkheim was aware of, or at least impressed by, the existence of forms of primordial solidarity organizing crime and persisting at the heart of modern society. Even more surprisingly, Georg Simmel wrote extensively about secret societies, but the terms 'mafia' and 'camorra' do not figure in his seminal text on the subject. This does not mean, though, that Marx and Durkheim and even Simmel are not used in research on mafia, nor that the 'classics' in the social sciences never contributed. In fact, at least one classic scholar did, the Italian Gaetano Mosca, author of the influential *The Ruling Class*, and there is evidence that Weber noticed the existence of both the 'mafia' and camorra – referring to it in a passage of his *Economy and Society* (1978 [1922]) about the informal funding sources of political groups. This relative neglect by classic sociological figures notwithstanding, mafia studies are one of the most enduring and lasting research streams in the social and human sciences, whose roots go back at least to the last three or four decades of the nineteenth century.

What we might call 'mafia studies' started in 1862 – at least, this may be a reasonably convenient date from which to depart in this review. In that year, the first book-length study on the camorra was published, and 'camorra' was at the time apparently the only word available to denote mafia-like behaviours and organizations. The author of the book, Marco Monnier, was a young Swiss writer living in Naples where his family managed a hotel. He was not an academic scholar, but a talented writer who had already published a book on brigandage. His definitions of the camorra are worth reading, as the continuities with mafia studies are as impressive as any conceptual or methodological breaks:

> The Camorra could be defined as organized extortion: it is a secret society among the lower classes whose goal is evil ... What the Camorra is, at least what it was not long ago, I will briefly state: it was an association of men of the common people, corrupt and violent, who used intimidation to obtain money from vicious and cowardly people. I strongly insist on these words: an association of men of the common people ... Among the lower classes there is a very special sect, very local, highly organized, extending throughout the ancient Kingdom of the Two Sicilies ... it reigns where the vicious and the cowardly gather, and especially in places where a sad necessity brings them together, that is, in prisons. (Monnier 2010 [1862], 7–8; my translation)

Monnier's book continues with detailed and apparently first-hand descriptions of activities and situations, as well as customs and rules, of supposed members of this sect, distinguishing between the camorra as it works in prisons and the camorra as it appears *in piazza* (in the open), also focusing on its origins and the 'social motives' for its reproduction.

It has been noted (see Benigno 2015) that the literary imagination has provided much of the original imagery used to assemble this early conceptual representation of mafia – and a central contribution seems to have been offered by the French novelist and journalist Alexandre Dumas, author of the *Three Musketeers*, *The Count of Monte Cristo* and many other successful novels, with his notes on the Neapolitan camorra written in 1862 while in Paris after a two-year period spent in Naples. Undoubtedly, the literary power of these exotically coloured descriptions is strong, and they impacted subsequent writing on the subject, even in Italy. But it is not clear what the point is here: whether it regards the reliability of these early representations (whose impact on following representations cannot be overestimated) or the fact that the literary imagination should be taken into account when assessing even self-claimed scientific or at least realistic representations – the kind of representations the social sciences aim to provide. Indeed, the circular relationship between literary imagination and sociological imagination is far from exceptional, and, as Wolfgang Lepenies (1988) has brilliantly shown, sociology has been, since its inception, suspended between 'literature and science'. What mafia offers is just another case in point, an especially enlightening one as the diffusion of the words 'mafia' and 'mafiosi' to identify what had until then been called 'camorra' and 'camorristi' is a consequence of a literary creation and its apparent success in the decades after unification.

In other words, we are dealing in the case of mafia, as in many others, with the mutual contamination, collaboration and cooperation, but also conflict and competition, between two different genres of discourse and writing, two different ways of telling the truth about social life, or two different claims to cultural authority: one rooted in the human capacity to create worlds of fiction, the other in the human capacity for logical reasoning and systematic observation. As Lepenies has shown, the confrontation between literature and sociology was very intense precisely at the beginnings of sociology – the same period that saw the 'discovery' of first the camorra and later the mafia. To see the world also through the eyes of a novelist is far from being anomalous, as a giant of sociology like Erving Goffman observed and, above all, practised (see, e.g., Goffman 1961). As Bourdieu admitted too, novels can 'say more, even about the social realm, than many writings with scientific preten-sions' (Bourdieu 1996 [1992]: 32) – something that resonates well with the declaration that 'some of the best sociology is in novels' (Ruff 1974,

368) and those who see novels as approaching a form of social inquiry, as does Boltanski (2014).

How much literary imagination and how much empirical social observation generated the first true classic in mafia studies is not easy to assess. Surely, the two volumes comprising *La Sicilia nel 1876* are the fruit of several months of travelling across Sicily looking for witnesses to and evidence of the social and economic conditions of the island. Not surprisingly, the 'mafia' looms large in these pages, written by a then young Jewish intellectual, Baron Leopoldo Franchetti, who arrived from Tuscany with the specific objective of documenting and establishing some firm bases upon which to build efficacious policies for helping the southern regions of Italy to meet the standards of social and civic life of the northern regions. Franchetti was born in 1847 in Livorno into a family of good social standing – who had come to Italy from Tunisia in the final decades of the eighteenth century to engage in trade, eventually becoming one of the most important families of the local Jewish community. The young Franchetti was strongly influenced by the ideas of John Stuart Mill, which made him a convinced liberal. This was the mind set with which he observed and then wrote his influential book on public life in Sicily, published in 1877, together with the book of his friend and co-researcher Sidney Sonnino (a future Prime Minister of Italy), on the working conditions of Sicilian peasants. Franchetti's half of the report, *Condizioni politiche e amministrative della Sicilia*, was an analysis of the mafia in the nineteenth century that is still considered authoritative today, much quoted and utilized by contemporary scholars. As historian John Dickie says, Franchetti would ultimately influence thinking about the mafia more than anyone else more than a century later, and *Le condizioni* is the first convincing explanation of how the mafia came to be (see Dickie 2004, 43–54). Most influential nowadays is Franchetti's suggestion that we see in the mafia something like an 'industry of violence', a suggestion that would become the cornerstone of the economic theory of the mafia – the subject of my next chapter.

Given its impact on current research, it is worth noting here how Franchetti arrives at this suggestion and how he elaborates on this conceptualization. The following quotation is helpful in this endeavour:

> The complete fact of which only one phenomenon is covered by the common meaning of the word ['crime'], is the way of being of a given society and the individuals comprising it. As a consequence, to speak efficiently and in a way that makes the idea clear, it is better to express it with an adjective and not a name. The Sicilian usage, competent judge in this matter, expresses it precisely with the adjective 'mafioso', which does not mean a man devoted to crime,

but *a man who is able to make his rights respected, independently from the means he uses for this objective.* And, as in the social context we have tried to describe, violence is often the best means he has to make himself respected, so it was natural that the word used in an immediately derivative sense ended up meaning a man devoted to blood. Thus the term mafia found a class of violent criminals ready and waiting for a name to define them, and, given their special character and importance in Sicilian society, they had the right to a different name from the one defining vulgar criminals in other countries. The importance gained by this social class of independent thugs (*facinorosi*) had the effect of assuring them of the moral authority enjoyed by every private force able to become superior in Sicily for the reasons above. As a consequence, on the island, this class of thugs has a very special status, which has nothing to do with that of delinquents in other countries, as much as they may be numerous, smart and well organized, and you can almost say that here it is a *social institution ... a class with industry* and interests of its own, an independent social force. (1993 [1877]; my translation, emphasis added)

As this quotation makes clear, Franchetti's vision of the mafia was much wider and deeper than the one for which he is nowadays recalled – the 'industry of violence' may be just one aspect of the 'complete fact' that manifests itself in the 'way of being of a given society and the individuals comprising it'. In addition, industry was used by Franchetti not as the name for a sector in the production of goods or related services within an economy (as in the modern English use), but in the old Italian sense of *operosità* and *attività*, i.e. industriousness and productivity. We will elaborate on this point in the next chapter. What has to be emphasized at this point is that Franchetti's analysis is only apparently focused exclusively on Sicily and the mafia. Indeed, what he is continually doing while describing and making sense of social and cultural features is a comparison between what he observes, what he listens to, what he reads (in local newspapers, for example) and what he considers the model of modern political and social organization, i.e. the rule of law, as he could see – along with many of his contemporaries with liberal attitudes and beliefs – in the British constitutional system. The image of mafia we find in Franchetti's pages is an image depicted in contrast with the image of a liberal, market-oriented society based on the rule of law.

Not surprisingly, Franchetti's analysis was attacked, disbelieved and labelled as 'fiction' by a host of Sicilian intellectuals and politicians (for a contemporary account, see Alongi 1977 [1887]; for an example of a pamphlet against Franchetti, see Conti 1877; see also Capuana, 1898). Today, the same text is considered one of the most coherent and comprehensive accounts of the Sicilian mafia and its social causes. Indeed, there is much to be praised in that book. But this should not make us blind to the positioning of the author and the bias that his political objectives and, above all, his mind set could have produced in his analysis. Franchetti's interpretation of the mafia is embedded in a cultural frame in which the state – in its liberal, constitutional form – is assumed to be a sort of universal institution, an incarnation of reason, freedom and modernity. The same is true for the 'rule of law' – an ideological pillar of the whole edifice that sets the standard for the assessment of any institution.

The parameters of the debate on mafia, camorra and the like in the last decades of the nineteenth century were, however, less a legacy of Franchetti than of an eclectic scientist, one of the most influential scholars of the time, indeed – whose scientific standards, according to the current vision, were so flexible as to make his work more interesting nowadays as evidence of human fantasy than for its research results. It is difficult to imagine today just how influential Cesare Lombroso, the author of scientific bestsellers such as *L'uomo delinquente* (1876) and *L'uomo di genio* (1893), could have been in those decades, in Italy and elsewhere. The number of pages Lombroso devoted to southern peculiarities and mafias in his numerous publications is not that large (even though he started to devote himself to these issues very early, see Lombroso 1863), but we could say that much of what was written on mafias in the latter decades of the nineteenth century was in some way related to him and his ideas. This is the case of Giuseppe Alongi's *La maffia* (1887) and *La camorra* (1890), both published in a book series edited by Lombroso, as well as Abele De Blasio's *Usi e costume dei camorristi* (1897), with a preface by Lombroso, and Antonino Cutrera's *La mafia e i mafiosi: origini e manifestazioni. Studio di sociologia criminale* (1900). Alongi and Cutrera were not academics but policemen, attracted to the social sciences thanks to the new discipline Lombroso had founded: criminal anthropology. A physician by education, De Blasio was a follower of the Lombroso School and one of the early academic practitioners of anthropology in Italy as well as the author of dozens of articles and books on phrenology, prehistory and the sociology of deviant behaviour. While influenced by Lombroso's idea of the 'born criminal' and other aspects of his biological theory of crime, neither these writers, nor Lombroso himself, were so blind, or so consistent, as not to notice other causal factors linked to history and social context. All in all, the Lombrosian legacy had a massive impact on the social study of the so-called 'dangerous classes' in *fin de siècle* Italy.

This is also the case of Napoleone Colajanni's *Nel regno della mafia* (1900), a booklet whose contents are maybe less interesting than its author. A participant in the *Risorgimento* as a young man, Colajanni would become a socialist leader and an accomplished social scientist – a professor of statistics, demography and even sociology at the University of Naples, and author of many pioneering books in these disciplines.

Today his name is especially remembered for his intellectual conflict with Lombroso (a socialist himself) and his School: whereas the latter insisted on the biological foundations of social and cultural divides (such as the one between northern and southern Italians, or between normal and criminal men/women) captured by the category of 'race', Colajanni was firmly against any form of biological determinism and a strong supporter of the argument that social inequalities and institutions are the unique real determinants of criminal conduct (Colajanni 1890). He published extensively on the divide between northern and southern Italy on poverty, on backwardness and deviant behaviour, especially in Sicily (e.g., Colajanni 1895). His pamphlet on the mafia adds a special sensitivity to political issues to his usual arguments, claiming that it is the Italian state – its ruling class, i.e. its government – that is primarily responsible for the mafia's existence and persistence, thanks to the diffuse practices of corruption and their general acceptance as ways of governance (Colajanni 1900).

Whereas the socialist Colajanni could point his finger at the Italian national state, the liberal Mosca was at more pain to specify exactly the political agents behind the mafia. As an insider of the 'ruling class', he himself had theorized in his sociological writings (he started his career as an officer in the Parliament, then, while pursuing his academic career, he also spent time as a deputy; in the new century, he also became a member of the government in charge of colonies), but Mosca was less interested in looking for who or what was responsible than he was in providing descriptions and possible explanations – historical and sociological – for the existence of this strange phenomenon called mafia – 'strange' at least to people foreign to Sicily, as Sicilians knew very well what mafia was, according to Mosca. The intellectual strategy that Mosca, a founding father of modern political science and political sociology, used for conceptualizing the mafia is worth quoting at length:

> First of all, we need to eliminate a certain lack of precision in our spoken language. It should be noted that with the word Mafia, the Sicilians intend to express two things, two social phenomena, that can be analyzed in separate ways even though they are closely related. The Mafia, or rather the spirit of the Mafia, is a way of thinking that requires a certain line of conduct such as maintaining one's pride or even bullying in a given situation. On the other hand, the same word in Sicily can also indicate, not a special organization, but the combination of many small organizations, that pursue various goals, in the course of which its members almost always do things which are basically illegal and sometimes even criminal. (Mosca 1980 [1900], 3)

Moving from the mafia as a 'spirit', a set of perceptual schemas and dispositions towards acting in certain ways (that is, of habits), Mosca was able to derive the social organization which the second meaning of the word intends to capture. He focuses the major part of his essay on this second meaning, making it clear that only the combination of a way of thinking that is not unique to Sicily and certain features of Sicilian social and political structure could generate the mafia as a special, and criminal, institution. This is possibly the clearest and most profitable definition of the word in terms that are fruitful for social research. Mosca's (short) writings on mafia are possibly the last relevant contribution of Italian social science to mafia studies before the demise of positivist sociology in the early twentieth century. Indeed, mafia never emerged as a legitimate subject in this early sociology – no article esplicitly devoted to mafia was printed in the *Rivista Italiana di Sociologia*, the first professional journal in sociology published in Italy from 1897 to 1921. In the fascist period, sociology did not disapper, but reduced its public role – becoming a strictly academic discipline taught in the newly founded Faculty of Statistics as a disciplinary sideline of demography. While in Italy mafia more or less disappeared as an object of social research (leaving space to literature and even cinema), scholars in the US were busy discovering a new research object.

However, there is another research stream worthy of notice: folklore studies. Due to a coincidence that probably was not really a coincidence, folklore studies developed in Italy mainly as a Sicilian specialty thanks to the impressive collection and published work of physician-turned-ethnologist Giuseppe Pitrè. His name is famous in mafia studies because of his early description of the mafioso as a psychological type and of *omertà* as a cultural code (of silence) (see the etymology of 'mafia' in Chapter 1, pp. 5–7; also see Chapter 4). Located in a chapter in one of Pitrè's many published books, these descriptions would probably have remained known only to a few experts and scholars interested in folklore if not for a political scandal that occurred in Sicily at the end of the nineteenth century. With the assassination of the banker Emanuele Notarbartolo in 1893, and the subsequent indictment of a deputy from Palermo, Raffaele Palizzolo, as the instigator of that homicide, the 'mafia' surged to national notoriety, with Notarbartolo as the mafia's first eminent victim. Mosca's most influential work, 'Cosa è la mafia?' (What is mafia?), was written as a contribution to this public debate in the mass media of the time. A 'Committee in defence of Sicily' – and of Palizzolo – was founded in Palermo. Pitrè, the dean of Italian folklore studies, used his persona and his speech to act as the ideological weapon of the committee, casting a long, dark shadow on the reliability of his opinions on and knowledge of the subject. However, he was among the few who could claim insider knowledge of the rich social phenomenology referred to by the name 'mafia'.

Towards a Comparative Approach: Hobsbawm's Pioneering Contribution and the Neglect of American Research on Organized Crime

In very general terms, and in a loosely sketched form, this is the history of mafia studies in Italy during the last four decades of the nineteenth century. Rarely can you find references to other countries in this literature, or to other possible experiences of supposedly mafia-like phenomena. That similar phenomena or institutions could exist elsewhere – for instance, triads in China or yakuza in Japan – does not seem to have been noticed by any of these writers.

It is through Hobsbawm's historical imagination (an author writing in English) that mafia – indeed, always written as 'Mafia' – moved from its narrow localization on an island in the Mediterranean Sea to its insertion in a comparative framework alongside other historical experiences deemed to be similar in certain ways. In his book *Primitive Rebels: Studies in Archaic Forms of Social Movement in the 19th and 20th Centuries* (1959) – which happens to be his first book and one of the most influential books in social history ever written – the Marxist historian considered mafia as a primitive form of social movement. Building mainly on the texts published in Italy after unification, especially Colajanni and Alongi, plus some more recent contributions in political magazines, Hobsbawm offered a fully developed and consistent portrait of the mafia which is compatible with our common standards of academic scholarship – better, of mafias in the plural, as the Sicilian one was just an instance of a wider phenomenon for him. According to Hobsbawm, primitive rebels are those engaged in 'pre-political' forms of social mobilization; their politics are often ambiguous and perhaps even reformist, if not conservative; and they are more often rural and poor, coming on the scene on the cusp of dramatic socioeconomic transformations (see also Hobsbawm 1973; Shanin 1971). The social bandit is their archetypical outlaw form:

> Social banditry, a universal and virtually unchanging phenomenon, is little more than endemic peasant protest against oppression and poverty: a cry for vengeance on the rich and oppressors, a vague dream of some curb upon them, a righting of individual wrongs. Its ambitions are modest ... Social banditry has next to no organization or ideology, and is totally inadaptable to modern social movements. (1959, 5)

In his book, Hobsbawm tests his argument against a series of case studies: social bandits, mafia, millenarian movements (Italian Lazzaretti,

Spanish anarchists, the Sicilian peasant leagues), the city mob, labour sects. His main claim is that these forms of social protest emerge in the absence of what he considers the 'modern' forms of political organization (parties, unions, etc.): 'The bandit is a pre-political phenomenon, and his strength is in inverse proportion to that of organized agrarian revolutionism and Socialism or Communism' (1959, 23). The chapter on mafia is the longest and possibly the most interesting of the book. Hobsbawm notes three meanings of mafia: (1) a general sceptical and dismissive attitude towards the state and state law; (2) a highly mediated and decentralized form of power and patronage; (3) the control of a community's social life by a secret – or officially unrecognized – system of gangs. In his own words:

> *Mafia* (in all three senses of the word) provided a parallel machine of law and organized power; indeed, so far as the citizen in the areas under its influence was concerned, the only effective law and power ... The apparatus of coercion of the 'parallel system' was as shapeless and decentralized as its political and legal structure, but it fulfilled its purpose of securing internal quiet and external power. (1959, 35, 38)

Hobsbawm's understanding of the mafia has not been very influential in mafia studies – at least not compared to the influence his thesis on social banditry has had on sociohistorical research. This is a pity, as there was much to recommend in his first book, including the suggestions of reading mafia as a (pre-)political phenomenon and pursuing its study in a comparative perspective. In this early book, and even more explicitly in a later one (1969), Hobsbawm makes passing references to other countries, including China, Colombia and Japan. Indeed, even though it is not evoked directly, this was an expansion of the comparative framework for reading mafia (in addition to social banditry) that would only be furthered in later years with the explicit comparison of Italian mafias to other similar social formations such as triads, yakuza and, since the 1970s, Colombian cartels.

Of course, all these subjects have their own intellectual histories, historians and social analysts. The problem is that, too often, they remain almost unknown to Western scholars writing and researching on mafias – and are difficult to locate even in available books on the history and sociology of these forms of 'organized crime' (but see sources referred to in Ownby and Heidhues 1993; Betancourt and García 1994; Wang 2017). Indeed, you cannot expect to find sociological analysis of the triads and yakuza until the post-Second World War period or even later, when the social sciences – and sociology among them – eventually had the opportunity to enter these Eastern countries and their academic systems. However, official reports, and even a few books on these foreign forms, have been written by Western observers since the nineteenth century, as well as on other exotic criminal institutions – such as the Thuggee phenomenon and other so-called 'criminal tribes' in India, the subject of a rich literature produced by British colonial officers or ethnographers as well as indigenous observers well before the arrival of colonial rule (see Wagner 2007; Piliavsky 2015; see also Benigno 2011).

The publication since the 1930s of the fifteen-volume *Encyclopedia of the Social Sciences* was a major achievement in the history of these sciences, including sociology. For mafia studies, it was the occasion to see its object recognized as a social phenomenon worthy of attention on its own and therefore of an autonomous entry, authored by the same Mosca whose name and ideas, in the meantime, had been travelling beyond Italy and Europe (in 1939, the English translation of his *Elementi di scienza politica* would be issued in the US as *The Ruling Class*). The only novelty with respect to his previous writings on the subject was a political acknowledgment of the fascist regime – presented as able, like no previous one, to defeat the mafia (Mosca 1933). Unfortunately, this was simply not true. Fascism fought the mafia, it is true, but the lower branches of it rather than its highest ranks, so that the mafia persisted behind the scenes, sometimes well camouflaged within the same fascist ruling class (on mafia during fascism, see Duggan 1989).

Meanwhile, 'mafia' was becoming the name of a major social problem in the US, where it emigrated together with millions of Italians in search of luck and a new life across the Atlantic. This is not the place to tell the story of the transplantation of 'mafia' from Italy to the US and elsewhere (see Anderson 1965; Lupo 2008; Lombardo 2013). Suffice to say that the research on gangs and organized crime that started at Chicago in the 1920s and 1930s (e.g., Thrasher 1927; Landesco 1968 [1929]; Whyte 1943) had almost no impact on the Italian debate on the mafia. Social and criminological research on organized criminal activities in the US were conducted in those years under labels such as 'racketeers', 'mobsters', 'gangsters' and the like. Rarely, if ever, was 'mafia' a common name for these activities and the people in charge of them. What in the United States was becoming a major political issue – with the institution of committees especially devoted to its study and investigation – was considered in Italy a legacy of history to be overcome with modernization, a folkloric appendix, or simply not an issue at all. Based on research conducted in his capacity as a consultant for the President's Commission on Law Enforcement and Administration of Justice in 1966 and 1967, sociologist and criminologist Donald Cressey was able to write a whole treatise on so-called 'Cosa Nostra', as the Sicilian mafia was named in the US according to Joe Valachi's witness (see Maas

1968), with the suggestive title *Theft of the Nation* (1969), and later the smaller *Criminal Organization* (1972a), in which he extended his conceptualization of organized crime to include criminal groups other than Cosa Nostra. Both the government and Cressey viewed the mafia – as embodied in 'Cosa Nostra' – as a secret society with rituals and a highly bureaucratic structure that included 'bosses', 'underbosses' and 'soldiers'.

After Cressey's influential 1969 study, many other social scientists entered the fray. Some challenged Cressey directly, arguing anew that the mafia did not exist (Hawkins 1969; Smith 1990 [1975]), that it was not nearly as organized and sinister as he had implied (Albini 1971; Chambliss 1978; Reuter 1983), or that organized crime was more ethnically than organizationally based (Ianni 1972, 1975). Others used Cressey's framework to study a specific example of organized crime (Anderson 1979). All these studies recognized the centrality of Cressey's study and took it as their point of departure (cf. Colomy 1988; Akers and Matsueda 1989), but they also revealed that, rather than using rituals and being bureaucratic in structure, their group structure was based upon network models otherwise known as forms of patron–client relationships. Among these revisionist scholars were Joseph Albini and Dwight Smith (sociologists), Francis Ianni and Elizabeth Reuss-Ianni (anthropologists), Peter Reuter (economist) and Mark Haller and Alan Block (historians). These revisionist authors helped lead the way in challenging the governmental (or bureaucratic) model of organized crime that viewed the mafia as the top criminal organization that had a monopoly on rackets in the US and around the globe (see Albini and McIllwain 2012, 4–5).

The Modern Wisdom (or Mafia Studies since 1970)

Indeed, it was not only in the US that something new about how to study mafia was in the making. Since the 1960s, the social study of mafia and mafia-like organizations had experienced a sort of turn. In those years, foreign scholars of Sicily, 'swayed by that decade's profound distrust of policing institutions', began to do research on mafia conceived 'with a small *m* and without the definite article' (Schneider 2008, 550–1). Rather than a criminal association with clear boundaries, rules and goals, mafia was now seen as the sum of individual mafiosi wielding power through their skills, including the ability to use private violence. This reading has been highly influential, and we could say that mafia studies definitely came of age in the 1970s with the publication, one after the other, of three outstanding and seminal contributions to the social science literature on mafia in Europe and especially in Sicily: Hess (1970), Blok (1974), Schneider and Schneider (1976). To them we could also add dalla Chiesa (1976) and Arlacchi (1983b [1980]), the two first substantial contributions to mafia studies from Italian sociology after the demise of the discipline in Italian culture (and academia) in the 1920s and its recovery in the 1950s (for a sociohistorical portrait of Italian sociology from its inception to the 1950s, see Santoro 2013).

What had already been happening in the US beginning in the 1950s was also starting to happen in Italy, however. After decades in which it was difficult to even assert the existence of something like the mafia in Italian courts, in the 1980s and 1990s some brave Sicilian prosecutors, responding to the mafia's assumption of a commanding role in trafficking heroin to the US, were able to 'turn' several mafiosi into justice collaborators, eliciting ethnographically rich personal narratives. (Palermo-based Tommaso Buscetta was the first of these, offering testimony to the prosecutor Giovanni Falcone, who was assassinated in 1992.) This and a corresponding citizens' antimafia movement encouraged new research, much of it by Sicilian scholars, which revealed that the mafia had a greater institutional capacity than had been imagined before (see Jamieson 1999; Schneider and Schneider 2003; Santino 2009; Rakopolous 2017; Ben-Yehoyada 2018). This section is devoted to this double, partly contradictory move.

A German sociologist, Henner Hess published in 1970 what was possibly the first academic book-length text on the Sicilian mafia (and any Italian mafia at all) from a modern sociological perspective – where for 'modern' we mean post-Weberian sociology (including some aspects of US functionalism). It was also the first truly empirical study on Sicilian mafia, mainly based on archival sources – something not all social scientists at the time would have considered empirical research, especially in the absence of numbers and statistics. The main argument and general approach of Hess's book are well captured by the following quotation from the preface to the second English edition:

> My theory about the *mafia* phenomenon is based above all on my most important source material, the Sicilian archival police records and court files which contain nothing about 'the Mafia', but a great deal about individual *mafiosi* ... I have used them as criteria to assess other research material and as the basis for the portrayal of the *mafioso*, the structure of *mafia* groupings and the functions of *mafia* behaviour ... *Mafia* has to be understood as a plethora of small, independent criminal organizations rather than as the secret society of common belief. This is the first point I want to make. The second point is that *mafia* is (or at least was) more than just crime. To treat it as crime alone misses much of its essence and fails to explain the reasons for its

strength and durability. To really understand and explain it, we have to see the phenomenon as deeply rooted in the structure of Sicilian society and in its subcultural values. (1998 [1970], x–xi)

Locating the origins of mafia in the political structure of Sicilian society and, above all, in the 'tradition of dual morality' which lies at the core of its local, subcultural system, Hess was trying to find a way to encompass both social structure and culture in explaining the genesis of this social phenomenon and grasp its 'essence'. Although he devoted at least one chapter to the structure of the mafioso groupings, the primary factor in its explanation was played by the regional cultural system, i.e. the subcultural code of *omertà* – to the point of saying that only mafiosi, with their subcultural values and individual behaviours, exist, and not 'the mafia' as a real organization. As Bell (1953) did in the US case, Hess saw the mainspring for mafioso behaviour as lying in people's aspirations for social mobility within a social structure with limited opportunities but valuable (sub)cultural resources. Clearly, he was reacting to the US debate on 'the Mafia' as a single centralized organization. Translated into Italian in 1973 with a preface by the Sicilian writer Leonardo Sciascia, Hess's book soon became a central reference in the Italian public and academic debate on mafia. It was, conversely, relatively uninfluential in the American debate, a foreword by Cressey to its English edition notwithstanding.[1]

However, Hess was only the first of a series of modern social researchers to contribute to the social science literature on Sicilian mafia starting in the 1970s. Anton Blok, a Dutch anthropologist, spent several months during the early 1960s in Genuardo, a village in western Sicily, doing participant observation and archival research. With a preface written by the then Michigan-based sociologist and historian Charles Tilly (who, at the time, was conducting his pioneering research on mobilization and state formation) and opening with a long quotation drawn from Barrington Moore, with strategic rhetorical references to Eric Wolf and Norbert Elias, Blok's book (1974) positioned itself firmly in a tradition of studies focused on the *structural* dimensions of social life (see Watts 2016), though it was also very sensitive to history (a legacy of Elias, who had spent a lot of time teaching in Amsterdam where Blok had been studying for his PhD). Indeed, it was under Jeremy F. Boissevain's supervision that Blok wrote his dissertation and subsequent book.[2] Blok's position towards approaches like those adopted by Hess was very clear: 'All such arguments in terms of values and subcultures alone are innately circular, and thus beg the very question they propose to answer' (1974, 176n; the explicit target of this passage, however, is not Hess but Wolfgang and Ferracuti 1967). Moving from Elias's sociology of the state and his theory of social figurations, Blok proposed reading mafia as an aspect of the formation of the state in Italy. His main innovation was to understand mafia and mafiosi as elements in a wider configuration of social relations spanning different localities and an array of subjects, including officials and politicians. What mafiosi furnished, according to Blok, was mainly *mediation* between the administrative centre (i.e. Palermo at the regional or Rome at the national level) and the periphery:

> Villages like Genuardo [the community under study] are part of larger complex societies. Many of their particular characteristics are dependent upon and a reflex of the larger society and can only be explained with reference to their specific connections with it. This is especially true of *mafiosi*, rural entrepreneurs of sorts, who were until recently [*sic*] an outstanding feature of peasant communities in Sicily's western interior. Recruited from the ranks of peasants and shepherds, and entrusted with tasks of surveillance on the large estates (*latifundia*) of absentee landlords, they constituted a particular variety of middlemen – individuals who operate in different social realms and who succeed in maintaining a grip on the intrinsic tensions between these spheres. *Mafiosi* managed those tensions by means of physical force. Poised between landowning elite and peasants, between city and countryside, and between central government and the village, they sought to control and monopolize the links between these various groups and segments of society. (1974, xxvi–xxvii)

Like Blok, Peter and Jane Schneider spent months in Sicily in the 1960s studying demographic patterns and fertility, gender relations and land tenure – and this is the background to their book specifically devoted to the mafia as an aspect of class relations and cultural life in western Sicily, published in 1976 in a book series edited by Tilly (who had also written the preface to Blok's book). Like Blok, the Schneiders had been doing ethnographic research on a small town in western Sicily, called Villamaura.[3] Unlike Blok, though, their outlook was more sensistive to constraints rather than choices, to structure rather than agency. They moved from a concern with the ways peasant communities were encapsulated within larger systems (following their mentor, Eric Wolf) and collected ethnographic and historical data to document them until they discovered that Immanuel Wallerstein's world-system theory, which he had just started to elaborate in 1974 with the publication of the first volume of his masterwork, was very apt for making sense of their data. In their words:

> Wallerstein uses the concepts 'core' and 'periphery' to describe relation-ships between the various regions of Europe as they developed from the

mid-fifteenth century. In particular, his analysis of Poland – which was also a wheat-exporting peripheral region – helped us to clarify our own understanding of western Sicily. Yet we did not have the benefit of his work until 1974, and were led to a similar 'world-system' perspective by a somewhat different route, namely as a consequence of anthropological field work conducted in western Sicily from 1965 to 1967 and again during the summers of 1968 and 1971. We did not begin our field work with that perspective. Our initial intent was to examine the structures through which peasant communities are articulated with the nation-state. Yet we soon discovered the importance of labor migration and the ways in which it connected our field site not only to the state, but to an international labor market as well. (Schneider and Schneider 1976, x)

Like Blok, the Schneiders' target was the concept of culture – and the associated approach to cultural explanation – in terms of norms and values related to socialization, a concept they proposed to overcome by suggesting the idea of *cultural codes* as historically adaptive determined structures to be used as symbolic tools and resources – a move that, in many senses, anticipated the one taken more famously by American sociologist Ann Swidler (1986) in the following decade. It is worth remembering that Swidler's work was built, in part, on the shoulders of the anthropologist Ulf Hannerz, a participant in the same intellectual network as Boissevain and Blok. The Schneiders' position with respect to the status of culture and cultural analysis is well captured in this excerpt:

Scholars and others concerned with underdevelopment often link it to the presumably reactionary and traditional qualities of peasant culture. In our view, such cultural determinism is incorrect, yet it is seductive ... In the course of anthropological study in a west Sicilian agricultural community we identified three cultural codes as particularly interesting and salient. The code of family honor (*onore*) asserts the primacy of the nuclear family in society and establishes women as symbols of familial worth. The code of friendship (*amicizia*) and hospitality helps solidify the omnipresent coalitions and cliques through which business affairs and other ventures are conducted. *Furberia*, the code of cleverness or astuteness, focuses on the individual and his immediate family, and helps legitimate the idea that almost anything goes in defense of one's personal interests ... Local as well as foreign observers frequently attribute the island's economic difficulties to the codes in question, noting, for example, that preoccupation with family honor undermines the kind of trust that is necessary to collective organization for long-term gain, while friendship and cleverness rationalize foul play and corruption. We see these codes, however, in another light. We intend that this volume should provide a clear case for *a different understanding of the role of culture* in change, and that it should do this by demonstrating (1) that exogenous colonial and neo-colonial forces have had an overwhelming impact on Sicily, not only in the recent past but also over centuries, and (2) that the cultural codes at issue were instruments of adaptation to these secular forces, and not simply residua of a 'traditional' preindustrial past. (Schneider and Schneider 1976, 1–2; emphasis added)

A question we could raise at this point is the following: do these contributions and their authors amount to what could be termed a scientific or intellectual movement (Frickel and Gross 2005)? As a matter of fact, Hess and Blok worked independently – Blok refers to Hess, saying he became aware of his work after he had finished writing his own book (1974, 13) – and with different methods (ethnographic and archival for Hess, only archival for Blok) and from different intellectual traditions (respectively, historical-anthropological research strongly influenced by Elias's sociology, and Weberian sociology). Blok and the Schneiders – who indeed confess in the acknowledgements of their books that they met each other several times while doing ethnography – were closer in terms of disciplinary affiliations, personal networks (with Wolf and Boissevain as common nodes) and even research sites.

The Schneiders' Marxist approach was shared by the Italian authors – the aforementioned Arlacchi (who was a student of Giovanni Arrighi, at the time teaching in Calabria before moving to the US and joining Wallerstein at the Braudel Centre at the State University of New York at Binghamton) and Nando dalla Chiesa, whose book *Il potere mafioso. Economia e ideologia* (1976) was explicitly framed in Marxist-Gramscian terms and was conceived and written in the same intellectual milieu in which Arrighi had studied and trained. So, it seems that all the books published on mafia in the 1970s, except for Hess's, shared a set of personal relations and conceptual strategies. Of course, there was enough difference in accents, topics and writing styles to make the individual books worthy of attention in their own right.

Indeed, while the research of the 1970s was conducted under the aegis of Marx, the 1980s saw the discovery of Weber's insights by mafia studies. Arlacchi's second book on the mafia is paramount: originally published in Italian in 1983, *Mafia Business: The Mafia Ethic and the Spirit of Capitalism* was pivotal in suggesting it was time to make the turn from culture to economics – and possibly from anthropology to economics – also in the study of Italian mafias. Arlacchi's solution was ingenious: while culture worked in making sense of traditional mafia, it did not work in accounting for the newly emergent forms of mafia, much more oriented towards profit (instead of honour) and business (instead of social control) than the earlier ones. The concept of the 'entrepreneurial mafia', aka *mafia as business*, was born – and the way towards an economic theory of the mafia began to be paved.

The first to profit from this turn-in-the-making was a Canadian-Italian political scientist, Filippo Sabetti – the author of the third historical-ethnographic study on Sicilian mafia worthy of consideration, after Blok, and Schneider and Schneider (see Figure 2.1). Sabetti's approach in *Political Authority in a Sicilian Village* (1984) was highly original: indeed, his book was the first to make use of institutional theory to make sense of the mafia. The challenging perspective that Sabetti adopts – inspired by American political scientist Vincent Ostrom and future Nobel prizewinner Elinor Ostrom, as well as Italian liberal economist Francesco Ferrara – is made clear from the very first page of his book. After quoting an imaginary conversation between a Sicilian and a Neapolitan that the French political writer Alexis de Tocqueville had used as an expedient to present his thoughts after his southern travels in 1827, Sabetti continues:

> Against the stark backdrop of governmental failures and general social disintegration, local outlaw societies or mafia groups stand out as the most successful long-term efforts at collective action in Sicily. These mafia groups have, however, been viewed, especially from outside of Sicily, as gangs of malefactors, as expression of fundamental asociality of islanders … as outlaw protective agencies of large landowners or urban capitalists, and, more generally, as impediments to human development … The study of mafia groups and how they actually work in Sicily has, in fact, become impenetrable on any premise except that of killing or murder. The multitude of problems inherent in governmental failures, general social disintegration and outlaw societies has often been characterized as the Sicilian problem or in Italian as *sicilitudine*. The present study is an effort to provide a more satis-factory explanation of *sicilitudine* within the microcosm of a single Sicilian community. (1984, 3–4)

Drawing upon a suggestion included in Alongi's early book (1977 [1887], 45), Sabetti makes sense of *mafia* as an instance of self-government, a regime of self-reliance rather than a criminal institution: 'Villagers [of Camporano, the community under investigation] attempted to obtain satisfactory remedies to local contingencies through a pattern of social organziation outside of the formal institutions. This pattern of social organization is the outlaw regime of mafia or what a sociologist policeman characterized as "primitive self-government"' (1984, 95).

Through intensive fieldwork and, above all, the analysis of various documentary sources (including archival ones), Sabetti claims to identify in the career and doings of Mariano Ardena, the local mafia boss, an instance of a 'profitable altruist', i.e. 'a villager who by helping others also helps himself' (1984, 6). Clearly, people like Ardena were playing at the borders of legality, and it was easy for them to get involved in

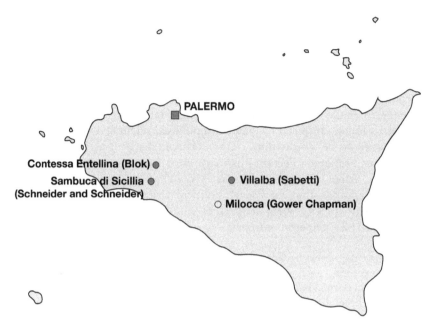

Figure 2.1: Map of Sicily with the location of the three case studies (Blok 1974; Schneider and Schneider 1976; Sabetti 1984)
Note: the map also includes the location of the first ethnographic study in Sicily (Gower Chapman 1971), originally done in 1928–9.

veritable outlaw societies along with more established and legalized ones, such as social clubs or cooperatives. A crucial insight in Sabetti's reading of the mafia is that '[s]uch outlaw societies are confronted with all the problems of political organization, including the possibility that their rule-making and rule-enforcing mechanisms can become mechanisms for tyranny and shakedown rackets' (1984, 12). This is an insightful conjecture, which I will build on in Chapter 4.

Sabetti's contribution to mafia studies is controversial and has not exerted an appreciable impact on the field – its merits notwithstanding. His idea of 'the mafia' as a set of outlaw groups working to solve local problems of collective action is possibly too accommodating to mafiosi's own self-representation as 'men of goodwill' to sound acceptable to readers and even scholars. But his interpretation of 'mafia' as an institutional arrangement capable of fulfilling political functions in certain social locations had analytical potentialities that later scholars eventually missed.[4] In contrast, Raimondo Catanzaro's book, published in Italian in 1988 and translated into English in 1992, is much more referenced than

Sabetti's. It has the merit of introducing a systematic historical, temporal dimension to mafia studies and a more balanced understanding of the political aspects of mafia groups with respect to economic ones. Key to a sociological understanding of the mafia is, for Catanzaro, the notion that the latter provides a 'violent regulation of the market' – a concept that permits the author to put together a sensitivity to political issues linked to the use of violence in social relationships and a focus on mafia's involvement in economic activities.

Indeed, Gambetta has taken this kind of institutional analysis of mafia to the extreme. His 1993 book *The Sicilian Mafia* (published in Italian in 1992) acted as a watershed in mafia studies, introducing the notion of the Sicilian mafia as an instance of a more general type of economic organization, the 'industry of private protection'. We will focus on this book in the next chapter. Suffice it to say here that Gambetta proposed an *economic theory* of the mafia conceived as an 'industry' specialized in the provision of a special commodity, private protection, capitalizing on Franchetti's early suggestion of mafia as an industry on its own (even though with a different objective) and, above all, on Thomas Schelling's and Peter Reuter's pioneering contributions to an economic analysis of organized crime. What Gambetta added to this mix was a massive documentation drawn from recent Italian trials against Cosa Nostra (the *maxi processo* organized by Judge Giovanni Falcone and the Palermo *antimafia* pool on the basis of Tommaso Buscetta's testimony in 1984–7) and a rich sociological imagination, able to 'translate' economic insights into sophisticated understandings of mafia as both an economic organization and cultural reality – with the former accounting for the latter. Academic writings on mafias after 1992 may be divided according to their position with respect to this book and Gambetta's more general approach to mafia (for followers, see, e.g., Varese 2001, 2010; for critics, see, e.g., Paoli 2003; Santoro 2007).

Attempting to review all the relevant production on Italian mafias since these pioneering empirical studies would require much more space than I have here. Instead of a review of texts and their authors (the most influential of which I will refer to in the following chapters, partly as sources and partly as targets of my critical readings), I will here propose a simple classification of approaches, each with some examples.

First, we can distinguish between perspectives that are economic in orientation (e.g., insisting on both material and rational dimensions of human conduct and life), and perspectives that put greater emphasis on nonmaterial and nonrational aspects – be they symbols or status positions or identities – or even power management and regulation. The first group includes approaches as different as rational action theory (RAT) and political economy, i.e. individualistic and holistic approaches.

But the most important distinction relates to the identification of the mafia phenomenon: is the mafia something pertaining to economic life or to some other sphere/life order, such as politics or social solidarity (e.g., communal life)? Putting it bluntly, is the mafia an economic phenomenon or a political one? Is it business or government? To be sure, *mafia seems to be precisely 'the' institutional order that makes such conceptual distinctions problematic*: the distinction between spheres of life which comprises so many parts of modern society's identity and structure looks less clear when seen through the prism of mafia and mafia-like phenomena.

I would say that what makes the mafia sociologically interesting is its resistance to being easily captured by the established categories of the social sciences – categories generated by the meeting of a certain gaze with a certain historical, and geographical, experience. This is more than the usual 'essentially contested concept' (Gallie 1956) syndrome that social scientists are well aware of. The problem is not that the concept of the mafia is a contested one, but that almost every sociological concept applied to it shows some weakness or inadequacy to capture its working. Letizia Paoli's (2003) reference to the notion of 'multi-functional brotherhoods' tries to capture this lack of differentiation, of course. However, since scholars are eager to make sense of the mafia by translating its puzzling phenomenology into our common categories (which include the distinction between economics and politics, as well as between public and private), it is still possible and plausible to use these institutional distinctions as tools for distinguishing between theories of the mafia. Gambetta's economic theory of the mafia as 'an industry of private protection' is the most explicit among current theories on this aspect. But it is relatively easy to classify other theories according to the same conceptual structure as well. So, it is apparent that Sabetti sees the mafia as belonging to the realm of government and politics more than to economics, and the same is true for scholars as different as Santino and Hess – the latter with his more recent (2011) identification of mafias as para-state organizations.

Things are more complex, however, because authors can change their dominant perspective over time: this is the case of the Schneiders, for example, who moved from a neo-Marxist political economy approach to an interpretation of mafia that is much more sensitive to both 'culture and politics' (e.g., Schneider and Schneider 2003; see also Tarrow 2006). Something similar could be said for Federico Varese, who moved towards the acceptance of a more blurred distinction between mafia as business and mafia as government (compare his 2001 and 2011 works). However, I suppose that the conceptual map offered in Figure 2.2 still roughly works.

		Perspective		
		Economic*		Non economic
Mafia *Identity*	Economic (e.g. mafia as a business, an industry, a form of capitalism)	Gambetta Varese	Schneiders	Arlacchi
Mafia	Not economic (e.g. mafia as government, as political mediation, as mutual help society, etc.)	Sabetti	Catanzaro	Paoli Santino Blok Hess

Figure 2.2: Mafia studies, after 1970: a conceptual map (I)
*Includes political economy
Note: position in the cells is representative also of distance from other perspectives (e.g., Varese is less distant than Gambetta from an identification of the mafia as a 'non-economic entity', which means that Varese takes more distance from the notion of the mafia as a business or an industry than Gambetta)

This conceptual map would be incomplete, however, if not supplemented by a second one, built on the now traditional distinction between action, structure (e.g., social structure), and culture (e.g., cultural structure). Figure 2.3 shows how current authors and theories can be mapped onto this set of distinctions, whose analytical space partly overlaps with the perspective/identity map. For the 'action' side, the main difference is between scholars who adopt a rational choice perspective and scholars who follow a less constraining theory of action.

Rational choice theory in the study of organized crime was pioneered by Reuter in the early 1980s, and then applied to the study of the mafia by Sabetti (1984). Gambetta (1993) made it a cornerstone of his economic theory of the mafia as 'an industry of private protection' (for an application of RAT to an important historical case that exhibits some resemblance to the mafia – an application apparently independent from Gambetta's and with somewhat different results – see Leeson 2009). The idea of 'social structure' is not a uniform one: for some (e.g., Gambetta),

		STRUCTURE	
		Social structure	Cultural structure
ACTION (RAT theory)	YES	Gambetta Sabetti Varese	
	NO	Schneiders Arlacchi Catanzaro Santino Blok	Hess Paoli

Figure 2.3: Mafia studies, after 1970: a conceptual map (II)

it roughly means the structure of property rights; for others (e.g., Blok), it is the structure of social relations; for others again, it is mainly the class structure (e.g., Santino). 'Culture' is conceived of in terms of norms and values by Hess, who wrote in the 1960s, but not by Paoli (2003) or Santoro (2007) – both of whom make use of a 'revised' concept of culture in terms of symbols and cognitive schemas. This is the same concept of culture we can find in the economic theory of the mafia, even though it is almost never named as such (the term 'culture' is reserved by Gambetta for norms and values; skills and cognition are not called culture in the economic theory of the mafia, even though they are 'culture' in the most recent cultural theory which capitalizes on Bourdieu, Geertz, Douglas and so on: see, e.g., Smith 2001). In the economic theory of mafia, mafia culture has a regulative status, whereas in Paoli (2003), and even more so in Santoro (2007), it plays a constitutive role (on this distinction between regulative and constitutive, see DiMaggio 1994).

Last but not least, it is useful to try to locate and make sense of sociological (or anthropological, or political science) works on the mafia according to sociological types or genres (extending the classifications used for sociology to other disciplines). I have in mind here, in particular, the fourfold distinction between professional sociology, policy sociology, critical sociology and public sociology (Burawoy 2005). Let me say that these distinctions are frequently collapsed or blurred in the literature on the mafia, mainly because of the strong presence of a critical and public attitude even among followers of 'professional' sociology (this is why I have decided not to include a diagram for this classification). In a sense, we could say that a critical stance is implicit in every piece of sociological work on the mafia. This criticism is usually addressed towards the mafia itself, and secondarily towards the social structure and/or the political system making the mafia possible. Moreover, it is a common ambition of mafia scholars to write for, and to be read by, an audience that is larger than their peers or students: this makes room for frequent incursions into the territories of public sociology, with their typical features (readability, communication strategies useful for reaching large audiences, etc.). This is what makes a book like *Gomorrah* (Saviano 2006, 2007) less an instance of public sociology of mafia (but recall that Saviano, even though he is a professional writer, has an educational background as a philosopher and anthropologist) than a successful performance in creative writing grounded on readings of public documents and backed by direct (and sometimes participant) observation. The ambition of offering policy advice or suggestions is very common among scholars on mafia as organized crime – who often act or have acted (or hope to act) as advisers to governments or other public organizations (including NGOs), and are often asked to provide advice and recommendations for them.

An important point: it is often difficult to locate a given text in one or another class (or genre) because of the gap between explicit or manifest aims, and/or self-representation, and hidden or latent ones. It is not rare that texts or approaches presenting themselves as pure exercises of social analysis conceal (and commonly presume) a political or at least a normative stance towards a certain state of the world. It is not rare that this stance is communicated through the adoption of a linguistic register that sometimes exemplifies what has been termed – not without a normative bias – as 'expressive sociology' (Boudon 2002). As I will argue in the next chapter, this seems to be the case with the economic theory of the mafia, which presents itself as the most analytical and detached, if not scientific, representation of the mafia and mafia-like things, but it is grounded on a strong commitment to a well-defined political philosophical tradition, the liberal one running from John Locke to John Rawls, passing through Adam Smith and Alexis de Tocqueville (see Santoro 2007). With Weber, we would say that this 'relation to values' is a necessary prerequisite and ingredient of any social study. With the same Weber, however, we could ask whether scholars working on mafia make every effort to put aside those same values or keep them under control when doing empirical research, theorizing about their data, and writing their texts on mafia.

In conclusion, we could say that the last four decades of mafia studies, at least in Italy, have been marked by a series of features that we can synthetize as the 'G effects' (dalla Chiesa 2010b; Santoro 2010). The first is the Generation effect. The second is the Justice effect (*giustizia* in Italian). The third is the Google effect. To these three we should add at least three others: a Gender effect, a Gambetta effect and, finally, a *Gomorrah* effect. In short, we are thinking of the following aspects:

1. New generations of researchers often move ahead forgetting the contributions of the previous generations of scholars. This is apparent in the almost total lack of references to classics of mafia studies as well as to scholars who have not entered the pantheon of contemporary authorities in these studies – e.g., Hess, Blok, the Schneiders, Arlacchi.

2. With the testimony of Buscetta, the maxi-trial, the assassinations of judges Falcone and Borsellino, and the rise of an antimafia movement, the justice system and its products have become the major source of reference, of information and even of symbolic legitimation in research on mafia. Today there is a large industry of articles and books almost exclusively built on court testimony and documents. The risk is to take as neutral what is inevitably the application of a point of view on mafia, losing sight of the technical legal constraints to which judges are subject and therefore of what cannot be captured by the judicial apparatus.

3. Google has become a relevant source even in mafia studies because of its readiness and its apparent completeness. But Google and the internet in general are not so transparent or so reliable as people often think as sources of data about a complex topic like mafia.

4. Gender considerations entered mafia studies only in the 1990s, with the first studies devoted to the role of women in mafia organizations and the increase of female mafia students sensitive to issues of gender identity and inequalities. Mafia is indeed a big topic for gender analysis, with its patriarchical organization, its references to honour and its gender-based and biased division of labour.

5. We already have introduced the Gambetta effect, and in the next chapter we will focus on this.

6. As everyone knows, *Gomorrah* has been one of the major bestselling publications in the world in recent decades. Saviano's background

as a graduate in philosophy with some anthropological education influenced the way the social sciences entered his writing as symbolic and intellectual resources in this sort of fictionalized ethnography of camorra life in some areas of Naples and its surrounding area (though the book's final chapter is focused on a case of 'mafia export' to Scotland). Surely, the impact of *Gomorrah* on social research has been more indirect than direct – as a reference point for debating issues such as the comparative merits of academic writing and literature, or the impact of a certain kind of writing on public debate, or even the realibility of the sources used by Saviano in writing his book.

This impact might be measured by the number of articles devoted to the book in sociological, historical and criminological journals, at least in Italy. However, its impact can follow much more subtle routes, as the vehicle for a certain vision of what the mafia is (and for Saviano the mafia is first and foremost a mark of incivility and something to be denounced and combatted, and in light of these objectives it has to be described, understood and denounced). The success of a bestseller is not only in the number of copies sold or its position in bestseller lists, but also in its capacity to shape the public debate according to its own terms and in its even wider circulation through other means, such as films and TV series (and both have been made from *Gomorrah* the book).

Global Mafia (or a Globalization of Mafia Studies)

The story of mafia research in Italy and the US accounts for the greatest part of mafia studies as we know them today. But something still remains to be covered – which may, indeed, account for a seventh G effect. We have seen how the historian Hobsbawm approached the mafia and similar phenomena such as social banditry in a comparative framework. This is not that common in mafia studies, where national cases – sometimes even regional ones – have been typically studied as individual and sometimes even exceptional cases, the product of a very local and contingent array of events and factors. Only rarely have the Sicilian mafia or the Neapolitan camorra been approached as instances of a more general class of social phenomena. In the case of mafia studies in the US, this parochialism has been so strong as to render Italian research on Italian mafias irrelevant or unknown to scholars – who very often do not read Italian. The same has been true for Italian scholars or even foreign students of Italian mafias, who have rarely compared their research objects to what was known about their American counterparts.

Of course, the research on regional forms of (organized) crime is a well-established genre in both the social and the historical sciences. The point is how these studies may be said to pertain to a common research area, a supra-local one, that could contribute to the knowledge and understanding of a whole new class of social phenomena.

For many years, studies on organized criminal forms have typically been regionalized, i.e. remained local. There were studies on triads in the nineteenth century as well as on Indian thugs, many undertaken by British (colonial) observers. There were local studies (not many, as far as we know) on Japanese yakuza, the subject of a well-established genre of film production in Japan since at least the 1950s. More recently, there have been studies on gangs in Mexico and Colombia – many only available in Spanish. None of these books has been able to overcome the borders of their original language and enter the international debate, i.e. the debate written or spoken in English. When this has occurred, it has happened because of certain institutional arrangements or innovations in scholarly toolboxes. The 'organized crime' category has helped, of course, in looking for patterns across cases – regional and even national. After all, ethnicity has been a central variable in this research area for a long time. But you can study Mexican gangs without thinking you are contributing to the study of Sicilian mafia, a few similarities, for instance in terms of the concept of honour and masculine culture (after all, both Mexico and Sicily were influenced by Spanish baroque culture), notwithstanding.

In the 1980s, and even more in the 1990s, however, something changed in literature on mafia. The implicit message found in Hobsbawm's first book was to become reality. Hess had already suggested a move towards comparative research in his introduction to a new Italian edition of Alongi's (1977 [1887]) classic text on mafia. Gambetta's book raised issues of comparative analysis, and a few of Gambetta's students applied his model to other instances of the 'industry of private protection', such as the Russian mafiya (Varese 1994, 2001), Japanese yakuza (Hill 2003) and Hong Kong triads (Chu 2000). Other scholars also started to analyse local criminal experiences as if they were instances of a wider class of mafia phenomena, subsumed under some more general conceptual categories, e.g., as 'patrimonial alliances' in Collins's (2011) interpretation.

This move notwithstanding, almost nothing of this literature can be found in the bibliographic references of books and articles devoted to Italian mafias written in Italy – as if they were, indeed, very diverse phenomena. Some brief references would suffice, just to acknowledge one's awareness of the existence of similar phenomena in other parts of the world. It is easier to find attempts to locate Italian experiences and stories side by side with similar or apparently analogous experiences – such as Nigerian trafficking and cults, Colombian cartels, drug trafficking in Turkey, and so on – when there are documented connections among these geographically different species of criminal organizations.

The globalization of organized crime has surely pressed observers to focus on this network of interconnections as well as on their similarities. Nor is it surprising that books by journalists have been among the first to have arrived in bookshops and libraries – with the pioneering contribution of Manuel Castells (2000), who was neither a mafia specialist nor an established name in mafia studies but, rather, a sensitive and reputed analyst of social change. Comparative studies on mafias are far from common; we can count them on the fingers of one hand (see Varese 2010, 2017).

A big issue lies at the centre of this literature, however: how can we be sure we are making sound comparisons among things so far apart in space and with such different histories as the Sicilian mafia, the yakuza, the triads and even the so-called Russian *mafiya* if they are not supported by a theory, or at least a general concept (e.g., 'organized crime', the 'industry of private protection', and so on)? Indeed, a general concept of some kind is necessary when we are writing or talking about mafias in the plural – even if we restrict our range to Italian mafias such as the Sicilian one, the camorra, and the *'ndrangheta*, which are different enough among themselves to make it difficult to compare them without some conceptual structure (see, e.g., Paoli 2003). This set of concepts is exactly what we need when constructing our research object.

To conclude this chapter, it would probably be useful to offer a final diagrammatic representation about the main distinctions that have structured the discussion on mafia since its inception in Italy in the nineteenth century. Instead of an image, I syntetize them according to the following set of conceptual, even epistemological, alternatives: individual/collective; centralized/decentred; ethnically based/diffused; economic/political; culture/structure; culture as regulative/culture as constitutive. Think of them as a series of nested, recursive oppositions. We will see in the next chapter how this set of oppositions has been managed in what looks like the single most influential of contemporary theories of mafia – i.e. the economic theory set forth by Gambetta working on the shoulders of pioneers such as Schelling, Reuter, Tilly and economic historian of Venice in the Middle Ages and early modern times, Frederic C. Lane. The next chapter addresses a critical reconstruction of that theory.

3

What is Right with the Economic Theory of the Mafia?

The conspiracy theorist will believe that institutions can be understood completely as the result of conscious design; and as to collectives, he usually ascribes to them a kind of group-personality, treating them as conspiring agents, just as if they were individual men. As opposed to this view, the social theorist should recognize that the persistence of institutions and collectives creates a problem to be solved in terms of analysis of individual social actions and their unintended (and often unwanted) social consequences, as well as their intended ones.

Popper 2002 [1963], 168

The previous chapter has provided a general overview of mafia studies, identifying the competing theories and comparing and contrasting the approaches used by different theorists since the inception of these studies in nineteenth-century Italy. My aim has not been to offer a complete history of mafia studies but only to show how the mafia has been variously constructed as an object of social research – an operation of construction that, in the case of the mafia, is indispensable given the ambivalent, confused, mysterious and elusive nature of the object or series of objects called by this name.

Among other things, we have seen that there is a common thread running through the history of mafia studies, uniting theories and approaches that, in other aspects, look very different: this thread is the idea that the mafia is an economic activity, a business, and that mafiosi are first and foremost interested in economic gain or profit.[1] Since the very beginning of mafia studies, indeed, mafia has *also*[2] been conceived of as a kind of enterprise devoted to supplying some 'good': as an *industry of crime* (*industria del delitto*) in Leopoldo Franchetti's terms.[3] While *violence* was the typical 'good' supplied by mafiosi for this nineteenth-century liberal scholar and politician – the author of one of the very first systematic analyses of mafia based, at least in part, on fieldwork, what was called a 'social survey' at that time – it was the provision of *protection* from a variety of risks in a variety of activities that was the essential function of mafia according to Franchetti's contemporaries. While the main representative of this line of thought today is the Italian sociologist Diego Gambetta, we should recall that the equation of mafia with an 'industry' had its proponents among contemporary sociologists, such as Catanzaro (1992 [1988]), as well as economists, such as Reuter (1983). However, it is with Gambetta and his 'school' that the equation between mafia and 'industry' as well as business has been conceptually exploited and brought to its ultimate effects, making it the cornerstone for the emergence of what Gambetta himself (1987) named an 'economic theory of the mafia'.

With Gambetta, what was originally just one element in a wider puzzle (like the one depicted by Franchetti), and what was being suggested in those years as a turning point in the historical evolution of the mafia and mafiosi – the transition 'from men of honour to entrepreneurs' (Arlacchi 1983a, 1983b [1980]) – was promoted to a transhistorical, essential feature of the mafia itself. Far from being the outcome of some recent change, business, according to Gambetta, is part and parcel of the mafia being mafiosi; they are businesspeople involved in the market: not the market of land or drugs, but of protection. When acting in the land or drug markets, as they often do, mafiosi are there less because of their interests in the land or drugs, but first and foremost because of their services to the operation of these markets, as in any other market in which protection may be a precious asset that cannot be taken for granted. And if this were the case, if mafia were, *ab origine* and by its very nature, an economic activity, then the best theory of the mafia could only be an economic one.

Not surprisingly, the spread of economics and economic thinking that has been occurring in the social sciences since the 1960s at some point reached the relatively insulated and peripheral research area of the mafia. In just a few years, the diffusion of economic thinking impacted on the study of law as well as crime, politics and administration and also drug trafficking and corruption. The study of the mafia would not be immune to this development and, in fact, a tradition of mafia studies inspired by economics and distinguished by its recourse to an economic way of thinking has developed, and is now well established in the field.

This is the focus of this chapter as it tries to 'rationally reconstruct' (as Hungarian philosopher Imre Lakatos would have said), in a 'rational but nonrationalistic' way (Ginzburg 1986, x), a set of principles and themes that substantiate what I would call the rational/public choice tradition of mafia studies. First, I locate this tradition alongside its foils. Second, I will illustrate the tenets of the most influential stream of economic theory of the mafia, the one centred on the idea of a market of protection. Third, I will discuss the strengths and limits of this research stream. Fourth, and lastly, I will focus on a sort of minority school in this tradition, which is more directly linked to public choice and the economic analysis of *political* life.

The main objective of this chapter is, therefore, to expose and dissect this economic theory of the mafia, showing its strengths and its weaknesses. The strengths of the theory will be located in the identification of protection as the central object of mafiosi's work, and in the claim that it is possible to work on mafias in rigorous terms, moving from analytically forged concepts and clearly stated theories, and elaborating them in order to account for the research object in genuinely fresh ways.

The weaknesses of the theory are contingent upon a series of traits, such as the surreptitious adoption of a politically grounded point of view (that may be described as liberal universalism or universal individualism) which constrains the analysis along implicit but powerful normative (politically and morally engaged) grounds; the aspiration to hyperrationalize in order to account for social life which misses the opportunity to give emotions and other 'irrational elements' their due; and the recourse to narrowly conceived notions of the state, of politics and of culture – the latter fundamentally reduced to its flawed Parsonsian definition, and for this same reason understandingly expunged from the framework.

Of course, these are conceptual strategies that are far from specific to Gambetta's perspective alone and that may prove to be helpful in doing social research and sociological theorizing – *on the condition of clarifying what is gained and what is lost by adopting this paradigm, and that concurrent paradigms are not reduced to flawed and already surpassed embodiments*. Simplifying a bit, the central problem with the economic theory of the mafia (as with any other 'economic theory') is – to use Bourdieu's words – that it has an immanent tendency to substitute the model of reality with the reality of the model. There is more in the mafia than what the economic theory and economic reasoning/modelling can capture. The point, of course, is how to assess the nature and weight of this 'more'.

The Rationalist School and Its Foils

As pointed out in Chapter 2, mafia studies may be thought of as making up a research field in Bourdieu's sense of the term 'field' (*champ* in the original French), that is a structured space of positions which function as a space of forces and struggles for what is at stake in the field – with intellectual reputation being the principal stake in the intellectual field. To have an idea of how strong these struggles can be, it is sufficient to scan the relevant academic journals and read the reviews of this or that book on the mafia, through which the tensions and fault lines traversing the field are made visible and readable.[4]

In Chapter 2, we have also seen that some authors and texts are positioned better than others in this field, at least for the amount of attention they command and the visibility they enjoy. What we have seen up to now, however, pertains more to individual scholars than to research groups or 'schools', more to individual positions (or works) in the field than to clusters of positions (and works). In order to account for these more encompassing sets of interlaced authors and works, it may be useful to refer to the tripartite classification of ideal-typical research schools originally proposed for comparative political analysis, but easily transferable to most fields of social enquiry (see Lichbach 1997, 2003). Briefly, the scheme identifies three major camps in the social sciences: structuralist, culturalist and rationalist. Each of them has an ontology, an epistemology and a methodology. The first sees the world as made of social relationships among individuals, groups, institutions, organizations – relations among things, and not the individual things themselves, are what count. Individuals are always embedded in bundles of relations, and it is the way in which these bundles are generated and work, and with what consequences, that is of relevance. Intentions are relatively unimportant, if they are important at all (strong structuralism). The second is focused on the more immaterial social substances, such as beliefs, norms, values and, above all, meanings. Individuals are capable of action, but always in historically given contexts: interests are shaped by symbolic universes and cannot be abstractly posited. In a somewhat extreme version, people are exactly what the system of values, norms, beliefs and meanings in which they have been educated and in which they live asks them to do; but this is just an extreme case, made famous by Parsons in the 1950s but discredited after the 1960s and 1970s and replaced by more interpretivist (Geertz 1973) or practice-oriented (Bourdieu 1977) perspectives. The third is made of methodological individualists for whom only individual agents may choose, prefer, learn, believe, etc. Collectivities have no autonomous status; they are simply what the individuals comprising them make of them. People are to be understood as endowed with intentions and purpose and an intimate capacity of rational calculus. Social problems arise because the aggregate consequences of even rational decisions and actions may be quite irrational or, in the preferred language of this school, are unintended and unwanted, albeit inevitable. In sum, 'rationalist ontology depicts a world populated by rational individuals and possibly irrational collectivities. The rational pursuit of individual interests explains the all-too-common occurrence of irrational social outcomes' (Lichbach 1997, 246).

This scheme provides another way of accounting for the varieties of mafia studies I outlined in the previous chapter – a very efficacious, though less precise way, I think, than the way I used. While less precise, this classificatory framework has the merit of making the major fault lines splitting the field clear, and of directing the focus on this chapter's subject: the economic theory of the mafia with its internal articulations and foils (see Table 3.1). Moving from this classification, we can say that, because of its associations with, and sometimes even roots in, Marxism, on the one side, and social anthropology, on the other (to which we could add the Chicago ecological-institutional tradition from Thrasher and Landesco to Cressey, passing through the almost-Chicagoan William Foote Whyte and even Elias's figurational sociology), mafia studies, especially as it developed after the Second World War, has privileged a structuralist approach – an approach centred on the analysis of social structures and their consequences on both cultural codes and behaviours (e.g., Hobsbawm, Blok, the Schneiders, Sciarrone, dalla Chiesa, Santino, etc.).[5]

This structuralist tradition has been accompanied by a more scattered stream of cultural(ist) research whose roots may be traced back to nineteenth-century folklore studies (and to Sicilian positivism, especially through the ethnographic research by Pitrè, one of the fathers of cultural anthropology in Italy) and whose developments in the post-war decades were informed from time to time by Parsonsian value theory, Weberian and Chicago-based subcultural theory, labelling theory or symbolic interactionism, phenomenological sociology à la Schutz (see Hess 1970; Smith 1990 [1975]; Albini 1971; see also Siebert 1996 for an exemplar of Frankfurt School-inspired critical theory *cum* phenomenological analysis of the mafia in everyday life). This research stream has probably been more influential in the public sphere than in the academy, and endured strong scholarly criticism after the 1970s. As a consequence of its ongoing marginalization, the cultural(ist) school was paradoxically impervious to the sea change that was occurring in contemporary cultural studies and cultural theory from the 1980s, through and after the so-called 'cultural turn' (for an early plea to make a cultural turn in

Table 3.1: Three ideal-typical research schools/approaches in the field of mafia studies

Properties	Structuralist	Culturalist	Rationalist
Periodization • beginnings • spread	1880s 1950s	1880s 1970–80	1960s 1990-present
Ontological assumptions	Relations among actors Social structures as systems of rules and patterns of resource distribution	Meanings and rules, identities, intersubjectivity, shared values, practices	Rational actors with beliefs and desires, unintended, even irrational aggregate outcomes
Epistemological assumptions	Structures with laws of dynamics Social types with causal powers	Cultural constructionism (culture constitutes reality)	Intentions explained, methodological individualism
Methodological preferences	Comparative social history Social ethnography	Case studies Cultural history, ethnography	Comparative statics, modelling, analytic narratives Social Network Analysis, ethnography
Main (classical) references	Marx Weber Gramsci Wallerstein Elias	Pitrè Weber (Parsons) Becker Schutz	Adam Smith Schelling Lane Nozick Coleman
Criticism	Determinism, misrecognition of agency	Determinism, risks of tautology, conceptual vagueness	Instrumentalism Mechanical-behavioural view of subjectivity
Sub-traditions	Marxism/ Gramscism Social anthropology Figurational sociology	Folklore studies Subcultural theory Symbolic interactionism Interpretative socio-anthropology	Economic theory of the mafia Protection theory (PT) Public choice theory of the mafia
Exemplars	Hobsbawm (1959), Blok (1974), Schneider and Schneider (1976)	Hess (1970), Smith (1990 [1975]), Siebert (1996)	Gambetta (1993), Sabetti (1984)

Source: adapted from Lichbach (1997, 245).

mafia studies, see Santoro 1998, 2000). After a period of decline, if not demise, during the last two decades of the twentieth century, the cultural approach in the new millennium was revived by scholars like Deborah Puccio-Den, who applied tools drawn from French social and cultural theory (e.g., 2019) to the case of the Sicilian mafia and antimafia, and Randall Collins (2011), with his attempt to produce a general theory of mafias (and gangs) as patrimonial alliances built on a mix of Weberian analysis of patrimonialism and Durkheimian ritual theory. They were not alone, however, in this revival of the culturalist approach, aware of the pitfalls and traps of the old culturalism and endowed with the resources made available for the study of cultural objects by three decades of the cultural turn (see Bachmann-Medick 2016).

To be honest, it is not an easy task to locate mafia studies along the fault line separating structuralist from culturalist approaches (and the just-cited Collins is a case in point), as a feature of many studies, especially since the 1980s, has been the attempt to merge structure and culture as a way of acknowledging multidimensionality of mafia (e.g., Arlacchi 1983a, 1983b [1980]; Catanzaro 1992 [1988]; Paoli 2003; see also Schneider and Schneider 2003). Rarely, however, has 'culture' in mafia studies been approached along the lines of interpretative, post-Parsonsian, meaning-centred cultural approaches (of the type pioneered by Geertz and developed by many others in anthropology, sociology and history), of what has been called a 'strong programme' of cultural analysis (Alexander and Smith 2001), or even allegedly 'weaker' but well-established programmes, such as the practice-based varieties of cultural analysis that are common currency in contemporary cultural studies and the sociology of cultural life (e.g., Bourdieu, Turner, Ortner, Willis, etc.).

The case of Bourdieu's (missing) place in mafia studies is enlightening and, in many ways, surprising, considering his centrality in current research in the social and human sciences (Santoro et al. 2018). However, scanning the wide literature on mafias, only a few passing references to his work (nowadays at the core of the social sciences and humanities) can be found, typically in contexts that are not really congruent with the kind of epistemological commitments his concepts require. 'Rites of institution' (Paoli 2003; for the original concept, see Bourdieu 1993 [1982]) and symbolic domination (e.g., Dino 2007) are possibly the most visible borrowings from Bourdieu's lexicon that can be found in the literature – but when you encounter the concept of social capital, something quite common in current scholarship on the mafia (e.g., Sciarrone 2009, 2014; Pottenger 2014), you may bet that it is James Coleman or Robert Putnam, and not Bourdieu, who is the author referenced (but see Santoro 2007; Santoro and Solaroli 2017; Sciarrone

2018).[6] Habitus, field, cultural and symbolic capital are concepts still waiting to be systematically employed in mafia studies – at least in those segments of mafia studies 'that count'. Another missing presence in mafia literature is that of Durkheim – the third father of sociology after Marx and Weber, the latter being authors well represented in mafia studies (through direct references or associations with research traditions inspired by them). This means that symbolism and rituals as well as systems of classification, concepts so prominent in Durkheim and among (neo)Durkheimians, are far from core subjects in mafia studies. As we will see, this also means that no serious use has been made in research on mafia of a model strongly associated with Durkheim's school, that of the 'gift' (Mauss 1990 [1925]), its potentialities for enlightening mafia practices notwithstanding.

As a consequence of these missing references, which clearly amount to missing resources, it is far from unusual in mafia studies to read harsh complaints about the faults of the cultural concept in offering explanations of the mafia, whereas the 'cultural' argument, when explicated, would amount to the following:

> [I]ndividual agents are *pushed-from-behind* by an immaterial substance called 'Sicilian' culture. People's behaviour is considered as mechanically shaped by a set of beliefs, norms and cultural values, which determine the preferences and the set of feasible alternatives. Hess in particular provides an account of Mafia activities in terms of a sub-cultural system which would explain the resistance of Southern Italy to change. (Varese 1994, 230; see also Gambetta 1993, 10)

I am not saying these complaints are without foundation. It is true that the concept of culture has often been used to generate circular explanations of social facts and analytically flawed accounts of social phenomena. But a complaint like this says nothing about the concept of culture as such, nor about the structure of a cultural argument *per se*, but only addresses *a certain* version of the culture concept and *a certain* way of practising cultural analysis, a version and a way that have been criticized inside the fields of cultural sociology and cultural anthropology since the 1970s and which are no longer used by serious students of culture and practitioners of cultural analysis in the social sciences (see, e.g., Swidler 1986; Alexander 2003; Sewell 2005). Paradoxically, these complaints in the literature on the mafia emerged most loudly precisely when the 'cultural turn' was already producing its first effects in other research areas, creating the conditions for the emergence of what has been called the 'new sociology of culture' (Smith 1998).

Also, as a consequence of the growing dissatisfaction towards the weaknesses and deficiencies of the old culturalist approach as they were apparent in the more specialized literature on the mafia, a new school in mafia studies (and in research on organized crime more generally) has been growing since the 1980s, a rationalist school that has established itself at the very centre of the field since the early 2000s. The movement started with the pioneering work on crime markets and criminal strategies by economists Thomas Schelling (1967, 1971) and Peter Reuter (1983) – both located at the famous RAND Corporation in the US while researching on this topic (see Amadae 2003) – joined a short time later by the specifically mafia-centred work of (at the time) UK-based Italian sociologist Diego Gambetta (1987, 1993, 2009; see also 2011 for a retrospective assessment), and soon followed by multiple generations of PhD students trained mainly at Oxford (prominent among them Federico Varese) and an array of followers all over the world.

Published in 1993 (in 1992 in Italian, but only because the Italian publisher 'has been faster' – Gambetta 2011, 1), Gambetta's *The Sicilian Mafia. The Business of Private Protection* was a book that in many ways changed the game in the study of the mafia; the previous chapter has already shown its impact on mafia studies as measured by that imperfect, but still useful, proxy of influence that is the rough number of citations. What may still be worth noticing is how this impact or influence has changed over time, and there is no doubt that the trend has been a growing one, at least until 2017 (see Figure 3.1). Other studies belonging to this camp have already been referred to and comparatively 'measured' in their relative weight in the previous chapter, to which I refer the reader. It is always difficult to identify and locate the mainstream, but it would be difficult to dispute the claim that if there is something like a hegemonic bloc in the field of mafia studies, that built around Gambetta and the 'economic theory of the mafia' is what comes closest to it.

To have a precise grasp on the latest developments, we should however distinguish between two rather different versions of rationalism in mafia studies. One is what has been defined as the 'economic theory of the mafia' (at least since Gambetta 1987), which comprises the bulk of this school, also due to its subsequently constructed linkage to a more broadly encompassing protection theory (see below). The other is a minority, 'public choice' variant mainly represented by the Italo-Canadian political scientist Filippo Sabetti, whose 1984 book has been briefly presented in the previous chapter (but see also Sabetti 2002, 2011). Combining fieldwork, historical research and analytical theory, Sabetti has demonstrated the feasibility of informal and outlaw regimes such as the mafia as tools and arguments originally developed to make sense of formal political arrangements and rules used in democratic regimes (e.g., Buchanan and Tullock 1962; Ostrom and Ostrom 1971).

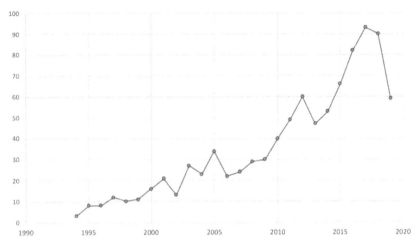

Figure 3.1: Number of citations of Gambetta 1993–2019
Note: The total sum of citations according to Scopus is not that large
compared to other texts (according to the Scopus citation database, it is less
than twenty times the number of citations of a classic reference like Bourdieu's
Distinction (2010 [1979]), to give just one example). It is, however, the most
cited text among those dealing with the mafia, almost double that of the work
in second place (i.e. Blok 1974).
Source: Scopus database

Roughly put: the former variant is an institutional theory of mafias
conceived as a kind of business, as an *industry* (a *sui generis* industry
dealing with protection understood as a special kind of commodity); the
second is an instance, and application to the mafia (especially Sicilian
mafia), of the economic analysis of *political decisions and organizations* pioneered in the 1960s by highly creative economists like Kenneth
Arrow, James Buchanan, Gordon Tullock, Anthony Downs, Gary S.
Becker, Mancur Olson and Elinor Ostrom (for a critical appraisal of this
tradition of thought, see Udehn 1996). This is an important point, one
already suggested in Chapter 2. An economic approach does not necessarily result in an economic definition of the researched object. Applying
economics to the state or democracy does not necessarily produce a
definition of the state as an economic institution; symmetrically, you may
see in the mafia an economic structure, even if your approach is sociological and anthropological, as the Schneiders' case shows.

In what follows, I will focus mainly on the first brand of rationalist
studies of the mafia, on the economic theory of the mafia (ETM) in
particular and on protection theory (PT) as its generalization, but I

will still reserve a few lines at the end for the public choice brand, as it offers a bridge to introduce the reader to the chapters that follow, where I develop the main argument of this book, i.e. that when we talk of mafia(s), we are talking about a kind of political organization or 'political form of life', and that we would do better to look for conceptual tools that are different (and more adequate to the object) from those offered by the economists' way of thinking.

The Economic Theory of the Mafia

We already know it: ETM has developed from the identification of mafia with an industry – a special kind of industry, the industry of protection. Indeed, the first tenet of the theory is that protection lies at the heart of mafia: this is what mafiosi provide; this is the good they specialize in. In Gambetta's sharp words:

> The hypothesis developed here is that the mafia is a specific economic enterprise, *an industry which produces, promotes, and sells private protection.* The mafia represents this industry as it has developed in Sicily over the last one hundred and fifty years ... To consider the mafia an industry is not a novel idea. Writing in 1876, Leopoldo Franchetti called it *'l'industria della violenza'*, and he meant *industry* in the literal sense.[7] As his definition suggests, however, the commodity with which the mafia has been most closely associated is violence, not protection. (1993, 1; emphasis added)

Contrary to a widespread argument according to which mafiosi were violent entrepreneurs (e.g., Blok 1974) or men involved in illegal and illicit trades (from blackmail to rackets), Gambetta identifies the proper object of mafiosi industry in the provision of protection:

> Mafiosi may sometimes be dealers in a variety of commodities both legal and illegal – and for that matter they may also be doctors, politicians, or even priests – but this is not the *differentia specifica* separating Mafiosi from ordinary entrepreneurs. Mafiosi are first and foremost entrepreneurs in *one particular commodity* – protection – and this is what distinguishes them from simple criminals, simple entrepreneurs, or criminal entrepreneurs. (1993, 19; emphasis added)

Moving from this apparently simple definition, and after elaborating on the alleged properties of the special, immaterial commodity that is protection, an *economic theory* of the mafia is developed analytically with respect to resources, symbols, equilibrium conditions and so on. In the end, Gambetta (1993, 155) is able to describe the Sicilian mafia as 'that set of firms which (1) are active in the protection industry under a common trademark with recognizable features; (2) acknowledge one another as the legitimate suppliers of authentic mafioso protection; and (3) succeed in preventing the unauthorised use of their trademark by pirate firms' (see Bandiera 2003, with reference to Gambetta 1993).

A more detailed presentation of Gambetta's theoretical argument may be worthwhile, and for this a good starting point is a vignette, a story Gambetta draws from Marco Monnier's book (see Chapter 2) on the camorra published in Naples in 1862 (that Gambetta moves from a book on the Neapolitan camorra to write a book on the Sicilian mafia may sound bizarre, but it is consistent with one of the assumptions of the economic theory, i.e. the comparability of mafias as instances of a more general model of industry; I will come back to this point later, however). From this vignette, Gambetta is able to extract what he presents as the main characters and the essential logics behind what he proposes to see as the industry of private protection. There is a buyer, there is a seller and, finally, there is a 'third person': let's call him Don Beppe. There is also a fourth character, indeed never considered by Gambetta: the object to be exchanged, which in this case is an animated one, a horse. I will not elaborate on this point now, but as we will see in a next chapter (in which I focus on violence and strategies of 'distancing from otherness'), this is not an irrelevant feature.

The problem at stake in the vignette is simple (and originally suggested by Akerlof 1970): who can guarantee that the horse to be exchanged is a good one, that it is not a 'lemon'? Clearly, the seller has an interest in representing the horse as being a very good one, but how can the buyer be sure he is not being ripped off (*fregato*)? A third agent enters at this point, as the man who has the standing to guarantee the quality of the object to be exchanged (the horse). This 'third' is, of course, the mafioso (in the vignette the camorrista). We can diagrammatically represent the network as shown in Figure 3.2. This simple insight – which could be presented as a historical solution to the 'lemon problem' – is developed by Gambetta into a fully-fledged model that could be roughly specified according to the following set of propositions (for a different way of modelling this, specifically focused on the problem of the origins of the mafia, see Varese 1994):[8]

a. Those who are called 'mafiosi' are best conceived of as agents dealing with a very special and specific good, i.e. protection (so, they are not just 'criminals' but, first and foremost, economic agents).
b. Protection as a service or good in itself (with the accompanying act of protecting, it seems, but this is not really clear) is to be distinguished

from the protected goods or services, which may change from time to time and in different places, and have been in fact multifarious (from gambling to money laundering, from kidnapping to alcohol or drug trafficking, from subcontracting to loansharking, and so on).

c. Mafiosi are rational agents in a market specialized in the exchange of one good in which they act as suppliers. They sell protection to anyone who wants to buy it, even if there are some tensions regarding the choice of how many to protect (it is convenient to them to limit the number, but it may be more convenient to enlarge this number in order to increase their autonomy from individual clients. As rational suppliers, mafiosi have, however, an interest in limiting their supply of protection in order to ensure a certain level of insecurity, thus sustaining demand for protection).

d. This protection business is independent from other activities in which mafiosi may be engaged individually, in both licit and illicit industries (as traders, shopkeepers, carpenters, drug and organ traffickers, gamblers, capital investors, managers of property or casinos, middlemen or brokers between centre and periphery, etc.); being protectors, they may protect their personal business at no or low cost, and this is a big incentive for sideline activities (note: students of mafia often confuse the proper activities of the mafia with the activities that individual mafiosi may perform as private citizens, so to say, using the protection that, as mafiosi, they can produce to further their activities).

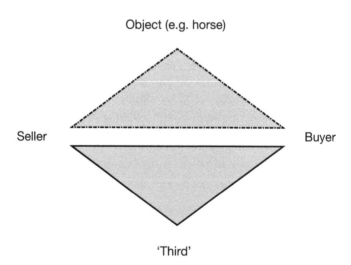

Figure 3.2: Minimal social network in the mafia

e. As it is sold, mafia protection is to be conceived of, and analysed as, a commodity and not a public good; it is private protection and, as such, it is totally different from the public, universalistic and non-selective protection furnished by state agencies on behalf of 'the state'.

f. Collectively understood, the mafia is an industry specialized in the provision (i.e. production, promotion and selling) of protection; the whole industry is made of both mafiosi as suppliers and their clients/customers as purchasers and consumers of protection.

g1. Mafias arise when states are not strong enough to protect their citizens/subjects – i.e. their bodies, their properties and their property rights (this point and the next are at the root of what is known as the 'property rights theory of mafia emergence'; see Varese 1994, 2010 and Bandiera 2003).

g2. For a mafia to exist, free markets of goods have to exist and property rights have to exist as well. Monopolies of the means of production have to be broken and private properties have to expand for demand for protection to develop. This is what happened in Sicily after 1812 (with the demise of feudalism) and in Russia and other ex-Soviet Bloc countries after the fall of the Soviet Union (indeed, a bit earlier with the reforms that led up to its fall).[9]

h. Symbols and rituals of the mafia (part and parcel of mafia representation in the media, from photography to cinema to literature), as well as documented practices like religious sponsorship, are to be conceived of and analysed as marketing devices (to create and reinforce brands) and advertisement tools for the industry (especially if mafiosi have to compete with other potential or actual suppliers of protection, including state agencies) (Gambetta 1993, 2009; see also Varese 2006, on the case of yakuza cinema).

i. Violence is just a means (a necessary one when dealing with a special commodity like protection) and not an end or a perverse taste for mafiosi, who are always rational agents careful to calculate the pros and cons of violence and regulate its use accordingly (the model assumes they want to minimize their costs in order to maximize their benefits, so they calculate when it is convenient for them to make use of violence, to simply threaten to use violence, or to not use violence at all).

j. Protection is a special commodity with special features, and this makes the industry of protection a special case among industries; the special features of the mafia are an implication of protection as a commodity with special properties.

k. Protection always runs the risk of transforming itself into extortion (when it is ineffective as a service, when it is bogus) or to being perceived as such (it is indeed a question of perspective).

l.   Most of the morally reprehensible features of the mafia, like deception and recourse to violence (including murder), are prerequisites for or, alternatively, unintended effects and externalities of, the protection industry's normal workings.

There is much to be praised in the identification of mafia with a single, core activity, especially such a complex and consequential one as *protection*, and we will come back to this issue in the next chapter. What I want to highlight here is the special character of the protection mafiosi deal with in the economic theory of the mafia. According to Gambetta (1993; see also Varese 1994, 2001), mafia is to be understood as an industry specialized in the supply of *private* protection in a context of state weakness. When the public protection supplied by the state is lacking or inefficient, there are opportunities for *private* entrepreneurs to specialize in the supply of this particular good, and its selling in a market. This is, Gambetta says, what happened in Sicily in the first half of the nineteenth century (after the fall of feudalism and before the unification of Italy; see also Bandiera 2003), what happened in Russia after the fall of the Soviet Empire (see Varese 1994), and what can be shown to have happened elsewhere (on Hong Kong triads, see Chu 2000; on Japan, see Hill 2003; for the case of Syria, predictively, see Haidar 2019). More recently, Varese has suggested that:

> Two authors advanced similar claims in the nineteenth and early twentieth centuries, respectively: Leopoldo Franchetti, an Italian aristocrat who published a report on Sicily in 1876 – *Condizioni politiche e amministrative della Sicilia*; and John Landesco, an American ethnographer employed by the Chicago Crime Commission who published in 1929 *Organized Crime in Chicago* as part of the 1,100-page Illinois Crime Survey. (2014, 343)[10]

Putting all this information together, we can generate the stylized portrait of this 'theory group' (for this concept, see Mullins 1973) collected in Table 3.2.

From the Economic Theory of the Mafia to Protection Theory

In an effort to provide further generalization and theory-building, but also retrospective intellectual legitimation, ETM has recently been presented by one of its main proponents as an extension, and at the same

Table 3.2: Social and intellectual properties of the ETM as a 'theory group'

Intellectual ancestors	Franchetti 1993 [1877]; Landesco 1968 [1929]
Intellectual sources	Lane 1958; Schelling 1967, 1971; Nozick 1974; Elster 1986
Intellectual leaders	Gambetta; Reuter
Training centres	Cambridge; RAND; University of Maryland
Disciplinary references	Economics; sociology; criminology
Paradigm content	The mafia is an instance of an industry of private protection. Mafiosi are rational agents of this industry
Program statement	Reuter 1983; Gambetta 1987, 1993
Exemplars	Gambetta 1993, 2009; Varese 2011
Applications	Varese 1994, 2001; Alexander 1997; Chu 2000; Frye 2002; Bandiera 2003; Hill 2003; Anderson and Bandiera 2005; Wang 2011, 2017; Campana 2011; Campana and Varese 2013, 2018; Pottenger 2014; Skarbek 2014; Haidar 2019
Examples of critical work	Santino 1995; Paoli 2003; Santoro 2007

time a component, of a supposedly more long-lived and more encompassing 'protection theory':

> Protection Theory (PT) is a set of propositions that describes the properties of the commodity 'protection' and predicts the actions of its providers. It has been used by economists, historians and political theorists to explain the emergence of the modern state (e.g., Lane 1958; Nozick 1974; Tilly 1985; Olson 1993, 2000). Recently, several authors have adopted it to account for the behaviour of gangs, organized crime and the Mafia. This literature spans several disciplines and suggests analytical links between the behaviour of states and that of criminal groups. The key insight of this theory is to distinguish between those who commit a crime and/or trade in criminal commodities, from those who make sure that promises are kept and more broadly 'protect' the exchange. (Shortland and Varese 2014, 1; see also Varese 2014)

In a sense, this relocation of ETM into the context of a more general theory of protection looks like a necessary integration. After having widely exploited insights spread throughout a dispersed and unconnected corpus of texts (a corpus including writings authored by a network of very disparate scholars, including the economic historian Frederic Lane, the political and analytical philosopher Robert Nozick, the historical and political sociologist Charles Tilly and the institutional economist Mancur Olson, whose research on political development and stationary bandits of the early 1990s has probably contributed much to the 'discovery' of this apparently new theory), the supporters of ETM made it explicit that theirs was just a part – indeed, half – of a more general theoretical picture whose other half had to do with the most authoritative political institution of our modern times, the state – in a symmetrical position with respect to the mafia. The not-so-implicit implication is that a theory that works for explaining the state should also work for explaining the mafia, and vice versa. This is a strong assumption, however, whose implications for ETM are not yet entirely clear and still need to be explained.

To help in this exercise of critical theorizing, in Table 3.3 we offer a sketch of the social and intellectual properties of this larger 'theory group'. Like ETM, and as an instance of the rationalist approach more generally, PT shares[12] key assumptions with rational choice theory (Elster 1986) – i.e. rationality of agents' minds and invisible-hand types

Table 3.3: Social and intellectual properties of PT as a 'theory group'

Intellectual ancestors	Machiavelli; Hobbes; Smith
Intellectual pioneering sources	Lane 1958; Schelling 1967, 1971; Nozick 1974; Tilly 1985; Elster 1986
Intellectual leaders	Gambetta; Olson; Varese[11]
Disciplinary references	Economics, political theory, sociology, criminology
Paradigm content	A set of propositions describing the properties of the commodity 'protection' and predicting the actions of its providers
Program statement	Varese 2014
Exemplars	Gambetta 1993; Olson 1993; Sabetti 1984
Applications	Varese 1994, 2001; Chu 2000; Frye 2002; Hill 2003; Wang 2011, 2017; Pottenger 2014; Haidar 2019
Examples of critical work	This book

of explanations à la Smith (e.g., Nozick 1994); it also makes strong assumptions about motivational self-interest on the part of the actors involved. Among the key theoretical propositions developed by PT are, for example, the idea that, because most trading engenders the risk of predation and unfulfilled promises for the trading partners, a demand for protection tends to emerge in order to insure both producers and traders against predators and unfulfilled promises. But the list of propositions is a long one:

> Division of labour leads to the emergence of specialists in enforcing promises and security as distinct from those specialized in the production of goods and services that do not require the use of violence. When protectors have a long-time horizon, they are expected to provide a genuine service from which clients/customers benefit. However, protection is a special commodity that is subject to economies of scale – it is cheaper to protect several customers rather than just one – and it is a (contestable) monopoly: there can only be one protector in a given domain. Because they are monopolists, protectors charge for their services more than what it costs them to produce those services and fight off attempts to encroach on their domain. Finally, building and maintaining a reputation for effective protection has the effect of enabling the protector to save on the production of the good itself.[13]

What makes the theory even more interesting beyond the alleged special case of mafia and other criminal organizations, proving some further bit of symbolic legitimacy, is that it has been used to explain state-building, in particular by Tilly who, in 1986, had already identified the key stimulus to building and centralizing state authority in war-making as both a practice and an event (or, better, a series of events). States, it is argued, need to mobilize resources internally (through taxation and debt) and to neutralize internal rivals (what state-making consists of, in the last instance) when they face external threats. In this scenario, which is normally applied to early modern Europe but which can evidently (at least this is the underlying assumption) be extended to cover other continents and times, rulers also *effectively* protect those who support their efforts. This 'protection thesis' (as it is also sometimes labelled) has indeed been used to account for a number of recent cases of illicit activity in Africa, and it looks like a potentially powerful tool for analysing the use and application of violence – always violence, indeed! – to protect illicit flows of resources (Shaw and Mangan 2014; Shortland and Varese 2014). How difficult it is to separate the study of protection from the analysis of violence is demonstrated by the fact that all this work has been built upon past research on shadow, felonious or predatory states, 'warlords', 'big men' and what Reno (2011) dubbed, with a much-used term that scholars are clearly reluctant to leave behind, 'violent entrepreneurs' (see more on this, with references, in Shaw 2015).

What remains to be shown, however, is how a theory intended to explain the rise and the functioning of a political institution like 'the state' could be appropriate for and capable of explaining the rise and functioning of a kind of specular institution that persists in being described as a business and an industry.

Some Problems with the Theory

It is time to take stock. ETM has to be praised for its quest for analytical strength and knowledge cumulativity, and for the rigour it aspires to in a research field that has long been marked by conceptual confusion and few attempts to find a common language. It has contributed to elevating the standards of research on mafia, demanding more cogent forms of reasoning. And it has contributed to locating the study of mafia close to the centre of intellectual debates in sociological theory and the social sciences more generally. It has also contributed – maybe unintentionally – to making the symbolic dimensions of the mafia a serious object of study – even though the interpretive efforts have been reduced to a minimum, moving from the assumption of supposedly more foundational economic factors deemed responsible of their generation, strategic use, and reproduction.

But this theory, like any other, has its flaws and biases, and it has been the target of a series of criticisms that can be summarized as follows:

a. *Substantial essentialism.* Is protection really what the mafia can be reduced to? How can we decide, against the historical and ethnographic evidence of a multifunctional mafia, for a reduction of all the varieties of functions and activities performed by mafiosi over time to a presumed single core function (Paoli 2003)?[14] What about mediation, which is the core role of mafiosi according to at least two of the most important studies of the mafia (Blok 1974; Schneider and Schneider 1976; see also Pizzorno 1987, who insists on the coupling of the two functions). As David Nelken (1995) has indicated, there is a strong risk of essentialization in Gambetta's model, which is not easy to harmonize with the historical argument (i.e. the history of property rights and other market institutions in Sicily in the wider context of the Italian *Mezzogiorno*) on which the model has been constructed. To be sure, it is not clear how much room exists in the model itself for accommodating the addition of other activities/functions without shaking the model up too much. Consider the following. Clearly, the more plausible cases in which demand for protection arises are those of illicit markets and industries which, by their nature, cannot enjoy the protection of the state, such as smuggling, prostitution (where and when it is illegal), the drug trade, and so on. However, the protection of property rights in both licit and illicit markets was not the only activity the mafia was involved in; it also provided cartel enforcement. Indeed, cartel enforcement is one of the few services that the mafia has provided throughout its history, from its origins (there is evidence of this activity in the neighbourhood of Palermo as early as 1876 – see Bandiera 2003) to Depression-era Chicago (Alexander 1997) to the contemporary US and Sicily (Gambetta and Reuter 1995). Is cartel enforcement just an extension of protection, or does the latter amount to such a general kind of activity that it encompasses almost everything someone can do for some other?

b. *Rough schematism.* Apart from historians' obvious criticism against any formal model because of the constraints it implies (but this is the price we must pay if we are looking for more than historical descriptions and detailed narratives, useful in any case for reminding the social scientists of the complexities and contingencies of the social world, but not sufficient to justify the neglect of any efforts towards modelling and theory-building), the point here is substantial and has to do with the phenomenological structure itself of the phenomenon under scrutiny. The point is not just formalism and schematism, but *how much* of them exists. Formalized (or quasi formal) models are useful for clarifying and controlling reasoning, being always careful not to commit excessive violence on the historical and empirical evidence. A major point has been raised by scholars of more structural/cultural persuasion: how can mafiosi *qua* protectors be distinguished from their alleged 'clients' – e.g., landowners, factory owners, managers, even politicians? The distinction between sellers and clients in matters of protection is hard to sustain, both empirically and conceptually, because those whom Gambetta calls 'clients' (and Varese 'victims') are often in collusion or strongly associated with mafiosi; not to mention the instances in which the selling of protection is subtly imposed through ways (morals and manners, so to say) that could also be thought of as essentially mafiosi (i.e. very typical of the mafia as a *sui generis* social and cultural structure), and whose simple presence makes it difficult, when not ridiculous, to speak of clients or a market (e.g., Santino 1995)

c. *Abstract economism.*[15] The model posits the demand for protection, in contexts marked by pathological shortages of trust, as the real and genuine source of its supply and, therefore, of the formation of something like an industry. However, it is difficult to pretend that mafiosi, as suppliers, never play an active role, in other words, that they do not produce the social conditions that create the demand for their services by capitalizing, first of all, on the resources of power they control, in terms of physical force and disposition to violence (see Catanzaro 1993). As an abundant literature never ceases to show, power and violence are not simply means that can be economized and calculated in terms of their use, but constitutive features of the mafia as a structure of power (dalla Chiesa 1976; Catanzaro 1992 [1988]; Raith 1992; Santino 1994; Volkov 1999, 2002). Historically, looking at the generative moments of the mafia, it would be very hard to find uncontroversial evidence strong enough to solve this puzzle. It would be better to move away from the assumption that mafiosi, as a Machiavellian would predict, always look for power and are always making allowances for it (as chimpanzees and other nonhuman primates do, according to ethologists: see de Waal 2007 [1982]; Maestripieri 2007). The point is: which kind of power, in the end, is the power of mafiosi?

To these critical points we should add insiders' self-criticism – i.e. that which has been criticized in the model by its own supporters. A major refutation has been made by scholars who, like Varese (2010), have worked in recent decades on the circulation of mafias and, more specifically, on the 'transplantation of the mafia'. Gambetta (1993, 351–3) excluded this possibility on the ground that the original social conditions that permitted the emergence of the mafia in Sicily, as in other regions all over the world comparable to Sicily, e.g., Japan (see Hill 2003), are not exportable as such. Also Reuter (1983, 21–2), referring to the US, has emphasized the 'local character' of mafia enterprises and their resistance to moving.

However, this is exactly what the first two decades of this century[16] have shown precisely *not* be the case – unfortunately for those who had to recognize the presence of the mafia even in places where it would never have been imaginable, such as in Emilia-Romagna, the region of Italy that international social scientists may know because of its consistent and deeply rooted reputation as the capital of *civicness* (Putnam 1993). Mafias travel and, it seems, are able to establish themselves relatively well and with some ease in more unsuspecting places. The reality of social life – as made manifest by police investigations, journalistic reports and trial proceedings (see Sciarrone 2009 [1998], 2014; Varese 2006; dalla Chiesa and Panzarasa 2011; Santoro and Solaroli 2017; dalla Chiesa and Cabras 2019) – has, in the end, prevailed over the model of reality. This is not so bad for the original theory, as only a scientific argument, one with enough details and clarity, could have been refuted with empirical evidence.[17] But this case also suggests the need to use some caution with respect to other tenets of the model, and sounds a warning against an excess of confidence in the model instilled by the boldness with which it has been presented and defended.

Still, I would point out how, in the literature, a certain dose of ambiguity arises in the way in which the economic theory has been read and received by scholars – an ambiguity partially produced by the same supporters, to be sure. It is not so uncommon, for example, to find references to the *economic* theory in writings focused on the *political* dimension of social and cultural life (e.g., Berezin 1997), a clue to some unresolved conceptual tensions in the model. At the same time, this ambivalence is apparent occasionally in the writings of authoritative proponents of the theory:

> Mafiosi are stationary because the service they provide is inherently local. They ensure selective access to resources in a given territory. In order to do so, they build long-term relationships with the place in which they operate as well as with the people, officeholders, and police. Rather than with a CEO, a more apt comparison is with a politician – say, a British Member of Parliament or US Senator. Candidates who have built their power base in a given constituency do not simply pack up and try their luck in the French or Italian political system, even if the salaries and allowances are larger. They would not have enough local knowledge and therefore cannot hope to get things done because they do not have connections to local power holders. As a rule, political (and criminal) reputations are local and are the product of costly investments. To start afresh somewhere else is expensive. (Varese 2011, 191)

Let me add some further considerations to these points. It would be unfair to expect a precise representation of reality from a theoretical model – it would not be a model. What we could fairly ask of a model – or, better, of its supporters – is a clear statement about what elements remain outside the focus of the model because they are not interesting to its creators and followers or because the model is poorly equipped to account for them (see Albert 2012 [1963]; Marchionatti and Cedrini 2016). There are at least three phenomenological areas that, in my view, do not enter into the framework, the claims of the model's supporters notwithstanding. The first is the religious dimension, which is undoubtedly more than the simple sponsorship of religious ceremonies considered by Gambetta in his analysis of the mafia's symbols (as a brand). Fortunately, in recent years, a large amount of research has been devoted to this dimension that has much to offer to students of the political dimension of the mafia as well (for the Sicilian mafia, see

Schneider and Schneider 1984; Puccio-Den 2011; Dino 2008; Ceruso 2007; Cavadi 2009; for Chinese triads, see ter Haar 1998; for mafia and witchcraft, see Albini 1978; Geschiere 2002; Puccio-Den 2019; see also Stewart and Strathern 2004; Armstrong and Rosbrook-Thompson 2016). The second area is what goes under the umbrella term of the terror–crime nexus (e.g., Ballina 2011; Haidar 2019), whose relevance for an understanding of what the mafia is and how mafias work cannot be trivialized; paradoxically, Gambetta's book was published in Italy the same year as the bombings of the judges Falcone and Borsellino, but nothing in the book seemed able to make sense of these acts of extreme violence against high representatives of the state (on the implications of the terrorism–crime nexus for mafia studies, see Schneider and Schneider 2002; Rossi 2014). The third area is aesthetics, something that may surely be approached in economic terms, but *not only* in these terms, of course. There seems to exist a strong bias in ETM in favour of a conception of aesthetic symbols as tools or vehicles for communication, especially business communication (Gambetta 2009 is built on this equivalence; and see also Varese 2006, 2017), but this cannot be the last word on the topic. Tattoos, song lyrics, films, cartoons, graffiti, literary texts, clothes, even mafiosi musical tastes and artistic practices – issues on which there is a growing literature in the humanities as well (e.g., Edberg 2004; Sneed 2007; Castagna 2010; Ravveduto 2019; Plastino 2012; Pine 2012; Dainotto 2015; Renga 2019 [2011]) – cannot be reduced to devices for marketing campaigns. They can be instrumentally used for this, for sure, but any expressive form, by its very nature, goes beyond mere instrumentality. Clearly, here we are touching on problems/limits/biases of the rational approach per se, including what is known as the economic approach to politics, about which there is already a rich literature (see, in particular, Green and Shapiro 1994; Udehn 1996; Lichbach 2003; see also Bourdieu 2017).[18]

The fact that an economic model grounded on the notion of the market and on the assumption of rational action cannot explain everything is something that an economist like Schelling, who has devoted almost his entire career to the extension of the economic paradigm to areas of social and political life that are not strictly economic (e.g., Schelling 1960, 1984; see also Dixit 2006; Sent 2007), has been careful to highlight. The example he gives has something to teach even readers of a book on the mafia,[19] and is worth being quoted at length:

> [N]ow look at an activity that at first glance is like a 'market activity' but upon closer inspection isn't. To make my point I'll choose a non-controversial illustration familiar to most of us, the 'non-market' for Christmas cards. There is a literal market for Christmas cards – a market for buying them,

and a federally monopolized market for sending them by mail. But I mean the choosing of whom to send a card to, what kind of card, how expensive, by what date to mail it, whether to pen a message, and what to do about non-Christian addressees. In addition to personal greetings we have cards from teachers to students and students to teachers, elected officials to their constituents and insurance salesmen to their policy-holders, and, of course, from your paperboy or papergirl.

My impression – and I've found nobody who doesn't share it – is that the sending of Christmas cards is an 'interactive process' greatly affected by custom and by expectations of what others expect and what others may send, by cards received (and not received) last year and already received this year, conditioned of course by the cost of cards and postage and the labor as well as the fun or nuisance of selecting cards and penning inscriptions.

People feel obliged to send cards to people from whom they expect to receive them, often knowing that they will receive them only because the senders expect to receive cards in return. People sometimes send cards only because, cards having been sent for several years, cessation might signal something. People send cards early to avoid the suspicion that they were sent only after one had already been received. Students send cards to teachers believing that other students do. Sensible people who might readily agree to stop bothering each other with Christmas cards find it embarrassing, or not quite worth the trouble, to reach such agreement. (If they could, they might be so pleased that they would celebrate by sending 'voluntary' cards, falling back into the trap!)

My casual inquiry suggests widespread if not unanimous opinion that the system has some of the characteristics of a trap. Even people who, on balance, like Christmas cards find parts of the system ludicrous, preposterous, or downright infuriating. Some wish the whole institution could be wiped out. Some wish for a 'bankruptcy' proceeding in which all Christmas-card lists could be obliterated so people could start over, motivated only by friendship and holiday spirit, without accumulated obligations.

Nobody claims that the system reaches optimal results. Even if everybody guesses correctly the cards he will receive, and ends the holiday season with no regrets for the cards he sent and the cards he didn't send, the outcome is a long way from ideal. And there isn't much that anybody can do about it. Fortunately, it doesn't matter much.

At first glance someone might call this exchange of greetings a 'free market activity'. But 'exchange' is an ironic metaphor. And 'market' is a remote and unhelpful analogy. Things don't work out optimally for a simple reason: there is no reason why they should. There is no mechanism that attunes individual responses to some collective accomplishment. (Schelling 2006 [1978], 31–2)

Moving ahead in exploring the limits of the market model, Schelling admits even the institution of marriage comes as a source of embarrassment for the economist (Gary S. Becker notwithstanding, we should add).[20] The fact that something can be usefully examined through a market model is not a good reason for applying the model of the market to everything, or to every aspect of something.

Towards a Political Theory of the Mafia

ETM centred on the idea of protection comprises the core of the rationalist approach to the mafia but does not exhaust it. Although surely in the periphery of the field, a place apart is occupied by Sabetti (1984), whose public choice-inspired theory of the mafia as an outlaw regime of self-government has been briefly illustrated in the previous chapter. What we could still add at this point is that this book is an ingenious empirical case study, both historical and ethnographic, on an influential mafia town (Villalba) and an important figure of mafioso (don Calò Vizzini, in the book disguised under the name of Mariano Ardena) whose social background, career in the mafia as well as in other spheres of life, organizational skills, talent for leadership, lifestyle, and influence on other mafiosi and common people are reconstructed with biographical details and theoretical concerns (see Varese 2014 for implicit words of praise in this light).[21]

Still more importantly, the book also shows a strong sensitivity for the political dimension of mafia life and a proclivity to go against the 'state mystique', or what Bourdieu (2014) has called 'state thinking', *une pensée d'état,* which thinks according to the categories the state has impressed on our minds. This is a distinctive feature of Sabetti's book, which positions itself at the antipodes of Gambetta (whose praises for the virtues of the constitutional state of liberal tradition are revealed in the introduction of his 1993 book and in other places), of all the students of the mafia moved by civic commitment (and they are legion), and of course of almost all the criminological literature on the mafia, strongly biased in favour of the (state) definition of lawfulness and ready to accept the (state's) official definition of what is crime. I would add that Sabetti's introduction of the concept of 'profitable altruism' has the merit of going to the core of the mafia not only as a regime of self-government but as a regime of value as well, and as an order of justification (Boltanski and Thevenot 1991; Stark 2013): as Mosca (1980 [1900]), a Sicilian by birth, already had reason to underline, the mafia has an implicit moral claim that social scientists are still reluctant to investigate in its nature and structure.

However, like any other research grounded on the application of economic theory to social and political life, Sabetti's study also suffers from the limits and lacunae highlighted by critics of this tradition (Udehn 1996; Lichbach 2003). Three kinds of assumptions ground ETM like any economic theory (and there are plenty of them in the social sciences, after so-called economic imperialism): assumptions about human motivation, about the chosen unit of analysis, and about the kind of order we are thinking to account for. Alternatives to these assumptions are diverse: whereas rationalists are disposed to see only 'individuals', other paradigms see relations and relational configurations; whereas rationalists see economic interests, other paradigms see a plurality of interests not reducible to instrumentality; whereas rationalists see calculus and transparency, other paradigms see tacit knowledge and practical reasons and logics of practice; whereas rationalists see market exchange, other paradigms are open to seeing other kinds of exchange (including that crucial form of exchange that is the gift); whereas rationalists see a rigid alternative between the private realm and the public sphere (or collective order), other paradigms are open to investigating how the boundaries between these spheres are drawn, negotiated, manipulated, trespassed, misunderstood, even destroyed; whereas rationalists see rational orders, other paradigms see normative, affective and cognitive orders.

Take the qualification of protection as a private good or, more specifically, as a commodity – clearly a major tenet of PT. Of course, it is possible to sell protection services, and specialized agencies active in this business exist all over the world: think of bodyguards, or companies offering security services in cities and for commercial enterprises. However, it would be difficult to propose an immediate identification of an ordinary protection agency with a 'mafia': the latter should have some additional special features that are not necessarily present in an agency operating in the open market of protection services. Still, in order to be classified as a commodity, a good has to be exchanged on a market for money (rarely as a barter), it needs to have an exchange value besides its use value. In short, it needs to be conceived of as something that can be sold. But does the categorization of a concrete instance of exchange like 'selling' suffice to qualify a sequence or a web of exchanges as a market, and to make a commodity of the exchanged thing? For economists, commodities simply exist (Kopytoff 1986, 64). But commoditization is far from a simple and linear process, and anthropologists and historians have alerted us to the difficulties of classifying an individual act of exchange as an act of 'market exchange' and not of something else, say a gift. The classification of human actions is far from immediate and is often more a matter of definition from the outside or from above, rather than an outcome of experience or assessment by those who are acting. Still, forms of classification and ways of classifying exchanges change over time and space, and according to the perspectives at play (Appadurai 1986; Kopytoff 1986).

By way of conclusion, and schematically, we may summarize this chapter's argument in these terms: while ETM and its PT derivation (or matrix, this depends on the point of view adopted) have to be praised for elevating the analytical standards of mafia research (a kind of analytical strength not necessarily to be emulated but that could be taken, at least, as a benchmark), for introducing cumulative research in mafia studies, and for claiming to have identified a *differentia specifica* capable of identifying, in a rigorous way, the mafia as a bounded object (to the cry 'if everything is mafia, nothing is mafia'), it has to be criticized for both the (economic, rationalist) approach adopted and the argument eventually advanced (that the mafia is a kind of business to be compared with the state as the political institution *par excellence*). In his turn, Sabetti may be praised for his argument (the mafia as an outlaw political regime), notwithstanding the (economic) approach he follows which presents the same flaws as PT. It is not only a matter of taste at the basis of my critical reading (after all, theories are cultural objects like any other that elicit preferences and enjoyment according to tastes), but of intellectual efficacy – what we gain as contrasted to what we lose by following a certain approach instead of another (I am aware of the almost economic thinking implied by this consideration; this sounds like an inner contradiction to my whole argument, indeed). A final point of merit for the economic approach is its comparative claim: the Sicilian mafia is just one instance – albeit a crucial one – of a more general something, and it searches for patterns of commonalities with other phenomena sharing a 'family resemblance', to employ Wittgenstein's terms.

In order to set the stage for what follows, two issues have to be raised at this point. (1) Is the qualification of mafia protection as *private* protection conceptually and empirically sound? (2) Is the market exchange the only kind of exchange available to mafiosi and their clients (in other words, is protection furnished by mafiosi necessarily *a commodity*)? In the next two chapters I will address these questions, which, together, amount to my central argument against ETM. This bring us to a further argument against it (to be addressed widely): its critical reference to a misleading concept of culture, and its grounding upon a really weak theory of culture.

4

The Public Life of Mafiosi

… questi uomini, che la voce pubblica vi indica come capi mafia.

Sciascia 1961

Finally, we enter this book's core argument. Many themes will return – from the interplay of rules and strategies to the force of invitations, from the public settlement of accounts to the establishment of boundaries among friends and enemies, to the use of gossip and silence as political means in the game of social life. This chapter is the first of three that will develop what I call a *political anatomy of the mafia*. This anatomy is articulated in three major parts, each corresponding to a chapter: the first (this chapter) deals with the joint issues of publicness and secrecy in mafia life; the second (Chapter 5) examines the nature of the social exchanges and social bonds in which mafiosi are engaged and that together make up the social texture of the mafia. This analysis will be further developed in the subsequent chapter (Chapter 6), which addresses the issue of how to sociologically account for the mafia as an organization – i.e. how to categorize the mafia as a social organization, keeping what is credible from the 'industry' analogy (or metaphor) without doing cognitive violence to the available evidence. Why these investigations will amount to a *political* anatomy will become apparent, I hope, in the course of the following pages.

The Publicness of the Mafia

Contrary to a widely accepted idea, the mafia exists and performs its existence in public. Secret and mysterious as it is, with its legitimacy and legality unrecognized by the modern embodiment of public power par excellence, that is, the state, the mafia has participated in the public sphere since its very inception, even though its nature would seem to be the opposite. In fact, the mafia as well as mafiosi are often public characters – even when, for security reasons, they live hidden from the (state) law. This does not mean the mafia and mafiosi *only* exist and *always* perform in the public sphere. Clearly they do not. But neither do public officials or public authorities. In an insightful article on 'the difficulty of studying the state', Philip Abrams (1988) made the useful distinction between the state as a system (state-system) and the state as an idea. The system side is made up of official, tangible, mostly government institutions, whereas the idea side consists of what is generally expected from the state and its human agents. The idea of the state is a powerful one – especially because of its global and therefore 'universal' reach (e.g., Meyer et al. 1997) – so powerful it may be employed to evaluate the 'not yet' of the state as a system, even with reference to institutions that effectively exercise public authority of one kind or another. The point is that often, even in state societies, more institutions than those provided by the state exercise public authority. This is apparent in Africa, where 'a wider variety of institutions are at play in this enterprise' (Lund 2006, 685), as well as in other regions of the world (e.g., Southeast Asia: see Scott 2010). The long-lasting existence of something like the mafia in Sicily and other Italian regions prompts us (this implied 'we' being any reader of this book with a Western-based education in the social sciences) to ask whether this is also the case much closer to home, in peripheral regions of the continent where the state as a political institution *sui generis* was born: Europe.[1]

The definition of the mafia as a 'something' (we will see in Chapter 6 how to conceptualize this social entity) dealing with *private* protection needs be scrutinized and possibly have its appeal significantly reduced – to the point of limiting its scope of application to borderline cases in which mafiosi truly behave *as if* they were acting in a market. This is a difficult task to the extent that our conceptual categories are those shaped by the institutions of the state – from the law and the courts to the academic system and scientific establishment: 'state thinking', as Bourdieu (2014) called it. One way to (critically) read the economic theory of the mafia is the following: it has willingly chosen to (uncritically?) adopt as a *conceptual assumption* for its theoretical architecture a positive-legal (in the sense of legal positivism), state-backed definition of the boundary between the private and the public realms, potentially blinding itself to the reality of a social world grounded on the refusal, or at least the local rearticulation, of the very terms of this boundary itself. The economic theory of the mafia thus prevents itself and its followers from exploring whether or not, in places where the mafia has emerged (and probably not only in these mafia places), what is public and what is private follows the binary logic of the classificatory schemas embedded in (Western) 'state thought' (Bourdieu 1998 [1994], 2014). Introducing a concept we will refer to again below, I would say that the economic theory of the mafia adopts the *epistemic authority* of the state (Glaeser 2011) in accepting the ways in which the state, as a 'thinking institution' (Douglas 1986; see also Scott 1998), has come to articulate, more or less since the eighteenth century, the boundaries of the public versus the private.[2] This is far from being a novelty in mafia studies, in fact. As Paoli noticed:

> Today we are used to thinking that government and business have always existed as separate organizations. Nonetheless, until after the beginning of the modern period neither governments nor business enterprises had the forms familiar to us. As Joseph Schumpeter pointed out, our terms 'state' and 'private' enterprise can hardly be applied to the institutions of feudalism without eliciting a distorted view of those institutions (1981, 169, 201). The separation of force-using enterprises from the profit-seeking enterprises that we now call business firms took place at different times in different areas of Europe and in the rest of the world. In the case of mafia-type organizations, such a process of differentiation has even nowadays taken place only to a minimal extent. The latter, in fact, emerged in contexts where this separation had not yet been fully achieved and where the use of violent means was almost an unavoidable pre-condition of social ascent and have been impeded by state institutions from taking part in the wider process of differentiation because of their criminal nature. (2002, 74)

However, it seems to me this point has not been sufficiently exploited as yet, and that in research on the mafia a state-centric perspective is still dominant, fostered by the policy implications this research clearly has. A closer look at the state is worthwhile – a look as far as possible unencumbered by the weight of the 'state-as-idea' as a standard setting device. As a matter of fact, the assumption of a full translation of the qualifying claim of the state – the Weberian *Monopol legitimen physischen Zwanges* ('monopoly of legitimate physical force') – into social reality has often been recognized as impossible. In his influential book *Community, Anarchy and Liberty*, for example, political theorist Michael Taylor has little doubt about the unreality of this claim:

> My starting point is Max Weber's well-known definition of states as 'human associations that successfully claim the monopoly of legitimate use of physical force within a given territory'. Either as a necessary or as a sufficient condition for the existence of a state, this clearly won't do. Claiming the monopoly of the legitimate use of physical force (which, admittedly,

states do – well-developed states at any rate) entails *nothing about the actual possession of means of exercising force*. Any group can claim a monopoly of the use of force or of the legitimate use of force, but this does not make it a state. To be a state, it must actually possess at least some means of exercising force. So Weber is right to require that this claim must be successful. But then his test is far too stringent; and no instances of a state in this sense could be found. *Obviously states never do possess an actual monopoly of the use of force* (there are always individuals and often organized groups, other than those which are part of the state system, which continue to use force, even under a powerful, highly developed state), and presumably this is not what Weber meant by a 'successful' claim. But nor could a claim to a monopoly of legitimate use of force ever be fully successful in the sense that everyone or nearly everyone granted the state legitimacy. (1982, 4–5)

Linked to this claim of a monopoly of legitimate force is another claim that has become a recurring mantra in mafia studies, especially when scholars are rooted in criminology and political science: that publicity and publicness are self-evident, given, almost common-sense properties of the state and its functions, activities, services and provisions. Talking about the state, even thinking about the state, means *ipso facto* introducing a distinction between the 'public' (what belongs to the state) and the 'private' (the rest). As Bourdieu once put it, in order to posit what would be the object of his sociological deconstruction:

What we call the state, what we point to confusedly when we think of the state, is a kind of principle of *public* order, understood not only in its evident physical forms but also in its unconscious symbolic forms, which apparently are deeply self-evident. One of the most general functions of the state is the production and canonization of social classifications. (2014, 9; emphasis added)

The distinction between 'public' and 'private' is indeed one of the most longstanding and consequential among these social classifications. The distinction has been a central concern of Western thought since classical antiquity, and has long served as a point of entry into many of the key issues of social and political analysis – including, as we have seen in Chapters 2 and 3, 'the mafia'. As the Italian legal theorist Norberto Bobbio (2017 [1989]) famously wrote, the public/private distinction stands out as one of the 'grand dichotomies' of Western thought, in the sense of a binary opposition that is used to subsume a wide range of other important distinctions and that attempts (more or less successfully) to dichotomize the social universe in a comprehensive and sharply demarcated way (see also Weintraub 1997, 1). In Bobbio's words:

It was in two much commented-on passages of Justinian's *Corpus iuris* ... where public law and private law are defined in an identical manner – the first as *quod ad statum rei romanae spectat*, and the second as *quod ad singulorum utilitatem* – that the pair of terms 'public' and 'private' first entered the history of Western political and social thought. Through constant and continuous use, and without any substantial changes, they have since become one of the 'great dichotomies' used by several disciplines – social and historical sciences as well as law – to define, represent and order their particular fields of investigation. (2017 [1989], 1)

It is a claim of this book that to sociologically understand the mafia we need to call these categories and classifications into question without accepting the official, formal and normative drawing of this 'great divide' as it stands in legal documents backed by the state. This does not mean, it is hardly necessary to emphasize, that the mafia has to be approached without any sense of the law or, better, of the juridical. On the contrary, there is wide evidence of the existence of something like a 'juridical order' in the mafia – without which no socially patterned mafia life would exist at all, and it would be difficult even to write a book like this. Evidently, the 'juridical' is not to be confused with the law of the state – as legal theorists would recognize, especially followers of so-called institutional theories of the law, and sociologists and anthropologists of the law would simply consider as a necessary, preliminary assumption of their research field.

Allow me a brief note. The refusal of a juridical grounding of the mafia qualifies the economic theory of the mafia – in a certain sense because of its logical coherence. Although it has never been explicated by its supporters, the economic theory of the mafia is grounded on an implicit adoption of a legal perspective, firmly based in the same liberal tradition to which this theory is clearly indebted. Indeed, as the Introduction to his 1993 book makes apparent, Gambetta selected one specific tradition of legal thought as if it were the only appropriate tradition – from a scientific but also, and even more, from a political point of view. This is the tradition of liberal positivism whose canon runs from Locke to Kelsen. Refusing to grant any intellectual value to the institutional theory of the law – on the argument that it represents a kind of illiberal and politically dangerous theoretical ground from which to assess social institutions like the mafia – Gambetta has, indeed, deprived sociological theory of the insights potentially coming from the brand of legal theory that is more closely linked to the social sciences and the sociological imagination. Even more, he has deprived the sociological gaze of the extraordinary analytical lens offered by Santi Romano's work, one of the few masters of Western legal thought whose thinking is rooted at least in part in a direct experience of social life in southern Italy.[3] What may be striking to a sociological reader is that what, for the sociologist Gambetta, amounts to a misleading and surely illiberal understanding of the mafia as a kind of order was, for the legal theorist Romano, one of the paradigmatic instances from which to develop a more exhaustive and more compelling (with respect to the positive and formal theory of the law by legal scholars like Kelsen) theoretical understanding of the legal order in its social, if not sociological, groundings. Paradoxically, we could conclude, today's more influential sociological theory of the mafia is not only self-designated as 'economic', but is also based on the firm rejection of one of the most sociologically sensitive legal theories of the state and its (public) law produced in the twentieth century. The fact that this theory was created by a scholar socialized, if not educated, in Sicily, in the region where the mafia first developed and was identified, adds further value to this neglected and negated perspective.

The point is that, like every social classification, even this is far from being consistent and conceptually satisfying. Jeff Weintraub's remarks are especially insightful for us:

> Unfortunately, the widespread invocation of 'public' and 'private' as organizing categories is not usually informed by a careful consideration of the meaning and implications of the concepts themselves. And, even where there is sensitivity to these issues, those who draw on one or another version of the public/private distinction are rarely attentive to, or even clearly aware of, the wider range of alternative frameworks within which it is employed. For example, many discussions [included those on the mafia, we could add] take for granted that distinguishing 'public' from 'private' is equivalent to establishing the boundary of the political – though, even here, it makes a considerable difference whether the political is conceived in terms of the administrative state or of the 'public sphere'. But the public/ private distinction is also used as a conceptual framework for demarcating other important boundaries: between the 'private' worlds of intimacy and the family and the 'public' worlds of sociability or the market economy; between the inner privacy of the individual self and the 'interaction order' of Erving Goffman's *Relations in Public*; and so on in rich (and overlapping) profusion. The public/private distinction, in short, is not unitary, but protean. It comprises, not a single paired opposition, but a complex family of them, neither mutually reducible nor wholly unrelated. These different usages do not simply point to different phenomena; often they rest on different underlying images of the social world, are driven by different concerns, generate different problematics, and raise very different issues. (1997, 2)

Lying behind these different forms of public/private distinction,[4] there are (at least) two fundamental and analytically distinct frameworks in terms of which 'private' can be contrasted with 'public': (1) what is hidden or withdrawn versus what is open, revealed, or accessible; (2) what is individual, or pertains only to an individual, versus what is collective, or affects the interests of a collective of individuals. As Bourdieu puts it:

> The public is thus opposed to the particular, to the singular. Secondly, it is opposed to the concealed, the invisible ... Once again, the theatrical analogy is apt: the public is what takes place on stage ... Private acts are invisible, they take place behind the scenes, backstage; the public, on the contrary, is conducted in view of everyone, before a universal audience, in which it is not possible to select. (2014, 49)

The two meanings of the dichotomy should be clear at this point: the first is related to the nature and scope of power, the second to its degree of openness. The two issues – secrecy and the public/private divide – are indeed closely connected (see Ku 1998). Recalling that 'public and private are paired to describe a number of related oppositions in our thought', sociologist Paul Starr (1988, 7–8) has described this connection in these terms:

> At the core of many uses are the two ideas that public is to private as *open* is to *closed*, and that public is to private as the *whole* is to the *part*. In the first sense, we speak of a public place, a public conference, public behavior, making something public, or publishing an article. The private counterparts, from homes to diaries, are private in that access is restricted and visibility reduced. *The concepts of publicity and privacy stand in opposition to each other along this dimension of accessibility.* Public is to private as the transparent is to the opaque, as the announced is to the concealed. Similarly, a person's public life is to his or her private life as the outer is to the inner realm. On the other hand, when we speak of public opinion, public health, or the public interest, we mean the opinion, health, or interest of the whole of the people as opposed to that of a part, whether a class or an individual. *Public in this sense often means 'common', not necessarily governmental.* The public-spirited or public-minded citizen is one concerned about the community as a whole. But in the modern world the concepts of governmental and public have become so closely linked that in some contexts they are interchangeable. The state acts for the whole of a society in international relations and makes rules binding on the whole internally. Public thus often means official. In this sense a 'public act' is one that carries official status, even if it is secret and therefore not public in the sense of being openly visible. Indeed, according to the *Oxford English Dictionary*, private originally signified 'not holding public office or official position' ... Now, of course, private is contrasted with public to characterize that which lies beyond the state's boundaries, such as the market or the family.

However, it would be better not to confuse the public/private dichotomy as used to discuss the nature of power and authority, as well as the scope of the law (first set of meanings), with the distinctions in which public means 'open to the public', 'performed in front of spectators', while private, in contrast, is that which is said or done in a restricted circle of people or, taken to the extreme, in secret (second set of meanings). They are, to be sure, not be confused as they belong to two different conceptual and even historical contexts. The concept of private protection may foster this confusion: it suggests as evidence of privateness the secrecy surrounding the protecting agency, forgetting that, historically, political power has systematically implied the production and management of secrecy (Ku 1998). Political power is always public power in terms of the great dichotomy, even when it is not publicly visible, does not act in public, is hidden from the public and is not controlled by the public. Conceptually, the problem of the publicity of power is used to highlight the difference between two forms of government: the republic, characterized by public control of power and, in the modern age, the free formation of public opinion; and the monarchy and even the dictatorship, whose method of government includes recourse to the *arcana imperii*, that is, to state secrecy, which in the modern constitutional state is allowed only as an exceptional remedy and under legally established and enforced guarantees (Ku 1998). This does not mean, however, that the power and authority of a king or a dictator are not 'public' because of their use of secrecy.

To complicate this issue even further: besides their descriptive meaning, the two terms of the public/private dichotomy also have evaluative meanings which are mutually exclusive in both cases:

> We are dealing with two terms which in descriptive use commonly function as contradictory terms, in the sense that in the universe defined by them no element can be both public and private simultaneously or even neither public nor private. Similarly, the evaluative meaning of one also tends to be opposed to the other in the sense that, when a positive evaluative meaning is attributed to one, the second acquires a negative evaluative meaning and vice versa. (Bobbio 2017 [1989], 9)

Still, in descriptive as well as evaluative terms, the conceptual relevance of the public/private dichotomy is demonstrated by the fact that it is associated with other traditional and recurring dichotomies of the social sciences that both converge within it and fill it out, but which can also replace it. These two sets of dichotomies are synthesized in Table 4.1.

It is easy to locate the mafia, as it is imagined in economic theory, in this dichotomous framework, with any item of the private pole comprising

Table 4.1: The great divide of public vs. private and its extensions

Public	Private
Politics	Economy*
(State)	(Market)
Associations of unequals	Associations of equals
Law	Contract
Distributive justice[5]	Commutative justice (exchange)
Openness/visibility	Secrecy/invisibility

Source: compiled from Bobbio 2017 [1989]
*Not 'economics', as the translation of Bobbio 2017 [1989] says

one of its features: being an instance of the industry (business, economy) of private protection, selling private goods (commodities) in the market through contractual exchanges, making use of secrecy to protect the market and its agents. There is, indeed, a clear correspondence between the economic theory of the mafia and two other more general models which are well-established in political theory (see Weintraub 1997): the first is the liberal economic model, dominant in most 'public choice' analysis and in a great deal of everyday legal and political debate, which sees the public/private distinction primarily in terms of the distinction between state politics and the market economy. The second is the republican virtue (and Greco-Roman classical) approach, which conceives of the 'public' as a realm apt for political community and citizenship, to be analytically distinguished from both the market and, in this case, even the state as an administrative machine.

This is, after all, what stands behind the definition of mafia protection as private protection. As a matter of principle, economics as a science would be relatively open with respect to the 'public as state'-ownership of public goods – usually its owner is the state, but it could also be an NGO. However, in practice, it would be difficult to provide a public good through privately owned, nongovernmental institutions and means because of its very nature – what Paul Samuelson identified in the 1940s as its non-excludable and non-rivalrous character. A private good does not possess these properties in the sense that its owner can exclude others from using it, and, once it has been used, it cannot be used by others. To this latter kind of good would belong the protection offered by mafiosi: a *private* one, to be sold in the form of a commodity. This is, notwithstanding the acknowledged peculiarities of 'protection' as a good – peculiar enough to require a special theory (the theory of the 'industry of protection', to be integrated into a more general protection theory that includes the theory of the protection guaranteed by the state), but not to the point of preventing its exchange on the market as a private good. This is indeed what makes the mafia – our topic – just an instance of a larger phenomenon, the 'business of private protection', as in the subtitle itself of Gambetta's 1993 book. According to this line of thought, while the protection dealt with (if not always guaranteed) by the state is public, the protection offered (but read 'sold') by the mafia is, according to the model, private. Granting to the state the monopoly of publicness and publicity, the economic theory of the mafia cannot but confine the latter to the private sphere.

Protection can be a private good – and a commodity – to the extent that it may be consumed as such, singularly as it were. Only the state, the argument implies, can really guarantee the supply of protection in a non-exclusive and non-rivalrous form. The problem is that the available evidence is ambivalent about this, at least with respect to the Sicilian mafia. The same Gambetta seems to be aware of certain difficulties when discussing possible objections to the argument:

> The question arises why the mafioso should not offer his 'mark of guarantee' to *all* sellers on the market and allow customers to choose on the basis of taste, price, and quality. He would be providing a *public good* ... Transactions would then take place under ordinary market conditions. After all, it might be thought, the more sellers the mafioso protects, the higher his total [gain]. Evidence suggests, however, that the mafioso will guarantee (and therefore select) only a limited number of sellers at the expense of all others. (1993, 22; emphasis added)

Indeed, the evidence exhibited (see below) seems less relevant for the whole argument than the modelling constraints. Asking himself why mafiosi adopt – as it seems – a selective approach to protection, Gambetta (1993) proposes three main reasons. First, there is a problem of scale: if the offered protection were *too* public, the mafioso would be unable to enforce the collection of his gains from all his clients; the underlying assumption is that any customer would have an interest in enjoying the mafioso's protection but also in not paying for the supply. The point is that there is wide evidence from both autobiographies and trials that mafiosi spend a lot of time exactly in this activity of credit collection through the mafia's typical repertoire of more or less violent means (from intimidation to destroying properties to bombing). Second, a 'publicly oriented' mafioso would find it difficult to control and guarantee every transaction of every customer, 'risking the loss of his reputation' whenever something goes wrong (1993, 23). This seems to be a good reason, but we have strong evidence that mafiosi prefer to risk this loss *after the fact* than to lose their reputation from the start (it is not great publicity to be known for refusing to provide a service just because of uncertainty that the service will match expectations). Still, mafiosi are not short of means for restoring their reputation in case of problems: the recourse to extreme violence is a real possibility in the hard work of being a mafioso (or one of his agents), even when conceding that mafiosi employ such extreme means – which are dangerous not only for their victims but for themselves as well – only as a last resort. Third – and this an important caveat for us, because of the different meaning it can be given when read from a perspective that is not strictly economic – is that the intervention of a mafioso 'must be not anonymous and universal but rather clearly linked to specific transactions' in order 'to ensure that the buyer knows that if he gets a good deal, it is due to the mafioso's protection and the independent honesty of the seller' (1993, 23). A missing point in this reasoning is that you do not need to select your clients to have them be aware of your intervention: it suffices you make it clear, with the right means, that you, or someone linked to you, is behind every transaction. And this is easier to do when *every* transaction is known to be guaranteed precisely by the relevant local mafia group.

What this economic model lacks is an adequate consideration of the theoretical role of the context: *spatial* context *in primis* (this is a point made by Abbott 1999 in his criticism of mainstream sociology, which applies to economic modelling and rational action theories as well).[6] Mafiosi do not normally need to select the recipients of their services as if they were 'private customers' because they have already selected a spatially bounded jurisdiction for their services – typically the whole administrative jurisdiction of the *comune* (municipality) in the case of smaller towns, and neighbourhoods and *borgate* in the case of larger towns and cities. This is one of the constitutional rules, as it were, of the organization of Cosa Nostra, as described in the US by Joe Valachi and in Italy by Tommaso Buscetta, and repeated systematically and therefore confirmed by trial witnesses as well as in autobiographies of mafiosi (Arlacchi 1993, 1994; see also Calvi 1984; Stajano 1986; see also Gambetta 1993; Paoli 2003). This necessary territorial reference has been elevated by Umberto Santino (1994) to a definitional trait of the mafia itself, proposing the (Weberian in its spirit) concept of 'territorial lordship' (*signoria territoriale*) to account for the capacity of mafia groups to take and maintain a complete, almost totalitarian social control of a bounded portion of local space, be it a town, a piece of land or a neighbourhood (*borgata*) in a large city like Palermo. While this image makes the mafia look very similar to 'a state' (with its monopoly of legitimate violence on a given territory, a definition difficult to maintain indeed for the state itself as we have already observed), it also helps us to see the concept of *private* protection as a metaphoric projection of an abstract model (the economists' model) more than as a profitable way to capture the character of the 'master activity' of mafiosi, which is to offer protection not to individuals but rather to their 'public'.

As such, mafiosi do not act as private providers in a market – not even in the special market of security services. Seen in this light, the sort of protection the mafia is involved with may well be labelled not as private but instead as roughly 'public' because it is, first and foremost, public in the ways it is supplied and in its scope. It has to be public to be materially and symbolically effective. Inside the spatial niches in the territory under their jurisdiction, mafiosi do not set limits to their 'protection', at least nominally: every shop, every firm, every commercial activity exceeding a certain size and economic value (not rigorously established to be sure) has to pay for the simple fact of their geographical location in the portion of space officially, that is publicly, under the authority of the local mafia group (whether it is called a *cosca*, as in the past, or a *Family* as it has been termed by mafiosi turned state witnesses since the 1980s). Universal does not mean infinite or indefinite. And the publicly known fact that, in that specific territory, there is only one mafia group in control protects the intervention from the risk of being 'anonymous'. The reasoning behind this locally universal claim to a gratification in return for an offered protection service (whether it is genuine or extorted is a different point), is well captured in the following excerpt from a classic in the literature on the mafia, Leonardo Sciascia's novel *Il giorno della civetta* (1961), published in English as *The Day of the Owl* (2003, but originally translated as *Mafia Vendetta*). Captain Bellodi, the investigator for the Carabinieri, is trying to get information from a man named Giuseppe Colasberna, whose brother Salvatore has just been found dead (both were leading members of the Santa Fara Co-operative Building Society):

'Let's just suppose that in this district, in this province, there are ten contracting firms operating. Each firm has its own machinery and materials, that lie by the roadside or on the building site at night. Machines are delicate things. All you have to do is remove a piece, even a single bolt, and it will take hours or days to get it running again. As for the materials, fuel oil, tar, timber, it's easy enough to lift those or burn them on the spot. True, there is often a hut near the machinery and materials where some workmen sleep, but that's just it; they sleep. Well now, there are other people – and you know who I mean – who never sleep. Wouldn't it be natural to turn to these people – these people who never sleep – for protection? Especially when protection has been offered you at once and, if you've been unwise enough to refuse it, something has happened to make you decide to accept it ... Of course, there are the stubborn, the people who say no they don't want it, and wouldn't accept it even with a knife at their throats. From what I can see, you're stubborn ... or perhaps only Salvatore was ...'

'This is all new to us', said Giuseppe Colasberna, and the others, with taut faces, nodded assent.

'Maybe it is, maybe it isn't', said the captain, 'but I haven't finished yet. Now, let's say that nine out of ten contractors accept or ask for protection. It would be a poor sort of association – and you know what association I refer to – if it were to limit itself to the functions and pay of night-watchmen. The protection offered by the association is on a much vaster scale. It obtains private contracts for you, I mean for the firms which toe the line and accept protection. It gives you valuable tips if you want to submit a tender for public works, it supports you when the final inspection comes up, it saves trouble with your workmen ... Obviously, if nine companies out of ten have accepted protection, thus forming a kind of union, the tenth which refuses is a black sheep. It can't do much harm, of course, but its very existence is a challenge and a bad example. So, by fair means or foul, it must be forced to come into the fold or be wiped out once and for all.'

At least in a case like this, with a not-so-large number of potential receivers (let me use this word instead of the highly connoted 'customers'), it makes sense to argue that mafiosi have an interest in not selecting their counterparts and pretending that *everyone* in their territory pay their due. Gambetta himself at some point concedes that, 'although protectors have an interest in restricting the number of protégés, they are also subject to a countervailing drive to increase it in order to strengthen both their sources of revenue and their independence from any single source' (1993, 23). This happens, it seems, when protection is referred not to goods but to promises, especially promises to respect cartel agreements: in this case the role of mafiosi is that of agreement enforcers, a role closer to that of 'settlement disputer', says Gambetta (see also Bandiera 2003).

To analytically develop his exploration of mafia protection and the reasons why it is (or has to be) *private*, Gambetta is prompted by the logic of his (economic) model to advance strong claims. One of the strongest is that 'private protection is not supplied on the basis of principles, let alone universal principles ... it is supplied strictly on the basis of opportunity', exactly like any other market good (1993, 24). Certainly, there is evidence of opportunistic behaviour by mafiosi in their role as providers of protection, but this can be said of every agent endowed with strategic skills – including chimpanzees and other smart nonhuman primates (de Waal 2007 [1982]; Maestripieri 2007), not to mention political actors of any sort (e.g., Bailey 2001 [1969]; Barth 1969; Finley 1978 [1954]; Yang 1994; Gould 2003; Bourdieu 2014; Wilson 2015; Vaishnav 2017).

Opportunism is far from being a characteristic of the economic sphere or of the market (e.g., Goffman 1969), and this factor does not say much about the definition of a certain service as 'private'.

Moreover, there is good evidence in the historical and socio-anthropological literature on mafia that at least *some principles* have been and are relevant in the world(s) of the mafia. We may call them normative and value principles, and they embody much that is included in the mafiosi's *self-presentation* and even *representation* – ranging from the value of honour (limiting the range of what is possible to do in order not to be accused of being dishonoured and justifiably incurring strong sanctions), to the principle of *omertà* (see below), to the many reported debates, even struggles (concerning both opportunities and principles at the same time, it would be difficult, if not pretentious, to make a distinction) that have characterized the post-war history of the mafia over whether to engage drug trafficking and similar activities (to be protected by mafiosi themselves as protectors before being traffickers). In the past, debates like these occurred over the protection of prostitution – mafiosi often pretended to be different from, i.e. to have more status than, simple pimps. That the mafia as a social phenomenon includes elements belonging to what in the social sciences is commonly called 'culture' (e.g., Geertz 1973; Swidler 1986; DiMaggio 1997; Alexander 2003; Sewell 2005) is accepted, even in the economic theory of the mafia, and even though the way in which these cultural elements – such as honour, *omertà*, oaths, folktales and other normative, symbolic and even ritual and practical traits of the mafia – are named, conceptualized and modelled may be differentiated from more culturally sensitive, or explicitly cultural, theories (for an instructive example of what a rational theory of culture could be, see Chwe 2001).

The argument of this book, in any case, is not simply to invert that of Gambetta: I am not suggesting that mafiosi deal with public rather than private protection. No: things are more complex and ambivalent than that. Borders are never so neat, and the pertinent categories intermingle. Boundary work is an activity mafiosi are commonly engaged with. As their stories and memories testify, they are constantly busy in the difficult art of hermeneutics; they have a continuous and immoderate need to interpret, to make sense and even to explain to themselves and their mates what they themselves, their mates or other mafiosi are doing or experiencing. For example, whether the assassination of a member of the organization should be considered an episode in a private war (a conflict between two mafiosi for strictly personal motives) or should be read as a signal that a true 'mafia war' involving every member is beginning; or whether their or some other's investment in a drug deal is just a private business or is part of a more collective concern.

Externalities are rarely clearly predetermined in mafia life and ask to be negotiated through exercises of framing and meaning-making – activities that mafiosi autobiographies and reminiscences, as well as testimonies of trial witnesses, demonstrate are ubiquitous in mafia life.

The Public Lives of Mafiosi

To be sure, an insistence on the private character of the protection furnished by mafiosi is a must in the literature, not only on mafias but also on gangs and any other actor dealing with protection that is not comparable to the state or is not the state itself (Skaperdas and Syropoulos 1995). Apparently, there is not much room for alternative visions; if we identify the state as the realm of the public, everything that is outside the state or separated from it – or, even worse, against it – becomes by logical exclusion 'private'.

However, there are influential streams of thought and cultural practice (e.g., feminism, Marxism) that have questioned this simple equation, proposing to extend the public sphere to include issues previously considered private (e.g., family life and sexuality; see Landes 1988; Pateman 1989) or showing the various forms of entanglement of the two spheres in different places and times (see Habermas 1989 [1962]; Negt and Kluge 1993). Decades of research across times and places have, indeed, produced enough evidence – historical, ethnographical – to maintain, as we can read in the introductory chapter of an influential volume on the subject, that

> attempts to use the public/private distinction as a dichotomous model to capture the overall pattern of social life in a society – as opposed to using one or another version for specific and carefully defined purposes – are always likely to be inherently misleading, because the procrustean dualism of their categories will tend to blank out important phenomena. Thus, just as the 'public' realm (and politics) cannot be reduced to the state, the realm of social life outside the state (and its control) cannot simply be identified as 'private'. (Weintraub 1997, 15)

Unfortunately, this is exactly what the economic theory of the mafia and its twin, protection theory, seem to do in order to sustain their 'hard core'.

In fact, the sociological tradition offers various strategies for escaping this 'procrustean dualism'. A useful way is to address the issue from diverse perspectives, capitalizing on different research traditions. For example, we can move from the notion of *public* opinion – which is not the same as public power but is clearly linked to it. This point of entry is spectacular, indeed, putting ourselves directly on the scene where the mafia *as we know it* took life.

We cannot say whether the entrance of the mafia onto the public stage in the 1860s coincided with its discovery (after a period of more or less submerged life) or with its social birth. It could even be possible that the mafia really did not exist in the 1860s and, paradoxically, coalesced into something more concrete and even visible only after the proliferation of public discourse about its alleged, but not yet proven, existence (see Appendix). What is sure is that, when the mafia entered onto this stage in the early years of the new Italian national state, it was in a sufficiently *public arena* and under an intense enough spotlight to immediately become a *public issue*. And it is this publicness that the mafia has had to deal and cope with since then.

The relationship of the mafia to the sphere of 'public opinion' is indeed somewhat paradoxical. The more it was talked about, the more it appeared to be a mysterious entity. The lack of evidence and information, as well as the confusion about it, understandably, became a major source of both fear and fascination. We have strong evidence from mafiosi autobiographies and courtroom testimonies that fear and fascination are feelings that mafiosi themselves experience in their daily life. Still, it may be just a coincidence that the beginning of the perception of the mafia as a criminal organization or society dates back to the success of a popular drama – this was, according to contemporaries, the main reason for the semantic shift of the word *mafia* from meaning a positive human quality or virtue to naming a supposed bloody and dangerous association, as the Palermitan folklorist Pitrè reiterated both in his writings on the 'folkways of the Sicilian people' and as an expert witness in trials against the mafia.[7] A coincidence as it may be, it is a matter of fact that theatre has been the cultural and entertainment genre that spawned the very idea of the public – as spectatorship, but also as a critical voice. Paradoxically, a world famous for being hidden and secluded started to exist *in public*, really on stage, under a spotlight. There is enough, I think to question any simple confinement of the mafia to a 'private sphere' that is not very well defined.

Consider one of the more influential conceptions of *the public*, that of the American pragmatic philosopher John Dewey. His analysis of what the public is and how it can emerge even from the practical working of a (private) institution like vengeance or feud is enlightening and worthy of being quoted at length. First, Dewey's notion of the public:

> The line between private and public is to be drawn on the basis of the extent and scope of the consequences of acts which are so important as to need

control, whether by inhibition or by promotion. We distinguish private and public buildings, private and public schools, private paths and public highways, private assets and public funds, private persons and public officials. It is our thesis that in this distinction we find the key to the nature and office of the state. It is not without significance that etymologically 'private' is defined in opposition to 'official', a private person being one deprived of public position. The public consists of all those who are affected by the indirect consequences of transactions to such an extent that it is deemed necessary to have those consequences systematically cared for. Officials are those who look out for and take care of the interests thus affected ... it is necessary that certain persons be set apart to represent them and see to it that their interests are conserved and protected. (1954 [1927], 15–16)

It would seem that the public, so conceived, would have little to do with a social universe like the mafia – also because of this reference to the 'nature and office of the state'. Things take another sense, though, just a few lines later when Dewey illustrates the process by which a public emerges even from seemingly primordial situations such as feuds:

It is commonplace that legal agencies for protecting the persons and properties of members of a community ... did not always exist. Legal institutions derive from an earlier period when the right of self-help obtained. If a person was harmed, it was strictly up to him what he should do to get even. Injuring another and exacting a penalty for an injury received were *private* transactions. They were the affairs of those directly concerned and nobody else's direct business. But the injured party obtained readily the help of friends and relatives, and the aggressor did likewise. Hence consequences of the quarrel did not remain confined to those immediately concerned. Feuds ensued, and the blood-quarrel might implicate large numbers and endure for generations. The recognition of this extensive and lasting embroilment and the harm wrought by it to whole families *brought a public into existence*. The transaction ceased to concern only the immediate parties to it. Those indirectly affected formed a public which took steps to conserve its interests by instituting composition and other means of pacification to localize the trouble. (1954 [1927], 16–17; emphasis added)

Recall that the standard, classical definition of the mafioso sounds exactly like this: he is a person, he is a man, who carries out justice for himself (Pitrè 1889; Mosca 1980 [1900]). The idea of vengeance was inherent in the concept of the mafia even before it became an ingredient in mafia novels and film plots. The sources are ambivalent, however: they define the mafioso as a man who metes out justice for himself but, at the same time, they acknowledge that a mafioso may ask for the help of others in pursuing his own justice (e.g., Cutrera 1900, 38, 41; Mosca 1980 [1900]). Indeed, this is how things work in feuds: no one is really alone, since it is the kin group that becomes mobilized. Mafia groups, from what we know, emerged from, and coalesced through, variously assembled and composed associations with the aim of self-help 'without limits and measure' (Lestingi 1884, 453; see also Hess 1970; Sabetti 1984; Recupero 1987; Pezzino 1990; Lupo 1993). We can even imagine – it is not so difficult – that a person who is not really able to take justice for themselves but who is mafioso enough or untrusting enough towards the state could ask someone more courageous, more skilled or better endowed with friends and relatives to help them or even do justice on their behalf – a situation that Leopoldo Franchetti (1993 [1877]) clearly envisions in his seminal analysis of his (quasi) ethnographic research.

'People' like these – 'unofficial officials', as it were, but effective and with a clear enough mandate and licence, to borrow terms from Hughes's (1971) sociology of occupations, to be known even outside the mafia world – are well established within the mafia universe. Three extraordinary documents are relevant for us – extraordinary because they report the voices of mafiosi, as produced within the very world of the mafia to (self-)present itself, according to its own categories of knowledge and criteria of relevance. The first is an excerpt from an interview with Don Calogero Vizzini, Don Calò as he was also known, the real man behind Filippo Sabetti's Mariano Ardena (a name chosen in homage to Sciascia's *The Day of the Owl*'s mafioso main character, Mariano Arena), alleged boss of Villalba and long considered the leading godfather of all the Sicilian mafia (before being described by insider-turned-state witness Tommaso Buscetta, in 1982, as a relatively minor figure in the revealed organizational chart of Cosa Nostra). The interview was conducted in the 1950s by an authoritative journalist and published in a book of interviews with relatively well-known, albeit not very famous, public characters, entitled *Pantheon minore* (even this is a mark of publicness):

> You know, I believe that if one holds a position like yours ...
> What position?
> I mean: in the opinion of the people.
> Oh! (Pause) The fact is, he replied after a while, that in any society there must be a category of persons who puts things right again when they have become complicated. (Montanelli 1958, 282; as quoted and translated in Hess 1970, English edition 1998, 74)

The second source is drawn from a sort of autobiographical statement, collected by the social researcher and activist Danilo Dolci in the 1950s and published in one of his documentary books on Sicily and the mafia (a book whose title, *Spreco*, waste, speaks about the mafia more than it seems at first sight: see below). The person speaking is, probably, another alleged mafia boss, Giuseppe Genco Russo, 'godfather' of Mussomeli, a rural town close to Villalba, who was a local party leader of the Christian Democratic Party in those years:

> I was born that way. I act without purpose. No matter who asks me a favour, I'll do him the favour because, I believe, that is what my nature prescribes to me ... One man will come and say: 'I have a problem with Tizio, do see if you can settle the matter for me.' I summon the person concerned to me or else I go and visit him – according to what terms we are on – and I reconcile them. (Dolci 1960, 68; as quoted in Hess 1970, English edition 1998, 74)

Our mafioso does not say exactly how he plays this role of reconciler or what happens when this reconciliation fails. Clearly, sometimes it can fail. What we can read from this *padrino*'s voice is that it 'doesn't matter who asks him' – he follows a universalistic orientation and not a particularistic one, to use Parsonsian terms – but he also states that he is *personally* engaged in this service: a point the literature on the mafia has yet to explore in depth for its theoretical value (see below for some preliminary considerations).

The third document is the souvenir card prepared by relatives for the funeral of boss Francesco Di Cristina, head of the Riesi 'Family' or *cosca* in 1961 (this written document is also famous for being the first text released from inside the mafia world to include the name 'mafia', against any claim of the mafia's inexistence):[8]

> Fulfilled in all range of human possibilities
> He showed to the world how / a true man might
> Inside him virtue and intelligence
> Judgment and strength of mind / Happily married
> For the good of the humble / For the defeat of the superb
> He operated on the Earth / Imposing on his fellows (*simili*)
> The respect for eternal values / Of the human personality
> Enemy of every injustice / He demonstrated
> With words and works / That his mafia was not delinquency
> But respect of law and honour / Defence of every right
> Greatness of soul / It was love. (Quoted in Sciascia 1979, 28; my translation)

Independently from the pomp and rhetoric exhibited, we can have little doubt that 'this' mafia, and its human representatives, had a public as their target and considered their position in the local social world at least as a public position – 'unofficial official', as it were.

Let us continue our exploration of this public side. We have seen how two influential approaches in the social sciences manage the distinction between public and private: the public choice approach and the republican model. Both would sustain a relatively clear-cut distinction between the state, as the public sphere of politics, and economics, as the private sphere of market exchange. We have also observed how both of these models resonate with the economic theory of the mafia. These two models, of course, do not exhaust the various social science approaches relevant to the public/private divide. There is, for instance, a third approach, common in social history and anthropology, which sees the 'public' realm as a sphere of fluid and polymorphous *sociability* and seeks to analyse the cultural and dramatic conventions that make it possible (this approach could be called, with Goffman, dramaturgic) (see Weintraub 1997, 7).

Public places offer an interesting way to address the issue of the publicness of mafia life, bypassing the public/private dichotomy as it is assumed in the legal discourse backed by the institutions of the state. Public spaces have no definite borders – just think of what an open window can offer to the vision of one who is looking out of the private space of the family home. There are public places that are privately owned, such as bars, restaurants, shops, workshops, discotheques, nightclubs, hotels, gambling houses and casinos – and here we have just written a list of typical places where you can typically find mafiosi, as both dwellers and owners themselves. There are, finally, public spaces that are public also in legal terms: plazas, parks, public gardens, corners, sidewalks and streets. Just as, for African Americans, the street corner functions as a foundational social institution (Liebow 1967), along with sidewalks as the site for Black book vendors – living in a grey zone where legal and illegal pursuits intermingle (Duneier 1999) – so mafiosi can be found in the bars, taverns, plazas and sidewalks of the villages, towns and neighbourhoods where they live and/or practice their activities.

Their visibility is not serendipitous, but rather an integral component and requisite of their mandate, as it were. Far from living in the closet, mafiosi have for long conducted their lives in public – at least many of them have, including some of the alleged bosses of the mafia, the godfathers. This is the case, for example, of the aforementioned Don Calò whose iconic picture depicts him standing in the square of his native village, Villalba, and whose funeral was adorned, according to reports of the time, by dozens of wreaths that arrived from all over the island, together with notables of local party politics and other Sicilian bosses (Dickie 2004; Marino 2006).[9] This was also the case of other influential mafiosi, such as Francesco and Giuseppe Di Cristina, father and son, both bosses of Riesi, near Caltanissetta, as well as Girolamo Piromalli, boss of the Calabrian 'ndrangheta, whose funerals, respectively in 1961, 1978 and 1979, were occasions for grand processions.[10] Rituals marking community life – from baptisms to weddings to funerals, passing through widely attended religious ceremonies such as processions – play a central role for mafiosi and mafia organizations. It is through these ritual moments that they (intentionally) communicate and (unintentionally) express symbolic messages and representations about themselves, about their identities, and their actual and potential position in the local social life and structure. It is through these (by definition, public) rituals that organizations like mafia groups make themselves visible and find channels of public recognition. Funerals represent, possibly, one of the most strategic moments in this public representation of the mafia, as occasions for the celebration of their (more or less) charismatic leaders capable of connecting them with the highest authority of God and, at the same time, for the public communication of who is going to succeed the dead boss, an especially delicate step when the latter has died a violent death. As observed by Alessandra Dino (quoted and translated in Gavini 2017, 289):

> In the general economy of the social relations that a funeral is called to represent, important elements by which it can be evaluated include the number of participants in the funeral procession, the presence or not of flowers and wreaths, the overall atmosphere of affection and esteem by which the dead man's nearest and dearest are surrounded, and the degree of attention manifested by the context in which the deceased and his family have operated ... Even more important than the procession and the scenic apparatus by which it is surrounded is, in some cases, the religious ceremony celebrated in church; because the liturgy in commemoration of the deceased member of a Mafia association may become the pretext to reaffirm its privileged relation with God – the only entity to which authority and legitimacy of judgment is recognized – and, hence, may be useful to justify through a minister of the church – whether conscious of the objective or not – the clear and decided rejection of the canons and prescriptions of earthly justice.

The symbolic strength of such public representations is so significant, to the point that a 'funerary model' (Gavini 2017) has developed in most mafia organizations, in Italy as well as elsewhere, from the *splendide esequie* ('splendid funerals', as the Neapolitan daily *Il Mattino* termed it on 6 December 1892) of the camorrista Ciccio Cappuccio, to the golden coffin of boss Vito Rizzuto in Canada in August 2016; from the funeral of Girolamo Piromalli celebrated in Gioia Tauro in 1976 with the whole establishment of the *'ndrangheta*, to that of Giuseppe Di Giacomo in March 2014, accompanied by the closing of shops in mourning in the working-class Zisa neighbourhood in Palermo.[11] As has often been noticed, the fostering of the symbolic force of these rituals has also been the work of cultural producers such as journalists, novelists and film directors, whose activities have unintentionally contributed, we could say, to the very creation and reproduction of what they may think of as representative of mafia history since its beginnings in the 1860s (Maltby 2001; Gambetta 2009; Puccio-Den 2019; Morreale 2020).

Sure, not *all* mafiosi can live and even die so publicly – it is not safe when you are wanted by the police. Fugitive mafiosi – hidden by necessity – are the counterpart of those mafiosi who are happy to make themselves visible in public spaces, showing off their signs of power and masks, or simply living their lives normally in front of the admiring eyes of their public. The last few decades have seen a recrudescence of the state's fight against the mafia, with a consequential rise of wanted mafiosi evading imprisonment. What this could mean for the nature of the mafia as a social world is hard to say – even if, as far as we know, this social transformation is not enough to change the (semi-)public status of mafia life and mafia groups. As it happens, many fugitive mafiosi still live close to their native towns or neighbourhoods, and there is evidence that, at least in the past, they have been able to marry and have families.[12]

Curiously enough, Gambetta's sources offer many glimpses of this public presence of mafiosi. A case in point is Carmelo Colletti, one-time mafia boss of Ribera, near Agrigento, who 'could welcome his friends ... in a little glassed-in box which stood inside the car showroom he owned with his sons' and where 'he was shot dead ... in 1983' (1993, 58). We can imagine that any customer, actual or potential, in the showroom would have noticed these friends' meetings, especially given the transparency of a glassed-in box. A telling case is Joe Bonanno's description of his headquarters: 'My office was a small private room in the back of a political club which I had set up for the benefit of my friends. It was called the Abraham Lincoln Independent Political Club ... My office was in the back. A tag on the door said "Private"' (Bonanno 1983, 150; quoted in Gambetta 1993, 58). What we can read in these words is, I think, less a cue to ownership of a protection firm than the adamant admission of the political nature of this protection activity, including the distinction between the public stage and the back room of the political sphere. Still relevant for us are the references to bars as public places, of which Gambetta is well aware. The case of the aforementioned Colletti is still worthy of consideration:

> After Carmelo Colletti's death a meeting was held at Gennaro Santino's house to patch up what remained of the family. At the end of the meeting the participants proceeded to the town's main bar in full public view, respecting an *ordine di parata* (parade order) based on hierarchy ... According to investigators, this parade served to inform the public of the position Santino had attained within the family. (Gambetta 1993, 60)

It would be strange to make the Family's new pecking order public if only a few selected people were interested in it for its 'business of private protection'.

To conclude this brief commentary about these analytical efforts to support the economic argument, a glance at the relevant issue of the ownership of these firms for private protection (a crucial feature that commonly defines property rights) may be revealing. Unfortunately, the evidence is missing: 'There are, to my knowledge, no recorded cases in which the actual sale of a mafia "firm" has taken place' (Gambetta 1993, 60–1). While Gambetta speculates about this apparent mystery, I wonder what Schelling would have said – maybe that, just as the exchange of Christmas cards does not constitute a market, the same could be said for mafia 'firms': there are no recorded cases of sales because they are not firms.

Protection as a Field (A First Instalment)

Mafiosi live both private and public lives – with the latter strongly influencing the former. Even when focused, their activities easily extend beyond their narrow aims. To confine their work and services to a 'private dimension' is therefore a mistake, not only because it univer-salizes a distinction that is historically and geographically grounded (as even an economist like Schumpeter recognized), but also because it freezes what, in real life, is a very confused and fluid ongoing concern into clearly delimited categories. The relevant point is that mafiosi have a sense of the distinction between spheres (more or less public, i.e. communal) and have even developed, within their own organization – whose name, it is worth underlining here, is Cosa Nostra, 'Our Thing' – institutions to manage their interrelation; for instance, there are proce-dures for arranging their personal involvement in drug-trafficking affairs independently from their membership in a 'Family'. The way in which they draw the line, however, is not necessarily the same as ours (that is, as Western, liberal, secular observers). This was clearly acknowledged by the sociologist Gaetano Mosca, born in Sicily and knowledgeable about Sicilian customs or folkways, when he wrote:

> The Sicilian, even if you may think the contrary, is widely endowed with moral sense; however, he has a moral sense that is very different from that of northern Italians. His morality, for instance, is expressed preferably in his relationships with private others instead of in his fulfilling public duties as a citizen. Therefore, on the island even a gentleman (*galantuomo*),

independently from any spirit of the mafia, faced with the choice between denying the truth in court or embarrassing a friend or acquaintance who has trusted him by giving him some serious information, and showing himself light-spirited or faithless, will almost always solve the moral puzzle against [the state] justice. (Mosca 1980 [1900], 10–11; my translation.)

This does not mean that every Sicilian is a mafioso, but that mafiosi draw their self-concepts, beliefs and values from a common wisdom they may share with their fellow citizens. So, living in a market society and having experience of the commodity form like any other, mafiosi may sometimes offer protection as if it were a commodity and as if they were operating in a market, but this does not exhaust their activity and function qua mafiosi. Indeed, we could say that this market activity accounts for only a minor part of the affairs of mafiosi as they are more commonly and typically involved, as we are trying to show with the help of documents and witnesses, less in the 'business of private protection' than in the 'business of rule' (Poggi 1978). In this 'business', protection is not a commodity but a service to be furnished in the least exclusive and secluded way possible – offering it not just to someone who might pay, but to everyone who can pay enough to be worth the effort (since it is work) of imposing and extracting revenue, as well as to anyone who happens to live in the area for which the mafia group has jurisdiction and who might be in need of their help. This view recognizes that what is at stake in the mafia is the protection not of abstract individuals, but of those particular persons belonging to the ecological niche of their competence. Mafia protection implies an ecological system with relatively well-bounded niches and a distribution of rights and duties according to this ecology – including norms and practices to solve potential (and sometimes actually occurring) jurisdictional conflicts.

This introduces us to a further issue, i.e. the way in which the subject itself is conceptualized. I have insisted on the impact of 'state thought' on the economic theory of the mafia, as this model lies on an unrecognized state effect, as it were (where the state itself is conceived of in the guise of the liberal and constitutional doctrine of the state). This is not how things look on the surface. Indeed, analytically, the economic theory's argument moves from the other side: not top-down, so to speak, or from structure to agency – that is, from the assumption of the state's structural monopoly of publicness, as I am saying – but bottom-up, moving from the alleged peculiarities of the situation in which the mafia operates to arrive at its identification as an agency that deals with *protection as a commodity* – which is what remains once the possibility of publicness beyond the sphere of the state has been expunged.

Something like a logical fallacy is at play here: if mafia protection is genuine – as the economic model argues – this means state protection does not work. If this is so, then there are no grounds for maintaining the public/private distinction, since the alleged (by definition) 'public' is in fact missing. We can even go so far as to claim that, in a situation like this, the only truly public protection would be that furnished by the mafia – with the state seeming to exist only on paper, but not in real life. On the other hand, if the state were really able to furnish protection, the mafia would simply be one of those security agencies that sells supplementary protection to anyone who is willing and able to pay for their services, e.g., bodyguards or bank security and so on. Of course, when the transactions to be protected are legal and potentially under the public protection of the state (in the case of illicit transactions, say drug trafficking), the mafia would still have the option to simply sell its protection or find other ways of exchanging protection (an option we will explore in Chapter 5). Clearly the mafia is more than this, also because its field of action is much wider and goes much deeper than that of these private agencies.

Let us return now to the vignette of the equine 'lemon' and its players (see Chapter 3): a horse-seller, a horse-buyer and the camorrista, here playing as the (Naples-based) representative of the mafioso type. If this were the case, if just three agents were playing the game (putting aside the fourth element, the object of the transaction, that a horse can be animated as well and as an agent in itself),[13] things would be fairly simple – and economic modelling would work relatively well. The point is that the mafia is far from being a universe populated with *individuals* – and *individual sellers* and *buyers alone*. Protection rarely refers to single individuals, as every individual's safety can have implications for the safety of other individuals as well, beginning with relatives and friends. Protection as a 'good' is less for individuals than for social circles: in other words, it is referred to persons as bundles of social relations (for this relational concept of the agent as 'person', see Smith 2011). Family members, as well as a firm's workers – not to mention owners – are to be included in the protection services given by a mafioso. Evidence for this relational property of the 'market of protection' is widespread, from literary sources to autobiographical narratives, from court witnesses to empirical research.

This means the mafia is active in a much larger environment than a 'market of protection' – an environment that we could name a 'field of protection' in the sense given to the word 'field' by Bourdieu. Let us recall this concept (see Martin 2003): for Bourdieu, fields are arenas of production, circulation, appropriation and exchange of goods, services, knowledge or status, and the competitive positions held by actors in their struggle to accumulate, exchange and monopolize different kinds of power resources (capitals). Fields may be thought of as structured spaces that are organized around specific types of capitals or combinations of capitals. In fields, actors strategize and struggle over the unequal distribution of valued capitals and over the definitions of just what are the most valued capitals. Like a magnetic field, the effects of social fields on behaviour can be far-reaching and not always apparent to the actors involved. The concept of field stands as an alternative analytical tool to concepts such as institutions, markets, individuals and even groups, though all of these can be key components of fields. Field analysis brings these separate units into a broader perspective that stresses their relational properties rather than their intrinsic features and therefore the multiplicity of forces shaping the behaviour of each (see Martin and Forest 2015 for a concise but precise overview).

This implies the substitution of the notion of the market (as opposed to the state) with a more encompassing conceptual device, the state being one of the field's actors (clearly, a major one, a macro-actor as it were), and the market a different metaphor able to capture aspects of the system of social relations at work (see Bourdieu 1977, 1998 [1994] on the concept of the 'cultural field' as a more encompassing and articulated model for capturing the exchange of cultural goods and their logics than the model of the cultural market).

In a field, what is public and what is private is not defined a priori, but is the outcome of the system of forces and struggles constituting the field. Public and private cease to be essential identities and become relational properties. The 'field of protection' is where the mafia and the state are relationally co-involved, sometimes through direct interaction, peaceful or violent, but always in terms of *objective* relationships for the mere fact of their coexistence and activity in the same field.

In this 'field of protection', some individuals and firms demand (and even do not demand, but are in some way involved in the play of forces active in the field) protection, and there are agencies ready to offer/provide protection – including agencies of the state. In the same field, however, there are other agents, individual and collective, whose inclusion has to be guaranteed in order to get the whole picture rather than a partial one. Mafia agencies are among these, together with others that compete with the state's agencies – sometimes in a coordinated game, sometimes even through bloody fighting. From the point of view of the individual, it is clear that if two protection agencies insist on occupying the same ecological niche, their protection risks being redundant and, above all, costly – as he may have to pay for both. The real point is not who has the legal title – though this is a point, albeit a minor one – but who has the force to protect or to persuade someone to be protected. The world has plenty of situations and places in which the state is only nominally the guarantor of protection, while the real protectors are other agencies.

A common argument is that mafia agencies emerge when the state is weak or not strong enough to offer effective protection. Things look more complicated, however (see also Migdal 1988). Does the state guarantee protection to everybody in its territory? This is hard to sustain if we are not happy with formal claims but prefer concrete evidence of protection. First, recall that states are imperfect machines – like every complex organization, they may fail to provide what they claim to be able to furnish. Second, if states – including liberal states – were so universalistic in their deeds, there would be no evidence upon which to ground sociological theories of the state like the Marxist one; in fact, there is wide evidence that states have long been and sometimes still are political class structures, closer to one social class, e.g., landowners, bankers or even peasants, than to others, whose members may feel unprotected or less protected than their class counterparts (e.g., Poggi 1991; Jessop 2016). Third, the same could be said for other identity categories based on gender, race, ethnicity, region and so on. There has, indeed, long been a line of thought and writing in Italy specifically devoted to bringing to light and analysing the inequalities in state protection according to regions, with southern regions, but also some peripheral areas of northern Italy, allegedly being less protected than others that are more central or powerful or economically relevant (e.g., Zitara 2010, 2011). Still, the weakness or insufficiency of state protection against rape, typically perpetrated by men, is a well-known bias of the state, with its formally universalistic claims clashing against its patriarchal features (Pateman 1989; MacKinnon 1989). Fourth, citizenship in liberal states is intrinsically a form of social closure, with citizens constitutively better positioned with respect to public protection than foreigners, refugees and migrants (Metha 1990; Brubaker 1992; Soysal 1994).

Populating this field are the families of the firms' owners and their workers, as well as the families of anyone living in the territory where the firms operate – which is the ecological niche over which the local 'Family' or *cosca* has jurisdiction. All these families are social molecules, as it were, enriched in their scope and integration with what anthropologists call spiritual kinship – a major ingredient of the mafia as well as of the popular culture of Sicilian and other Mediterranean societies, the same that generate the formidable social institution that is friendship and the human figuration known as 'friends of friends' (Hess 1970; Blok 1974; Boissevain 1974; Sabetti 1984). This 'field of protection' is a much wider and more complex social arena, and this is where mafiosi have to play: a social world, an arena in more Weberian terms, made not of individuals but of social relationships. Looking at individuals as units of analysis can miss the point when what needs to be investigated are social universes that are not immediately traceable back to (northern and continental) European history and social life (Rudolph 2005; see also Bourdieu 1977, 2017; Granovetter 1985; Chakrabarty 2000; Connell 2007). Located at the extreme southern border of Europe, the Mediterranean is sufficiently 'other' to put in question well-established conceptual tools of the social science repertory (e.g., Elster 2007), while asking for differently shaped tools. This changes the picture enough to ask for a different framework, I suppose.

The Public Secrecy of the Mafia

The moment has come to focus on the crucial issue of secrecy – a theme associated with privateness, as we have seen, but extending beyond it. This is, after all, the most famous, easy-to-understand, feature of the mafia and mafia-like organizations: their existence as secret societies. A common source of confusion is the ambivalence of the word 'secrecy': it may signify something that is hidden, but also something that is closed, not open. We should therefore distinguish between the two meanings of this 'quality': the first is the condition of being concealed or hidden; the other is the feature of being reserved to an elected few. This distinction makes it possible to pursue a double objective: first, to come to terms with one of the qualifying features of any mafia, that is, its being *secret* and hidden as a social phenomenon – its illegality and alleged criminality being just one of the conditioning factors of secrecy;[14] second, to directly address again – but from a different perspective – the economic theory of the mafia regarding one of its pillars, i.e. the confinement of the mafia qua industry of protection to the *private* world of markets and firms.

Secrecy, 'one of man's greatest achievements', according to Georg Simmel, 'produces an immense enlargement of life: numerous contents of life cannot even emerge in the presence of full publicity. The secret offers, so to speak, the possibility of a second world alongside the manifest world; and the latter is decisively influenced by the former' (1950 [1906], 330). This sense of otherness, this impression of living in a world that they themselves have brought to life and have been reproducing and performing through their gestures and their minor or major decisions, shines through in the words mafiosi use to communicate to outsiders what it means to be a mafioso (see, e.g., Arlacchi 1993, 1994; Lodato 1999).

To be a mafioso means, indeed, to be a member of a secluded organization. Exactly how secluded and how organized it is has been an issue since the beginning of discussions about mafia. We had to wait until 1984 to have an apparently definitive answer, with Buscetta's testimony, the first by a *pentito* to be taken seriously. His revelations solved, once and for all, the old debate about the real nature of the mafia that had started in the aftermath of unification: was this so-called 'mafia' an organized entity (and just how organized?) or was it just a 'way of doing things', an attitude, a 'spirit' as scholars once used to say? Was there simply a 'spirit of the mafia', as Mosca called it, four years before Weber made the expression 'spirit of capitalism' famous, capturing the cultural dimension of what was, in its way, becoming the major point of reference in economic debates and the name for what is possibly the most creative and most dangerous form of economic organization humanity has ever generated?

After more than a century of discussions, contestations, criticisms, proposals and retreats, at least there was no longer any doubt on one point: the mafia is – or at least, is *also* – an organization, with rules, statutes, positions, career trajectories and, as in any organization, narratives and myths. It was discovered that this organization had a name and an organizational history, with recognized leaders, organs, mandates, even offices and officers to fulfil them. Even though none of its members really knew who had started it or when it had been established – the common story believed and repeated by mafiosi in both Sicily and the US (e.g., Bonanno 1983) is the mythical narrative of an ancient structure dating back to the Middle Ages (a popular theory says it began at the time of the Vespers, the Sicilian revolt against the dominating and hated French-born Angevins in 1282, but another even more popular version puts Cosa Nostra in a genealogy originating from the mysterious and mythical sect of the Beati Paoli)[15] – we have sufficiently hard evidence that something like a unique organization encompassing western Sicily has been in existence since the post-Second World War period, with weaker evidence of an organized presence of more or less coordinated translocal groups of mafia since the end of the nineteenth century (for evidence of a large organization of coordinated mafia groups in Palermo and the surrounding area at the turn of nineteenth century, see Santino 2015). Organized *local* groups or associations variously involved in the 'field of protection' as self-help associations, sometimes protecting rackets in specific economic sectors, more frequently acting as agencies of generalized protection, have been shown to have existed, through police and court evidence, at least since the 1870s (Franchetti 1993 [1877]; Lestingi 1884; see Crisantino 2000 on the important case of Monreale). In many cases, evidence has been collected about initiation rites – a major clue for a secret society – and even written statutes.

While not the first to break the secret, Buscetta was surely the first to be believed by judges when he started to talk about Cosa Nostra, the name he revealed for the organization – not a big novelty to be sure, as the same name had already been revealed on the other shore of the Atlantic by a wise guy called Joe Valachi in the early 1960s. But the Cosa Nostra described by Valachi, a low-level member of the organization, was located in the US and was, in many ways, isomorphic vis-à-vis the kind of economic organization that had emerged and flourished in that country (we have seen in Chapter 2 how this discovery was received among social scientists, reproducing the old controversy in a new key). Strange as it may seem, Buscetta's revelations in 1984 (partly anticipated, with less detail, by Giuseppe Di Cristina in 1978, and still earlier, in 1974, by Leonardo Vitale, who were both killed shortly after their revelations) found a positive reception in Italy, not only among judges and other state officers but even among scholars: it was like the launch of a new paradigm, with the shift from a conception of the mafia as belonging to a not-so-hidden world (because there was nothing, indeed, to conceal, apart from individual participation in occasional illegal activities and weakly arranged crimes) to a view of the mafia as a recognizable and institutionalized secret society, whose secrecy, however, had just been broken – in spite of the protection that secrecy is supposed to be guaranteed to the organization that chooses it.

What this dynamic reminds us is that even secrecy has a temporal structure; its shape and its contents change, and, while changing, still projects its aura on what is at least partially revealed. This movement has been captured by Simmel, with his typical penetrating insight:

> The historical development of society is in many respects characterized by the fact that what at an earlier time was manifest, enters the protection of secrecy; and that, conversely, what once was secret, no longer needs such protection but reveals itself ... How this is distributed among the various formations of private and public life, how this evolution leads to ever more purposeful conditions inasmuch as, at the beginning, the range of secrecy is often extended much too far, in clumsy and undifferentiated fashion, and, on the other hand, the utility of secrecy is recognized only late with respect to many other items; how the quantum of secrecy is modified in its consequences by the importance or irrelevance of its contents – all this, even as mere question, illuminates the significance of the secret for the structure of human interaction. (1950 [1906], 330–1)

Independently of what we know today about the organization of the mafia – which is, in any case, only a portion of what the past sources and partial evidence accumulated during more than a century of investigation may suggest and offer to scholarly questions – it is a matter of fact that life in the mafia and in mafia places has to do with the manipulation of knowledge (information) and silence (or secrecy). Catino (2019) offers a systematic analysis of the logic underlying the use of secrecy in mafia organizations. While referring to these analytical efforts, the next section will focus on the meanings of secrecy and their consequences for the production and negotiation of mafia identities.

Simmel has taught us to consider this manipulation of information and silence as quintessentially sociological: all relationships, in fact, 'can be characterized by the amount and kind of secrecy within and around them' (2009 [1908], 331). The theme of secrecy lies at the very heart of the mafia, as one of its apparently essential features. Almost all the available historical sources depart from this quality. In Sicilian dialect, there is indeed a word that was coined in, or has at least been in use since, the second half of the nineteenth century (witness of its existence runs parallel to that of the word 'mafia') to capture and convey the value of being able to remain silent – one of the conditions for a secret to persist or, better, for a secret to be *protected*. This word is *omertà*. It is a feature we have yet to investigate. Here we will offer some first reflections (others will be given in the next two chapters).

As we know, Pitrè identified in *omertà* the core of the mafioso's identity. In more detail, he describes the meaning of this word thus:

> *Omertà* does not mean humility (*umiltà*) as it might seem at first sight, but *omineità*, the quality of being an *omu* (a man), serious, solid, strong. It is a proper way of being, consisting in making oneself independent from society's laws … in resolving all controversies with force or, at most, with the arbitrage of the most powerful representatives of *omertà* in the quarter (*contrada*) … The base and support of *omertà* is silence: without it, an *omu* could not be an *omu*, nor maintain his unquestioned superiority … *Omertà* endures because it is sure of its impunity, and it goes unpunished as long as nobody denounces it; and even when it is denounced, if nobody talks. (2008, 14–15; my translation)[16]

Two things are worthy of notice here. The first is that *omertà* has to do with the idea, and ideal, of a 'government of oneself' (Pitrè 2008, 14n). Following Foucault, we could conceive of *omertà* as a *technology of the self* – technologies of the self being those that 'permit individuals to effect by their own means or with the help of others a certain number of operations on their own bodies and souls, thoughts, conduct, and way of being, so as to transform themselves in order to attain a certain state of happiness, purity, wisdom, perfection, or immortality' (1988, 18).

As such, *omertà* really belongs to moral discourse, but above all to a regime of practices intended to put that discourse into practice. As a technology, it is associated with a certain kind of domination and implies several modes of training and modifying individuals, not only 'in the obvious sense of acquiring certain skills but also in the sense of acquiring certain attitudes' (Foucault 1988, 18). Translating the so-called 'code of *omertà*' into a system of skills, as the economic theory of the mafia does, is just the first step for going beyond the problematic concept of a subcultural normative system acting on the back of agents (Hess 1970), but misses a potentially important point: the attitudinal, or dispositional, dimension of this cultural code; in other words, the way it is an embodied symbolic structure orienting and shaping the interpretations, decisions and actions of the people subject to this code. Skilled persons are not simply those with technical knowledge to put into use whenever they need to and according to some calculus: they are people with a certain posture, a certain idea of themselves, a certain mind-frame, a certain – to introduce a term I will come back in the next chapter – habitus even as a lasting effect of bodily techniques (Mauss 1973 [1935]; Bourdieu 1977, 1998 [1994]).

Second, *omertà* may go beyond the individual level to characterize a whole neighbourhood or local area. In other words, it can denote a *collective identity*. The individual quality of being an *omu* is contingent upon the qualities of others living and acting in the same area, in the same ecological niche, a system of qualities that can be represented by those better endowed with them and possibly coordinated, if not stably organized. 'Even without knowing the person he uses as a means for doing justice for himself and to whom he relies on, the merest eye and lip movement, half a word, suffices to make himself understood, and he goes ahead, sure that the offence will be repaired' (Pitrè 2008, 13). The evidence of a *medesimo sentire* (common feeling) that the sources insist upon asks for more than simple skills: it asks for a theory of practical action explaining the organization even in the absence of organizers and explicit rules or norms. The more this 'human/manly' (*omu*) quality is spread, the more it can be relied upon and the easier it is to behave *as if* this was your quality too: you can trust your fellows so that, if you act according to the rules of *omertà*, they will not say or do anything that could make you vulnerable in the face of official, state justice. This is a strong incentive to enforce the demonstration of having this quality *as if* it were a normative principle – without neglecting or refusing the immanent normative force some ideas and ideals may have, at least for some people (including mafiosi).[17] The list of proverbs celebrating the ability and the wisdom of staying silent is witness to at least the historical existence of a doxa, a universal common sense, functioning as a collective cultural capital and a shared system of meanings through which common understandings are produced.

Less known, and much less quoted, is what Pitrè wrote about *omertà* as a 'social and moral effect' of another institution, well known among anthropologists of the Mediterranean (but also of other parts of the world), *comparatico* or *comparaggio* (often translated as 'co-parenthood', but more usually left untranslated), the local name and practice for what is known more generally as artificial or spiritual kinship (Jussen 2000; Alfani and Gourdon 2012; Thomas et al. 2017). *Comparatico* is a transaction between two men (but even women and children may make use of the institution) in order to establish a strong bond between them. According to scholars of popular culture, this artificial, willingly chosen, social tie is stronger than blood kinship, even though the people consider themselves to be brothers. Historically, this kind of kinship has been developed in order to provide protection in situations where other agencies, especially public ones, were missing or too weak. Often the bond is asymmetrical – one of the partners is more powerful than the other. But the tie may also be symmetrical. We will return to this institution in the next chapters.

Moving from this institution, whose scope clearly extends well beyond the mafia universe, Pitrè offers a structural mechanism that accounts for the enforcement of the cultural code of *omertà* – making a case, surprisingly, for even a *structural* and not a uniquely cultural explanation:

> We have here a moral consideration which explains many facts that are almost unexplainable regarding the social life of a part of our people. Given that San Giovanni is the greatest of the saints, that he is the avenger of the *comparatico*, that an offence done to the latter is an offence done to him, that through him (*in lui*) the strongest and most sacred bonds in the world are established, it is easy to imagine the influence it exerts among the lower classes (*basso popolo*) and the miracles he has to perform. Among a people dangerous for their vengeful nature, among people who follow the principles of the so-called *mafia* as norms of conduct, the *comparatico* is a great good, but also a great evil: a great good for them, a great evil, sometimes impossible to separate from some good, for society. (2008, 110; my translation)

Let us suppose that among men of this kind, says Pitrè, some bad words are exchanged: 'then from these words they pass to acts in a short time; revenge cannot wait very long; thus, conciliation is necessary, with the intervention of some friend of goodwill'. We already know how this device may work: read again the words by Genco Russo and Don Calò, cited in the previous section. The outcome is so described by our ethnologist:

> Peace is made through wine, and under the aegis of San Giovanni it ends with a *comparatico*, which will produce effects with the baptism of the first child born to one of those who made peace. From that day on, these two men, who would have slaughtered each other knowing no other way to

overcome offences among people of this kind, have become friends, more than brothers, and trusting of one another. This is the good side of *comparatico*. But what can we say when this spiritual kinship is contracted with bad will? The *comparatico* wants blind trust, fidelity in every trial, scrupulous silence about the most dangerous secrets; and at the lower the level of society, the convictions about the duties the *comparatico* demands from its contractors are even stronger. Hence the great damage done by a violent person to his *compare* who, bound by these ties, secretly gives the other a hand, without restrictions, without reserve, without hesitation, ready to risk any danger to help his *compare*, and when he has fallen into the hands of Justice, disposed to suffer whatever difficulty, whatever condemnation, in order to maintain silence about what he knows and which, if honestly revealed, might reveal his innocence. (Pitrè 2008, 110–11; my translation)

Interestingly, Pitrè's arguments resonate here with those advanced years later by Giuseppe Marchesano, the lawyer representing the family of Emanuele Notarbartolo, the banker and politician murdered on the orders – at least this was the charge brought at trial – of Raffaele Palizzolo, the aforementioned Palermitan politician suspected by many of being a member of the mafia but enjoying the intellectual and moral protection of Pitrè himself, who even at the trial was unable to see in Palizzolo anything other than a *galantuomo* – and for this reason said to be an 'excellent folklorist but a terrible witness' (Marchesano 1902, 292). For this lawyer, the puzzling nature of the mafia could be addressed only by considering the whole scope of the concept: because if it is true that the mafia consists in taking the law into one's own hands, this is also the source for what he calls 'the anti-social instinct' replacing 'the forms of civil society with the forms of barbarian and remote societies' (Marchesano 1902, 294). And he develops this consideration of the changing times, the teleological horizon against which even an alleged 'virtue' like *omertà*, and therefore the mafia, should be read to grasp its actual meaning:

But what does this degeneration depend on? ... When the State was a tyrant, was the enemy, was for example the foreign invader, then the sentiment of rebellion against the State could dwell within noble souls, could be a social spirit of resistance to arrogance that was rooted in the State!

Nowadays, the concept of the State has changed very much, it is no longer the tyrant, it is no longer the oppressor, the enemy. What is it instead? It is the citizens' emanation, an organ of civility, and rebellion against the State today means rebellion against the form of civil life itself. Once the mafioso was the rebel to a foreign power, the rebel even to an internal oppressor, but now the mafia is a rebel to the rules of civil life. The mafia has changed by necessity, because its enemy has changed.

And what is the mafia today? An organization, as some believe, with bosses and underbosses? No. This does not exist if not in the dreams of some police commissioner (*questore*),[18] and I do not say anything I do not think is true … Thus, this is not the mafia, but rather a natural sentiment, a spontaneous bonding, a solidarity bringing together all the rebels against the law of civil society. And therefore it is a scary thing, sirs! (Marchesano 1902, 294–5)

Interestingly, we find in this forgotten text the adumbration of much social theory elaborated in the last three or four decades with respect to symbolic means of resistance, subaltern politics, the naturalization of domination, everyday forms of resistance, tactics of everyday life, counter-public spheres and other 'saturnalia of power', as James C. Scott (1990) would say. This kind of infrapolitics or parapolitics (Hobsbawm 1959) had some validity, so the argument goes, when the state was in oppressive hands, maybe those of foreigners. But this is no longer the case, it is argued. Clearly, only faith in a state depicted in a positive light – as 'the citizens' emanation, the organ of civility … the form itself of civil life' (Marchesano 1902, 294) – could logically support the argument *against* the mafia. Otherwise, very different scenarios and arguments might be advanced. The final thoughts 'about the mafia' of this well-born and well-connected lawyer[19] who perfectly represents and embodies the doxa of the liberal state with its corresponding civil society, the state as the supreme defender of (high) civility against primitivism and barbarism, are worth reporting as well, since they unintentionally suggest a research path that we will follow in the next two chapters by relying on the intellectual resources social theory nowadays offers to us:

In the same way that in a society all those who are of a distinct and separate race tend to form a faction, so these bad elements of rebellion to civil life and the State have a special bond of solidarity that binds them spontaneously, from the profiteers to the brigands, from the so-called *guardiani* (none other than blackmailers) to the so-called *sensali* (camorristi of market exchanges), from the so-called *trafficanti* (exploiters of workers) to the lower form of the *soutener*, who exploits the poor wretches in brothels. Bring together these and all other forms of high and low delinquency, make sure that the most despicable has a feeling of solidarity with the most elevated malefactor, and you get the spontaneous, terrible organization of the mafia, more dangerous than any other artificial organization indeed because it is not an agreement, but a way of living, something from which the existence itself of all this people depends, bound with natural ties that make it into a unity. And it lacks a general organization, though there is no shortage of organizations. Rebels are organized in *cosche* (this is a technical word) which have their bosses. The members of these *cosche* make up this monstrous organism of violence that is nowadays the mafia in Sicily. The *cosche* have among them an ideal bond, their common interest. (Marchesano 1902, 295)

Anthropologist Michael Taussig has coined the term 'public secret' to denote 'that which is generally known but cannot be articulated' (1999, 5). His examples were drawn precisely from those 'barbarian and distant societies' referred to by our Sicilian lawyer, who on that occasion articulated for us what everyone knew but could not explicitly say. There are secrets inside the mafia, of course. Ontological questions apart, and accepting a range of different interpretations of even the same data/ information, the reality of the mafia has been presumed and even talked about, described, debated in books, reports, newspapers and conversations, and at the very least it has been negated in trials and police offices and even media interviews.[20] Everyone knows there is something like a mafia, but only a few can say it really exists or that they really know it – but of course these few do not speak unless they are defeated (and revealing the secrets of the mafia world means defeating or betraying the mafia and its associates to which an oath has been made). There is only one, and certain, sanction for betrayal – which is what revealing the secret to outsiders means, especially if they are state officials – namely, death. This death horizon is not a minor feature: it is what gives a mafia life its special tension and pathos, typical of politics (see Pasquino 1986).[21]

What, exactly, is the content of the secret? Apart from details about contingent events or occurrences (what happened on that occasion with that participant, or who did an act and why), the content of the secret may by subsumed under four rubrics: (1) the effective existence of a social entity or organization; (2) the rituals and norms of the organization, including the initiation rite with its (variable) formula; (3) the names and status/positions of its members; (4) the history of the organization and information about its members' pasts. None of these 'secrets' is very complicated; nothing is so exoteric as to require a special, long education and master/student relationships. What is difficult is not understanding and learning the contents of the secrets, but carefully managing them in order to survive in an environment where trust is crucial but, for this very reason, there can never be enough of it, especially enough to be trusted (see Dino 2016; Catino 2019).

This does not mean that the 'Families' or the *cosche* willingly and openly teach – this is something one has to learn by living in that world, by keeping one's eyes wide open, by understanding how and when to communicate and express oneself. This is tacit knowledge as personal knowledge (Polanyi 1958, 1966; see Collins 2010). The world of the mafia is, in this respect, not that different from the world of spying and spy novels (Goffman 1969; Boltanski 2014). Education as training and socialization start before the sharing of secrecy (see, e.g., accounts by Vitale, Buscetta, Calderone, Brusca, Zagari and Spatuzza, respectively, in Stajano 1986; Arlacchi 1993, 1994; Lodato 1999; Zagari 2008 [1992]; Dino 2016; see also Paoli 2003). In a sense, entry into a 'Family' – intended as a mafia group, what was once called a *cosca* – implies a successful 'anticipated socialization' (Merton et al. 1957), a socialization that, for the sons of mafiosi, begins the day they are born and that for others starts in an unspecifiable moment, usually during adolescence. A point that is too neglected by scholars of the mafia is the gender structuration of this world (but, on women and, indirectly, on men, see Siebert 1996; Dino 2007); the secrets of the mafia are first of all male secrets. This locates the mafia in a much wider, extended and deeply rooted social phenomenon: that of ritual secrecy (Herdt 2003) The men's houses studied by anthropologists in Guinea, Melanesia and other 'primitive societies' are not an institution you would find in the mafia, but their functional equivalents are far from rare – places where men of different ages meet and spend time together enjoying bonds and situations of homosociality; a social club, a café, a bar, a showroom, a pizzeria or even a street corner (see Whyte 1955 [1943]; Pileggi 1985), in any case, places legitimately frequented only by males in groups, men among men. Secrecy is a social technique for boundary-setting and boundary-maintaining. Being a member means sharing a body of knowledge/information. Sharing information is what citizens do when ritually reading newspapers every morning – they imagine the nation they reproduce, as Benedict Anderson (1983) noticed – or watching newscasts at dinner. Mafiosi do not have to read newspapers every morning to imagine 'their thing': it suffices just to know of their commonly shared knowledge of the real existence of this 'thing' they have created, inherited, transformed, destroyed (sometimes it happens) and reproduced, and which they are still reproducing. Their everyday activities suffice to make their public think they have something to share that is not perfectly known to the outsiders. The boundaries between insiders and outsiders is created. Everyone has an idea of what this thing called the mafia is. Only a few may be sure about it. Sometimes even they can doubt that what they are supposed to be is real. After all, nobody has full control of what happens in and around the mafia, its bosses included.

What I have tried to do in these last paragraphs is underline what Simmel taught us more than a century ago: more than the content, it is the *form* of the secret that is interesting to sociology. But secrecy in the mafia is something we have just started to elucidate: we need other tools for this, and we will further develop our analysis by connecting it to a still more central topic: the nature of *mafia exchange*. In terms of game theory, what Pitrè was depicting in his culture-structural analysis of *comparatico* (see above) is a typical prisoner's dilemma scenario, but one where the players act as if only one equilibrium were possible: the one in which both players can be sure that the other will remain silent. The joint interest to avoid prison is pursued through the 'blind trust, fidelity in every trial' demanded by the *comparatico* in the name of a transcending agent as a saint (San Giovanni) who put the two players in a mediated relationship with God – and recall that secret has the same etymology as *sacer* (Johnson 2002, 3).

But from where does this bond take such an extraordinary force? Making sense of this exceptional resource in the mafia's hands is one of the objectives of the next chapter.

5

The Mafioso's Gift, or: Making Sense of an 'Offer You Cannot Refuse'

Lu dari è magaria ('To give is magic')

Pitrè 1880, 187

In the previous chapter we have seen how the protection offered by the mafioso is far from being simply *private*, and how the mafia universe offers wide evidence for being understood as embedded in forms of publicness, if not in a veritable public sphere (albeit a counter-public and 'personalized' one). The same secrecy – what remains of secrecy in the mafia after you have eliminated this quantum of publicness – makes sense only against the backdrop of a widely shared public representation of its being and working. The mafia protection may be defined as *private* at the risk of missing all this, as well as its consequences. Having questioned the private character of the protection offered and managed by mafiosi, its status as commodity has to be questioned too. Is the protection offered by a mafioso a commodity, as the economic theory of the mafia and its cousin the protection theory claim, or would it be better captured by other models of exchange? In other words, is the mafia grounded on market exchanges, or are the kinds of ties it is built on different from those of the market? As you may expect, my answer veers in favour of the second option, and this chapter is intended to offer arguments in its support.

The economic theory of the mafia has the merit of having pointed out to scholars a crucial feature of the mafia as a social phenomenon, i.e. the nature of the social relationships the mafia is essentially made of: its *differentia specifica*, as it were. The issue had already emerged, of course, in previous literature, but never with this precision and clarity. The challenge has to be met with adequate intellectual weapons, however. As is well known to anthropologists and sociologists, but strangely forgotten by mafia scholars, there is a major alternative to the idea of the market: namely, *the category of the gift* – the notion of an institution-alized practice '[e]conomists have systematically neglected' (Elder-Vass 2019, 1; but see Offer 1997; Belk 1979).

In this chapter, I will argue for a conceptualization of the bond at the core of the mafia as belonging to the species of the 'gift' rather than that of 'commodity exchange.' This involves two different operations: to collect and comment on empirical evidence concerning exchanges in the mafia that make plausible a reference to the idea of the gift in order to make sense of them; to conceptually elaborate on this idea, showing where it may lead us in our understanding of the mafia as a social phenomenon, in what we could name – paraphrasing a classic study in the anthropology of law (e.g., Llewellyn and Hoebel 1941) – 'the mafia way'. Bur first of all, we have to introduce the category of the gift.

Of Gifts and Commodities (and Goods as Well)

It is fair evidence of its intellectual force and fascination that Marcel Mauss's *Essai sur le don* (*The Gift*, 1990 [1925]) is still the starting point for most analysis of gift exchange. Sure, his text has been subject to a vast amount of discussion and refinement (e.g., Lévi-Strauss 1987 [1950]; Sahlins 1972; Carrier 1990, 1991; Gregory 2015 [1982]; Hyde 1983; Parry 1986; Camerer 1988; Thomas 1991; Bourdieu 1998 [1994], 2017; Testart 1998; Pyyhtinen 2014; Caillé 2019, 2020), but its status as a classic in sociological and anthropological theory is nowadays indis-putable. If there is anything like a gift theory in the social sciences, it is because of the lasting legacy of Mauss's exceptionally long article (more than 150 printed pages in its original version); it was published in the first issue of the new series of *L'Anneé sociologique*, the journal founded by the *doyen* of French sociology, Émile Durkheim, of whom, as it happens, Mauss was a favourite nephew and most distinguished pupil. At the time of publication, Durkheim himself, like many other members of the Durkheimian school, was no longer alive; the First World War had seen the death of many very promising young scholars (e.g., Robert Hertz). The atmosphere that is palpable between the lines of *The Gift* is one of sadness but also of hope and reconstruction – the building of a new society on the ruins, or the ashes, of the present one, moving from the reconstruction of social theory, as it were, shedding light on the hidden potentialities of this only apparent 'sociological anomaly'.[1]

The essay's subject is set out from the very start: Mauss intends to speak of 'exchanges and contracts tak[ing] place in the form of presents; in theory these are voluntary, in reality they are given and reciprocated obligatorily' (1990 [1925], 3). The programme looks immediately appealing to students of the mafia who have in mind the debate between those who insisted on the 'demand of protection' from potential clients of the mafia business as being the analytical key social fact in mafia life, and those who see in this move a patent undervaluation of the notion of power as a necessary tool in any serious analysis of the mafia (see Chapter 3). Well, it seems there is a whole class of social facts – Mauss moves from documentary evidence drawn from Scandinavian civilization, adding that the same exists 'in a good many others' (1990 [1925], 3) – that exhibit this double nature: voluntary and obligatory at the same time. Actually, Mauss starts with some caution, distinguishing between theory (appearance) and reality (the true nature of the exchange): but his whole argument and the mass of evidence he presents implicitly lay open for discussion exactly this initial distinction (a point emphatically made by Mauss's followers and benevolent critics, as Claude Lévi-Strauss and Pierre Bourdieu). It is Mauss himself who emphasizes the complex nature of the phenomena he is addressing, introducing for the occasion, by way of close empirical illustration, his seminal concept of the *total social fact* (Karsenti 1997). After having restricted – again, cautiously – the scope of the analysis to the so-called 'primitive' and 'archaic' societies, Mauss explains:

> This embraces an enormous complex of facts. These in themselves are very complicated. Everything intermingles in them, everything constituting the strictly social life of societies that have preceded our own, even those going back to protohistory. In these 'total' social phenomena, as we propose calling them, all kinds of institutions are given expression at one and the same time – religious, juridical, and moral, which relate to both politics and the family; likewise economic ones, which suppose special forms of production and consumption, or rather, of performing total services and of distribution. This is not to take into account the aesthetic phenomena to which these facts lead, and the contours of the phenomena that these institutions manifest. Among all these very complex themes and this multiplicity of social 'things' that are in a state of flux, we seek here to study only one characteristic – one that goes deep but is isolated: the so to speak voluntary character of these total services, apparently free and disinterested but nevertheless constrained and self-interested. Almost always such services have taken the form of the gift, the present generously given even when, in the gesture accompanying the transaction, there is only a polite fiction, formalism, and social deceit, and when really there is obligation and economic self-interest. (1990 [1925], 3–4)

Two points are worth noticing. The first is to reiterate what should be at this stage apparent: that in the 'gift' as an exchange model – as a veritable type of social exchange different from others, including the commodity exchange – there is a possible key to one of the most formidable puzzles of mafia research and to one of the dangerous features of the mafia as a social experience: the fact that it is extremely difficult to detect, to identify, to recognize its full contours and contents, and, for the same reason, to prove legally its existence according to the rule of law. The second point is even more surprising. Mauss is here suggesting that there are societies – better, there are social phenomena – in which the usual division among institutional spheres does not work, in which the same practice or institution functions as if it had at the same time a religious, an economic, a moral, a political meaning – even an aesthetic one. This passage has always reminded me of another passage in a text apparently very different from *The Gift*, a text Mauss surely never had occasion to read or even to scan: Leopoldo Franchetti's *Condizioni politiche e amministrative della Sicilia*. Look at what Franchetti says about the word 'mafia' after warning about the improper way in which it is commonly understood 'on the Continent':

> It is generally believed that the phenomena encompassed by this common meaning [i.e. as violent crime] alone comprise a **complete social fact** even though they are just partial manifestations. Therefore it is common to search inside these for their causes and in the end is found only a mess of disordered facts, often mutually contradictory. The complete fact of which only one phenomenon is covered by the common meaning of the word *mafia* is *the way of being* of a given society and the individuals comprising it. (Franchetti 1993 [1877], 103; my translation, italics in the original, bold added)

Far from suggesting you read this as an instance of (Italian) foreshadowing of what would have been a central (French) contribution to social theory,[2] what I propose to see in this alleged similarity is the common experience of the scholar attempting to solve a puzzle with a move – a heuristic gambit (Abbott 2004) – supposedly able to change the perspective from which to look at it and figure out how to recompose its dispersed items. In both cases, what was puzzling was a set of phenomenic manifestations intermingling with each other and asking for a superior point of view from which to reduce the chaotic complexity. I would suggest that in part this convergence might be accounted for by the hypothesis that the two puzzling social phenomena – the 'gift' and the 'mafia' – have something in common in their structure. At the very least, their manifestations show such numerous overlaps that their similarities cannot be random.

To investigate these manifestations we have first to identify instances of gift exchanges. Are they merely presents or do they encompass a wider field? Mauss had few doubts about the range of acts and experiences to be subsumed under the more general umbrella concept of the gift. As he has little doubt about the *identities* of the subjects engaged in these exchanges. Since this amounts to a sort of empirical operationalization of the concept – or at least a set of instructions about what to look for – a long quotation is worth the space:

> In the economic and legal systems that have preceded our own, one hardly ever finds a simple exchange of goods, wealth, and products in transactions concluded by individuals. First, it is not individuals but collectivities that impose obligations of exchange and contract upon each other. The contracting parties are legal entities: clans, tribes, and families who confront and oppose one another either in groups who meet face to face in one spot, or through their chiefs, or in both these ways at once. Moreover, what they exchange is not solely property and wealth, movable and immovable goods, and things economically useful. In particular, such exchanges are acts of politeness: banquets, rituals, military services, women, children, dances, festivals, and fairs, in which economic transaction is only one element, and in which the passing on of wealth is only one feature of a much more general and enduring contract. Finally, these total services and counter-services are committed to in a somewhat voluntary form by presents and gifts, although in the final analysis they are strictly compulsory, on pain of private or public warfare. We propose to call all this the system of total *services*. (1990 [1925], 6–7)

Looking for an explanation of how this system works, Mauss finds help in an indigenous theory, a Maori legal doctrine focused on the notion of the *hau* (one of the most influential and puzzling ethnological objects, as any anthropologist well knows).[3] This is not the place to go deep into this part of *The Gift* and or even of Mauss's model of the gift; suffice it to say that Mauss follows here a strategy this book shares: it is good practice to find evidence for the reasons of some social institution in the mindscapes, even the words, of the social agents who make use of it. Let the subaltern speak, as it were. This phenomenological moment is a necessary step in analysis – not the final step, however, as, famously, Lévi-Strauss (1987 [1950]) and, later, Bourdieu (1997, 1998 [1994], 2017; see Silber 2009) took Mauss to task for, because the social agents cannot have the whole picture of the structural pattern. We will come back on this point later. Now we will go ahead with Mauss's analysis.

> What imposes obligation in the present received and exchanged, is the fact that the thing received is not inactive. Even when it has been abandoned

by the giver, it still possesses something of him. Through it the giver has a hold over the beneficiary just as, being its owner, through it he has a hold over the thief. This is because the *taonga* [the valuable, exchanged object] is animated by the *hau* of its forest, its native heath and soil. It is truly 'native': the *hau* follows after anyone possessing the thing. It not only follows after the first recipient, and even, if the occasion arises, a third person, but after any individual to whom the *taonga* is merely passed on. In reality, it is the *hau* that wishes to return to its birthplace, the sanctuary of the forest and the clan, and to the owner. The *taonga* or its *hau* – which itself moreover possesses a kind of individuality – is attached to this chain of users until these give back from their own property, their *taonga*, their goods, or from their labour or trading, by way of feasts, festivals and presents, the equivalent or something of even greater value. This in turn will give the donors authority and power over the first donor, who has become the last recipient. This is the key idea that in Samoa and New Zealand seems to dominate the obligatory circulation of wealth, tribute, and gifts. (1990 [1925], 15)[4]

It is not relevant for us, here, to investigate further the deep causes of this obligation to return the gift to its first owner, this obligatory counter-gift. A wide anthropological literature has developed around this. More useful for us is to follow Mauss in his attempt to make sense of the total system, creatively elaborating this piece of indigenous legal theory:

First, we can grasp the nature of the legal tie that arises through the passing on of a thing ... it is clear that in Maori law, the legal tie, a tie occurring through things, is one between souls, because the thing itself possesses a soul, is of the soul. Hence it follows that to make a gift of something to someone is to make a present of some part of oneself. Next, in this way we can better account for the very nature of exchange through gifts, of everything that we call 'total services' ... In this system of ideas one clearly and logically realizes that one must give back to another person what is really part and parcel of his nature and substance, because to accept something from somebody is to accept some part of his spiritual essence, of his soul. To retain that thing would be dangerous and mortal, not only because it would be against law and morality, but also because that thing coming from the person not only morally, but physically and spiritually, that essence, that food, those goods, whether movable or immovable, those women or those descendants, those rituals or those acts of communion – all exert a magical or religious hold over you. Finally, the thing given is not inactive. Invested with life, often possessing individuality, it seeks to return to what Hertz called its 'place of origin' or to produce, on behalf of the clan and the native soil from which it sprang, an equivalent to replace it. (1990, 15–16)

In this way Mauss is able to account for one of the elements in the exchange, the obligation to return. But this is just one of three.

> To understand completely the institution of 'total services' ... one has still to discover the explanation of the two other elements that are complementary to the former. The institution of 'total services' does not merely carry with it the obligation to reciprocate presents received. It also supposes two other obligations just as important: the obligation, on the one hand, to give presents, and on the other, to receive them. (1990, 16–17)

In sum, Mauss speaks of (a class of) givers and (a class of) recipients who are bound together through the objects or services given in an interdependent relationship. The Maussian gift is *inalienable*, in that something of the original owner always remains with it, and it establishes ties of reciprocity or interdependency between people. In Levi-Strauss's extension of the model (1969 [1949]), the gift is an inalienable *thing or person* (e.g., a woman for marriage) exchanged between two reciprocally dependent transactors.

The model is relatively simple in its elemental structure and may be synthetized as the temporal organization of three distinct acts, three separate obligations: the obligation to give, the obligation to receive, and the obligation to return. However, the category of the gift is far from being a simple one. Indeed, its intellectual success is proportional to the degree of controversy it has engendered since its inception in Mauss's seminal essay. One of the major sources of controversies, besides the explanation according to a Maori legal doctrine, is the ambivalence Mauss shows in his location of the model in historical time.

At a certain point in his text, in fact, Mauss placed societies on an economic evolutionary scale, a linear move from a system of total prestations, to gift economy, to commodity exchange (see Mauss 1990 [1925], 90). Both Sahlins (1972, 186–7) and Gregory (2015 [1982], 19) have followed the French sociologist along this path, distinguishing between 'clan societies', where the gift predominates, and 'class societies', where private property and the commodity are the rule. To be sure, even before Mauss, gift exchange had been viewed as part of a socioeconomic totality found mainly in traditional premodern, preindustrial societies, even if its traces and remains can still be seen in our present societies. In the northern West, home of industrial capitalism, in fact, it is commonly accepted, at least after Marx, that alienable commodities change hands in market exchange for a price; Mauss himself was in part concerned enough in his investigations of the gift to address what he saw as the historical separation in the West between economic relations and social relations. Commodities are usually seen, in social as well as economic theory, as (manufactured) products intended for market exchange within the capitalist mode of production; they are marked by the alienation of their production and the impersonality of their exchange. In contrast, gifts, especially in the Maussian tradition, are socially engaged and a binding force in society. In contrast with this evolutionary scheme, Mauss's main point was, however, to envision a future for the gift as rooted less in some linear development than in its *longue durée*, the same through which it is also possible to detect signs of market presence even in primitive and archaic societies.[5] Even if rooted in the Maussian main argument, this interpretation of the gift as a structural ingredient of human societies was not how the model of the gift has been received in subsequent literature – as a matter of fact, the model of the gift is still much more known among anthropologists, especially those working in exotic societies, than among sociologists and even anthropologists of Western societies, and mafia studies show this clearly.

In the words of Christopher Gregory, commodity relations occur in 'the exchange of alienable objects between transactors who are in a state of reciprocal independence', while those of the gift occur in 'an exchange of inalienable objects between people in a state of reciprocal dependence' (Gregory 1980: 640). To be sure, Gregory elaborates this simple bipolar opposition into a continuum of related forms of technology, distribution and exchange of which he writes: 'At one end of the continuum there is the moiety or dual-clan system of organization, at the other end the proletarian or capitalist system of organization. As one moves from one extreme to the other, equality and unity give way to inequality and separation' (2015 [1982]: 37). This notwithstanding, gift and commodity remain firmly located at the two extreme poles, and they have been constructed as inherently opposed to one another in much of the anthropological literature (e.g., Gregory 1980, 2015 [1982]; Hyde 1983; Taussig 1980). 'In this view', Appadurai observed, 'gift exchange and commodity exchange are fundamentally contrastive and mutually exclusive' (1986, 11).

However, some scholarly attention has focused on formulating a more nuanced view of this oppositional gift–commodity relationship (see Herrmann 1997). While some hold to the gift–commodity distinction, others explore how the two types of exchange can coexist in differing contexts within and on the borders of the same society. Such fundamental notions have been challenged by some because of the inalienability of the gift (Parry 1986), commodity exchange occurs only among independent transactors (Stirrat 1989) and the social cohesion engendered by gift relations (Bercovitch 1994). Valeri (1994) argues the need to view gift and commodity in marriage exchange as engaged in a dynamic, transformative tension with each other. Appadurai's attempts to overcome the tension between gift and market exchange through the construction of what he terms the 'politics of value', while focusing on how exchange creates value and insisting that 'it is the things-in-motion that illuminate their human and social context' (1986, 5), is an especially welcome move, except that it obscures the analytical distinction between gift and commodity that has been a major conquest of this whole research stream since Mauss. As Nicholas Thomas once noticed, '[t]o abandon the distinction altogether seems to obscure precisely the factors which mark the biographies of objects and sometimes break them apart through recontextualization and transgression' (1991, 29). Like Thomas, I find the distinction a fruitful *analytic* way of elucidating the complex web of social relationships that people create and navigate in their lives through exchanges of things and services whose values may surely change in time because of the agents' strategies and skills, but always through their combining and mixing of differently organized and differently labelled kinds of relationships.

Before moving ahead, a note about terminology and concepts. Gregory (2015 [1982]) offers a useful insight for mafia studies with his insistence on a distinction between a theory of commodity and a theory of goods, that is, respectively, political economy and economics. While the former implies that a set of historical and social conditions are fulfilled – in other words, it implies a certain economic structure – the latter has a subjective and universal character, with no 'objective empirical basis for distinguishing between different economic systems'. In this sense, while the commodity concept is compatible with the gift concept, they 'together stand opposed to the theory of the goods' (Gregory 2015 [1982], lxii). The theoretical status of the category of commodity in protection theory is not really clarified. It shows features of both 'commodity' in the political economy sense and 'good' in the public choice/economics tradition. It is conceived of as endowed with exchange value and embedded in an economic structure. Contrary to the Marxian tradition, in particular, it is proposed as if it had universal meaning and scope – as it were merely grounded on the subjective relation of a prospective consumer and the object of her desire (for protection).

It is true that the alleged socioeconomic environment in which mafia(s) emerge(s) is one where property rights are at work (Gambetta 1993; Bandiera 2003; Varese 2001, 2014). But this is more a matter of definition than of (ethnographic) substance: simply, it is assumed that, given the historical existence of a certain formal institutional frame (backed by the state's official institutions and inscribed in its legal structure), property rights as well as commodities do exist and work *as they should do* in a (free) market universally open to anyone who has the formal requisites to compete. There is enough historical and ethnographic evidence to suggest, however, that this is often not necessarily the case – indeed, that it is rarely the case. Even in our postindustrial, capitalist societies there is wide room for noncommodity exchanges that are not forms of gift economy, be it in the case of very special 'goods', such as blood-giving (e.g., Titmuss 1997 [1970]), or more prosaic Sunday garage sales (Herrmann 1997). In this neoclassical model (what Gregory calls the economic model), even when there is evidence of gifts and presents, they are not treated as such but, rather, more generally as goods – of a traditional kind, maybe, just as 'commodities' are treated as just 'modern' goods. But gifts may circulate widely in 'modern societies' as commodity exchanges may be detected in ancient settings.[6]

The Gift and the Mafia

We can return to the former saying that, around the world, in societies we used to call primitive or archaic, there are social phenomena whose boundaries we take for granted – those that allow us to distinguish between the economic, the juridical, the religious, the moral, the political and the aesthetic – fail, and things appear mixed. One of the profound features of these complex phenomena in which things mix, 'total social phenomena' as Mauss proposes to call them, is their ambivalent character: indeed, they are apparently free and gratuitous services that are, instead, compelled and interested. These services often take the form of a gift, of a generous gift; however, behind all appearances, behind its forms in the sense of formalism, there is 'obligation and economic self-interest'. In short, in many archaic societies, one can observe social relations that are manifested in forms that do not correspond to their objective content and that are, therefore, fiction, generating 'social lies'.

In an article published a few year before the *Essai sur le don*, Mauss had introduced the theme in the following way:

> Long before the war [First World War], our attention (that of G. Davy and me) was drawn to certain forms that contracts and exchanges of wealth normally take in a large number of societies, Australian, African, Melanesian, Polynesian, North American. There, contracts and exchanges do not have the individual and purely economic aspect of bartering, a system that has been given the name of 'natural economy' without having determined whether a society in which this economy has worked in an exclusive or regular way has ever existed. In general, it is not individuals, but collectivities, clans and large families that commit themselves to each other, often in the form of a perpetual alliance, particularly in the case of marriage, an alliance in the full sense of the word. The reciprocal obligations that these collectivities impose on each other not only encompass all individuals, and often subsequent genera-tions, but extend to all activities, to all kinds of wealth: thus, in exchange for dances, initiations, the clan gives all that it owns, with the obligation of

reciprocation: women, children, nourishment, rituals, inheritance, everything is set in motion. *These exchanges are therefore not of an exclusively economic nature.* On the contrary. They are what we propose to call a 'system of total services'. (1975a [1921], 57–8; my translation, emphasis added)

Among these 'normal forms of collective exchange', continues Mauss, is a 'very notable one', widespread above all – for what was at the time known – in the Pacific Northwest and in Melanesia. North American ethnographers called it *potlatch*, a word generally used among the tribes, or at least the confederations of the Pacific Northwest. According to Mauss, there were two fundamental characteristics of this Indigenous institution, as described by the ethnologist Franz Boas with the help of his Tlingit British informant, George Hunt:

[T]he first [is] that almost all exchanges, which are often very complex and actually involve a quantity of services of all kinds, begin in the form of apparently gracious gifts of objects which the beneficiary will, however, be obliged to return not just the equivalent but an overabundance. The transaction has a sumptuous aspect, a real waste … The second aspect of the institution of potlatch is its intensification, an aspect quite evident in Melanesia and even more so in North America. It has a *competitive nature*. The clans, represented by their leaders, face off against each other much more than they ally. It is a *constant rivalry which can go as far as fighting and killing*. (1895, 58–9; emphasis added)

It is worth noting here that the Boasian description of potlatch upon which Mauss draws (and many others after) is an integral part of a more comprehensive ethnographic description of the social organization of the Kwakiutl indigenous people and, in particular, of their system of secret societies (Boas 1895).[7] Although Mauss in 1921 could not yet make explicit reference to them, it was instead the research on the kula system conducted in the Trobriand Islands by the anthropologist Bronislaw Malinowski (1922) that was the classic source in which to find the most in-depth and influential description of the gift in Melanesia. Also in this case – and it is one of those cases from intellectual history that the sociology of ideas could perhaps explain – an interpretation in a political key was later added to an originally economic, though not economistic, interpretation (Malinowski's), presented as better adhering to the ethnographic data and better able to account for it (Uberoi 1962; but see also Landa 1983; Lee 2011; Corriveau 2012).

Let us compare this model with another, this time taken directly from the literature on mafia, precisely from one of its classic texts: Gaetano Mosca's lecture 'Che cosa è la mafia' ('What is mafia'?; see Mosca 1980 [1900], 3–25). After affirming, in an apparently simplistic way, that in the final analysis mafia groups (i.e. *cosche*) have only one aim ('to obtain the maximum prestige and the maximum illicit gain for the benefit of the organization or its most influential members, minimising criminal acts so as to face investigations and the rigours of justice as little as possible'), Mosca adds that, in order to achieve this result, the *cosche* usually

> not only try to violate the penal code as little as possible, but they also try to preserve those forms, those appearances, that do not excessively offend the self-esteem, and even the mafia spirit, of the victims of their freeloading. Thus, they act in such a way that the victim himself, who in reality pays a tribute to the *cosca*, can *flatter himself that it is a gracious gift* or the equivalent of a service rendered rather than something extorted by violence. (Mosca 1980 [1900], 12; my translation, emphasis added)

Only apparently simplistic, I wrote above, because carefully reading what Mosca says we see that the objectives of the mafia groups are diversified: 'maximum prestige' and 'maximum illicit gain' (if the gain were legitimate, what is called mafia would not be a problem) in favour of the group as such or some of its members (the most influential ones), making the minimum effort and therefore risking 'as little as possible'. In summary, there are objectives of both an economic (earnings) and noneconomic (prestige) nature, for two categories of subjects (more or less influential individuals and the collectivity), following principles of economy or efficiency (minimum effort) – probably a homage to the typical reader of the *Giornale degli economisti*, the main academic journal in the field of economics in liberal Italy, in which Mosca's text was originally published. According to Mosca, the *cosche* would therefore be both economic and status groups (in the sense that today we would call Weberian), capable of institutionally distinguishing between the individual and collective levels and capable of rational calculation – a capacity that does not identify its bearer as an economic agent any more than it would the 'Prince' that Machiavelli instructs and indeed constructs with his teachings, inspired by the principles of loyalty and honour (principles to be followed even when deceiving oneself) more than those, not yet 'thinkable' in Renaissance Italy, of efficiency and competition.

However, it is on the second part of the quotation that I want to focus here, and in particular on the passage: 'Thus, they act in such a way that the victim himself, who in reality pays a tribute to the *cosca*, can flatter himself that it is a gracious gift.' Mosca published this text, which had already been presented at conferences in Turin and Milan, in 1901. We infer that, also in this case 'long before the war', at least one of the studies on the mafia destined to become classics had glimpsed in the gift a mechanism for the functioning of mafia groups, a principle of mafia practice, insisting on the distinction between 'appearance' and substance (but we already know that the gift as a mechanism of social exchange works precisely in the form of appearance) yet failing to develop this intuition in a way that would provide useful elements for a social theory of the mafia. We can assume that, unlike Thorstein Veblen (whose classic *Theory of the Leisure Class* (1994 [1899]) was inspired by the description of this institution and its related practices, which the Scandinavian-American sociologist found, hidden in other forms, in the conspicuous consumption of the American upper classes), the Sicilian Mosca – jurist by training and political scientist by vocation – had no knowledge of the studies then under way on the other side of the Atlantic on the secret societies of the Kwakiutl people and on potlatch, that central institution of social life among these indigenous tribes. For his part, Malinowski was still far from the Trobriand Islands and from identifying kula as the central institution of Melanesian social life. When Mauss published *The Gift* in 1925, introducing this enigmatic subject into sociological and anthropological debate, Mosca's attention was far from the theme of the mafia, though it was a theme to which he returned in the early 1930s, writing the short entry 'Mafia' for the American *Encyclopedia of the Social Sciences* (Mosca 1933; cf. Mosca 1980 [1900], 99–102), but this time without making any reference to the 'forms' and 'graces' of the gift.

None of the studies in the following decades that could have guaranteed the mafia a place in the history of the social sciences would return to Mosca's intuition. Certainly none of the seminal contributions to the literature on mafia – not even anthropological ones (including Blok 1974; Ianni 1972; Schneider and Schneider 1976) – was able to find useful conceptual and theoretical references applicable to the study of mafia in the influential and substantial literature on the gift.[8] How can this absence be explained? The simplest answer is obviously the following: because that theory does not work in the case of mafia. Since what I am trying to demonstrate in this article is exactly the opposite, this response cannot be the answer for me. A possible alternative, then, could be that none of the anthropologists who have worked on mafia has thought of referring to the tradition of studies on the gift, for reasons that have to do with intellectual genealogies and/or paradigmatic criteria of relevance. In fact, none of the anthropologists who have dealt with mafia seems to have profited from the extensive literature on the gift, in their studies neither of mafia nor of anything else, whether birth control in Sicily or Dutch banditry. The case of the Schneiders is emblematic: while recognizing the omnipresence of favours and mutual aid in the social life of mafia, and while noting the effect of creating obligations that these practices generate (2003, 115), they never use the anthropological theory of the gift to further an interpretation of the mafia as a politically relevant, if not truly 'political', phenomenon – even though they have constructed a 'political anthropology' to thematize aspects of mafia phenomenology (Schneider and Schneider 2004). To my knowledge, Pipyrou (2014) is the only scholar who has mobilized the notion of the gift to study the mafia (in its Calabrian variant); however, the analysis suffers in my view from a substantially normative vision of both the gift (assumed to exist solely in its exceptional, and difficult to anthropologically accept, variant of the 'free gift' – see Laidlaw 2000) and the mafia in a conceptualization that cannot give up its underlying state-oriented definition of mafia as a criminal organization.[9] I would also mention the important work of Moss (2001), though it focuses only on *pentitismo* (repentance). Neither of these studies, however, goes towards the type of integral analysis of mafia phenomenology I am advocating here, starting from a comparison with the anthropological theory of gift and an interrogation of the presumed universal model of market exchange based on rational-instrumental action.

That a certain 'family resemblance' may have escaped the few anthropologists who have dealt with mafia since the 1960s is, however, unlikely in my opinion. The answer, then, is probably another: the moral cost of the effort has been judged to be too high. The risk, of course, is not only that of an anthropological justification of the mafia, but also of a 'mafiosization' of forms of social bonds that, from Mauss to MAUSS (Mouvement anti-utilitariste dans les sciences sociales / Anti-utilitarian movement in the social sciences), anthropology apparently desired and recommended as an antidote to the drifts of contemporary capitalist, consumerist, materialistic society. It would be to say that those antagonistic, violent and potentially harmful traits for collective life that are recognizable in the extreme case (as presumed by Mauss, though his quasi-pupil Georges Bataille would have radically questioned this judgement) of potlatch, traits that could throw a dark light on the phenomenon of the gift if not adequately handled in the analysis, should not in any case have crossed the threshold of anthropological otherness (after all, the indigenous tribes of the Pacific Northwest are far away) to find space in modern capitalistic societies where mafia and phenomena similar or comparable to it (the various 'mafias' that police, journalists, judges and political authorities, as well as scholars of social and political sciences, find almost everywhere) not only persist, but even seem to thrive, held together, however, and so to speak secluded from the rest of the good social order in the equally legal and moral (and certainly not very scientific) category of 'organized crime'. Aware of this risk, and assuming its burdens, we will try to shed some light on the nature and functioning of the Sicilian mafia – and probably of other 'mafias' with different historical forms but similar by virtue of structural similarities to the one that gave the name to these phenomena – making use of insights from the now centuries-old anthropological research on the gift.

Identifying a system of exchanging gifts in the mafia may certainly seem bizarre, if not really misleading: isn't a 'gift', by its nature, free and disinterested, and as such antithetical to the usual image of the mafia? It is also true, as anthropologists tell us, that there have been primitive and archaic societies that seem to know the gift only in the form of fiction and social mask (in Mauss's words), but mafias exist and thrive in modern market societies where the distinction between gifts and commodities is clear and foundational (e.g., Gregory 2015 [1982]). However, many of the gifts that mafiosi may give are not authentic gifts but manipulations and exploitations, deviations and distortions, of practices that have a very different logic and that refer to moral universes far removed from those of mafias.

Yet, what makes the gift anthropologically interesting far beyond the classic case studies (Melanesia and the Pacific Northwest) is precisely the repeated and almost ubiquitous discovery of its excess with respect to the conception of the free and disinterested gift – the 'pure gift' – typical of modern, industrialized, liberal societies (e.g., Offer 1997; Caillé 2001; Elder-Vass 2015). If this is the normative (ideal) conception prevalent today in Western societies by virtue of an already well-studied historical and ideological process (Silver 1990; Carrier 1995; Liebersohn 2011; Mallard 2019), it is not the prevailing concept either across human history or in the practical experience of gift-giving typical in our societies. Perhaps the ambivalence of the gift (like that of the mafia) has to do with its own logic and not with the distortions to which it may be subjected (on the very nature and place of sociological ambivalence as a common feature of social structure, see Merton 1976). Moreover, the social theory of the gift has developed precisely to account for its ambivalence, its 'double truth' (Bourdieu 1998 [1994], 160).

The Gift of the Godfather: Giving Evidence to the Argument

So, here we are, back to the heart of our topic, which we could summarize using the words of Mauss himself: in the mafia – that social form that we call mafia – 'exchanges and contracts take place in the form of presents; in theory these are voluntary, in reality they are given and reciprocated obligatorily' (1990 [1925], 3). It is this trait, 'that goes deep but is isolated', of the gift that interests us, just as it interested Mauss: '[T]he so to speak voluntary character of these total services, apparently free and disinterested but nevertheless constrained and self-interested' (1990 [1925], 3)). There is much, obviously, in this classic characterization of the gift that would sound familiar to a scholar of mafia. Paradoxically, Mauss introduces us to one of the most insidious and unanimously condemned traits of mafia behaviour from a perspective that would apparently seem to have nothing to do with it. It may be for this reason that the connection between mafia and the gift – that air of familiarity that can be perceived between the two phenomena – either has escaped scholars of mafia (but also those of the gift, it would seem) or, if noticed, has been set aside, archived, if not outright denied.

To empirically support this argument, we will come across clues (according to that 'evidential paradigm' that Carlo Ginzburg (1979) has shown to be 'widely operating in fact' in the human and social sciences, 'though not explicitly theorized': here another case of invisibility) that can be traced through a variety of sources: judicial and police records, of course, but also journalistic, autobiographical, literary and academic texts. The material we use is not unpublished, and this is its probative power: as we shall see, it is a question of testimonies, stories and documents that are available and often very well known, at least to specialists. It is material that, as such, does not really say anything new about the 'facts' or the 'factuality' of the mafia, but which, re-read in light of a new interpretative scheme, seems capable of bringing out neglected aspects and dimensions of the mafia phenomenon and shedding new light on its generative and reproductive mechanisms. Therefore, we will look for fragments of text from which to sift the circumstantial evidence with which we will try to give substance, depth, support and scientific validity to the thesis in the interstices of these pages and sources, scattered and interspersed among other themes and, for this reason, mostly unnoticed, though in some cases they are clearly visible even though neutralized within interpretative models that conceal even evident meanings (think of banquets, of which we will say more below). For reasons of space, I will limit my probing to a few circumstantial fragments, taken from sources of different types, referring to different phases and moments in the history of mafia (Sicilian, as well as its Italian-American variant) yet converging at the heart of our topic.

'An offer you cannot refuse'

We will start with a very well-known literary object. The argumentative strategy we are following will expand, starting from the most uncertain sources, bordering on fiction (but no less effective), gradually enriching them with more and more concrete sources, eventually incorporating documentation that has already been validated by the academic community.

The father of the bride, Don Vito Corleone, never forgot his old friends and neighbors though he himself now lived in a huge house on Long Island. The reception would be held in that house and the festivities would go on all day. There was no doubt it would be a momentous occasion. The war with the Japanese had just ended so there would not be any nagging fear for their sons fighting in the Army to cloud these festivities. A wedding was just what people needed to show their joy.

And so on that Saturday morning the friends of Don Corleone streamed out of New York City to do him honor. They bore cream-colored envelopes stuffed with cash as bridal gifts, no checks. Inside each envelope a card established the identity of the giver and the measure of his respect for the Godfather. A respect truly earned.

Don Vito Corleone was a man to whom everybody came for help, and never were they disappointed. He made no empty promises, nor the craven excuse that his hands were tied by more powerful forces in the world than himself. It was not necessary that he be your friend, it was not even important that you had no means with which to repay him. Only one thing was required. That you, *you yourself*, proclaim your friendship. And then, no matter how poor or powerless the supplicant, Don Corleone would take that man's troubles to his heart. And he would let nothing stand in the way to a solution of that man's woe. His reward? Friendship, the respectful title of 'Don', and sometimes the more affectionate salutation of 'Godfather.' And perhaps, to show respect only, never for profit, some humble gift – a gallon of homemade wine or a basket of peppered *taralles* specially baked to grace his Christmas table. It was understood, it was mere good manners, to proclaim that you were in his debt and that he had the right to call upon you at any time to redeem your debt by some small service. (Puzo 1969, 8–9)

As the reader will probably have recognized, this is a piece from the first chapter of the Italian American writer Mario Puzo's *The Godfather*, a novel that quickly became a bestseller and upon which Francis Ford Coppola based his famous film, a milestone in the history of US cinema. It is not a classic text like the Scandinavian Edda from which Mauss's essay on the gift starts, but it has a paradigmatic immediacy of its own that is worth deploying immediately. The passage introduces us to the theme with the elegance and expressive power that are typical of the literary imagination. With these words, Puzo frames one of the central events of the story (and later of the film), the wedding of Costanzia 'Connie' Corleone, the Godfather's daughter. The image of the Godfather – interpreted in the film by Marlon Brando, who created an iconic figure that has since entered global popular culture (not to mention the imaginary of the Sicilian mafia, as revealed by some *pentiti* – see Gambetta 2009) – that this description conveys is that of a generous dispenser of aid to anyone who has requested it, assistance that is effective and, at the same time, concrete. Yet it is assistance that is only apparently disinterested because, as the narrator explains, 'it was understood' that there was an exchange. To the requester went concrete help, to the Godfather things like 'friendship', verbal 'gifts' (compliments), some 'humble gift'; however, the Godfather's aid was 'never for interest': the debt was, in fact, understood, and was expressed in the tacit right of the Godfather to be able to ask at any time for 'some small service' to 'redeem' the debt (we will return to the meaning of this verb later). The passage represents the mafia as a system of exchanges, favours, credits and debts, of help in exchange for friendship, for compliments personally given. It is aid that creates debts, and therefore bonds, their terms never explicit, their conditions never defined – but for the fundamental one that to ask for help, to 'beg', the person involved ('he, himself') became personally committed to assuming the burdens as well as the honours of the proclaimed 'friendship'.

Again from this text, in the same chapter but a subsequent scene, there is an image and an expression whose capacity to evoke the mafia universe – a universe of meaning as well as of force and violence – cannot escape the reader. 'I'll make him an offer he can't refuse' (1969, 43), says the Godfather to his protégé, Johnny Fontane, a singer and actor linked to the 'Family' who complains about a lack of engagement by a Hollywood producer, who will later find himself, for not wanting to accept the offer, with the head of his beloved racehorse in his bed, dripping with blood. Having entered common usage, this expression has lost its original anthropological meaning, perhaps even to Puzo himself. What else is an offer that cannot be refused if not the second moment of the exchange of Maussian gifts? It is the moment that imposes the obligation to receive what one has given, and a prelude to the third obligation, that of reciprocating the gifts received.

The literary imagination has an advantage over the sociological one, to which it is also related: the ability to encompass universes of meaning and scenes of life in just a few effective words, which the sociologist, like the anthropologist, can only reconstruct starting from a series of disordered and incomplete data and information, rarely so perfect and coherent as to combine into a complete and well-rounded image. This joking exchange about the Godfather between Michael, his third son who had originally been destined for a legal career, and his girlfriend Kay (the epitome of a WASP), testifies to the power of literature to 'plunge the reader into the immediate atmosphere of ideas and facts in which our exposition will unfold' (Mauss 1990, 1):

Kay said thoughtfully, 'Are you sure you're not jealous of your father? Everything you've told me about him shows him doing something for other people. He must be goodhearted.' She smiled wryly. 'Of course his methods are not exactly constitutional.'

Michael sighed. 'I guess that's the way it sounds, but let me tell you this. You know those Arctic explorers who leave caches of food scattered on the route to the North Pole? Just in case they may need them someday? That's my father's favors. Someday he'll be at each one of those people's houses and they had better come across.' (1969, 47–8)

In short, three properties of the gift and its exchange are condensed here: the temporal dimension ('the interval of time that separates the gift from its reciprocation', which Bourdieu has especially emphasized in his re-analysis of the exchange of gifts after Mauss and Lévi-Strauss), ambiguity (which is expressed in the form of both individual self-deception, that of Kay that Michael takes care to correct, and the collective one, the self-deception of all those who participate, so to speak, in the game of the Godfather) and, last but not least, the symbolic violence inscribed in a relationship whose apparent disinterest and affection masks its truth as an act of domination (Bourdieu 1998 [1994], esp ch. 6; see also Bourdieu 2017; for a reconstruction of the analysis of the gift in Bourdieu, a sort of leitmotif of his work, see Silber 2009).

One could, indeed, re-read the entire novel *The Godfather* in light of the gift paradigm. There are so many narrative elements that can be easily accommodated in the paradigm that perhaps the reason such an intellectual operation – one of those operations that Andrew Abbott calls 'gambits of imagination' (2004, 4) – has never been performed is for an excess of immediacy: it is too obvious, too 'already there', to really work. But perhaps the opposite is true: that this evidence presupposes, in order to be exploited, a certain familiarity with a discipline, an anthropology, and with a line of anthropological research on the gift that started from Mauss's essay, which we cannot take for granted among Puzo's readers or mafia scholars.

Of course, in the field of social sciences, a literary source does not have the same probative force as a verified source that is not produced by the researcher. And this is true despite knowing that Puzo, author of the novel and screenwriter of the film based on it, was not Sicilian but, rather, Lucanian, and thus had to spend months researching articles and reports at the New York Public Library in order to write the novel that would make him famous (for an account of this preparatory work, the so-called *Godfather Papers* drawn up by the author himself, see Puzo 1972). But our path is only at its beginning. We proceed with another fragment, another source. This time it is not literary fiction, but an insider's testimony from within the mafia world. This is a report that I draw from a wider narrative testimony recently collected by the journalist Anna Vinci, an account whose value with respect to our thesis is rather remarkable. The speaker is a genuine member of Cosa Nostra, Gaspare Mutolo, former bodyguard of the head of the Palermo Family, Rosario Riccobono, and later driver of the Corleonese boss Totò Riina, who, as a *pentito*, or rather a 'dissociated' mafioso, helped magistrates as well as scholars and observers learn more about his world:

> The ties of kinship and those of old friendships formed during adolescence in the neighbourhood (the only ones usually permitted besides friendships between mafiosi) are of vital importance: the first dances, the first love affairs, the alleys, the first thefts. For example, when you want to influence a lay judge, you don't necessarily have to resort to corruption. You try to reach him through a relative, a friend ... it is precisely through these bonds of friendship that the mafia try to influence the person nominated. The lay judge who, for example, has been seeing a certain woman since adolescence will never think that she's asking him for consideration for the benefit of a mafioso, especially if she makes the request using phrases such as: 'Have you heard about that murder? There is a friend of mine who has been investigated, but you know ... it's a mistake.' It is she who does the convincing, and her words will work better than any threat. (Vinci 2013, 56; my translation)

And if the network of obligations interwoven by simply living in the neighbourhood since adolescence, with the sedimented network of favours and exchanges that this implies (a network evidently built over time through a continuous exchange of even the most minute and apparently negligible services), is not enough, the mafia strategy does not seem at all to be that of buying and selling favours, of *do ut des*, of the contractual link typical of the market economy (of the 'economic economy' as Bourdieu would say), but the politics of the gift:

> Several times – Mutolo continued – they asked me: 'But were these people paid?' No! Mostly, when we had to 'encourage' someone to help us – and not just lay judges – we tried to convince him through gifts of respect to his wife, sister-in-law or even his lover. To make them feel, let's say, a little bit obliged and respected, and the most appreciated gifts were a diamond, a necklace, a piece of jewellery for a special event or an anniversary. Never money: cash is tactless. It is better that they realize the value of (and reasons for) the gesture without the vulgarity of money. And the more important the gift is, the stronger the bond: it is a game of upping the ante. When you create a relationship with the mafia, you can never go back: *you don't just pass through our world*. Often people don't understand this or, rather, prefer not to understand it. (Vinci 2013, 56–7; my translation, emphasis added)

'You don't just pass through our world': because the micro-dynamics of the gift necessarily require time, the accumulation and sedimentation over time of favours and, therefore, of obligations, which multiply 'with interest' in a 'game of upping the ante' – a mechanism that exists not only in the monetary economy but also in the symbolic economy of favours and social relations (on the indefinite, till-death's horizon of mafia life, see next chapter).

'I am someone who has always cried over the pain of others'

Admittedly, such precise and explicit testimony about the use of the gift in the mafia *modus operandi* are rare in the literature on the mafia, witness accounts, reports and autobiographies themselves. This should not be surprising: this is not the issue on which either investigators and agents of the state insist in their questions, or indeed journalists, who are sensitive to other topics (killings, brutal violence, corruption, collusion, etc.). But if we are willing to accept as circumstantial evidence even minor reports that only implicitly, indirectly, refer to the pervasiveness of the gift system in the daily life of the mafia, the testimony is plentiful.

Here is a sample of what a necessarily selective reading, searching for traces and clues, of certain bestsellers of this genre can offer our topic.

> It's in my nature. I have no ulterior motives. If I can do a man a favour, no matter who he is, I will; because that's how I'm made. It's just a question of the sort of character and feelings that a man's born with. I'm made that way … A man will come to me and say: 'I'm having trouble with So-and-So. Can you see if you can settle the matter?' I either send for the other person or go and see him, according to the terms we're on, and I settle the business. But I don't want you to run away with the idea that I'm blowing my own trumpet … I'm only telling you this to be polite, because you've come all this way to see me …
>
> I'm always here. If a person comes and asks me a favour, I'll do it for him. I can't say 'no' to anyone … This is my way of life, Signor Dolci. How else would you have me be? Very often warm-heartedness will win a man gratitude and friendship, and then the time comes to ask for one thing or another in return.
>
> Living a certain sort of life, brings its consequences; one thing leads to another. First one man came to me and I did him a favour, then another and another; and so it went on until it became a sort of habit with me, and more and more people came to hear of my name. … Folks come and ask how they should vote because they feel the need for advice. They want to show that they are grateful to those who have worked for their good; they want to thank them for what they've done by voting for them; but they are ignorant, and want to be told how to do it. (Dolci 1964 [1960], 121–2; emphasis added)

Sharing his story with the sociologist Danilo Dolci, doing it 'to be polite, because you've come all this way', explaining the reason for the sense of gratitude and appreciation that people nurtured towards him – and this was undoubtedly the reason for Dolci's interest in this man – is Giuseppe Genco Russo, landowner and farmer of peasant origins as well as an exponent of the Christian Democratic Party of Mussomeli, a town of fifteen thousand inhabitants of the Caltanissetta area, considered by many observers to have been the 'boss' of the Sicilian mafia in the 1960s. It is a presentation of the mafia self that, read in light of the 'gift paradigm', certainly loses much of its cultural specificity but acquires sociological comprehensibility: there is nothing exceptional about participating in a system of services, exchanges of services and assistance, but for that predisposition of character (Bourdieu would say: habitus) which, due to its relative rarity, makes it easier for some to occupy a strategic position in the system of exchange. It could be more than a coincidence that the title of the book in which this testimony is documented (anonymized, but whose source is easily reconstructed; see also Hess 1970 – new edition, 1998, 74) is *Waste* (whose subtitle clarifies the subject as *An Eyewitness Report on Some Aspects of Waste in Western Sicily*): for is it not precisely waste, expenditure, that is the most significant trait of potlatch, that form of extreme gift, bordering on violence, of which Bataille (2001 [1949]) traced a personal 'theory' in the framework of his analysis of 'the accursed share'? And it is certainly not out of place to recall here that, in 1884, the Canadian government went so far as to outlaw the indigenous practice of organizing collective celebrations and ceremonies (which continued, however, secretly and at risk of prosecution for participants) precisely because of the deleterious consequences for their economic life and, of course, for public order that the Canadian government, in the wake of pressure from Catholic missionaries as well as local officials, saw in this competitive practice (Ringel 1979; Cole and Chaikin 1990; Bracken 1997).

According to press accounts of the time (a judgement that was partially disavowed by the testimony of *pentiti* who, a few decades later, would greatly reduce the effective weight and power of these rural figures in the history of Cosa Nostra), Genco Russo had inherited his 'godfather' position from another country 'gentleman', Don Calogero Vizzini, *gabellotto* (a sort of overseer) of large landholdings and sulphur mines, who had always resided in Villalba. Upon Vizzini's death in 1954, his family (which included the town's archpriest, Don Calò's brother, as well as two uncles who were bishops) wanted to commemorate him with an enormous written text on a black-edged cloth overlooking the church where the funeral was held: 'enemy of all injustice / a humble man among humble men / a great man among the greatest men / demonstrated with his words and deeds / that his mafia was not a crime / but respect for the law / defence of every right / greatness of spirit / it was love (Marino 2006, 246; my translation). Moreover, Don Calò himself had already taken steps, a few years earlier, to create his autobio-graphical profile (dictating it instead of writing it himself, as he was, it seems, illiterate). Here is an excerpt, which is self-explanatory enough not to require comment:

> I am someone who has always cried over the pain of others, over the material miseries of men, and I have given all of myself to soothe them. I must admit that I have often returned home without a penny in my pocket, since I had given everything to those in the streets who had asked me for it. I have always reacted when someone wanted to overpower me and, for this, I did not use transactions as, respecting all my peers, I wanted the respect returned ... So I am a mafioso in our own way, in the Sicilian way, giving what I can to those who need it, respecting and making myself respected, not tolerating the oppression of the weak, respecting the honour of others and making mine respected. (quoted in Marino 1986, 281–2; my translation, emphasis added)

And, to those who, in the columns of a local left-wing newspaper, accused him of being not only a mafioso and a fascist but also a business failure, he replied:

> This is true. In 1926, the date of my bankruptcy, I had a sulphur business, and still do, as well being a landowner. I have never been interested in admin-istration, and someone, indeed more than one (what do you want?) took advantage of it. The sulphur crisis was raging, *I gave money away, and I keep giving it away*. I was arrested for that damned mafia and therefore was forced to leave everything in the lurch. And there is the failure. (quoted in Marino 1986, 283; my translation, emphasis added)

In the 1980s, the literature on the mafia, as we know, changed. In addition to journalistic inquiries and interviews with alleged mafiosi, as well as a few academic studies, there was also a new editorial trend, almost a literary genre: the publication of confessions by people who were no longer just allegedly mafiosi, but who had confessed – above all, the *pentiti*. Dispersed across many judicial orders and decisions, variously repeated but, mostly, supplemented and reworked with targeted inter-views, these confessions opened up to the sociological eye a world of symbols, practices and feelings previously revealed almost exclusively only through police investigations and descriptions by third parties, and only in a few very rare cases (of which we have seen two examples) through the measured words with which alleged mafiosi presented themselves, naturally denying their affiliation to the mafia as well as its very existence as being anything more than a way of feeling or a 'spirit'.

Although written in the third person by the journalist Fabrizio Calvi, the following text evidently derives, in its contents if not directly in its words, from autobiographical testimony that is among the most authoritative ever gathered. It was given by Tommaso Buscetta, a new *pentito* who, in 1984, had turned state's evidence, to the then little-known investigating judge Giovanni Falcone. From this testimony, we can get an idea both of the breadth of services that the mafia bond entails as well as of the network of obligations in which it, almost naturally, ends up being translated:

> Stefano Bontate [head of the 'Family' of Santa Maria di Gesù, a small town on the south-western edge of Palermo, and one of the most powerful and influential leaders of Cosa Nostra in the 1970s, nicknamed 'the Prince' for his refined manners and elegant clothes, or rather for his more credibly 'bourgeois' and 'noble' lifestyle than the average mafioso] could not refuse anything, or almost anything, to Tommaso Buscetta. Doing him a favour was an honour for him. So, when in 1975 Buscetta was trying to find an honest businessman to provide his daughter Felicia with her wedding trousseau, Stefano Bontate sent him, without hesitation, to his trusted man, Pietro Lo Jacono, the vice capo of the Santa Maria di Gesù family, who took care of everything in his absence. In addition to being Stefano Bontate's second-in-command, Pietro Lo Jacono was the right man, above all, because he owned numerous fabric shops, including one, located in front of the central station of Palermo, that specialized in items of purely local taste. So Felicia Buscetta went to Lo Jacono's shop, mentioned her father's name, and was offered a trousseau worth one million lire, for which she was not allowed to pay. (Calvi 1984, 90–1; my translation, emphasis added)

Of hospitality and conviviality

Re-reading the confessions and autobiographical testimonies of the various mafiosi – including Buscetta, Calderone, Cancemi, Spatuzza, Di Carlo, as well as the aforementioned Mutolo (whose life story was collected and told, over a decade later, in two books) and many others, Sicilians and even Calabrians, whose interviews journalists and writers have been collecting, editing and publishing since the early 1990s – searching for clues that can adequately support my hypothesis of extending the gift paradigm to the mafia universe, is perhaps not a very exciting intellectual endeavour, though it has borne fruit. One theme emerges strongly, a theme that Mauss had brilliantly emphasized in his writing on the gift:

> It was a period of broad agreements, grand alliances in every corner of Sicily … in those years, we hosted Luciano Liggio in San Giuseppe Jato, and he was also welcomed in Cinisi, a village near Punta Raisi, by Gaetano Badalamenti. In short, we were a happy family. There were exchanges of favours: this also meant the possibility of killing people in order to lend a hand to those

who found themselves in difficulty with someone. (Lodato 1999, 49; my translation)

Thus recounts Giovanni Brusca, son of the head of the Family of San Giuseppe Jato and one of the members of the hit squad who killed Judge Falcone in Capaci, speaking of the 1970s when the so-called 'triumvirate' was born, the commission that would govern Cosa Nostra until the early years of the following decade. His 'confession' teems with references to episodes and occasions of hospitality between mafia members, including those of different 'Families'. This is one of the oldest and most characteristic services in the gift system, whose importance was underscored not only Mauss, but also, in his wake, by Moses I. Finley in *The World of Odysseus* (1978 [1954]) and Julian Pitt-Rivers in his anthropological research on hospitality (1968, 1977):

> There are relationships of family and friendship that have been handed down over the years in the villages. I would go to someone and tell him: 'You know … I have some problems at the moment …' and ask for a helping hand. And the other would respond: 'My house is available.' (Lodato 1999, 43; my translation)

Nor do these confessions by *pentiti* lack references to the munificence, generosity and physiognomic traits, evidently accepted as 'true' in their mafia circles, beyond the self-representation that mafiosi, like many others, can indulge in their 'presentation of the self'. Reducing these 'documents of life' (Plummer 2000) to the 'manipulation of cultural codes', a leitmotif in studies on the mafia, does not help us to understand the phenomenon very much. Speaking of his decision to dissociate himself from the mafia, which had come to be dominated by Riina, and to turn state's evidence, the logic that Giovanni Brusca puts forward is still, upon closer inspection, that of exchange, with its obligations of giving, receiving and, above all, reciprocating:

> It was Riina himself who committed the first betrayal against the Brusca family. It was he who broke a thirty-year tradition of disinterested friendship … of acquaintances between our families, of shared risks, by publicly scorning me … I came to know these people as friends of my father. I fought, I risked my life for them. From every point of view. And how did they repay me? (Lodato 1999, 16–17; my translation)

And about his former boss:

> If any of us had financial difficulties, Riina wouldn't make you say it twice and would reach into his own pocket. If, on the other hand, someone thought

of jerking him around by welshing on the hundred thousand lire, or a million or a billion, he would go mad. He is generous, in his own way. (Lodato 1999, 65; my translation)

Autobiographical accounts such as those I have been discussing are rich in details, but have a limit: they express the point of view of the *pentito*. Their authors now live outside the universe of mafia significance. The risk of a retroactive reinterpretation is inevitably present in their choice of words, selection of episodes to recount and the emotions that accompany their story. Thus, we must also look elsewhere, among police sources for example, or academic sources based on ethnographic observation.

Giuseppe Alongi was a police officer with a passion for (criminal) anthropology, a follower of Lombroso to whom he dedicated his book on the mafia. At the end of the nineteenth century, he used his professional knowledge to discover how the exchange circuits of products, the movements of people and goods between the mountains and coastal areas and livestock fairs, were the channels through which the mafia communicated, made common acquaintances and strengthened their ties. Thanks to these encounters, collective initiatives and enterprises could be planned: 'interprovincial congresses of the mafia' (Alongi 1977 [1887], 71; my translation), as this policeman-anthropologist called them, but they were also occasions for social relations and rituals that readers of Mauss's work will recognize as nothing less than ceremonies for the circulation of goods, favours, confidences and commitments: in short, as places for the binding of those total service systems of which gift exchanges are an integral and fundamental part.

What police sources can offer us – understandably they are not very sensitive to describing instances of the exchange of gifts except to the extent that they can shed light on the nature of a criminal link or the context of a crime – is demonstrated by works like the so-called 'Sangiorgi report', a document, certainly exceptional for its time (late-1890s to 1900) and for its breadth but, at the same time, ordinary in its style and form, which was recently published in its entirety, with all its related documentation, thanks to the meticulous work and tenacity of Umberto Santino. This document describes events from a period when mafia *pentitismo* was not yet institutionalized, but certainly the practice of giving gifts, hosting big communal meals, banquets and parties was an integral part of the daily life of those who, in the eyes of the investigators (and others), passed for mafiosi. And so, with regard to the murder of a certain Salvatore Castelli, which took place in August 1895:

It was said at the time that this crime had been preceded by a banquet held at Giovanni Vassallo's tavern in the district of Verano, and this circumstance was better substantiated later when, in December 1897, this office questioned La Piana Vincenzo di Santo and Alfano Domenico di Salvatore, convicted by this Court of Assizes for the murder ... These two, of course, protest their innocence of the crime for which they have been convicted and do not admit the existence of a criminal association in these districts; but they do not deny that banquets took place in Giovanni Vassallo's tavern on the day Castelli was killed as well as previously.

    These are characteristic banquets of the mafia, in which bloody vendettas are usually arranged or celebrated after being carried out. (Santino 2017, 564–5; my translation)

And, as we learn from Annex II to the Sangiorgi report, which includes the statements of the prisoner Vincenzo Piana:

It's true that eight days before the murder I was invited by a certain Salvatore Greco to take part in a banquet at Giovanni Vassallo's tavern. I remember that on that occasion there were Salvatore Greco, Rosario Megna, the pasta maker, Girolamo Varesi, known as Mommo, and a certain Nené Figlia. Varesi paid for the dinner. Then Salvatore Greco, to reciprocate, proposed a second dinner for the following Monday. On that occasion I bought ten cockerels which I sent to the aforementioned tavern where, at the designated time, I went with Domenico Alfano, who had not been invited. (Santino 2017, 568–9; my translation)

Far from being a folkloristic ingredient of local customs or colour, the theme of banquets emerges, in light of Mauss's model, as strategic for better understanding the mafia phenomenon which, in this perspective, can be seen as a historical and ethnographic manifestation of convivial practices whose roots go far back into the past and whose sociological significance has been clarified by Mauss's book. The relevance of this social institution – also remembered with emphasis and described in detail by Brusca in his 'confession' (see Lodato 1999, 181–3) – did not escape the attention of anthropologists Jane and Peter Schneider in the mid-to-late 1960s, when they conducted field work for what would become one of the first ethnographic studies on the mafia, a theme to which they have returned on several occasions (cf. 1976, 104–7; 2003, 2006, 2011).

The Schneiders' interpretation identifies some strategic issues. For example, there is the role of cultural practices, such as banqueting, in the production of the mafia phenomenon, as well as the existence of liminal spaces separated from those of everyday life (an observation that is open to, among other things, a Durkheimian reading that would provide support to the one attempted here). Further, they note the possible involvement of non-mafia members in networks of reciprocity centred around banquets and entertainment, even grotesque and satirical. In addition, there is the theme of cultivating an aggressive male identity (the same kind that, evidently, is at stake in the archaic exchanges between warriors). Finally, connected to this, is the containment function that these convivial moments perform for conflicts and violence – reportedly, the five banquets that Peter Schneider had the opportunity to attend in 1966 (Jane, as a woman, was excluded) were aimed at celebrating the resolution of a quarrel between two influential local people, a merchant and a wholesale butcher. Still, what is of value in their analysis is, on the one hand, the functionality of the cultural practice of banqueting to business and running economic enterprises and, on the other, the link with the institutional political system: 'The favour system most relevant to the mafia', in their view, is and always will be the one that 'had long hinged on the ability of mafiosi to mobilize votes for parties and politicians in a position to influence the criminal justice sector' (2011, 9).

Yet, there is something else that needs to be added to the discussion: once again, it is the theme of hospitality and its laws (Pitt-Rivers 1968, 1977), and through this, that of the exchange of gifts as an autonomous anthropological principle of social organization, different from or in addition to both the 'market' and the 'state', understood as a rational (modern) organization that claims a monopoly on political power. In the institution of the banquet there is, on closer inspection, something much more ancient and profound: namely, the persistence of cultural practices through constructing and delimiting areas that are removed from the grasp of both market exchange and state public authority, practices that are found in Sicily as well as in Jordan, among the mafia as well as the Bedouins studied by Shryock (2012; see also Shryock and Howell 2001).

These are practices through which not only networks of reciprocity are built, but also reputations and claims of sovereignty. What the Schneiders fail to detect is the importance concerning who organizes these banquets, who is the host and who is the guest, who invites and who is invited, who owns the spaces, the places, the territories in which these banquets are held, and not only what happens during the banquet but its effects on its temporal and spatial surroundings. Evidently, it is not ethnographic observation but, rather, the testimonies and stories of *pentiti* that explain to us what can happen in these banquets, what risks are run in accepting or rejecting invitations. Holding a banquet to carry out a concealed project of collective violence is an ancient practice, and its persistence in the mafia universe – and therefore within the 'horizon of expectations' of those living and experiencing that universe every day – is confirmed by a myriad of narratives that discuss one of the great obsessions of research, even anthropological, on the mafia: the search, at all costs, for traces of the pervasiveness of that monster called 'capitalism', as if it were the necessary correlation of every promise of modernity, whether maintained or not. But what if it were not capitalism, or even 'the state', that is at stake, but rather resistance to both one and the other? James C. Scott (2010) has alerted us to the 'art of not being governed' by the state, which, for centuries, has marked the history and collective life of numerous ethnic communities in Southeast Asia. For his part, Mauss tried to show, in his time, on what historical and ethnographic bases the art of not being governed by the (capitalist) market could be founded.

Politics of the Mafia Gift

If, in 1900, Mosca did not know the work that Boas was carrying out among the natives of the Pacific Northwest, and which had led him to the (re)discovery of potlatch, Mauss, for his part, did not know about the mafia. It is certainly not included in his examples of the persistence of the gift in contemporary societies. If Mauss had known more about the mafia than a French ethnologist-sociologist active in the first three decades of the twentieth century could possibly have known and, above all, if he had had descriptions of the practice of *schiticciata* (the local name for these banquets), a frequent and important institution in the mafia world involving up to a hundred men and which was, as Brusca reveals, 'usually' organized to celebrate the initiation of a new member (Lodato 1999, 181) – or of other, equally central practices, such as the request for *pizzo* (protection money) or hospitality between members of 'Families', without which the (in)famous decades-long periods of mafia bosses being on the run from the law would not have been possible – he would probably have analysed them for traces of those 'archaic contractual forms' he had researched for years in the Indo-European context, not as merely surviving remnants, but as practices that were still alive and consequential in certain areas of the Mediterranean well into the twentieth century.

That a political theory of the mafia can be based on the paradigm of the gift may sound strange to contemporary Western ears, but it becomes almost a truism when seen from a socio-anthropological perspective informed by Mauss's legacy:

> The gift, as reconstructed by Mauss, has nothing to do, at least early on, with charity, goodness or altruism. It is, above all, a political act, a strictly political act, one through which groups pass from war and hostility to alliance and peace. And vice versa. The gift is politics. Politics, in turn, that is to say the

generative moment of a given society, is nothing more than a set of gifts and refusals of gifts. (Caillé 2019, 65; my translation)

Let me be clear. Social relations, in the mafia as elsewhere, are richer and more varied than relations based on the gift, and the relations mafiosi have among themselves and with others are not fully subsumable under the category of the exchange of gifts and counter-gifts, or of the refusal of gifts. What the model proposes is a simplification of a social reality that is necessarily more complex and chaotic: it is a model created specifically for analytical purposes. Like Gambetta, on this point we invoke Alexander Zinoviev's distinction between scientific principles, which proceed by rigorous abstractions and necessary simplifications, and the anti-scientific principle that 'strives to bring in everything which can be brought in on any pretext' and thus tends to 'confuse the simple and make what is obvious incomprehensible' (1979, 209).

After Mauss, the model has known some further development mainly through a bunch of Mauss's French followers, who were academically outsiders but creatively engaged in various intellectual movements, including surrealism. Among them was Georges Bataille, who was especially fascinated by the implications of the model of the gift for a critical rethinking of modernity and its deepest, anthropological foundations. He developed the model, making it a key for exploring some of the more hidden, cursed and regrettable dimensions of social life. The gift features as the dispositive for nonproductive consumption, for that destruction of goods (through luxury, lust, war and death) which is necessary, says Bataille (2001 [1949]), for the reduction of what exceeds, for the re-establishment of the equilibrium the writer assumes as a universal mechanism for human survival. From this perspective, we could even say mafiosi contribute, with their regrettable, cursed acts and practices, to the proper functioning of the human world. A provocative perspective, indeed, that lacks sound evidence, based as it is on a general assumption that is impossible to demonstrate.

It was Claude Lévi-Strauss 1987 [1950] who offered the first sustained critical (but constructive) reading of the model, contrasting Mauss's alleged phenomenological interpretation with a structuralist one, only envisioned and certainly not developed by Mauss. With Lévi-Strauss, the gift exchange becomes the medium itself of social life through the move from the exchange of things to the exchange of women with their reproductive capabilities.[10] It is evident that the relevance of this addition to an interpretation of the mafia as based on gift-giving. As shown by many studies, women play a crucial role in the working of mafia groups and the persistence of a mafia culture (see Siebert 1996; Paoli 2003; Dino 2007; Fiandaca 2017), as both medium for alliance, valuables (think of their role in the management of honorific relations) and even organizational resources, especially in the case of males' imprisonment.

Building on both authors, sociologist Pierre Bourdieu proposed in the 1970s his own reading of the gift exchange, taking it to be a paradigmatic case for a more general social theory of practice. This is how, a couple of decades later, he synthetized the main terms of the debate, attaching to it his own proposal:

> Mauss described the exchange of gifts as a discontinuous succession of generous acts; Lévi-Strauss defined it as a structure of transcendent reciprocity of acts of exchange, where the gift results in a counter-gift. In my case, I indicated that what was absent from these two analyses was the determinant role of the temporal interval between the gift and the counter-gift, the fact that in practically all societies, it is tacitly admitted that one does not immediately reciprocate for a gift received, since it would amount to a refusal. I asked myself about the function of that interval: why must the counter-gift be deferred and different? And I showed that the interval had the function of creating a screen between the gift and the counter-gift and allowing two perfectly symmetrical acts to appear as unique and unrelated acts. If I can experience my gift as a gratuitous, generous gift, which is not to be paid back, it is first because there is a risk, no matter how small, that there will not be a return (there are always ungrateful people), therefore a suspense, an uncertainty, which makes the interval between the moment of giving and the moment of receiving exist as such. In societies like Kabyle society, the constraint is in fact very great and the freedom not to return the gift is infinitesimal. But the possibility exists and, for the same reason, certainty is not absolute. Everything occurs as if the time interval, which distinguishes the exchange of gifts from swapping, existed to permit the giver to experience the gift as a gift without reciprocity, and the one who gives a counter-gift to experience it as gratuitous and not determined by the initial gift. (1998 [1994], 94)

Bourdieu's reading of the gift looks especially promising for us because of its explicit political implications. For him, the model of the gift acquires a more political twist – a move that American anthropologist Marshall Sahlins (1968) also made in a seminal essay. Whereas for Sahlins (as it was for Bataille), the impulse is philosophical, with Bourdieu it assumes a strongly sociological tone, functional to the proposal of what Bourdieu has named a 'general economy of symbolic goods' and that others have identified, more aptly in my opinion, as a 'political sociology of symbolic forms' (Wacquant 1993, 3). The following excerpts from a later assessment of the model by Bourdieu himself make apparent its worth for a novel reading of mafia practices, a reading capable of making sense of the systematically ambivalent character of the mafia and its practices. A crucial point of Bourdieu's remodelling of the gift is in fact its insistency on 'the experience of the gift, which cannot fail to strike one by its ambiguity':

> On the one hand, it is experienced (or intended) as a refusal of self-interest and egoistic calculation, and an exaltation of gratuitous, unrequested generosity. On the other hand, it never entirely excludes awareness of the logic of exchange or even confession of the repressed impulses and, intermittently, the denunciation of another, denied, truth of generous exchange – its constraining and costly character. (2001 [1997], 191)

This 'twofold truth of the gift', as Bourdieu calls it, is what makes it possible to account for the surprising, weird combination of deception and sincerity, interest and disinterest, intentionality and habit that gift behaviours exhibit, and the gift experience suggests:

> If social agents can appear as both deceiving and deceived, if they can appear to deceive others and deceive themselves about their (generous) 'intentions', this is because their deception (which can be said, in a sense, to deceive no one) is sure to encounter the complicity of both the direct addressees of their act and of third parties who observe it. This is because all of them have always been immersed in a social universe in which gift exchange is instituted in the form of an economy of symbolic goods. (Bourdieu 2001 [1997], 192–3)

As the last sentence anticipates, there is a social and historical context for a gift system to work, an institutional framework whose existence and persistence presume the working of a whole system of education (pedagogical and socializing):

> Only if one brackets off the institution – and the labour, especially the pedagogic labour, of which it is the product and forgets that both the giver and the receiver are prepared, by the whole labour socialization, to enter into generous exchange without intention or calculation of profit, to know and recognize the gift for what it is, in its twofold truth, can one bring up the subtle and insoluble paradoxes of an ethical casuistics. (Bourdieu 2001 [1997], 194)

At this point, the striking difference of a gift economic system from the commodity exchange (the economy in its more restricted sense, we could say) becomes apparent:

> The gift economy, in contrast to the economy in which equivalent values are exchanged, is based on a denial of the economic (in the narrow sense), on a refusal of the logic of the maximization of economic profit, that is to say, of the spirit of calculation and the exclusive pursuit of material (as opposed to symbolic) interest, a refusal that is inscribed in the objectivity of institutions

and in dispositions. It is organized with a view to the accumulation of symbolic capital (a capital of recognition, honour, nobility, etc.) which is brought in particular through the transmutation of economic capital achieved through the alchemy of symbolic exchanges (exchange of gifts, words, challenges and ripostes, murders, etc.) and only available to agents endowed with dispositions adjusted to the logic of 'disinterestedness'. (Bourdieu 2001 [1997], 195)

Nothing can be further from the economic theory of the mafia, built on the general assumption of a commoditization of protection and the adoption of the market model by default. Far from selling protection in view of some economic profit, mafiosi are embedded in a web of social relations through which offerings (of protection but also of other services) and counter-offerings (i.e. returns in material as well as symbolic and personal terms) circulate continuously. What these considerations may offer to an understanding of mafia practices and mafia relationships (mafia bonds) – an understanding that goes beyond the economic one without losing sight of the economic dimensions of the mafia universe – can be described in the following terms.

'Mafiosi' exist and act as social agents in a historically conditioned social universe, where determined socializing institutions operate and where a certain kind of pedagogical labour is accomplished. In this historical and social universe, the purely economic, as based on calculation and maximization of economic profit, on 'the exclusive pursuit of material ... interest', has no full legitimation, or isn't established so far as to make it possible to organize and manage exchanges according to a purely economic logic. This doesn't mean there is no rationality or no logic in this social universe, but it is a practical reason, a logic of practice that governs it. In this universe, symbolic profits and symbolic capital are not mere ornaments, but constitutive elements of social reality. Mafia can work, mafia can be visible, and mafiosi may look as they are, only in contexts where there is a gap, an *écart*, between the rational economy of those practices that are purely economic, and a symbolic economy where economic practices are imbued with symbols and meanings irreducible to the mere accumulation of profit and material wealth.

This makes it possible to understand rationally (that is in their immanent logic) apparently irrational practices as conspicuous consumption or the generation of waste (recall the title of Danilo Dolci's 1960 book), the use and apparent abuse of euphemisms in mafiosi's requests of tributes, and the same self-presentation of mafia bosses as the altruistic, generous characters we have described. We surely could say that the latter, with their polite words and modesty, are simply deceiving their interlocutors, as well as their subjected clients or customers. But this would simplify something that is clearly more articulated, pluridimensional, ambiguous and ambivalent. It would also reduce the mafiosi's subjects (their clients and customers or even their victims) to dopes, ready to be deceived by smarter guys. This could sometimes be true, but it would be misleading to generalize as the standard situation. The point is that mafiosi apparently have easily understood a central point of social life – namely, the productivity of denials and self-deception in the formation of social bonds and in their reproduction. More correctly, they have understood this point in the same way as those who share the same social universe, the same institution. What mafiosi may have more than their followers is the mastery of this system of practices and their underlying codes, the skills in orchestrating the elements of this system of deception and denial. In a sense, in order to master, they have to believe, to always act as if they were also immersed in this universe as full members. They have to invest in the belief in their disinterestedness – as directly interested in its credibility. Mafiosi and their clients/customers/victims share the same social environment, the same institutional complex, the same socialization process. Complicity – an ontological complicity, grounded in the sharing of the same institutional universe – between mafiosi and their victims is what makes the mafia difficult to destroy and even combat.

Mafiosi are not unaware of the productivity of gifts, of presents, in the formation of social bonds. It is true this is not the first thing they recall when asked – by judges or interviewers – about their actions. This may be evidence of how mafiosi share the common undervaluation of the gift we all have with respect to allegedly more relevant things as paid work or budget constraints. However, the place of gifts and presents in mafia life cannot be underrated, as the following excerpts from autobiographies and trial proceedings show. I would like to point out, though, that the logic of the gift often remains disguised, 'invisible', even for the mafioso who is not always aware of it. Indeed, one of the merits of an anthropological approach is to be able to bring to light pervasive social mechanisms and logics that are often invisible to the agents who are affected or who put them into practice.

For example, it seems to escape most mafiosi that the *pizzo* – a sum of money requested from those operating commercially on the territory of a mafia Family – is more effective according to the logic of gift and counter-gift than that of a mere violent imposition or market exchange (in this case, the protection money would be payment for a service, which is the interpretation advanced by the economic theory of the mafia: see Gambetta 1993).

Indeed, the political character of mafia extortion was already noticed by Max Weber in his classic *Economy and Society* (1978 [1922]). Here he asserts that the financing of political bodies can be divided broadly into two ideal types: (1) financing that takes place 'intermittently, based either on purely voluntary or on compulsory contributions or services'; (2) financing that is 'organized on a permanent basis' (1978 [1922], 194, 195). The first type may take one of four forms: 'large gifts or endowments', 'begging', 'gifts, which are formally voluntary, to persons recognized as politically or socially superior', and extortion, often in the form of protection money (1978 [1922], 194). The second type can also be divided, into at least two subtypes: a regular financing can take place 'without any independent economic production on the part of the organization', or it can 'be based on the existence of a productive establishment under the direct control of the organization' (1978 [1922], 195, 196). When Weber made these ideal-typical distinctions, he had in mind different forms of organization. For example, financing that is organized in the form of begging is, in his opinion, 'typical for certain kinds of ascetic communities' and can be found in 'secular castes of beggars' in India. The ideal-typical organization based on intermittent financing by extortion was indeed, for Weber, 'the Camorra in Southern Italy and the Mafia in Sicily' (1978 [1922], 194). He even tells the conversation he had with a 'Neapolitan manufacturer' who,

> replied to my doubts concerning the effectiveness of the *Camorra* with respect to business enterprises: 'Signore, la Camorra mi prende X lire nel mese, ma garantisce la sicurezza, – lo Stato me ne prende 10 • X, e garantisce: niente.' [Sir, the Camorra takes X lire a month from me, but guarantees me security; the state takes ten times that amount, and guarantees me nothing.] (1978 [1922], 195; Italian in the original text)

What Max Weber could not know, however, was the way in which requests were managed and received – something we have seen the Sicilian Mosca was in a better condition to know.

An insightful and precious document about the ways in which the request of *pizzo* may happen is in the following transcript of a verbal exchange between a building contractor active in the Borgo Nuovo district of Palermo and an emissary from the local 'Family', recorded by a hidden video camera in December 2018, which shows how mafiosi, even today, are concerned about dressing up their requests with those 'forms' and 'appearances' whose resemblance to the practice of the 'gracious gift' Mosca had already grasped. A brief excerpt will suffice:

> [Mafioso] We didn't ask you for protection money …
> [Entrepreneur] Really? Then what did you come to ask for? You asked me for 3% …
> – No, we asked you to give us a hand …
> – A hand? You bring me a worker and he can work if he wants to work. You have to work in life, you don't ask for protection money

– No, I'm talking here ...
– No? So what are you asking me?
– I'm not asking you for protection money
– So what are you asking for?
– I'm just asking you if you could help us
– Help you? I can't help you. What help do you want? Charity? Are you asking for charity?
– No, you know
– What should I know? You have to talk
– eh, I already told you ... [11]

In fact, the phenomenology of the *pizzo* shows it to be – both in its collection and payment practices – a mixture of elements, including a lack of awareness of the implications of the total system, which the model of the gift makes fully understandable without the degree of forcing required by economic theory. The underlying mechanism, however, emerges with particular clarity when we understand that not only are mafiosi themselves not exempt from the application of the *pizzo* when they engage in their normal (or 'private') economic activities in territories under the jurisdiction of other mafia 'Families', but that, in this case, the 'payment' takes place through gifts rather than money transfers. In the passage below, the aforementioned *pentito* Brusca is speaking during a trial held in Palermo in 2000:

Judge: Well, I ask, have there been exceptions, have there been cases in which a business owner hasn't made the protection payment to the Family that runs the area?

Brusca: Well, I can ... I can tell you about my own experiences. For example, it happened to me once, but then I paid it in another way. They didn't want money, but I had to pay them back in another form ... to pay off my debt.

Judge: And so it happened with one of your businesses?

Brusca: Yes, with LEDEL, the work in Altofonte and Monreale.

Judge: In that case, who did you have to pay?

Brusca: The boss ... the head of the Altofonte Family. Even though it belonged to our territory, as a rule, since I wasn't building my own home, it was a business, and so ... Also because I wasn't having any money problems, it's not like I was on the streets, so ... It was a business and so, working, earning, it was right that I paid. Then they, the men of honour of the territory, didn't want the money, and I, in the form of ... gifts, clothes, gifts to their wives, or whomever, paid off my debt. (Court di Palermo, second criminal section, trial of Simone Castello and five others)

Furthermore, the model certainly does not deny the violent taking of goods and, at its limit, of human lives (biopower), but places it in a theoretical framework that changes its analytical meaning, projecting it into a different universe of meaning. In order to be able to give gifts, a mafioso must, in fact, acquire goods and money with the means at his disposal, which certainly includes the use or threat of physical force as a last resort: 'violence', as it is commonly said when talking about the mafia and other 'pathological' social forms (see Chapter 6), is always a possible outcome of gift-giving practices. Life and death are ancestral, primordial elements of gift-giving.

Mauss himself noted the rapidity with which one passes, in gift-based societies, from parties to battles, from banquets to combat. Even the cycle of blood feuds, with the alternation of obligations of reparation and reciprocity of losses, repeats and exemplifies Mauss's model of the gift (Anspach 2001, 2002). However, the *cosche* do not have illicit enrichment as their ultimate goal (*pace* Mosca and his many followers who insist on this point). The acquisition of economic resources is not an end for the mafia, but a means: it is a necessary condition for the circulation of goods and people in a system of total services that sustains the members of the group. It is, undoubtedly, a system of particular rather than universal rights, like – on a different scale but, upon closer inspection, according to a similar logic – that of the territorial state, with its distinction between citizens and foreigners (see Brubaker 1992; Shryock 2012). The tributary system of the *pizzo* is an instrument of acquisition with a view to redistribution in the form of gifts – of money and goods. But it is either an intimation to give, thus a solicited gift – the creation of that obligation to give which constitutes the starting point of the cycle of giving – or often a courteous and veiled request (which follows 'those forms, those appearances', as Mosca observed) to reciprocate what is claimed to have already been received, payment for which is past due: protection, or even prior, authorization to operate in the jurisdiction of a mafia Family, with the consequences that this mere presence has for the control and order of the territory. Yet, paying the *pizzo* does not get rid of mafia pressure, but fully enters you into the mafia relationship as a system of exchanges of indefinite duration, potentially eternal. The transfiguration – as ascertained from various judicial proceedings – from victim to supporter and even to affiliate is a manifestation of the social alchemy that the logic of the gift can produce. The strength of the mafia lies not in its illegal wealth, or even in its supporters ('the strength of the mafia is outside the mafia', as the saying goes), but in the system of services that combines its wealth and supporters in a structure that needs to be fed and reproduced, day by day, through exchanges of gifts and counter-gifts.

Banquets are occasions not only for socializing, but also for the circulation of goods, favours and commitments with which to strengthen existing relationships and create new ones. But so are the more or less violent and illegal acquisitions, often disguised in the form of guardianship or management of villas and estates – indispensable places not only for the display of wealth through which the status competition between mafia families is conducted, but also for the exercise of the rights and duties of hospitality among mafiosi and their families. Without this availability of autonomously managed spaces and shelters, long-term fugitives such as Provenzano, Riina and Matteo Messina Denaro would not be able to remain free for so long.

The fact that an individual mafioso might be caught pursuing his own self-interest and profit does not say much about the mafia system as an institutional system (in the same way that a doctor or lawyer who fails to fulfil their professional duties does not invalidate the professional model, though it may cast a dark shadow over it that requires redress in the form of a fine or, in more serious cases, being struck off). Being a man of his time, the mafioso is not immune to the (self-serving) tendencies and temptations of his age. But every institution has its deviations. The question is whether this self-interested and profit-oriented behaviour – perfectly legitimate in the context of the capitalist system – is legitimate and justified in the mafia system with all its rules, rituals, forms and ideals. The fact that it is not considered legitimate is demonstrated by the many times in which, in their confessions, *pentiti* refer to these unexpected and disappointing 'utilitarian deviations' (of this or that mafia boss) to justify their disillusionment with, dissociation and ultimate exit from, this system. It is as if they have lost the illusion that sustained their affiliation up to that moment, with all that it entailed in terms of dedication, duly evoking a past time when this was unthinkable and the mafia – the alleged 'real' one of the past – was still faithful to its presumably ancient noble ideals of justice and solidarity.

In these pages, I have tried to advance an argument about the constitutive presence in the mafia, in what we call mafia, of a total service system of the kind that Mauss identified in the 1920s and defined with the mechanism of the 'gift', supporting it with evidence (necessarily evidential given the nature of the sources) in view of a more complete theoretical systematisation. How far can Mauss help us to explain the literary and cinematic topos of the 'offer you cannot refuse', is not easy to assess. What I can say is that the traces and clues here presented are only the tip of the iceberg. Very well-known manifestations of the mafia world, such as marriage alliances (of blood, but also, through them, of obligations) between families can be traced back to this same system of exchange practices, which appear to be free and gratuitous but are in reality compulsory or generative of obligations. Other examples of such practices are the ties of *comparatico* (godparenthood), the financial support of religious brotherhoods with concomitant control of processions (see Palumbo 2020) and initiation rites, which mafia scholars have studied in their occurrences and forms, but never really in terms of meanings and symbolic structures (see next chapter). If they had done so, the combined cognitive and affective, symbolic and practical, strength of one of the institutional pillars of the social and political world of the mafia could not have escaped them. It is a world built, represented and, above all, lived by its own inhabitants, the mafiosi, in terms that can only be made understandable if we are willing to put aside the two dominant principles with which the social sciences – born to respond to the emergence of modern Western societies – conceive of the human world in its variety and generality, both positively (in the sense of recording what is, what has already been found) and negatively (in the sense of noting what has not been found, or not yet found but which will presumably emerge with due interventions): that of the market and the state, with their convergent logic and rationality.

Seen from this perspective – rigorously 'beyond the state', but also aware of the Eurocentric nature of the social sciences and their need to 'globalize' by incorporating concepts drawn from other historical and spatial experiences into their analytical instrumentation – the mafia is not merely 'on the same level as kula and potlatch' in order to 'fully and legitimately constitute an object of study for anthropology' (Li Causi and Cassano 1993, 10) but belongs to the very same kind of institutions as both the kula system and, above all, potlatch, the indigenous North American institution that manifests itself, as we know, through a competitive system of total services. Like potlatch, the mafia as a system of exchanges and services has aspects that are juridical, economic, religious and political – although it could be said that the latter two perhaps have a stronger grip than the others, in the sense that they capture better than the others the structure and function of these institutions, which are political even before they are economic or religious; and it should be noted that we are still using a Western-centric system of categories that is essentially rooted in ancient Greek and classical Roman culture. We know that Mauss, even in 1921, admitted that he struggled to find traces of these competitive systems of total services in (Indo-) European societies, except for some traits uncovered in an ancient form of contract among the Thracians documented in the Iliad by Thucydides and, above all, in Xenophon's Anabasis. But evidence of the selective survival of these ancient forms of sumptuary contract was also traceable, according to Mauss, 'in the reciprocal invitations that our peasant families give and receive' (1975a [1921], 58; my translation). Since then, research on the forms and modalities of the exchange of gifts has been growing, encompassing new spaces, new historical experiences and, above all, new manifestations – those that Bourdieu would put under the common label of 'the economy of symbolic goods', like exchanges of honour in pre-capitalist societies, the philanthropic action of foundations, exchanges between generations within the family, markets for cultural, artistic and religious heritage, and so on.

The ambiguity of the gift – the word *gift* in Germanic languages can be used at the same time for 'gift' (as in English) and 'poison' (as in modern German), a linguistic paradox on which the French ethnologist (Mauss 1975b [1924]) could not help but focus – reverberates in the ambiguity of the 'service systems' that are based on it, including the mafia. Reading the (Sicilian, but not only) mafia as an instance of a much more common, geographically spread and historically rooted institutional system of exchanges that the notion of commodity is unable to capture is what this chapter has proposed and attempted to do.

6

Blood, *Bund* and (Personal) Bonds: The Mafia as an Institutional Type

Man is much more concerned with what is near at hand, with what is present and concrete than with what is remote and abstract. He is more responsive on the whole to persons, to the status of those who surround him and the justice which he sees in his own situation than he is with the symbols of remote persons, with the total status system in the society and with the global system of justice.

Shils 1957, 130

In the previous chapter, I explored the model of the gift as a viable alternative to the model of the market exchange bond as the pillar of mafia social life. In this chapter, my attempt to elaborate a sociological picture of the mafia more attuned to its immanent political dimensions continues with an exploration of two areas: the institutional form and modes of communication.

Of Brotherhoods and Institutions

The mafia and the 'fraternization contract'

After both Arlacchi (1983a) and Gambetta (1993), as well as Ianni (1972) and Anderson (1979), the idea of the business firm as a good approximation to the sociological type of the mafia (the 'new, entrepreneurial mafia' for Arlacchi and Anderson; *any* mafia for Gambetta) has known success both in the academic literature and in the mass media as an alternative to the once common notion of the 'clan' – a term whose media appeal is usually proportional to the evanescence and sociological vagueness of its uses – on the one side, and to the equally problematic and provocative notion of 'bureaucracy', once privileged by those who were, especially in the US, prone to accept and promulgate a representation of the mafia as a wide and well-structured organization grounded on an ethnic basis (see Cressey 1969). In fact, if there is a structural model of social organization that is in direct contrast to the mafia, it is exactly the bureaucratic type as classically depicted by Max Weber: whereas the latter is grounded on the principle of impersonality, the mafia works, and even represents itself in its rich imagery, as grounded on personal ties in all their forms and figures. To miss this point is to miss what makes the mafia at odds with the core codes of the Western political and civil sphere as represented in the 'rule of law' and in the model of the 'civil society' (see Alexander 2003, 2006; Santoro 2007, ch. 7).

To be sure, the 'secret society' would have been an apt characterization of the social type of the mafia, if it weren't for the not-so-secret social life of mafiosi in the local community, where who is a mafioso or who is close to him, and how mafia works, is far from being secret (people in mafia's territories usually don't need legally valid evidence to identify someone as 'mafioso'). This is a pity from a sociological and anthropological point of view, as the study of secret society has a noble genealogy in the social sciences which goes back to authoritative scholars such as Franz Boas and Georg Simmel.[1] Anthropologists have been especially interested in the ethnographic study of secret societies since the latter figure prominently in the relatively traditional, if not 'primitive', societies they are concerned with (e.g., Webster 1908; Little 1965; Mair 1970; Herdt 2003). Scholars of religions, and especially sinologists, have also devoted much attention to this social form, widely spread in East Asia (e.g., Chesneaux 1971; Davis 1977; Murray 1994; Ownby and Heidhues 1993; Ownby 1996; ter Haar 1998). We have seen in the previous chapter that secret societies are involved in the social life of the gift – potlatch are typically organized by Native Indians' secret societies – and, as Herdt has suggested, commenting on the results of his ethnography of secret societies in Melanesia, 'ritual secrecy shares with gift exchange ... the qualities of indebtedness and relatedness attached to the original 'owner' of the secret who teaches and transmits its power though hidden rituals' (2003, 62). Indeed, there would be much to learn by insisting on the 'secret society' character of the Sicilian mafia even for our argument. Not only do secret societies have clear political functions, as recognized and famously argued by Kenneth Little (1965) with reference to the Poro in Sierra Leone, but, in the words of ethno-archeologist Bryan Hayden, 'It can be argued that secret societies were the first institutionalized manifestation of ritual organizations linked to political power, and that this was, in fact, the explicit goal of secret societies. Therefore, the political dimension of secret societies may be critical to understanding the evolution of political systems' (2018, 6).

However intriguing it may appear, this is not the main road that I am going to follow in this chapter. What I will explore here is another path, opened up a few years ago by sociologist and criminologist Letizia Paoli with her identification of Italian mafias (in particular, the Sicilian one and the Calabrese *'ndrangheta*) as *fratellanze* – i.e. brotherhoods. As the author outlined in the Preface to the US edition of her book:

> Italy's mafia associations cannot be reduced to any of the most common forms of sociability in the contemporary world: they are not mere blood families, nor are they bureaucracies or enterprises. Cosa Nostra and the *'ndrangheta* are confederations of mafia groups, which are called families by their members but are distinct from the mafiosi's blood families. Though consanguineous ties are sometimes very important, especially in the Calabrian *'ndrangheta*, the bond uniting a mafia family has a fictive, ritual nature and is reestablished with the ceremony of initiation of each new member. Since mafiosi are required to regard their associates as brothers, mafia families are – at least prescriptively, if not always effectively – brotherhoods. They are, in particular, male fraternities, as women are excluded from participation. (2003, viii)

The 'premodern contractual form' on which these brotherhoods are based is explicitly referred to by Paoli, with the authoritative support of Max Weber:

> On entering a mafia family, the new member does not bind himself – as utilitarian analyses maintain – to respecting a contract aimed at exchanging goods or economic performances. Instead, he underwrites what Max Weber called a 'status contract'. As opposed to 'purposive contracts', which are typical of market societies, the status contract 'involves a change in what may be called the total legal situation (the universal position) and the social status of the persons involved'. A status contract does not entail the mere promise of specific tasks in exchange for a monetary or material reward, but commits the party to 'make a new 'soul' enter his body' and to become 'something different in quality (or status) from the quality he possessed before' (1978: 672). The status contract is also a 'fraternization contract', as the members of a mafia *cosca* are obliged to consider themselves brothers. (Paoli 2003, 65–6)

The suggestion is quite intriguing and suggests a path that runs parallel to and, in part, overlaps with the ideas explored in this chapter. Paoli offers an alternative to the economic theory of the mafia that in many way shares our own criticism of that theory. However, some issues have to be considered before we can accept her solution as definitive. First,

Paoli's proposal makes us wonder how we did not think of this before. The notion of 'brotherhood' has, for some time, appeared not only in discourse *on* the mafia (by magistrates, police officials, journalists – e.g., Frederic Sondern's 1959 book, *Brotherhood of Evil*) but also in the discourses produced *by* mafiosi themselves. In fact, it was a common term used by members of some of the secret, or at least not officially recorded, associations that were uncovered by the new unified Italian government in the 1870s; they were accused of being criminal societies whose members were responsible for a wide array of crimes, ranging from property damage to murder. It was from these post-unification trials against such associations that the image of the 'mafia' as a phenomenon of collective and often mysterious deviance acquired substance and a semblance of reality, not only criminological but also social and even sociological (see Pezzino 1990; Lupo 1993). Famously, in the 1880s there was, in Favara, a small sulphur town in southern Sicily close to Agrigento, the criminal organization known as Fratellanza di Favara, whose precise formula of their oath is known to us, as well as a description of the initiation rite, thanks to a much quoted article signed by the public prosecutor (Lestingi 1884, 455):

> A solemn oath binds each associate to the others. It is taken in the presence of three members, one of whom, having tied a thread around the [candidate's] index finger, pierces it and lets a few drops of blood fall onto a sacred image, which is then burned and its ashes scattered to the wind ... According to a note seized by the police, the formula of the oath appears as follows: 'I swear on my honor to be faithful to the Fratellanza, as the Fratellanza is faithful to me. As this saint and these few drops of my blood burn, in the same way I will shed all my blood for the Fratellanza; and as this ash and this blood cannot go back to their former state, so I cannot leave the Fratellanza.' (See also Gambetta 1993, 262–3; Paoli 2003, 68, 180; Cutrera 1900, 125)

Sure, not all these early societies, labelled '*associazioni a delinquere*' (criminal conspiracies) by representatives of the state, and at the time already considered as associative manifestations of that mysterious spirit called 'the mafia', identified themselves or were especially identified, as 'brotherhoods', *fratellanze*. Some, for example, labelled themselves simply 'società' (societies), such as the so called Stoppaglieri based very close to Palermo (which numbered 150 members alone in the town of Monreale and was divided into sections, one for each neighbourhood, run by a boss and as many underbosses as there were sections, and overseen by a board. The Society even had 'by-laws' that imposed the following obligations on its members:

1. Help each other (this is why it was originally called a mutual aid society) and avenge offences to members with blood.
2. Arrange and support, by all means possible, the defence and release of any member who has had the misfortune to fall into the hands of the police.
3. Following the judgement of the bosses, distribute the proceeds of blackmail, extortion and theft among the members, having the greatest consideration for needy members in the distribution of the spoils.
4. Maintain your oath and keep it secret, upon penalty of death within twenty-four hours. (see Cutrera 1900, 118–19)

The model is clearly that of a mutual aid society, a social formation prevalent worldwide whose apparent similarities with modern trade unions can be easily explained with reference to more ancient traditions of work solidarities among members of the same trade or craft, well established in the Old Regime in Sicily (where they were called *maestranze*) as well as in France and elsewhere (see Sewell 1980; for a more general discussion, see Sundberg 2019). Interestingly, in the Old Regime – which was only a few decades old – members of the *maestranze* had the right to be armed and were trained to use weapons as they were held responsible for local order in towns and especially in Palermo (Hess 1970; see also Scherma 1896). Other alleged criminal associations called themselves by a variety of different names, sometimes evocative of their apparent brotherhood's nature (such as the *Fratuzzi* of Bagheria and Corleone, whose name is a vernacular word meaning 'little brothers'), but usually referring to other images (for example, the *Oblonica* of Agrigento, which repeated its name from an early secret society founded decades earlier by Italian revolutionary Giuseppe Mazzini; the *Scattaliora* of Sciacca; the *Scaglione* of Castrogiovanni, from *scaglioni*, which means canine tooth, a reference to an element of their initiation ritual) or place names (like the *Fontananuova* [new fountain] of Misilmeri).

The organization model
Police officer and criminal sociologist Antonino Cutrera (1900, 121), examining both the constitution and functioning of these associations just a few years after they were discovered, and also the trials against their members, noted that, 'while their names are different … their organization is the same in all respects'. Members were categorized into groups and subgroups, structured on a local basis, their numbers often determined by multiples of ten,[2] featuring omnipresent initiation rituals in the form of oaths and sworn agreements infused with various symbols, such as blood, fire and saints (on these symbols in the Sicilian

culture, see Buttitta 1999). Among many of these associations there were interorganizational relations through which they 'provided each other with good services', although it was absolutely impossible – according to nineteenth-century sources followed by our writer – to speak of a supra-local, federal-style organization (see Cutrera 1900, 127). These descriptions have been substantially repeated, with a few changes worthy of consideration, almost a century later, in the narratives of the very first *pentiti* (repented) turned state witness since the 1970s, before police authorities and during judicial investigations. Schematically, what these insiders have described is a social organization whose basic social unit is the 'Family' or even the *cosca* (Hess 1970), a primary group based on kinship and ritual friendship, strongly linked to a territory from which it usually takes its name and which it controls. This territory may be a town, or a township, or a neighbourhood in a town (this is the case in Palermo). The Family is ruled by a chief, usually elected, known as the *rappresentante* (a clear reference to the idea of a representative democracy, which existed even among pirates – see Leeson 2009), who, in turn, appoints a deputy (*sottocapo*), one or more advisers (*consiglieri*) and a few *capidecina* (heads of groups of ten people), whose function is to coordinate the activities of the members, and who are known, after their initiation, as *uomini d'onore* (men of honor). According to Tommaso Buscetta and others following him, there is a second level, called *mandamento*, comprising two or three adjoining Families, which is also ruled by a *rappresentante*. Apparently, since the 1950s, there has been, in each province (according to the state administrative layout of the national territory, including Sicily, a province is composed of an aggregation of adjoining towns, and a group of provinces makes a region) another level of governance, made up of three people: a provincial *rappresentante*, his deputy and a provincial counsellor. A further level was created in 1957 (after a meeting with representatives of the US-based mafia Families in Palermo), with the institution in the province of Palermo of a new organism, the *Commissione*, whose seats are held by the representatives of *mandamenti*, who elect a chief. The main function of this new organism was to coordinate among Families, but also to mediate in disputes between them. Subsequently (probably in the early 1970s), a new interprovincial committee was created, composed of the chiefs of each province, whose job was to effect coordination. In exceptional situations, as happened in the 1960s after a resurgence of law enforcement action, these organisms could be loosened, and replaced by extraordinary and more oligarchic structures, like the so-called 'triumvirate' created in 1969 with the objective of reorganizing the whole mafia social universe.

It is within this kind of organizational structure that almost all our best informants about the mafia have resided – a mafia whose real name was, according to *pentiti*, Cosa Nostra, 'our thing', the same name given to the US mafia confederation, as revealed in the early 1960s by Joe Valachi (Maas 1968). What the initiation ritual looked like in those years is described in the following excerpt from Antonino Calderone's testimony about his own initiation in 1962 and the many others in which he participated, possibly the most detailed and accurate description of the ritual we have (see Gambetta 1993, Appendix B for a collection of rituals' descriptions). Like others before and after him, Calderone describes what can be called a deliberate and patterned process of recruitment which is, at the same time, a process of co-optation and sponsored mobility. To enter a mafia Family, in fact, people have to pass a period of observation, even without the candidate's knowledge. The person being considered by members of Cosa Nostra as a possible new member is monitored to check the extent to which he possesses the qualities necessary for full membership status – for example, being able to commit serious illegal acts and to maintain silence when confronted by the police; in other words, to be trustworthy. In certain places, the candidate was required to commit a crime, to test his skills as a 'man of action' but also to trap him in a road with no return. This procedure does not apply to people who, like Calderone and many others, come from families already belonging to a mafia tradition.

> When the appropriate moment comes, so Calderone tells, the candidate or candidates are led to a room, in a secluded location, in the presence of the *rappresentante* and those who hold certain positions within the family, and also of the ordinary men of honor of the family. In Catania [the Sicilian city where Calderone's Family was based] we used to put all the men of honor on one side of the room and all the candidates on the opposite side; in other locations the practice was to shut the candidate or candidates in a room for a few hours and then let them out one by one. At this point the *rappresentante* of the family told the novices the rules which discipline Cosa Nostra, beginning by saying that what is known as 'mafia' is, in reality, called Cosa Nostra. After explaining the rules, he then informed the candidates that it was still possible to withdraw. (Gambetta 1993, 267–8)

These rules – which indeed comprise almost all that make up the so-called 'mafia code' – are very elemental, such as 'not to touch the women of other men of honor'; 'not to steal from other men of honor or, in general, from anyone' (a rule, we should add, that was often transgressed in order to exploit the situation); 'not to exploit prostitution' (this is a rule often emphasized by the *pentiti*, and in Sicily, but not in the US, is commonly followed); 'not to kill other men of honor unless strictly necessary' (where the real point of course is to assess exactly what 'strict necessity' means here); 'to avoid passing information to the police'; 'not to quarrel with other men of honor' (a rule that is difficult to respect, indeed, because is it through quarrels that a fight for power will start); to maintain proper behaviour (this is the reason why Buscetta, who was divorced from his first wife and had several sexual partners and even sons from them, although recognized as a charismatic and highly respected man, never had the title of chief); 'to keep silent about the Cosa Nostra around outsiders' (a rule that is one of the main bases for the so-called *omertà*, and a rule that only with *pentiti* has been really broken); 'to avoid in all circumstances introducing oneself to other men of honor' (which means that any introduction requires the presence of a third man of honor who knows both parties and who may confirm membership in the Cosa Nostra by saying, 'This is our friend' or 'This is the same thing').[3]

What these rules really mean – because rules are nothing other than texts to be interpreted even by those who are willing to follow them, or to follow an interpretation of them, especially in order to provide a justification for what has been done – has been made clear by the same Calderone on another occasion: 'Cosa Nostra has its rules, but then there are special cases with their own shadings and complications. There are those who follow the rules, and there are exceptions and abuses. There are those who are tolerated, those who are made examples of, those who come to be punished' (Arlacchi 1993, 110). There is good reason indeed to claim that, in the mafia, as indeed in other oral-based social formations (see Bourdieu 1980; see also Garfinkel 1967), rules work more as practical devices in orienting action in everyday life and as justifications useful to account for strategies that easily go beyond the rule or cannot be immediately attached to some rule – without, I would insist, an active effort at sociological interpretation of how rules work in practice, not only in the mafia but in every social organization.

Clearly, some rules are easier to follow than others: it seems one of these is the rule of the third as a necessary mediation in introducing oneself to some other. Probably, the least followed among all the Cosa Nostra rules is the one – not listed by Calderone but recalled among others by Tommaso Buscetta – 'to tell always the truth', unless there is the real risk that someone in the vicinity can prove you wrong (see Falcone and Padovani 1993, 42). But let us go on with Calderone and his description of the ritual:

Once these 'commandments' of the Cosa Nostra have been explained, and having received a positive expression of the will to become a member, the *rappresentante* invites each candidate to choose a godfather from among the men of honor in attendance, who are designated '*amici nostri.*' Generally the candidate chooses the man who introduced him to the family. Then the oath ceremony takes place. This consists first of all of asking each candidate which hand he shoots with and then pricking the index finger of that hand in such a way as to spill a little blood, which is used to mark a holy card (generally it is the holy card of Annunziata, who is said to be 'the patron saint of the Cosa Nostra and whose day is March 25). At this point the card is set on fire, and the novice, preventing the fire from going out and holding the card in his cupped hands, solemnly vows never to betray the 'commandments' of the Cosa Nostra, or else he will burn like that *santina*. I must clarify – so continues Calderone – that, when the index finger is pricked, the *rappresentante* informs him that he must take care never to betray the family, because in the Cosa Nostra one enters with blood and leaves only with blood. I must also clarify that to prick the index finger of the subject certain families use the thorn of the bitter-orange tree, while others always use the same large needle, like, for example, the family of Riesi, whose *rappresentante* kept a golden needle specifically for these ceremonies. In Catania we did not have anything of the sort but just used any needle. After that the *rappresentante*, while pointing out the men of honor as '*amici nostri*', informed the new man of honor of the hierarchies of the Cosa Nostra in the family and in the provinces and, in general, of the structure of Cosa Nostra in Sicily. He pointed out in particular the *capodecina*, to whom the man of honor had a duty to defer. (Quoted in Gambetta 1993, 268)

As Calderone has taken care to make clear:

[T]hese are the ordinary rules of initiation; however, if necessary, when it is not possible to follow these criteria, it is permissible to resort to a faster initiation procedure, so long as at least three other men of honor are present, even if they belong to other families, and even if they come from another province … In cases of absolute necessity one can even do without the presence of a member of the family to which the novice is going to belong. (quoted in Gambetta 1993, 269)

Indeed, there is wide evidence that simplified versions of the ritual were very common, at least in the last quarter of the twentieth century, also because of the precarious period that followed the maxi-trial of the 1980s and, still earlier, the chaos provoked by the so-called 'third mafia war', which transformed Cosa Nostra into a sort of dictatorship ruled by the heads of the Corleonese Family – i.e. Totò Riina and Bernardo Provenzano (see Dino 2012; Caselli and Lo Forte 2020).

It is from descriptions of mafia rituals and organizational structures like these (and others similar to these as collected through the investigations and trials of the 1980s) that Letizia Paoli has drawn empirical evidence for supporting her undoubtedly sociologically stimulating argument: that, at the base of mafia organizations, there is a specific contractual modality that, in her view, is precisely of the Weberian type of 'status contract', as distinct from the 'purposive contract'. Let us try to understand better what we are dealing with by going through Weber's referred text, which is none other than a fragment of the classic *Economy and Society*. The context is that of a decidedly ambitious genealogical reconstruction of contractual freedom as a principle for the creation of subjective rights, which appears at the start of the work (which, as is well known, remained unfinished and was later completed, rearranged and published by Weber's wife, Marianne) dedicated to legal sociology. The passage in its entirety is worth reading:

> The 'contract', in the sense of a voluntary agreement constituting the legal foundation of claims and obligations, has thus been widely diffused even in the earliest periods and stages of legal history. What is more, it can also be found in spheres of law in which the significance of voluntary agreement has either disappeared altogether or has greatly diminished, i.e. in public law, procedural law, family law, and the law of decedents' estates. On the other hand, however, the farther we go back in legal history, the less significant becomes contract as a device of economic acquisition in fields other than the law of the family and inheritance. The situation is vastly different today. The present-day significance of contract is primarily the result of the high degree to which our economic system is market-oriented and of the role played by money. The increased importance of the private law contract in general is thus the legal reflex of the market orientation of our society. But contracts propagated by the market society are completely different from those contracts which in the spheres of public and family law once played a greater role than they do today. In accordance with this fundamental transformation of the general character of the voluntary agreement we shall call the more primitive type 'status contract' and that which is peculiar to the exchange or market economy 'purposive contract'. (Weber 1978, 671–2)

But what is the difference between the two types of contract? Weber is very clear on the point:

> The distinction is based on the fact that all those primitive contracts by which political or other personal associations, permanent or temporary, or family relations are created involve a change in what may be called the total legal situation (the universal position) and the social status of the persons involved. To have this effect these contracts were originally either straightforward magical acts or at least acts having a magical significance. For a long time their symbolism retained traces of that character, and the majority of these contracts are 'fraternization contracts'. (1978, 672)

As in these 'fraternization contracts', notes Paoli, so mafia initiation implies a total conversion of the neophyte, together with an overall, generalized modification of his identity and status. In the mafia, there is no exit option, typical of purposive contracts and, in general, of economic contractual forms: as even Judge Giovanni Falcone once recognized, one never stops being a mafioso (Falcone and Padovani 1993, 85). The new status is defined, first of all, by the encoding of honour as an essential feature of the new member's identity: by becoming part of a mafia organization through ritual affiliation, one becomes – or better one is established as – a 'man of honour' (*un uomo d'onore*). And, with his affiliation to a mafia organization, the new member, the new 'man of honour', enters an 'almost religious communion' – note Paoli's words (2003, 77), as we will find them again but in a different conceptual context – with all the members of the group, thus becoming the 'same thing' (*la stessa cosa*) and thereby losing his own identity in a process of de-individualization that could even account, Paoli suggests, for the cruelty of certain crimes. The ritual of affiliation – the mafia initiation ceremony – is clearly crucial in this institutional model as it culminates in the initiate's oath of absolute and exclusive loyalty[4] to his new 'Family', in which this indefinite series of relationships of spiritual kinship become bound together.[5]

However ingenious and enlightening this argument may be, a few critical points could be made. Although the oath represents 'one of the most universal forms' of such fraternization contracts, always oriented 'towards the total social status of the individual and his integration into an association comprehending his total personality' (Weber 1978, 673–4), it is, however, clear that, for Weber, these contracts constitute premodern legal forms and represent stages of legal evolution that are destined to be overcome by the process of rationalization produced by Western modernity. Beyond being situated within a more general social theory of the origins of the West and of modernity, the concept of 'brotherhood' is undoubtedly a historical-institutional one, given to us by legal historiography which, thanks to Weber, also possesses a stamp of legitimacy in the sociological tradition.[6] Paoli's contribution to mafia studies offers indeed a precious counterargument to the economic model of the mafia. Instead of depicting the mafia as an 'industry of private protection' in Gambetta's sense, she has insisted on the *multifunctional* character of mafia organizations as *not business-oriented* collectives, but, we would say, as ritual corporations. Max Weber's notion of status contract – and Victor Turner's (1969, 1974) well-known ideas of *communitas* and antistructure – have offered the main tool for Paoli's reformulation. But perhaps this was not the best way to construct a sociological theory of *the mafia as a type of relationship between men* (which, according to Bill Bonanno, would properly identify the meaning of the word 'mafia': see Chapter 1). The effect of this recourse to the Weberian notion of the status contract – with an insistence on the contractual mode – is, indeed, a surreptitious retreat to a privatist (and therefore economic) view of the mafia and, at the same time, a suggestive confinement of the mafia to a somewhat premodern ('primitive') institutional world in which things could only be residual and, thus, destined to disappear.

To be sure, Paoli firmly distances herself from a merely utilitarian and economic vision of the phenomenon under examination, which ends up leading to an 'underassessment of the strength of cultural codes' (2003, 66), and therefore, we must suppose, of their ability not only to reproduce but also to renew themselves. Indeed, as Mary Ann Clawson (1989) demonstrated with reference to historical cases different from the mafia, even 'brotherhood' as an organizational model is a *cultural form*, strongly linked to gender issues (brothers are male of course). As Paoli justly reminds us, referring to Clawson herself among others, 'contracts of fraternization are not peculiar to mafia associations. Indeed, although this concept has so far been rather neglected by sociologists in general, fraternalism has been one of the most widespread forms of social organization from the times of antiquity until now' (2003, 78; see also, e.g., Jackson 2012; Sundberg 2019). To avoid any risk of latent evolutionism, it may be useful to ascend the scale of abstraction towards a more general concept in which the 'brotherhood' cultural form can be considered a historically given, but not exhaustive and ultimate, institutional manifestation. What I am looking for is a sociological category that allows us to capture the essential nature of brotherhoods – including the mafia type of social relations – without tying it, for the moment, to a specific historical model.

From brotherhood to Bund

A fundamental contribution towards a sociological theory of the mafia, neglected by Paoli, can be found in a classic but undervalued essay by the German philosopher and sociologist Herman Schmalenbach on the category of the *Bund*, originally published in German in 1922 and critically taken up by Ferdinand Tönnies in the introduction to the fourth edition of his influential *Gemeinschaft und Gesellschaft* [*Community and Society*].[7] In Schmalenbach's conceptualization, a *Bund* is a type of social relationship distinct from *Gemeinschaft* ('community') and *Gesellschaft* ('society', in the sense of modern 'market society'), because a *Bund* includes forms of social existence that are not assimilable to either the first or the second type, although it is easy to confuse them with both. Conventionally translated into English both with 'league' and the originally Cooleyan term 'communion' (see Schmalenbach 1961, 1977 [1922]), the *Bund* category does not really have an exact equivalent in languages other than German. Etymologically derived from the Indo-Germanic verb *bhend*, which means 'to bind', 'to constrain', it was already being used in the second half of the thirteenth century to describe something bound or constrained. The word more generally refers to all forms of association founded on the '*foedus*', that is, on the existence of pacts, which could perhaps be better rendered with terms of more marked political significance such as 'alliance' or 'federation'. But unlike the word 'alliance', as Kevin Hetherington (1994) has observed, *Bund* preserves the idea of sacredness, as in the English 'communion', but it also has an organizational significance – which makes the term 'league' an appropriate synonym. As there is no single term that can precisely express the network of meanings that Schmalenbach identified and defined as the *Bund*, we would do better to leave in the original. To introduce the concept, let's quote from the author's words:

> The members of every community [i.e. *Gemeinschaft*] are originally united with one another; the parts of society [i.e. *Gesellschaft*] are essentially separated from one another. The comrades of communion [*Bund*] have nothing at all to do with one another in the beginning. The communion is originally established when they meet each other (also after a community has already been established). The experiences that give rise to communion are individual experiences. While it appears here that the communion is closer to society, it approaches community after it has been established. (1977 [1922], 94)

Not surprisingly, to make his concept clearer, Schmalenbach repeatedly compares his ideas not only with those of Tönnies, but also of Weber, noting in particular the correspondence between the sociological category of the *Bund* and the category of 'affective action' – a comparison that some time later Raymond Aron (1950 [1935]) would further develop by emphasizing the convergence between the concept of the *Bund* and that of 'charismatic power'. For the sake of clarity, let us suggest an example taken from everyday life. The family is a (natural) community which we do not choose but in which we find ourselves existing; a young man emerging from adolescence and leaving his family to join, for example, a squatter community, some closed and sectarian ideological group or – a widespread phenomenon in the US – a student 'fraternity', does not simply exit one community to enter another, but rather does something different. This is because we have, on the one hand, a natural community to which we belong by birth and blood and, on the other, a social unit to which we belong by affective and total adhesion (as for the community), but which, at the same time, represents a relationship of a corporate nature since it is a chosen belonging, an elective membership. In the *Bund*, there is a complete, total identification with the group, but between individuals who were previously separated and who have chosen to unite to form a community based on spontaneous affection, feelings and emotions are shared.

Schmalenbach's essay is one of the last works of the great period of classical German sociology. The German historian and sociologist Otto Hintze (1980, 150) noted that this category 'has a value for the interpretation of history still greater than his inventor thought and would deserve much more attention than the one sociologists have given till now'. What follows takes up Hintze's suggestion, exploring the usefulness of the concept of the *Bund* for the interpretation of the mafia. This also makes it possible to review, in general, the interpretative line that leads from Pino Arlacchi (1983a, 1983b [1980]) to Paoli (2003), integrating it with references to the sociological tradition where it is most lacking – that is, with respect to an exquisitely sociological theorization of the model of mafia organization.[8]

There are two main immediate sources of inspiration for Schmalenbach: the artistic circle of Stefan George and the German youth movement of the post-First World War period (which will contribute to the rise of the Nazi movement in the 1920s). However, in the text, we find references to many other contexts and institutions, including the secret male sects widely studied by nineteenth-century ethnologists, primitive organizations that combined religious worship and the social control of sexuality.[9] There is also the 'knighthood' or, better, the 'following', the *Gefolgschaftswesen*, a typical social form of the ancient Germanic world, founded on the principle of fidelity, which Schmalenbach considers 'one of the most outstanding examples of communion relationships', which was not only typical of German populations, 'but a pervasive form found in every corresponding type of culture' (1977 [1922], 97). It is this socio-historical form that offers one of the most vivid examples of the concept:

> The jubilant followers who crowd around their leader, chosen in an inspired flood of passionate feeling, do not intend (at least, their feelings do not 'mean') to be bound up with one another on a naturally common basis. They are bound together by the actually experienced feelings, or at least are motivated by those affective conditions. (1977 [1922], 83–4)

This is obviously a *noncontractual* form of relationship, founded – like the 'community' – on the strength of emotions and feelings.[10] But unlike the community, which is based on a pre-existing 'fact' (that of consanguinity, or even ancient territorial proximity), which renders consciousness secondary, in the case of *Bund*-type associations, these emotions are manifest, lived in the moment as 'conscious experience of feeling', and clearly understood as the very reason for the existence (and foundation) of the association. Historically, this 'ethnic' reference to ancient Germanic experiences is less extraneous than it may seem from our topic: as the reader may recall from the very first chapter, the history of Sicily has been marked also by the invasion of a company of Norman warriors in the tenth century, who established themselves on the island and there founded one of the political organizations, the Norman kingdom of Sicily, whose institutional development anticipated what would become, albeit far away from Sicily, the early state. The bulk of the warriors' company was bound together by brotherhood ties, of the *Bund* type. Far from being just historical monuments, these archaic cultural forms of social life may spread and, while adapting to new social circumstances and changing accordingly, penetrate the local popular culture where other similar institutes may already exist (see Tamassia 1886 on the diffusion of Scandinavian mores, especially linked to these bonds, in southern Italy among other regions).

Like the institution of the ancient Germanic 'following' or religious sects,[11] the mafia is not as such a *Bund*, but a 'substantial' social formation that has a particular affinity with this essential form of social existence. The *Bund* is, in short – similar to the community and society – a modal category which manifests itself in certain contexts and institutions in preference to others. In fact, Schmalenbach finds the 'elemental model of the *Bund*' in friendship – coincidentally, one of the basic social forms that are most often associated with the mafia:

> As far as communion is concerned, I have designated original religious associations as having a special affinity to such a mode. Perhaps, I could have substituted the association of warriors or the camaraderie of the military. However, the simplest pattern of the communion is friendship, just as legal and economic relationships are critical instances of society, and the family, of community. Even so, there are occupational friendships in which goodwill and sincere affection are blended. But the occupational and political links are always basic. The term 'friendship' always seems misused in the case of these associations. (1977 [1922], 102)

Regardless of how much the use of the word 'friendship' may seem to be an abuse in the case of the mafia,[12] it has, however, been established that the language of friendship pervades the symbolic universe of the mafia and that it constitutes an essential ingredient of the repertoire which the mafioso draws on for his self-presentation as well as for the representation of his world (Blok 1974; Schneider and Schneider 1976). References to unspecified relations of friendship (*amicizia*) are omnipresent in trial proceedings and any document regarding mafia life – especially autobiographies. According to Bonanno (1983), friendship is the real core of his 'tradition' – the word he uses for the never-named-as-such mafia. But the code of friendship is not a universal, and its encoded meanings cannot be generalized on the basis of a single historical experience. As anthropologists well know, the word 'friendship' can connote different social practices in different places. And, indeed, one of the findings of the ethnographic research in Sicily is precisely that 'in Sicilian peasant society, patrons and clients were and still are conceptualized as friends (*amici*). Where the West European middle-class notion of friendship is largely bound to personal relations between social equals, the Sicilian folk classification of friendship involves personal relations crossing class lines' (Blok 1974, 151).[13]

The idiom of friendship, in effect, offers an exceptional 'vocabulary of motives' (Mills 1940) for the justification of power and control claims by those who, in an asymmetrical *personal* relationship, are in a position to exploit their superior position. But this vocabulary functions to the extent that it truly succeeds in producing the representation that people of different status are nonetheless equal because they share a common sense of belonging. And it is this idea of equality as a reciprocal belonging that is promoted by the frequent, almost obsessive, use of the term by mafiosi. One's 'friends' are not only from the same social place and milieu and, therefore, the people you celebrate special occasions with[14] and who come together for weddings[15] (*convivium et connubium*), but also your allies and comrades, those belonging to the same collective entity. Friends not only know each other, but recognize each other. And, reciprocally, they help each other, as the by-laws of the nineteenth-century 'brotherhoods', whose traces are still easily visible in current mafia groups, make clear. It is the 'we' that presupposes and together produces the representation of the mafia connection as a bond of 'friendship.' It is Cosa Nostra, *our* thing.[16]

The language of friendship also offers a crucial vocabulary for representing relationships of trust. 'Friend' is the one you can, indeed you must, trust. This is why between friendship and spiritual, ritual kinship – in the form of the *comparatico* (see Chapter 4), which could be thought as a historical and local manifestation of the Weberian status contract – there are large areas of overlap, so much so that it is common to substitute one term with the other. As Cutrera tells us:

> The word *compare* seems to express such a sentiment of trust that all Sicilians, when they have to speak to a farmer they have never met before, usually call him *compare* in order to avoid arousing suspicion should they ask for news or information. In this way, they tell him that it is a friend who is turning to him, and that he finds himself before a person he can trust. (1900, 59)

'Friends of friends' is the institutional expression of this chain of ritualized personal relationships (Boissevain 1974; Blok 1974; see also Collins 2004) that constitute the micro-foundations of the mafia's social system.[17] But perhaps the most profound meaning of mafia friendship emerges when we consider that allies in mafia wars and feuds are identified by this term (see, e.g., Stajano 1986, 66), in effect encoding group exclusive loyalties that definitively assume the character of 'public' political relationships, something that only the normative adoption of what Bourdieu (1998 [1994], 2014) has called a 'state thought' can prevent from being understood, reducing the feud or mafia war to merely a *private* conflict or simple crime.[18] What mafia culture seems to propose – beyond the meaning that the concept may have in the Sicilian peasant culture from which the mafia understandably draws at least part of its symbolic resources and codes – is thus an idea of friendship in its original political sense (see Konstan 1997; Althoff 1999; Digeser 2008; Haseldine 2013; Sigurdsson 2017; see also Brunner 2015 [1938]). This was the sense in which friendship was institutionalized in the ancient Greek and Roman worlds (from which it was inherited by the Christian medieval world) and which – after its 'privatization' in the liberal commercial world (e.g., Silver 1990)[19] – the twentieth century recovered with the work of Carl Schmitt (1996 [1932]) and the elaboration of his by now classic concept of the 'political' in terms of the friend/enemy distinction (Freund 1965). Seen in the light of Schmitt's model, asserting the political character of the mafia looks like a truism: how could a world be otherwise than one in which every person of some relevance in your life has to be categorized according to the main distinction between friend and foe? In fact, as I will show in the last paragraph of this chapter, things may be more complicated than they seem.

Rituals of blood

However, the *Bund* – Schmalenbach warns us – has an essential quality, an intrinsic limit; namely, its transience. This limitation typically exists at the *statu nascendi* – from the very beginning. Hence the search for institutional guarantees, for surrogates that can at least give the appearance of persistence, of duration – thus, in fact, slipping into the type of community or 'society', i.e. the market, commercial society. The institution of the mafia oath is a typical historical manifestation of these guarantees, a veritable 'rite of institution' in Bourdieu's terms, which Paoli (2003) as well as Catino (2019) both follow, losing, I suspect, the strong political meaning this reformulation of the more traditional *rite de passage* wants to convey: its reference to those sacred ceremonies through which humans have been producing, throughout their long history, the fidelities and loyalties that make up their political life:

> The communion is similarly transformed, through the vehicle of the oath with which comrades pledge loyalty to one another, on the one hand, into a society, and on the other, into a community. Among *these forms* one finds some that show this with enhanced clarity. Now comrades seal blood communions by drinking a few drops of one another's blood, and presume to establish a community as cohesive as blood bonds. Up to the final weakening, the name, 'brother' (communion brother), is the designation par excellence that binds comrades to the communion. (Schmalenbach 1977 [1922], 99)

With its initiation ritual centred on the blood oath, the mafia can easily be included 'among these forms'. To be sure, blood symbolism occupies a central place in mafia representations, and even in mafia social life, which goes beyond ritual friendship and even ritual kinship. This may explain why the mafia ritual never implies the drinking or even the mixing of bloods – and why blood kinship is so common in mafia Families. Indeed, both agnatic and affinal kinship are common in mafia structures, along with other social ties, with the metaphor of blood acting as a symbolic device to mark and foster reciprocity (see Blok 2002). Looking inside Families' social composition, we in fact find at first agnatic kinsmen – i.e. blood relatives on the father's side. The core is often constituted by a father and his son(s), or by a group of brothers, or even uncles and cousins, always linked on the father's side. However, there is some evidence of transmission of a mafia identity through maternal uncles (this is the case, for example, of Leonardo Vitale, who, in 1972, was one of the early *pentiti* but who wasn't at the time believed by state authorities and was institutionalized in a psychiatric hospital, only to be killed when discharged). It is important to remember that blood is here always a symbolic construction, in the sense that the 'facts of biological relatedness' play a role because of 'culturally formulated symbols in terms of which a system of social relationships is defined and differentiated' (Schneider 1977, 66).

Relevant kinship in mafia groups is also based on intermarriage, which produces in-laws and affines. To be sure, there is wide evidence of marriage among cousins, but this has always been common in Sicily, especially among families climbing the social ladder, in order to safeguard property within the same kinship group, and doesn't seem to be peculiar to families linked to the mafia. As well as brothers, and because of intermarriage, brothers-in-law may also be located in the core of mafia Families. This was the case of Totò Riina and Leoluca Bagarella's long-lasting friendship (Riina married a sister of Leoluca), the mechanism behind the Rimi–Badalamenti alliances, as well as the motive behind Rosario Di Maggio's transfer of his Family leadership to Salvatore Inzerillo. Kinship and marriage are indeed two institutional pillars of mafia social structures, whose social effectiveness has to be accounted for with reference to a long-lasting culture structure, whose roots go deep in the Indo-European heritage with its kinship systems – different from other systems discovered and studied by anthropologists since Lewis Henry Morgan's pioneering researches on the Iroquois League (itself a manifestation of *Bund*). In the Indo-European conception of blood, this latter may come from the outside into the agnates' circle through marriage; and to be fully incorporated in the kin group, it has to be shed through the sexual consummation of the marriage – which makes virginity and female chastity a cultural necessity. Mafiosis' sexual politics is still to be studied, but one aspect we can be sure of is that some traditional Mediterranean values (and value justifications), such as virginity, have persisted and still persist in their moral universe, sometimes leading to intergenerational trouble.

This brings us, again, to the imagery of blood in initiation rituals. As the aforementioned Antonino Calderone was informed during his mafia initiation ceremony, one 'goes in and comes out of the Cosa Nostra with blood. One cannot leave, one cannot resign from the Cosa Nostra. You'll see for yourselves, in a little while, how one enters with blood. And if you leave, you'll leave with blood because you'll be killed' (Arlacchi 1993, 68). Indeed, blood is not just a metaphor in mafia life, but a real substance that accompanies a mafioso career through to the concrete possibility of violent death, with all the pathos this expectation may produce. This is blood imagery too, the lived, experienced imagination of a tragic fate to be shared with others.

Ibn Khaldūn's concept of the *'asabiyya* offers an interesting complement to both Schmalenbach's and Blok's analyses of blood symbolism in the mafia. It has the further merit of locating social theory in long-lasting culture structures spatially close to our case study (see Chapter 1 for information on this early pioneer of social science). The concept takes inspiration from the need to make sense of social and political dynamics common in the Mediterranean world during the Middle Ages and earlier: this makes the concept close to the Sicilian historical and cultural experience, especially when we are reminded of the Arab and Berber presence in the ninth and tenth centuries, a distant past surely, whose lasting influences are however still very evident in Sicilian dialect and cuisine, among other things. As part of popular culture, organizational forms like brotherhoods and clientage, as well as *comparatico*, may also well find their deep roots in past experiences of cultural contact. We have seen how a fraternal culture could be genealogically linked to the Norman invasion in the eleventh century. When conquered by this northern people, Sicily was already dominated by another foreign civilization, the Muslim and Arab one. So, this is another lineage for mafia culture, whose roots go still deeper. 'Asabiyya is, for the Berber scholar (who lived in the fourteenth century and was recently rediscovered as an early and 'southern' founding father of sociology: see Alatas 2006b), the strong feeling of solidarity experienced and intimately felt by the nomads of the desert, by the Bedouins, whose political strength was grounded exactly on their deeply experienced group feeling, on their 'asabiyya. The word was already of common use in the pre-Islamic era, but become popular in high cultural circles thanks to Khaldūn. This is how the German orientalist Hellmut Ritter (brother of the political theorist Gerhard) commented on this concept, tracing a parallel with Machiavelli's thought as studied by his brother:

> What is 'asabiyya? It has been pointed out repeatedly that this conception is very near Machiavelli's idea of *virtù*. G. Ritter characterizes this Machiavellian conception ... as follows: 'With regard to the individual it means generally: political ability, a mere natural association of will power and cleverness ... This kind of *virtù* is a purely combative "ability", the virtue of mere active, organized force, not yet "ethical reason", its symbol being a combination of lion and fox ...' But that is not the only aspect of *virtù*. He continues thus: '... therefore still another kind of *virtù*, which forges stronger ties than the terror of open violence, is required. He, Machiavelli, traces it (as Cicero had done before) to the public spirit of the old Roman Republic, particularly in its older, better period.' Ibn Khaldūn's conception of 'asabiyya is somehow a synthesis of definite elements of both kinds of *virtù*. It is, as it were, the public sense in its dynamic aspect, 'the sense of solidarity', bearing in itself not only the will of the community for self-assertion, the readiness of its members to defend each other and the whole community, but also the combative will for attack, which longs to try the accumulated strength it has derived from the solidarity of the community, by proving it in a fight against opposed forces. 'It is the 'asabiyya with whose help men protect and defend themselves, bring their rights to bear and carry through all their common decisions' (K. Ayad 193). Ibn Khaldūn has in mind first of all the solidarity, the strength giving internal cohesion of a class of leaders, politically active and, as a rule, normally genealogically connected, striving for rule and obtaining it thanks to 'asabiyya. The most fertile moment for its realization is that of the seizing of power, the first of the five phases of State development, as assumed by Ibn Khaldūn (Rosenthal 17). Another substantial characteristic of the conception of 'asabiyya is that its supporters have a share of the power, though with differences in degree. In the second phase, in which the leader of the 'asabiyya circle rises to the position of an autocrat, he destroys the 'asabiyya precisely because he no longer needs it, i.e. he deprives his fellow-combatants of their partnership in the power and provides himself with an independent instrument of power, consisting of mercenaries and clients, which involves a very different character from the old 'asabiyya. (Ritter 1948, 2–4)

Ritter sees in this feeling of solidarity 'a primitive phenomenon', deeply rooted in 'the irrational depths of human nature, which appears and must appear in various degrees of strength wherever a community of men forms itself, a community which is more than a mere agreement, or convention for rational purpose, its leading value being the community itself, its aim consisting in maintaining its independence' (1948, 4). How does what we call the feeling of solidarity come about in practical life? Ibn Khaldūn mentions some special moments, which give rise to or foster that feeling. He starts by mentioning blood relationship as the cause. 'It is a feature of human nature – he writes – that one feels tied to relatives by blood.' However, the feeling of being tied together may also come about between allies, as well as between protector and protected, a relationship characteristic of the Arabian tribes. 'It is in the nature of men that they should join one another and make a bond, even if they be not related by blood.' Still, according to Ibn Khaldūn, *'asabiyya* comes about through social intercourse, through long reciprocal testing and trying, and through the activities of common occupations. It also comes about between men who were brought up together and who share the vicissitudes of life. While blood relationship is the strongest bond, especially for Semitic nations, at any rate for the Arabs, who, even after settling down, kept up the organization of tribes in the desert, the second cause for the rise of solidarity seems to have been stronger for the Indo-Europeans than for the Semites, at least after they had settled down. At any rate, in the later period we see semi-military and social alliances of various kinds, which have nothing to do with kin relations, and whose newer, harmless forms are the innumerable clubs, comradeships, youth associations, etc., which, according to circumstance, show a stronger or looser solidarity.

We don't need to go ahead with Khaldūn's elaboration on the sources of solidarity. Suffice it to say, with Ritter, that

[t]he ethically most valuable quality of a true irrational solidarity circle is the readiness of its members to help and sacrifice. In a true solidarity circle the members make sacrifices for the community as a whole, or for each other, without expecting any return for themselves individually. Here is the place where genuine altruism thrives. The highest degree of such readiness for sacrifice is the sacrifice of one's life in fighting for the community or as a martyr ... That such feeling may be misused is another thing. But even such altruism and readiness for help show that solidarity inside its circle ignores injustice. The ancient Arabs said: 'Help your brother, whether he suffers injustice or does injustice.' One could produce a whole series of old Arabic poems, in which the chivalrous poet proclaims his will to rush to the aid of his tribe, no matter whether they are right or wrong in starting the fighting ... The instinctively felt obligation for solidarity eliminates the question of right

or wrong, which partly accounts for the attitude of the population even in unpopular wars. (Ritter 1948, 7–8)

One of the main tenets of Ibn Khaldūn's historical theory is that domination moves through cycles linked to the dynamics of the *'asabiyya*. Strongly felt solidarities help groups possessing them to seize power, to conquer lands and town, but, once established, the ruling group has a tendency to relax, to institutionalize we would say, and to lose the original group feeling which was at the core of its strength. This happened, in the history of Arabs, when Bedouin, nomads from the desert, settled down in cities, At that point, the ruling class is ready to be defeated by a new-born solidarity group, coming from the desert, where life conditions are favourable to the cultivation of the *'asabiyya*. This may explain why mafia groups typically do not last for long – at least, they don't last for long with the same organizational identity and are subject to continuous change in configuration and, above all, of leadership. We do not have measures and data about the average duration of a mafia group (a *cosca* or a Family), but we can say from the dispersed evidence that mafia dynasties are relatively few, and that the rule is what Vilfredo Pareto called the *circulation of the elites*.[20] Probably, it would be better to reverse the causal chain: it is because mafia groups are so unstable, as a consequence of internal fighting (competition for leadership between established and newcomers, especially when not linked through blood) and external contrast (by other mafia groups longing for hegemony, and by state agencies engaged in antimafia activities) that the mafia as an institutional system is able to persist and reproduce itself, and even grow as it did after Italian unification: the weak institutionalization of the individual mafia group, of mafia individual Families, their going up and down in the overall hierarchy, their passing through moments of real chaos if not destruction from which eventually to be reborn or to definitively disappear, is clearly a big issue for the individual Family, but a strength for the whole system, as always new or renewed sources of group feeling may emerge in this ongoing system. This is what both Schmalenbach and Ibn Khaldūn suggest with their respective analyses of the structural basis of solidarity and its dynamics.

To finish: the characteristics of mafia sociality that seem to be related to this ideal type of the *Bund*, to this form and mode of social existence, are indeed numerous and suggest a further examination of Paoli's central concept – the mafia as a system of sworn brotherhoods – not in terms of further specification but, rather, of an analytical extension and a more meaningful categorization in theoretical terms. More than as brotherhoods – a descriptive category of an institutional model determined in time and space – mafia organizations and, above all, mafia bonds should perhaps be read and analysed as being historically given, but not anachronistic, manifestations of a form and way of social grouping of which there are still numerous traces in contemporary society. This throws new light on a question that has long been debated in the literature and without apparent solution: the apparently contradictory, or double-edged, character of the mafia as a form of social organization. Investigating the economic and social conditions of the genesis and reproduction of the mafia phenomenon, Arlacchi (1983b) has, for example, observed that the social structure from which 'mafia behaviour and mafia power' is 'derived' shows a characteristic undulating movement without any apparent conclusion:

> Society restructured itself from time to time but remained unaltered. It rewound itself about its own central axes. This fluctuation of *corsi e ricorsi*, to use Vico's famous expression, gave rise to a situation which was neither community (*Gemeinschaft*) nor society (*Gesellschaft*). In short, it was a society in permanent transition. (1983b, 6)[21]

Catanzaro (1984) proposed to resolve this fundamental ambivalence of the mafia by taking it head on: perhaps, he suggested, what the mafia is, what identifies it as a social and sociologically relevant phenomenon, and which explains its persistence, is precisely its being a 'a form of social hybridization' in which both modern and premodern are combined together, giving those who control it the resources of both. The introduction of the concept of *Bund* suggests yet another reading, or at least a clarification. What the mafia indicates, or allows us to trace, may in fact be less the persistence of archaic forms of social organization in a context of incipient modernization and more the cyclical nature with which certain modes of basic social existence – no longer just two, but three – emerge and develop, shaping, in combination, different societies or historical periods. The 'contemporary sociological significance of *Bund*' would be – as Hetherington (1994) notes – precisely in the variety of cultural associations and forms of this type that the 'postmodern condition', in which we supposedly find ourselves living today, seems to be constantly generating: those 'neotribal forms', as Maffesoli (1996) called them, through which sentiment and emotions, in a word, passions, emerge from the confines of family life to which modern bourgeois culture had essentially circumscribed them and spread throughout the social structure. That the persistence of the mafia may depend on its at least apparent capacity to satisfy a need for emotional investments, and even ideal passions, and for total belonging – a need not at all limited to the medium-high sectors of the social structure as a certain vision of postmodernity might suggest – in what are fundamentally modern contexts (such as an urban neighbourhood in a large city like Palermo, in full urban expansion), is what, in the end, an authoritative testimony like the following suggests:

> For a Tommaso Buscetta who was in his twenties or thirties, Cosa Nostra was something beautiful. It was everything: it was the means by which a man who had been the victim of injustice, trampled on by the rich and criminals, could acquire dignity and pride. (Arlacchi 1994, 11–12; my translation)[22]

The sociological tradition has many names for such ambivalent phenomena,[23] but one seems to me particularly appropriate for our case: the notion of 'bastard institution' advanced by American sociologist Everett C. Hughes, one of the leaders of the Chicago School in the 1950s.[24] After defining institutions as organizations that distribute goods and services, or even better as 'the legitimate instance of satisfaction of legitimate human needs', Hughes illustrates the curious concept of 'bastard institutions' (1971, ch. 10). Certain institutions, Hughes argues, are created by collective protest against the institutionalized definition of services, functions or goods. One type of protest is sectarian – against the doctrine and religious practice offered by the official clergy, for example. It can be a protest against the way in which religious practice is defined, against its distribution or against alleged connivance or alignments of the church and its officials with the vested interests of certain social classes. With the passage of time, these institutions, Hughes notes, often tend to reproduce those models that they had originally refused and from which they had initially dissociated themselves. In his words: 'Established institutional patterns are hidden traps into which the best of protest enterprises may fall' (1971, 98). But there are also other deviations from established institutions, other forms of distancing from legitimate channels, that persist over time and across generations:

> Let us call them bastard institutions. Some are illegitimate distributors of legitimate goods and services; others satisfy wants not considered legitimate. Among bastard institutions are gambling, prostitution (the second oldest profession), rackets, black markets ... the fence, professional crime, bootlegging ... All take on organized forms not unlike those of other institutions. (1971, 99)

And Hughes goes on, recalling that

> the tong courts of the earlier Chinatowns meted out the justice of a particular group that did not accept or trust established justice. The popular justice of the frontier and the lynchings that continued in several Southern states until the 1920s were bastard institutions, not formally legitimate but highly conventional and supported by popular opinion. (1971, 99)

The prototype of all bastard institutions is, indeed, 'that kind of thing which has come to be called "the racket" ... a sort of parasite on the shady side of the institutional tree' (1971, 105); this is a naturally valuable indication for us, considering the close association in American culture between the mafia and the racket. But let us see how Hughes continues his description of the concept:

> Some of these bastard institutions are directly against the law, or the declared moral values of society. They are in direct conflict with accepted definitions and institutional mandates. Others offer a less than fully respectable alternative, or allow one to satisfy some hidden weakness or idiosyncratic taste not provided for, and slightly frowned on, by the established distributors. Still others offer quite simply a way to get something not readily available to people of one's kind in the prevailing institutional system. They are corrections of faults in institutional definition and distribution. (1971, 99)

So, what lessons can we learn from Hughes?[25] I would say this: that there are institutions in the social world whose legitimacy is not to be sought in the law, but rather in the functions that they knowingly carry out – against the dominant morality, and sometimes against the law – for the maintenance of the institutionalized legal system, the one that is positively sanctioned and approved. The task of the sociologist is not to judge, but to understand why and how 'bastard' institutions like the racket – and, we can easily add, the mafia – exist and survive. The methodological insight that Hughes derives from the consideration of these functions is very important here:

> Whatever they be, and whatever they have in common, these bastard enterprises should be studied not merely as pathological departures from what is good and right, but as part of the total complex of human activities and enterprises. In addition, they should be looked at as orders of things in which we can see the social processes going on, the same social processes, perhaps, that are to be found in the legitimate institutions (1971, 99–100)

The bastard institution is a neglected sociological category that has much to offer to our understanding of the mafia and its persistence, though it focuses on the relationship between the institution and its environment rather than on internal institutional life.[26] What a category like 'bastard institution' (as well as 'greedy', or 'total', respectively proposed, moving on from Hughes, by Lewis Coser and Erving Goffman) suggests to us is that the mafia is not a sociological oddity, but, rather, a system of social relations that can be found in numerous incarnations featuring various combinations of characteristics across different places and periods. In terms of institutional comparison, sociological research on the mafia still has much to do. Here, we are content to indicate some promising directions of inquiry that could come in handy in the next and final chapter. Now, let us return to our original path.

Culture, Writing and Communication

> *Tutto è messaggio, tutto è carico di significato nel mondo di Cosa Nostra.*
> Falcone and Padovani 1993 [1992], 51

> I believe one's point of reference should not be to the great model of language (*langue*) and signs, but to that of war and battle. The history which bears and determines us has the form of a war rather than that of a language: relations of power, not relations of meaning.
> Foucault 1980, 114

Let us now pass from the ways and means of social organization to the ways and means of cultural communication.[27] The focus here is not so much on a mafia communication system itself, whose modes and features we have already looked at in Chapter 5, but on the implications that a certain mode of communication has, or may have, on the nature and the social organization of the mafia. An in-depth study of the changing forms of communicative mediation in the mafia remains to be done, but its volatility has long been considered an essential issue. As a (relatively) *secret* and criminal (i.e. illegal) organization, the mafia has been primarily conceived, more or less explicitly, as a social form based on *oral* communication, inevitably marked by the structural characteristics of this communicative mode, superbly delineated by scholars of language such as Basil Bernstein[28] and Walter Ong. This structural characteristic of mafia organization has been reaffirmed, with reference especially to the Sicilian Cosa Nostra and with less cogency to the Calabrian *'Ndrangheta*, by Paoli:

> In both associations, it is forbidden to write down any information concerning the mafia group. In Cosa Nostra this prohibition is categorically respected, so much so that no exception has yet been recorded. In the *'Ndrangheta*, instead, exceptions are the rule. Ever since the late nineteenth century, in fact, written documents listing rites and esoteric formulas have been periodically discovered in southern Calabria and in Canada and Australia. (2003, 113)

The archaic image that this has produced in the representation of the Sicilian mafia is quite evident: as a 'society without writing', the mafia would satisfy a major criterion used by anthropologists to distinguish simple and premodern from complex and modern societies.[29] Nevertheless, written texts have a long history even in the Sicilian mafia, as classic studies have shown: blackmail letters (*lettere di scrocco*), statutes, even notes about oath formulas, are rare but not impossible to find in the historical literature since the 1880s. However, it is true that orality has for long been the standard way of communication inside the Sicilian mafia, supported by what can be described as a standardized, almost codified, style of talking and even of being silent – or just speaking with gesture and eye movements. The mastering of these modes of communication has for long been a crucial skill of the mafioso, and a differential, i.e. distinguishing, source of social and even moral worth. It has also been a crucial ingredient of the cinematic representation of the mafia as a world of silence and secret, or better, minimal but effective communication. Clearly, orality strongly limited not only the state's knowledge of mafia life but also sociological knowledge.

The *pizzini* (small pieces of paper with written messages) discovered in 2006 with the capture of godfather Bernardo Provenzano[30] after forty years on the run put this representation of the mafia as the world of oral communication into crisis, not only opening the door to a reconsideration of the structure of mafia dominion in light of its previously undervalued models of written communication[31] but also – and more important for us – opening a window on the modes and forms of communication among mafiosi in their 'natural', as it were, environment, away from the gaze and hearing of police or other public, state authorities. *Pizzino* is a term that derives from the Sicilian word *pizzinu* and indicates a small piece of paper or note. With this term, the numerous, strictly typewritten messages discovered in the refuge of the fugitive mafia boss, with which he had corresponded for years with his family, both biological and mafia, were introduced into Italian judicial culture. The investigators involved in Provenzano's arrest recognized and understood:

> the extraordinary importance that this correspondence, the so-called *pizzini*, has for Provenzano, given that it is precisely through this dense network of messages that he manages to preserve – and indeed consolidate – his managing role of the entire mafia organization, reducing to a minimum, for obvious security reasons, direct personal meetings but maintaining, nevertheless, contacts with the families and men of honour of the various provinces of Sicily and continuing to give directives (though usually under the apparent guise of advice and recommendations), to send and receive sums of money, to be informed of all the events that in some way affect the organization.[32]

As one judicial document explains:

The investigations have shown that the entire system, despite its apparently crude and elementary nature, is actually carefully managed and continually fine-tuned with the aim, above all, of guaranteeing the absolute security of Provenzano and – as far as possible – his communications. ... With regard to the objective of personal security, which is at the centre of this intense exchange of correspondence, it is guaranteed by the shrewd choice of men of proven loyalty for the delivery of the notes and, above all, by the fact that the messages coming from various parts of Sicily are gradually concentrated among a limited number of people who, in turn, deliver them to an even more restricted number of subjects who are in direct contact with Provenzano.[33]

In sociological terms, we could say that Provenzano's *pizzini* are important because: (a) they highlight the multiplicity of strategies adopted according to situational and contextual needs;[34] (b) they highlight the existence and use of a 'communicative culture' and, in particular, of a 'written culture' in the organization of the mafia, through which methods, procedures and strategies are conceived, communicated, interpreted – and, naturally, legitimized. In short, Provenzano's *pizzini* open up the structure and culture of mafia dominion to reconsideration in light of its communication models. In particular, they create the possibility of what I would call an *ethnography of mafia writing*,[35] or, better still, a *political* ethnography of mafia writing, since *pizzini* constitute the literal, graphic, written representation of power relations captured in the very moment of their enunciation. Not only that, but they also make it possible to outline a cognitive sociology of the mafia focused on the implications that the adoption of writing has in the practical functioning of mafia organizations. Hence, the objective of the following paragraphs is, starting from the language of the *pizzini*, to reconstruct a more articulated and all-encompassing – in a word, multidimensional – image of the mafia; in other words, to study its organization through language and demonstrate its intrinsic complexity. This entails that we must study mafia culture and communication (the *pizzini*) in order to understand the conditions of possibility of even mafia economic strategies (which, with another Sicilian term, we can evocatively call *pizzo*).[36]

Mafia as mode of personal communication

The mafia is also a communication system based, above all, on direct, in-person oral communication. But this communication is also inevitably mediated, very often by technologies capable of overcoming the problem of meeting in person (see, e.g., Thompson 1995). Like any other modern agent, the mafia knows how to use and exploit technologies for communication over distance, such as the letter, and this is certainly not a recent acquisition of just the last few decades, following the cultural transformations that have modernized Italy since the 1950s with the spread of literacy and mass education (De Mauro 1963). Indeed, the afore-mentioned Antonino Cutrera already pointed out the presence of this communication medium in the repertoire of the late nineteenth-century Palermo mafia (specifically, the one operating in the citrus orchards of the Conca d'Oro):

> The mafia boss commands the right to send *lettere di scrocco*. What is a *lettera di scrocco*? It is an anonymous letter delivered by mail to a rich landowner in which, with a tone of resignation, almost of one asking forgiveness for bothering him, or with extreme arrogance and menace, and almost always with the threat of seriously harming his property or person, the orchard owner is asked for a specific sum of money because the *picciotti* (meaning his affiliates) need to be subsidised because the year's harvest was bad and the needs of their families are pressing. (1900, 64)

It is worth reading some of these letters, faithfully reproduced from the original sources in their syntactic structure and original dialectal vocab-ulary, taken from the Palermo police archives. An English translation of a representative one would read as follows:

> Dearest Friend,
> Don't trust the counsel that you keep with your *compare* Pietro ... and don't report this to the Carabiniere so that they come in disguise with the money. You must bring it. This will be the last letter you receive, so, if you want to die, come with your children. Bring what we told you, two thousand lire, to the place that you know, without talking. We won't write again. If you do not do your duty, think of us, because you deserve to die. Come with your *compare* Pietro at noon on 6 July, bring the two thousand lire, bring the two thousand lire. Kind regards.

The demand for money, the economic practice, is therefore mediated by a communicative strategy because it is evident that, at least from the point of view of those who wrote them, these letters are intended to convey not only the tone and linguistic register of a financial body (for example, in the way they indicate the amounts in Italian as '*lire 3 mila*', '*2 milaliri*') but also a claim whose value, whose meaning, is defined by the modalities and forms of the messages themselves. Generally, they start with a request in a resigned tone, and continue, if the initial message is not received (i.e. decoded) according to the intentions of the person who transmitted it (and had encoded it previously), with a threatening tone. That the mafia owes its sociological identity to some systematically privileged communication methods is, indeed, a recurring theme in the literature (see, e.g., Piccillo 1970). Already according to sources from the nineteenth century, mafiosi could be recognized by 'their jargon ... a somewhat metaphorical language, but that from a certain accent, from their intonation, from their arrogant and rigid attitude, from the whole of the person, reveals the mafioso at first glance' (Alongi 1977 [1887], 53; see also Mosca 1980 [1900], 21). Still, Alongi noticed the oddity that, contrary to the 'mellifluous, exaggerated, full of images' day-to-day language of Sicilians, 'the *maffioso* language is short, sober, clipped' and 'very poor, variable, inorganic': but this could be explained, he suggested, when you think that 'Sicilians, with a wink, with a gesture, with the very variable expression of the face and the voice, easily understand each other, even reversing the natural meaning of the words' (1977 [1887], 54). A century later, the *pentito* Tommaso Buscetta could still highlight this characteristic communicative style of the mafia also in autobiographical fashion:

> The fact is that men of honour have difficulty talking a lot. They speak a language of their own, made up of very compact speeches, short expressions that boil down longer ones. The guy talking, if he's good or if he's also a man of honour, understands exactly what the other guy means. The language of *omertà* is based on the essence of things. The specifics, the details, aren't interesting, the man of honour doesn't like them. I myself am this way. I'm not used to saying any more than is necessary to say what I gotta say. All my life I've developed a psychology that doesn't make me talk to people freely and easily. And that's why I hate long-winded people and people who go over the top. (See Arlacchi 1994, 67–8)[37]

Using well-known sociological jargon, we could say the mafioso's mode of speaking is an integral and magnificent manifestation of his habitus, of that embodied mode of thinking and acting that is transmitted and inculcated from parents to sons and daughters inside the family – the habitus is history made (second) nature, according to Bourdieu (1977) – which is revealed in the gestures and behaviours of everyday life as well as, in Sicily, in the *omertà*, the culturally based name to refer to the rule of mafia silence that is necessarily a rule of mafia's ways of speaking. Or perhaps, better, we may categorize this strongly disciplined mode of communication as a 'technology of the self' (Foucault 1988): a historically based way of shaping a person's attitude and posture, her gestures and voice, a mode of being, that can be learned, cultivated and improved through imitation and continuous practice by living among others who already master the code – not necessarily parents or relatives, even if usually this is the rule (indeed, Buscetta was not born into a mafia family; he entered the mafia world as an adolescent).

We can understand now how much the adoption, in the early 1990s, of the *pizzino* as an originally exceptional, but later common, communication tool inside the social world of Cosa Nostra introduced new accounts of the working and nature of the mafia that are worth reflecting on. But first, we have to take advantage of this new communication device as an unexpected and precious source of evidence for our main argument. Indeed, this is the first time we can enter inside the mafia *mentalitè*, the mafioso's universe of meanings seen through a direct detection of his words, his vocabulary, the conceptual schemas used by him while communicating with other insiders: the *pizzini* opens the door to the mafia universe of meaning as if it were 'from the native point of view'.

Hermeneutics of mafia communication

Let us examine a concrete example of a *pizzino*, which can give us an idea of how this form of communication works and in what sense and measure it has a 'political' nature even when it comes to economic affairs. I have chosen to analyse a typewritten letter that the mafia turncoat Giuseppe Maniscalco claimed was sent by Provenzano to the fugitive mafioso Salvatore Genovese of San Giuseppe Jato:[38]

> Dearest friend, I received your news with joy, I am so pleased to hear that you are all in excellent health. I assure you that the same is true for me.
>
> (1) I can understand the reasons pushing you to write to me. I appreciate your trust. And I am sorry if I may disappoint you in some ways.
>
> (2) Now I hear you when you tell me you are at my disposal, and you would like me to advise you if there is some friend that you could turn to for certain needs, thank you again for your trust: I could tell you that I don't understand you? But that isn't my way: Let me point out that I can always be of help to you, where my circumstances will allow me, but only as I see it ? on a personal basis without responsibility, in spite of what some poor bastards are made to say, I know nothing of what some people have done, and for this reason I don't know how things really stand: And so if, as old friends, we wanted to keep in contact, that would be great, but in another position, no; I don't feel like it ? and I can't, I can just tell you ? what I think about it ? or could think when you ask me, with these conditions I am at your complete disposal, and my door is open.
>
> (3) Now you tell me that you have a political contact at a good level that would allow you to manage a lot of big jobs, and before you continue, you want to know what I think. But not knowing anything, I can't tell you anything, I would need to know the names and know how they are changed. Because today being today, you can't trust anyone: they could be conmen? or cops? or infiltrated? or idiots? They could be great schemers, but if you don't know where you have to go, you can't walk, so I can tell you nothing.
>
> (4) It would be my pleasure to see not only you, but also your Father. If you can, please send him my greetings and give him an affectionate hug from me. But as you know, we have a lot of problems because we are not close, I'm a bit far away, and everything can be done with the will of God, but at the moment, if you can, and you think it's appropriate/right, write me, if possible

by typewriter, and if not write as clearly as possible because I can hardly understand your handwriting, in your area, this guy Vitale, who I've never met, will take care of it, as a legacy of/taking over for one of your countrymen, but I don't know how, what, or which of you he is in contact with.

We can analyse this text – and others like this – by highlighting the implicit *political* strategies inscribed in it as well as the more obvious literary dimensions. Starting from the latter, we have to say that this is *not* writing that presumes to have control of the Italian language, especially its grammar and syntax. Provenzano – as well as the organization he controls – is from a semi-literate background which betrays its lower-class origins, even though many members of Cosa Nostra are nowadays professionals and graduates. Cultural capital is far from being elevated in the mafia. Indeed, this is one if its characteristics. As an interclass social formation, it must conform to the lowest educational level, especially as this is the level at which recognized chiefs of the organization still are. This low cultural capital betrays the humble origins of those who are well educated, while confirming them for those of equally humble origins and who belong to the same milieu. This is a way of sharing a common background and even a common fate – as expressed by the routine recourse to the Sicilian dialect in mafia communication. This strengthens the representational capacity of the writing and its ability to produce identity. In the language of the *pizzini*, it is possible for mafiosi to recognize each other and, in so doing, to verify each other's identity. Bernstein (1971) would call it, without hesitation, a communicative culture based on a 'restricted code'.

Second, it is writing that always presupposes an 'unsaid', an empty space, an absence. The mafia is, indeed, made up of these absences, these voids, the unspoken, even more than it is of the secrecy (which, in fact, is less present in the overall communication system) that Provenzano's writing exhibits and almost celebrates. Each *pizzino* contains much more than what the material signs say, and this is not only because it acts at the level of connotation (with the use of terms such as 'friends', 'advice', etc.), but also because it tenaciously exploits the indexical character of *public* communication, in Bernstein's terms. Paradoxically, secrets are best preserved by using public codes, that is, those of ordinary orality, which always presuppose much more than they say.[39] The messages must be deciphered not only because they are written in an approximate Italian and partly in code, but because they take for granted a previous communication, if not a real shared repertoire of knowledge. The writing of the mafia is based on a (Bersteinian) restricted code, a code based on orality, as Ong (1982) has renamed it, which can, however, be as expressive and precise as an elaborated code if the context of reference is familiar and shared – as is the case in the mafia context (also in a literal sense: many of Provenzano's correspondents were family members).

Third, it is the content of the message itself that exudes politics. It is enough to cite some of the words typically used by Provenzano, which immediately refer to the vocabulary of politics (European, though not exclusively so):[40] 'trust', 'advice', 'friend', 'help', 'responsibility'. It is political frames like these that structure mafia communication and make mafia culture an eminently *political* culture, not so distant, when looked at from a certain epistemological distance, from the political culture of Renaissance Florence or that of Old Regime Austria.[41] Meshed with technicalities about the management of contracts and procurements, this is the vocabulary used by mafiosi to talk and think about their 'business'.

But then it is writing itself – as a specific communication technology – that it is important to underline. As demonstrated not only by scholars of communication (Walter Ong, for example) and philosophers (Jacques Derrida, above all), but also historians and anthropologists (Jack Goody, Marshall Sahlins, Peter Burke, and others), writing is not a neutral communicative form, but rather possesses and implements its own logic. It also has specifically political, as well as psychological, cognitive and, broadly, cultural consequences. It is worth turning to anthropologist Jack Goody's (1986) work on 'the logic of writing and the organization of society', the title of his book in which he developed ideas that he had originally proposed in a seminal article two decades earlier (Goody and Watt 1963) on the social consequences of literacy. In this way, we will again bring the study of the mafia back to the field of anthropological research, from which it has been lifted in recent years in favour of different disciplinary areas (and therefore perspectives and points of view), especially economic theory, criminology and economic sociology (e.g., Arlacchi, Catanzaro and later Rocco Sciarrone, who worked on the concept of social capital and the problems that the mafia, understood as a network of relationships, produces in terms of local development). This means, above all, putting the study and understanding of the mafia phenomenon back on a terrain capable of recognizing and valuing the importance of the cultural and symbolic dimensions of the mafia's activities and organization. In fact, Goody's research on the social consequences of literacy and the effects of the logic of writing on social organization evidently presupposes the idea that 'culture counts', where, by 'culture', we mean, in short, the systems of symbols and public meanings through which social actors communicate and transmit their ideas and conceptions of the world. As Goody (1986) noted in his pioneering study, the use of writing by a political organization (state or other) has multiple repercussions on social action as it allows control over space–time relationships. It makes it possible to extend the scale on which a political organization can operate, which in turn affects stratification systems (it is evident that writing and reading become necessary conditions to be subjects capable of acting and therefore covering organizational roles). It is in this sense that *pizzini*, as stated above, can be understood as the literal, graphic, written representation of power relations captured in the very moment of their enunciation. Not only that, but a careful analysis of them also makes it possible to outline a cognitive sociology (DiMaggio 1997) of the mafia, focused on the implications that the adoption of writing has for the mafia group's formation of representations, strategies and decisions.

From writing to structure

What consequences could Provenzano's writing have had for the social organization of the mafia, and what can we predict for the future (i.e. the long-term consequences)? We can advance some hypotheses, which will require serious testing in a more careful analysis and (textual and ethnographic) interpretation of the messages. Not only is it a communication system that follows certain ritual forms (a standard opening with greetings and wishes for good health, followed by reassurance regarding the health of the sender, Provenzano), uses a certain code, though an elementary one (letters and numbers instead of proper names), presupposes a certain production technology (the typewriter, which Provenzano usually uses and declares to prefer and even suggests using) and a certain organization for sorting and distribution (a system of trustworthy couriers); but also, in its own written form, it introduces institutional logics,[42] so to speak, that for a long time have not been considered as characteristics of the mafia – Cressey's influential but much criticized and now obsolete interpretation of the US-based Cosa Nostra notwithstanding. There is a strong temptation to say, for example, that the adoption of writing introduced a 'bureaucratic' institutional logic into the mafia. The debate over whether or not the mafia has a bureaucratic nature dates back to end of the nineteenth century, with Mosca's claim that the mafia was not a bureaucratic organization, a thesis reaffirmed by a number of anthropologists in the 1960s and 1970s against widespread opinion in the mass media, which was intrigued by the idea of a rigidly organized and structured mafia. These findings were then brought into question by what was learned during the maxi-trial of the 1980s, which in turn led to a redefinition of the mafia's structure as being formally defined, provided with a sort of organizational chart in addition to specific institutional rules (for an updated assessment of the whole issue, see Catino 2019). However, a crucial requirement of the bureaucratic type was still missing: the use of writing, a necessary condition for the formalization of administrative procedures. Do, therefore, *pizzini* provide the missing link in support of the 'bureaucratic argument'?

Well, from the analysis of the *pizzini* that have been found, this does not seem to be what they are about: there is writing, but it is not aimed at the formalization of procedures, although we can note a certain rituality in the content of the letters. The mafia that emerges from the *pizzini* is no more bureaucratic than the one that emerged from the anthropology books of the 1960s and 1970s. This does not mean that there are no effects in terms of administrative practices. But the mafia model continues to be characteristically equidistant from both the bureaucratic type of administration classically described by Weber, and craft administration, which Arthur Stinchcombe (1959) characterized in terms of short-term contractual relations, continuity of workers' status in the labour market (and not in the firm) and professional technical competence. Instead, the mafia seems to be better classified – from a political-cultural reading of the *pizzini* – as a form of 'brokerage administration', a type of administration characterized by ambiguity, informality and negotiation that is quite widespread, for example, in the culture industry precisely because of the unpredictable and not easily plannable character of its products (DiMaggio 1977)[43] – as are those of the mafia (protection, first and foremost). And writing is, nevertheless, compatible with this form of administration, without it being necessary to evoke the notion of bureaucracy. However, the use of writing influences the functioning of the mafia organization regardless of its structural identification. What seems most important in the case of the mafia is that writing involves a change in the nature, or, better, in the culture, of institutional responsibility. As Goody (1986, 124) noted:

> One aspect of the introduction of writing is the greater precision it gives to orders from above and to pleas from below. It is less easy to evade an order that has been committed to writing and carries an authoritative signature. Such personalized commitment 'in writing' also means that responsibility for giving and receiving orders is more highly individualized.

Now, as we have seen, mafia communications exist in the form not of orders but, characteristically, of advice and recommendations – which are, in fact, communicative modes typical of the role of mediators, and therefore of brokerage administration systems. This makes the use of the written form even more strategic. Or rather, the use of the written form allows the standard rhetoric with which the mafioso traditionally communicates its commands to be refined, disguising it as advice and suggestions. Above all, it allows the command–obedience relations that mafia culture tends to conceal to be further mediated. However, the written form objectifies this relationship, defining those responsible for the transaction more precisely. This is one of the effects of writing on social organization: the development of greater objectification and therefore also of greater reflexivity. As Ong (1982) noted, communication technologies are not mere external aids but involve transformations of mental structures: for example, writing raises the level of awareness and introspection, and it also creates a distance that enhances reflection and planning, decontextualizing communication. Writing also allows for retrospective thinking, much more than is possible in an oral culture. With writing, we would therefore expect a strengthening of the strategic capabilities of the mafia. The consequences of writing are also 'widely cumulative' and led to the formation of what can truly be described as 'memory archives' (Goody 1986, 162). Unlike verbal exchanges, *pizzini* can be preserved, and they are, as evidenced by the fact that hundreds of them were found both in the Provenzano farmhouse and in the homes of the mafiosi who were in written contact with him. In other words, the fact that written documents are used within the mafia organization reveals something that previous research did not consider: namely, a type of organization that, aware of writing and, indeed, exploiting it as a tool for the administration and even governance of its operations, experienced a series of institutional effects that made it into an institutional type that is different from the one that emerged from the long-believed thesis of the mafia as a system of interpersonal relations and/or as an organized structure of power based on customs and oral communication.

Naturally, the existence of 'by-laws', organizational charts and documents relating to the organizational structure and accounting administration of Cosa Nostra was already well known in the wake of the maxi-trials of the 1980s and 1990s. But the discovery of the *pizzini* has revealed something much deeper and capable of potentially modifying our idea of the mafia – namely, its adoption of *writing* and its *logic* as a resource for political communication and therefore for government. This also opens up consideration of the mafia in relation to the category of *institutional isomorphism* (DiMaggio and Powell 1983): that is to say, the progressive structuring and standardization of mafia organizations according to forms similar to those found in the surrounding environment, defined both by capitalist enterprise and by the bureaucratic state (writing is a form of rationalization). This brings to mind a (counterfactual) observation made by Charles Tilly half a century ago, but still valid, which goes more or less like this: if a mafia network were one day to succeed in expanding across the whole of Sicily, it would resemble a state, it would be a state (1974, xxiii). Provenzano's arrest and the discovery of the *pizzini*, which are presumably only the tip of the communicative iceberg and the most powerful expression of a web of personal relationships whose concrete size still escapes us, but which gives the idea of being very extensive, reminds us that this always remains a real possibility. I cannot, however, close this paragraph without asking myself a perhaps provocative but also fundamentally obvious question: that is, what relationship can there be between the use of writing and the scriptures, that is, between the adoption of a written communication system and a system of religious beliefs based on the strength of the (God's) Word and on its transcription? Provenzano was – or at least acted as if he was – a very religious person; we have evidence of his habitual frequentation, while a fugitive, of churches and of his everyday use of sacred water (a strong Catholic symbol); in his cottage refuge, two Bibles were found – in addition to several newspapers, a book from a policeman and a television – and his letters, his *pizzini*, are filled with religious references. Provenzano's writing may also have had another unexpected effect (in Merton's sense): helping to strengthen the sacred aura of a nearly invisible boss. In Provenzano's *pizzini* there are not only the material signs of written communication, but also the signs of a symbolic power expressed in and through writing. Exactly like the Word of God.[44]

Violence, Communication and Pathos

> Unfortunately, to speak of mafia, certain deaths are needed; otherwise nobody is interested in the topic, as has been said several times, and I am sorry that it must be me who repeats it.
>
> Giovanni Brusca, *pentito*; my translation

We have seen in the Chapter 5 that violence is an integral mechanism in the inner working of the gift as a social institution as it has been theorized first by Marcel Mauss and then by others following him. This can already shed light on the issue of violence in mafia life. But violence is so central to our common understanding of the mafia that we need to go deeper into this topic. Indeed, violence is apparently implicated in the very working of mafia organizations as based on a sacred oath. If we recall that the sacred oath is historically linked to the expectations of mutual aid among people who are risking their lives fighting as warriors, we must expect violence to be the normal sanction for traitors. As repented Francesco Marino Mannoia stated in 1989 with reference to his own organization, Cosa Nostra, 'it is a given and accepted fact that in betraying the oath of faithfulness made to the organization, there can be no other outcome than death, and this hounds the traitor for the rest of his days' (quoted in Paoli 2003, 108). It has been noticed that, with the prospect of maintaining a mafia prison system, death has, necessarily, to be the final, definitive sanction in the mafia order. However, death is not the only image we have of mafia and mafiosi; an extensive array of acts of violence, including torture, are also included. To make some order in this differentiated universe, it seems necessary to elaborate on the issue conceptually.

I begin with what may be a rather obvious, but I think necessary, observation: 'violence' is a word with very strong connotations. Unlike 'strength' (including physical strength) or 'power', the word 'violence' includes an implicit value judgement. 'Strength' is neutral, if not positive, 'power' is factual, but 'violence' is neither (for a different understanding see, however, Collins 2008). As Nancy Scheper-Hughes and Philippe Bourgois have perceptively observed: 'Violence can never be understood solely in terms of its physicality – force, assault, or infliction of pain – alone. Violence also includes assaults on the personhood, dignity, sense of worth or value of the victim. The social and cultural dimensions of violence are what gives violence its power and meanings' (2003, 1). It is for this reason that violence 'cannot be readily objectified and quantified so that a "check list" can be drawn up with positive criteria for defining any particular act as violent or not' (2003, 2). Slapping a child or hitting them with a belt can be a violent act, but, in certain contexts, it is considered a legitimate, culturally validated expression of parental authority and responsibility. International courts must decide whether, and how, to classify specific acts of 'violence' under legal categories recognized as criminally relevant, such as that of genocide. But these acts of classification are neither simple nor immediate because violence challenges easy categorization. It 'can be everything and nothing; legitimate or illegitimate; visible or invisible; necessary or useless; senseless and gratuitous or utterly rational and strategic' (2003, 2).

To speak of mafia 'violence' therefore means – simply by choosing this word – having already associated the practices and ways of acting indicative of that complex institution which is the mafia with a semantic surplus value and a moral interpretation (see, e.g., Massari and Martone 2018). The mafia is, indeed, 'a complete social fact', as Franchetti (1993 [1877]) acutely noted in an all-too-neglected passage of his classic book, which has been quite influential in contemporary literature on mafias – not for this insight, however, but rather for his definition of the mafia as an 'industry of violence'. But, if it is true, as Scheper-Hughes and Bourgois still claim, that 'violence is in the eye of the beholder' (and not inherent in the act itself), and that 'what constitutes violence is always mediated by an expressed or implicit dichotomy between legitimate/illegitimate, permissible or sanctioned acts, as when the "legitimate" violence of the militarised state is differentiated from the unruly, illicit violence of the mob or of revolutionaries' (2003, 2), then speaking about 'mafia violence' – and of mafia as an 'industry of violence', as did Franchetti in the nineteenth century and others following in the twentieth (e.g., Catanzaro 1992 [1988]; Pezzino, 1990) – may well lead those who talk about it, as well as those who hear about it, to focus on, question and problematize their perceptions, evaluations and categorizations. It might induce them to recognize that the object of analysis – 'mafia violence' – cannot be given as an immediate fact before the sociological gaze but must be constructed like any other object of analysis, also taking into account the fact that that object pre-exists the gaze of the analyst and is, so to speak, already the outcome of construction processes by social agents.

In other words, it would be a matter of recognizing that the object of this paragraph is not given to the world fully formed, but is the effect of construction processes and mechanisms that, in turn, ask to be reconstructed (also deconstructing/dismantling what others have already constructed), in order to avoid being unconscious victims of the biases and prejudices of common sense, or to that partial and interested 'uncommon' sense which is, in any case, the sense of institutions, especially state institutions. What follows are some ideas, some traces of a possible line of research on 'mafia violence', which take seriously Bourdieu's (2014) warning not to get caught up, in the analysis of the social world, in the network of categories which make up 'state thought'; this is the way of thinking that all of us, as citizens of that supposedly sovereign institution which is the state, absorb given the simple fact that we exist within a state and in a world of states, which naturalizes categories and classifications sanctioned by the state, but which are no less arbitrary than any other cultural categories or classifications.

One way to get around 'state thought' is to question what the people of the world we are studying think and believe, without blindly and uncritically accepting it. In our case, this means questioning the perspective of law enforcement and criminal investigators, and, with them, all those who act from the point of view of the state, who do not recognize the legitimacy of the mafia to exist and act, in order to expand the field of phenomena to which our object of investigation (in our case 'mafia violence') belongs as 'a case of the possible'. Indeed, the risk is that we close off the field of the possible a priori and surreptitiously, preventing us from grasping similarities and convergences so that we then end up raising something that is quite common, normal and, as such, understandable to the status of a pathological exception.

We are here dealing with the classic theme of 'sampling', not in terms of a statistical procedure but more generally the problem of the selection of case studies and units of analysis (Becker 1998). How do we choose what we need to analyse? Where do we draw the line between what is relevant and what we can leave out? One solution to the problem is that offered by the already cited Everett Hughes that sociological analysis should 'take some matter, some aspect of human life, which is highly institutionalized and is the object of much moral sanctioning, and ... treat the whole range of behavior with respect to it: the institutional norms and the deviations in various directions from the norm' (1971, 105). From this perspective, for example, as we have seen, it would not make much sense to study prostitution by isolating it from the wider social organization of sexual relations of which prostitution, as a social phenomenon, constitutes a fragment, along with marriage, de facto families, homosexual relations and the institution of celibacy itself.

Could we speak, in a similar way, of a 'field of violent relations' of which 'mafia violence' would be part, as one element in a 'range of behaviours' that includes it but is not exhausted by it? The usefulness of this concept of a 'field of violence' is twofold. On the one hand, it helps us avoid isolating mafia violence from other forms of violence that accompany it, in conditions of competition but also of convergence. On the other hand, it allows us to analytically distinguish, even within the mafia, between forms of violent action and forms of nonviolent action, which would stay out of the field as we are examining it. Thus, mafia violence would be placed together with other kinds of 'violence' to be analysed comparatively, looking for elements of continuity/overlap and elements of discontinuity/distinction. For example, what distinguishes mafia violence from the violence of other nonstate actors (such as terrorist groups, common criminals, youth gangs, etc.) and from that of the state itself (in its various institutions, from police forces to the military, prison guards and other agents invested with the power to act against the will of individuals, such as doctors and nurses)? In addition, the violent expressions of the mafia would be located within the larger system of mafia conduct, identifying the conditions under which these behaviours are translated into acts that are interpreted as violent by mafiosi themselves, thus distinguishing between acts based on the use of violence that are legitimated by the mafia's internal governing order and acts that, for the same mafia order, represent a 'deviation from the norm'. The autobiographies of *pentiti* often refer to such cases. One of the best known of these was the kidnapping and subsequent murder (by strangulation, followed by dissolution in acid) of the young teenager Giuseppe Di Matteo, killed in an attempt to silence his father Santino, a former mafioso turned police informant. Another is the murder of a six-month-old girl, Nadia, who died as a result of the bombing of Florence's Uffizi Gallery in 1993 as part of a terroristic strategy pursued at the time by some families of Cosa Nostra intent on persuading the state to change its policies of jailing mafiosi (even if there cooperation is suspected between mafia groups and political personalities interested in diverting public opinion from other political issues). In both cases, there is evidence that mafiosi felt themselves – albeit after the fact – to be out of their usual moral depth, including the traditional reference to some rules constraining the use of violence inside well-bounded categories and cases (see Lo Verso 1998; Dino 2016).

Indeed, we have to recognize that the use of violence is far from being a problematic issue for a political theory of the mafia – violence, or rather physical force, is the 'normal' and defining feature of political groups, as well as the foundation of that pathos and 'community of memories' that, according to Max Weber, characterize political bodies (1978 [1922], ch. 9). To identify mafia violence as political violence is, however, far from immediate, and makes a case for debunking more common understandings of the mafia as organized crime or even as a business specializing in a special commodity like protection – the argument Gambetta (1993) advances to make sense of mafia violence in rational terms, at the cost of a highly selective theoretical construct, elegant as well as extremely demanding in terms of assumptions and cultural – i.e. symbolic – reductivism. To reduce mafia symbolism of death and damage, as well as blood and bodily manipulation, to functional requisites of a special kind of business means to lose all the imaginative and emotional universe in which mafiosi conduct their everyday lives (e.g., Siebert 1996; Fentress 2000; Dino 2016; Puccio-Den 2019), always running the risk of being killed by competitors or captured by state agencies.

One of the implications of an epistemological stance that starts from the principle that the scientific/objective fact has to be conquered, and that the research object is not already given but must necessarily be constructed in such a way as to break with the biases and prejudices of common sense (including the common sense inscribed in the most legitimate institutions), is the recognition of the historicity of the phenomenon, its existence in time and space, with all the variations that this existence entails. A valuable contribution towards a sociology of mafia violence that fully recognizes the historicity of its object is Tilly's concept of 'repertoire', proposed in 1978 in order 'to improve on the prepolitical/political dichotomy employed by E. J. Hobsbawm and George Rudé' (1995, 28; see also Traugott 1995), a concept that would later be taken up and recontextualized by the cultural sociologist Ann Swidler (1986) in her influential revision of the concept of culture as a toolkit or repertoire of strategies. Considering manifestations of mafia violence as elements of a more general 'cultural repertoire of forms of violent action' allows us not only to order, almost catalogue, a phenomenology as rich as it is horrific – from the intimidating assault, to deliberate murder in its various forms, up to the terroristic bombing – but also to measure, so to speak, the deviations in time and space of mafia practices from other practices that are also 'violent' (or interpretable as such) but not specifically attributable to the mafia's cultural and symbolic universe. Once this repertoire has been reconstructed – possibly localizing it (for example, the repertoire of the Sicilian mafia versus that of the Calabrese *'ndrangheta* versus that of the Neapolitan camorra) and 'historicizing' it (recording the transformations of these repertoires over time) – the subsequent operation would be to classify the individual elements of these repertoires according to an analytical grid. Using, for example, the typology proposed by Bourgois (2001), we could distinguish between four types of 'mafia violence': everyday, symbolic, structural and political. In the following I will focus on the fourth type – the one that I consider to be the most important, yet also the least recognized and written about in the literature.

Unusually for a sociological work, I will work from a short text by a legal theorist – one of the most authoritative Italian jurists of the twentieth century, Costantino Mortati – extracted from a long essay published in 1973:

> Just as the elimination of the enemy presents itself as an extreme instrument for the preservation of the sovereign power held by the hegemonic class, an expression of a right of legitimate defence against attack which furthers the fundamental purposes that are centralized in it ... so the resistance to the same power, which contests its legitimacy and asserts the claim to replace that hegemony with their own group and become the state, is also coloured by the nature of the political and reproduces, in the opposite direction, the antithesis [friend/enemy] against those it addresses and which it intends to subject to its own domain. And it is this claim and purpose that differentiate the group itself from others, *for example the mafia*, that can also turn against the state. (1973, 519; my translation, emphasis added)

Mortati made this claim in the early 1970s, a decade after the establishment of the first parliamentary Antimafia Commission, but also, and above all, when public attention was focused on another form of 'violence', that of rising terrorism, left- and right-wing, which was both more visible and less comfortable for the government then in office. And it was to these people that Mortati presumably refers to when he speaks of 'groups' that resist sovereign power by advancing the 'claim to replace that hegemony with their own group and become the state', differentiating them from others that, like the mafia, 'can turn against the state' but without any pretension to replacing it. Leaving aside here the implicit stance taken by Mortati with respect to his teacher Santi

Romano (who, as a Sicilian, perhaps had no qualms about acknowledging the juridical and therefore the political autonomy of the mafia), it is significant that this argument was taken up and called into question just a little over a decade later by a Foucauldian philosopher, Pasquale Pasquino (1986), who was evidently more willing to acknowledge the same 'political character' in the mafia as in terrorist groups that Mortati had denied only a few years earlier. In the meantime, the mafia had changed its physiognomy – or rather, the state's knowledge of the mafia and public opinion had both changed, thanks to the testimony of Tommaso Buscetta and the investigative work of judges Falcone, Borsellino and others of the antimafia pool.

It is not a question here of attempting an archaeological sketch of scholarly discourse on the mafia phenomenon by starting from some little-known and decidedly contingent passages of legal and political theorists. Rather, it is a question of putting into perspective what the research on mafia – Italian mafia research in particular – assumes, in my opinion systematically, even though it is almost never explicitly stated as a postulate, axiom or assumed starting point: the criminal status of mafiosi, of their conduct, of their 'way of life'. It is a matter of recognizing and always remembering what the American criminologist and sociologist William Chambliss never tired of repeating, that 'crime is a political phenomenon and must be analysed accordingly' (1989, 183). And if we need help to remember this, if someone were to ask me to provide evidence of the political character that the mafia can have and, therefore, by logical implication, that its acting with 'violence' can take, I think the following text can make the case even more than many others that I have collected and analysed in my previous works:

> It is too simplistic for the Italian state to relegate the phenomenon of Sicily to a horde of delinquents and a gang of criminals; it is not so, we have more history than this Italian state. If I had been born two centuries ago, with the same experience as today, I would already have fought a revolution against this Italian state and I would have won; today, wellbeing, progress and globalization make the world function differently, and my methods are archaic, so I am only a deluded idealist ... When a state resorts to the most depraved tortures for revenge and, even more, to induce weaker people to become informants, tell me what kind of state it is. A state that bases its justice on informants, tell me what kind of state it is. Certainly, informants will have helped some individuals further their careers, but as an institution, the state has failed. (Messina Denaro 2008, 60–61; my translation)

The fact that the writer (in correspondence intercepted by the police with a former mayor of Castelvetrano, who ended up in prison for mafia-related crimes) is a powerful – and still on the run – mafioso like Matteo

Messina Denaro does not worry me. What emerges from this and other similar texts is an awareness by more recent generations of something whose traces, signs, 'clues' – in the sense given to these terms by cultural historian Carlo Ginzburg (1979) – can be found in various places and times in the history of the mafia, or of the Italian mafias; these are indications of a complexity of the phenomenon underlying the category of 'mafia' that mafia studies has systematically simplified, paradoxically also on the occasions when it promoted a 'complexity paradigm' (Santino 1995).

As often repeated, there is a foundational bias in the research on the mafia as it has developed over the past 150 years: a state-centred prejudice, and an intellectual prejudice. In the first case, the prejudice is what induces scholars – not only legal scholars or political scientists but, paradoxically, also sociologists – to take as a principle of perspective on and categorization of the world what Bourdieu has termed 'state thought': i.e. the system of categories and classifications on which the state apparatus is based, and which includes, to give just a few examples, the distinction between public and private, lawful and illegal, and normality and criminal deviance. It is only uncritical adherence to this 'state thinking' that can prevent the sociologist from seeing – and even from hypothesizing – the political elements that are inscribed in certain manifestations of mafia violence, thus reducing the mafia phenomenon, with a move entirely functional to the tactics and operations of the state, to the 'category' of economic crime, and the mafioso to the figure of the economic entrepreneur, albeit violent and therefore abnormal. However, there is another blind spot at the basis of mafia studies, less subtle but equally influential. There is, in the interstices of 'mafiology', a postulate, never explicitly made but whose traces continue to reappear, according to which mafiosi like the afore-mentioned Messina Denaro, Provenzano, and Riina, as well as their forerunners, their followers, their subordinates and so on, are products of a social environment, of a humanity – if it can indeed be termed such – that is fundamentally retrograde, archaic and ignorant, and, for that very reason, incompetent – a position that, upon closer inspection, presents analogies with the 'orientalist discourse' laid bare and denounced by Edward Said in a classic text (1978). I would invite readers who are unwilling to acknowledge the intellectual capacity and 'thinking' skills of so-called mafiosi to reread Antonio Gramsci's (1971) well-known passages on intellectuals – those which argue, in no uncertain terms, that all human beings are 'intellectuals', even if only a minority of them specialize in that function. The assumption that social agents are incompetent when it comes to accumulating and managing resources of power and wealth because they lack the necessary education and style that define society's elites under advanced capitalism means, once again, that we fall victim to an ethnocentric prejudice, in this case that of the 'middle class'. It means we neglect the fact that, in advanced societies, the circulation of ideas is enhanced by a media apparatus that reaches even the most distant corners and most hidden recesses of social life. Provenzano may have been eating chicory and ricotta and quoting Bible verses, but he also kept *L'azione. Tecnica di lotta anticrimine* on his bedside table, the anti-guerrilla manual of Capitano Ultimo (nickname of Sergio De Caprio, the chief *carabiniere* to have led the arrest of Riina in 1993).

7

Mafias as an Elementary Form of Politics

In the previous three chapters I have outlined the profile of a model of the mafia focused on the organization's political dimensions and implications rather than its economic or business aspects – those privileged by most current research on the mafia and other forms of organized crime. My *political anatomy* of the mafia has been articulated in three major parts, each corresponding to a chapter: Chapter 4 has dealt with the joint issues of publicness and secrecy in mafia life; Chapter 5 has examined the nature of the social exchanges and social bonds in which mafiosi are engaged and which, together, make up the social texture of the mafia social world; Chapter 6 has addressed the venerable and much debated issue of the mafia as an organization, i.e. how to categorize the mafia as a social structure and – if applicable – a formal organization, with norms, rituals and modes of communication. The Sicilian mafia (also known as 'Cosa Nostra according to insider testimony collected since the 1970s) has been the almost exclusive empirical focus of the previous chapters. My alternative interpretation can be summarized in three main points:

1. The mafia exists and performs its existence in public. Secret and mysterious as it is, with its legitimacy and legality unrecognized by the modern embodiment of public power (the state), the mafia has participated in the public sphere since its inception, even though its illicit character would imply the contrary. In fact, the mafia and mafiosi are often public characters – even when, for security reasons, they live hidden. In emphasizing the public life of mafia and mafiosi, I have made a case that the 'protection' offered by the mafioso is hardly reducible to a private good, especially when considering that privateness must not be confused with 'personalized.' Mafiosi deal with personal (i.e. *ad personam*) protection, and even perform

themselves as persons among other persons – which makes a different social and cultural universe with respect to a 'society of individuals'.

2. The protection offered by the mafia and mafiosi is not only personal, but is also offered as a gift, in Mauss's sense, rather than as a commodity. Mafiosi act not in a market of contractual exchanges, but in a universe (or field) of gift exchanges; surely, market exchange is not alien to them, but their speciality is framing their services as if they were not really bought and sold in a market but, as Mosca once suggested, generously provided as a matter of friendship.

3. Far from being assimilable to 'firms', mafia groups are better conceived, with Paoli (2003), as exemplars of fraternal organizations aimed at providing mutual help among their members – i.e. as brotherhoods. From here, we can theoretically frame the mafia as a local, historically and geographically grounded instance of a more general type of social structure, the *Bund* (usually translated in English as 'communion') which Schmalenbach proposed as a third necessary complement to the two more famous types of community and society. What the sociological construct of the *Bund* makes clear is that relationships among mafiosi are grounded on various mixtures of ascribed and achieved statuses, as well as emotionally charged though voluntarily chosen belongings, aimed at producing and supporting projects of personal empowerment and social domination. Fidelity, faithfulness and loyalty – structural features of the communion as a social type – account for both strong solidarity and betrayal as a concrete risk (and obsession). The rituals, ceremonies, norms, symbols, style and organizational forms that mafia groups are made of are not simple instruments for implementing market strategies or rational solutions to organizational dilemmas, but practical, meaningful and original enactments of socially diffused and *popular* (in the sense of folk) cultural systems with deep roots in local history, which make mafia practices and institutions understandable and familiar to local 'indigenous' people, even those extraneous to the mafia universe.

Putting these three points together, we could say that 'mafia' is the name, charged with local semantic associations that also include positive values and images (recall the original meaning-in-use of the word *mafioso* to identify something cool and cute), for systems of practices and institutions – what Mosca (1980 [1900]) aptly labelled as 'mafia spirit' – that may be enacted when the (right) people meet the (right) social conditions and opportunities. These are used in the pursuit of personal and collective projects of empowerment based on (usually) sworn commitments of mutual aid among associates (comrades, brothers, even 'friends') to offer help – in the form of aid that usually includes protection but is not limited to it – to outsiders potentially interested and/or useful for fostering, supporting and strengthening the project with both personal and material resources. This definition recognizes the place of contingency in social life (Abbott 2001; Sewell 2005): in Sicily, mafia did not exist in every moment or location, but only when social conditions and personal situations converged. For example, being a collective project, mafia activity can start only when a certain kind of people in certain numbers are available locally; still, to make the project meaningful and even appealing, certain conditions of both insecurity and wealth (in terms of various kind of resources, not necessarily money) have to be satisfied. This is what the economic theory of the mafia has analysed and even theorized as the supply and demand conditions for the emergence of the mafia as an industry of private protection (Gambetta 1993; Varese 2001). What is unsatisfying in this influential contribution to our understanding of the mafia is its reduction of what the theory calls the *core business* of the mafia to the 'production, promotion and selling of protection' – indeed, of *private* protection conceived of as a commodity. However, as the previous chapters have suggested, this may be an excessive simplification for the sake of modelling.

Refining the Model: The Political Nature of Mafia Obligation

A central, though perhaps less explicit, point in the interpretation proposed here is that the core activity of mafia groups – or what I prefer to call mafia projects – is larger than the provision (and promotion and selling) of protection, a category that has a surprisingly untheorized status in the economic theory of the mafia. Indeed, what exactly is this protection about? What does it mean 'to protect' someone or something? When can an action or service be framed as 'protection'? Tilly has alerted us, in an often-quoted passage, to the ambiguous nature of the thing behind the word, noticing that, in contemporary speech,

> the word 'protection' sounds two contrasting tones. One is comforting, the other ominous. With one tone, 'protection' calls up images of the shelter against danger provided by a powerful friend, a large insurance policy, or a sturdy roof. With the other, it evokes the racket in which a local strong man forces merchants to pay tribute in order to avoid damage – damage the strong man himself threatens to deliver. The difference, to be sure, is a matter of degree. A hell-and-damnation priest is likely to collect contributions from his parishioners only to the extent that they believe his predictions of brimstone

for infidels; our neighborhood mobster may actually be, as he claims to be, a brothel's best guarantee of operation free of police interference. Which image the word 'protection' brings to mind depends mainly on our assessment of the reality and externality of the threat. (1985, 170)

Protection becomes a source of racket when the one offering protection is the same one producing the need to be protected – by creating situations of insecurity, fear or real damage. The point, however, is that being a matter of 'assessment of the reality', it is far from easy to draw a clear-cut, objective line between a racket and a genuine protection service. The chance of simply being deceived about the reality of the menace is always with us. The major implication of this not only semantic ambivalence was, for Tilly, that concrete, historical states, as well as established modern political communities, have a formidable structural similarity to rackets,

> [t]o the extent that the threats against which a given government protects its citizens are imaginary or are consequences of its own activities ... Since governments themselves commonly simulate, stimulate, or even fabricate threats of external war and since the repressive and extractive activities of governments often constitute the largest current threats to the livelihoods of their own citizens, many governments operate in essentially the same ways as racketeers. (1985, 171)

As he immediately observes, however, '[t]here is, of course, a difference: Racketeers, by the conventional definition, operate without the sanctity of governments' (1985, 171). Gambetta's comment on this same passage is also worth noting: 'Rather than ennobling the mafia, this parallel makes us reflect on some disturbing aspects of the state' (1993, 2). I would say, on the contrary, and for symmetry, that both the mafia and the state may have both ennobling and disturbing aspects. This is, in any case, the epistemic assumption I have adopted, following Hughes's invitation to compare engineers or lawyers with thieves and prostitutes, respected professionals with deviant (or so considered under society's established conventions) practitioners. I will return to Hughes in the next section.

What I would like to add now to the proposed picture of the mafia is a better identification of what the economic theory of the mafia identifies as its core business. According to the theory, the protection that mafiosi deal with is, first of all, the protection of property rights (see Gambetta 1993; Varese 2001; Bandiera 2003). This is what puts the mafia and the state in potential competition as they 'are both agencies that deal with protection' (Varese 2001, 5). However, the protection mafiosi offer and manage as if it was a commodity (according to the theory) may be different from the protection a state can offer. First, mafiosi may protect other agents in the underworld, that is, criminals – whose goods and deeds (e.g., transactions) are by definition illegal and cannot be framed as 'property rights' in formal terms, that is, according to the state's laws. In other cases, what mafiosi offer is protection not of property rights but 'against potential or real competitors' (Varese 2001, 5) – which means offering muscular services the state would consider illicit and illegitimate. In some places, the protection said to be lacking where the mafia emerges is a very general one: a protection of social order as such. In conclusion, it seems that even for the economic theory of the mafia, 'protection' is a general category more than a specified and specifiable activity around which to build a business.

If we come back to the stories (real and fictionalized) and occasions in which mafiosi are said to act or perform on behalf of someone or give help, the notion of 'protection' takes on even more meanings. Indeed, it seems there are few social situations or transactions a mafioso considers out of his field of activity, alien to his 'professional' jurisdiction. Whatever can be done by way of social relations, personal contacts, interpersonal mediation, through polite words or brutal violence, is potentially his business. Like the ogre from the fairy tale (and the historian, according to Bloch), 'where he smells human flesh, there he finds his quarry'.

The core activity of mafiosi is indeed – as described in documents from inside the world of mafia, from nineteenth-century written statutes to oral narratives from mafiosi turned state witnesses – mutual aid or help, in a never fully specified form and for an indefinite amount of time. To enter into a mafia project means to convert oneself, until death, to a new collective identity. This identity – which mafiosi call 'men of honour' and which can be acquired only through a rite of initiation that functions, indeed, as a rite of institution (Bourdieu 1993 [1982]) administered by 'made' mafiosi – is such that, whatever the brotherhood or, better, its leader(s) may ask for, the alleged necessities of the organization must, in principle, be done. This absolute, and sworn, fidelity entitles one to what looks like the real object, or content, of the mafia obligation, at least in principle again: a general and undefined guarantee for every need the bearer of this identity may have in his life, including – because this is one of the original objectives of the pact upon which the earliest mafia associations were created – economic and even emotional assistance to one's family in case of imprisonment, as well as work opportunities and support for whatever business or trade a member may be involved in. This general, unspecified, temporally indefinite content is what makes a relation or obligation *political*. Its conceptual opposite is market exchange, the contractual relation, which works better the more the content and time of provision are specified

(Miglio 2011, 155–65). Like the gift according to Mauss and, even more, to Bourdieu, so too does Gianfranco Miglio's concept of the 'political bond' exist in a temporal dimension where nothing has to be specified *ex ante* – indeed, it is precisely the missing specification of contents and terms that forms the real foundation of the political bond, what Miglio terms political obligation and contrasts to the private, juridically enforceable, contract–exchange obligation. According to this perspective, we could say that the economic theory of the mafia misperceives political obligations as contractual relations. This is, indeed, a major point of this book.

The political dimensions of the foregoing definition of the mafia should now be apparent. First, the mafia has to do with empowerment, that is, with claims to (some) power. Second, it has to do with the creation, management and enforcement of *collective* identities (see Pizzorno 1993 on the intrinsically political nature of collective identity), which presents an argument for a veritable 'identity politics' even in the case of the mafia (quite apparent when mafiosi insist on their rights and privileges as both local notables and members of an alleged criminal elite). Third, politics is in the nature of the guarantee that mafia membership provides to its holder: an undefined, generalized, existential and, above all, temporally indefinite guarantee for life. The human cost of this guarantee for life, of course, is the concrete risk of losing it; the horizon of death in the very nature of mafia membership (from the mafia oath) implies a feature that, together with the community of memory (often linked to the memory of dead comrades), makes for *the political* body, according to Weber:

> The political community, furthermore, is one of those communities whose action includes ... coercion through jeopardy and destruction of life and freedom of movement applying to outsiders as well as to the members themselves. The individual is expected ultimately to face death in the group interest. This gives to the political community *its particular pathos and raises its enduring emotional foundations*. The community of political destiny, i.e. above all, of common political struggle of life and death, has given rise to groups with joint memories which often have had a deeper impact than the ties of merely cultural, linguistic, or ethnic community. (1978 [1922], 903; emphasis added)

To be sure, Weber is quick to point out that the political community never has been in the past, nor is it today, 'the only community in which the renunciation of life is an essential part of the shared obligations'. This is because the obligations of other groups may lead to the same extreme consequences. His examples are worth a direct quotation and a response:

To name but a few: blood vengeance on the part of kinship groups; martyrdom in religious communities; the 'code of honor' of status groups [...] of groups like the Camorra or, especially, of all groups created for the purpose of violent appropriation of the economic goods of others. From such groups the political community differs, sociologically, in only one respect, viz., *its particularly enduring and manifest existence as a well-established power over a considerable territory of land* and possibly also sea expanse. Accordingly, the differentiation between the political community on the one hand and, on the other, the groups enumerated above, becomes less clearly perceptible the further we go back in history. (1978 [1922], 903; emphasis added)

As I have already pointed out in Chapter 5, Weber could not have known then what we know now of mafia and camorra, for at least two reasons: at the time Weber was writing, mafia research was just starting, and mafia itself (and camorra as well) were still in the making. What we know of the Sicilian mafia – and the Neapolitan camorra, which has been outside our focus – since at least the post-Second World War period, is that both enjoy an enduring and manifest existence as a well-established power over a considerable territory of land. As Umberto Santino claimed in 1994, in what is possibly the first serious conceptualization of the Sicilian mafia as a 'political subject', mafiosi enjoy a 'territorial lordship' over the land they control. This lordship manifests itself in the social control of not only economic activities but also social life more generally within the claimed territorial jurisdiction, even including powers of adjudication and conflict resolution. As the previous chapters have shown, the analytical recognition of a political subjectivity of mafiosi and their organizations is just the logical implication of the precise individuation of the bonds and boundaries that are constitutive elements of their identity and mode of working. That mafiosi may be involved in official political life as providers of votes for aspiring candidates in state elections is just a consequence of their inner constitution as political subjects in themselves, even capable, as both autonomous choosers of party politicians to support in regional and national elections and as recognized interlocutors in secretly conducted negotiations (the so-called *trattativa* that allegedly occurred in 1992–3)[1] with high officials of the state, of acting as direct players in the political field allegedly monopolized by the state but de facto shared with nonstate actors like the mafia. The participation of mafia and mafiosi – typically behind the scenes, at the local or regional level but sometimes at the national one – in Italian political life is just a consequence of their more structural, immanent, political character as individual and collectively organized social agents. It does not take much imagination to make sense of this participation once mafia is recognized as another form of doing, and being, politics. But how special is the Sicilian case? It is time to extend the model, comparing it with other instances or historical cases – other terrains, as the French anthropologists would say. But what other instances, exactly? The issue at stake is how to select these cases (see Becker 1998 on 'sampling' as a major issue in the social sciences).

Testing the Model: Questions of Method

This book's aim is not just to produce another interpretation of the Sicilian mafia more attuned to its immanently political aspects; instead, I want to explore how the idea of *mafia politics* may work as a (relatively) new conceptual tool for understanding social life in situations where danger, unlawfulness, money, ambivalence and power are so intertwined as to be puzzling from a cognitive point of view, and critical, if not pathological, from a political one. That 'mafia' might be more than just a name for what Weber identified as historical singularities – in other words, that Sicily or Italy are far from being the only places where mafia exists – should be quite apparent to anyone who has read a newspaper or watched TV or film since at least the 1960s, when Joe Valachi's hearings before the US Senate were televised (reaching a not-so-average spectator like anthropologist Frederick Bailey: see Introduction). The worldwide success of *The Godfather* in 1972, after the eponymous novel, with its landmark performances by Marlon Brando, Robert de Niro and Al Pacino, made the Sicilian mafia, as well as its American offspring (called La Cosa Nostra according to Valachi), a globally enjoyable cinematic experience and the word 'mafia' a familiar label to people in almost every corner of the world. Indeed, there are very few Italian words that have enjoyed as much success as *mafia* – probably only *spaghetti*, *pizza*, *fascismo* and *ciao*.

This notwithstanding, the initial question Federico Varese asks in *The Russian Mafia* (2001, 4) is far from obvious and remains current. In any case, it makes sense for a book like this one:

> Although the starting point of this study is Sicilian history, are we entitled to search for a 'mafia' out of its original context in a faraway land such as Russia? Surely the move is controversial. For some, 'mafia' is a phenomenon typical of Sicily and such a word should be used only in reference to the Sicilian Cosa Nostra. My view is that the mafia is a species of a broader genus, organized crime, and various criminal organizations – including the American Cosa Nostra, the Japanese Yakuza, and the Hong Kong Triads – belong to it.

Following Varese, as well as many others who have emulated, or even anticipated, his steps (Gambetta 1993; Chu 2000; Hill 2003; Tzvetkova

2008; Skarbek 2011, 2014; Peng 2017; Catino 2019), a relatively easy solution would be to compare the Sicilian mafia to other well-known cases of 'organized crime', such as the camorra and 'ndrangheta (see also Paoli 2003), the American Cosa Nostra, the so-called Russian mafia, the yakuza ('the Japanese mafia'), Chinese triads, and so on. This comparative focus on nationally or ethnically based criminal organizations is a well-established research (and publishing) strategy. Take the following statement, drawn from what is possibly the most respected Western *scholarly* – as distinguished from journalistic – work on the yakuza:

> [E]xamining the available literature on organized criminal groups outside of Japan, it has become clear that the yakuza are not *sui generis*; they exhibit behaviour ... similar to that of groups comprising, inter alia, the Sicilian Mafia, the Hong Kong Triads, the Russian *vory-v-zakone*, and traditional Italian-American organized crime. As such, it is appropriate to refer to all such groups as examples of the same phenomenon ... I use the term mafia to refer to these. (Hill 2003, 1–2)

The problem with this conventional strategy is that it assumes what should be demonstrated, that is, the existence of commonalities among a predefined set of experiences of organized social life – vaguely identified as 'criminal' – without asking if and how much these commonalities extend to social forms not labelled as criminal, and therefore whether these 'criminal' organizations are the best cases to be used in comparisons if we want to understand the mafia phenomenon. Clearly, to limit our comparisons to criminal organizations implies that we have already selected one aspect, quality or attribute as the most relevant – their being criminal, that is, their *being criminalized* by one particular subject claiming the right and power to define what crime is: the state.

However, this is not our only option for doing comparative research on mafia. Tilly (1985) and Schneider and Schneider (2002) have shown what can be gained by comparing organized crime groups with apparently non-mafia institutions: the early European state, and the Al-Qaeda terrorist organization, respectively. Years earlier, Hess had also suggested a wider comparative approach as the best way to make sense of apparently unique social realities like the Sicilian mafia, focusing on what he termed 'repressive crime', 'those transgressions of law aimed at conserving, strengthening, or defending privileged positions, particularly those connected to power and property':

> The Sicilian mafia is undoubtedly the classic example of this 'repressive crime' ... [but] there are others as well. In agrarian societies similar to Sicily, I mention just the jaguncos in the Brazilian north-east, the goondas in India, the Ku Klux Klan in the American South. On the same typological basis, we

can also include illegal actions aimed at protecting the privileges of entrepreneurs in industrialized states: the use of strike-breakers against workers, cartel agreements, corruption and so on. In general, most types of crimes by people in power would be included: electoral fraud, police abuses of power, terroristic acts by organizations tied to the police (such as death squads in Brazil ...), government crimes, colonial crimes, war crimes or those committed by secret services when they have a stabilizing function in a predetermined sphere of influence. (1977, xi–xii; my translation)

I think Hess's point was well made: not so much in his categorization of these historical instances under the umbrella term of 'repressive crime', nor in his selection of relevant instances, but in the underlying epistemic strategy of not restricting the scope of comparative research along surface similarities suggested by popularized uses of the term or decisions of law enforcement. Instead, he looked for cases with some 'family likeness' according to some articulated cognitive interest. As happens now in both journalism and academic research, terms like 'organized crime', or even 'mafia', are often applied to social realities that are very distant in time and space, frequently with only vague and unexamined analogical correspondences. We could rightly question whether there are good reasons for adopting this label; indeed, we could argue that phenomena called 'criminal organizations' – and sometimes even 'mafias' – tend to be tied together only by what Wittgenstein famously termed 'family likeness'. Entities that we commonly subsume under a general term, he observed, need not have anything in common:

> They form a family the members of which have family likeness. Some of them have the same nose, others the same eyebrows and others again the same way of walking; and these likenesses overlap. The idea of a general concept being a common property of its particular instances connects up with other primitive, too simple, ideas of the structure of language. (1958, 17; see also pp. 87, 124)

Think of the notion of a 'game', which includes a whole series of different things with very different properties – from competition to strictly defined rules, from entertainment to prizes, from strategy to physical strength and so on. A game does not necessarily have to share all these traits to be a game. What makes chess a game is different from what constitutes the game of bingo. The same could be said for the twin notions of 'organized crime' and 'mafia.' Instead of looking for 'a general concept [of organized crime or mafia] being a common property of its particular instances', we could focus our attention on the family resemblance our gaze detects across various instances – a gaze that in our case would be made with a sociological eye (Hughes 1971). What a scientifically sound comparative analysis of the mafia should attempt is to search for, and explore, this 'family likeness' shared by a series of different (and differently named) historically grounded social institutions, with the qualification of 'criminal' being one of its possible attributes but not the necessary requisite for inclusion. What makes them 'resemblant' would not be their belonging to the realm of crime, nor necessarily their sharing of the label 'mafia' in media outlets, but rather the way they work and the kinds of human activities they embody. This is what we could name 'mafia politics', in honour of the Sicilian mafia, which is the historically grounded social institution whose discovery has, more than any other, created the intellectual conditions for suggesting the existence of such a 'family'.

But where exactly should we look? In his short masterpiece devoted to 'bastard institutions' (see Chapter 6), Hughes made a claim that should be precious to all social scientists, especially those devoted to studying deviance and crime. He noticed that every social phenomenon can exist in at least three states: its modal state (the normal and normative, as it were, followed by the vast majority of people), and two deviant states: the first of these, the diabolic, is the most well known; the second is the angelic. This distinction has nothing to do with value judgement but is the effect of the sociological gaze's inclusion of the common point of view of the society under investigation along with its definition of normality and deviance. Think of the family as a normal, well-established institution (leaving aside all the possible cultural and historical variations). While in some countries and some periods, prostitution and even homosexuality are considered deviations in the diabolic direction, celibacy, as backed and justified by the Roman Church and other religious institutions, would be the deviation along the angelic track (see Becker 1998, 103–8). Obviously, prostitution and celibacy exist in different forms in different places and times, and it is the scholar's objective to describe and make sense of these variations.

So, the issue at stake is, as often happens in social science, one of sampling. This problem may be easily overcome if we move away from a definition of the mafia as a *type* of organized crime (see Varese 2001, 4), as in this way the only other appropriate cases to compare would be other (already defined as such) organized crime formations whose investigation would be aimed at detecting possible 'mafia' elements. This is indeed what scholars engaged in comparative analysis of the mafia usually do – or, better, say they do, as in fact they often do much more; the comparison, more or less explicit, is also with some presumed 'normal' institutional asset like the state or capitalist corporations. In this vein, the mafia group conceived of as a company is contrasted with other supposedly normal firms – for example, those not clearly engaged in the supply of private protection through violent means. Usually, and more or less explicitly, the mafia group is also contrasted, however, with the state as both the legitimate holder of a monopoly on the exercise of violence in a given territory (according to the classic Weberian definition) and the provider of protection in its pure form, i.e. as public protection, according to protection theory. As Stergios Skaperdas puts it:

> [If the] defining economic activity of organized crime is the provision of *protection* or its more respectable variation, *security*, ... [then] the peculiarity of protection ... makes gangs and mafias less akin to firms and more similar to the traditional provider of protection, the state. In particular ... organized crime groups are more similar in their structure and economic impact to pre-modern forms of predatory states. (2001, 174)

Unfortunately, a common feature of the literature on mafia(s) is a reliance on a weak and acritical theorization of the only institution capable of identifying something as mafia: the state itself. This is the first obstacle to a better comparative approach to the mafia, an obstacle that can only be overcome by a sound and critical understanding of what states are, how they really work, and how far their actual functioning is from that prescribed by formal rules. One of the main sources of misunderstanding is the practice of assessing mafias and what they are and how they act in relation to the state not as it really works, but how it claims to work. Still, the state to be compared is not the state as a political institution in all its varieties, but the state in its *liberal and democratic* form; even more precisely, this form in its formalized and official self-description. In sum, the rough reality of the mafia is usually compared with the angelic ideal of the state – not exactly a symmetrical approach.

Tilly's provocative analysis of early European states – engaged in never-ending wars and continually demanding resources – as protection rackets not so different from organized crime is a classic investigation into the concrete functioning of the state from its birth. Gianfranco Poggi carries this further with his analysis of how the modern state developed into its liberal and democratic form:

> [T]he genesis and development of the modern state resulted largely from the strenuous efforts made by rulers ... to widen and secure their power base and to increase their own effectiveness and discretion in managing and mobilising societal resources. The continuity and earnestness of such efforts ... accounts for the ... tendency for political power to build up. This tendency, however, acts upon each of a number of autonomous and mutually competing subjects. Territorial rulers ... have to compete with magnates and with estate bodies ... Furthermore, each territorially (more or less) unified power actor must engage in the restless power struggle characteristic of the states system.

> Finally, institutions and groups deriving their identity and their interests from their control over non-political resources also seek to enlarge and secure each their own power base, and to that end seek to maintain their autonomy of the political power centre, and/or to affect its structure and its operations. (1991, 101)

This, however, is not the whole story. The enlarged, differentiated and increasingly autonomous administrative apparatus, whose creation and growth was necessary for state formation, became in turn the site of a different politics, less tied to the visible politics of the public sphere but also more protected from it, yet which constituted an increasingly significant component of the political process as such. This is the field of *bureaucratic politics*, to which we still have to add another field shielded from public monitoring and criticism: the so-called 'invisible government' made up of security agencies and other non-transparent governmental bodies that operate outside public scrutiny. This is something that liberal democratic states have in common with all other states, including authoritarian ones. Every state must be endowed

> with appropriate machinery for detecting and neutralising hidden threats to their external security ... or their internal public order ... By their very nature, the agencies established to that end must often operate covertly ... Whether and how they can do so without totally violating the principles of account-ability applicable to all public bodies is a difficult question for all liberal democracies. But if the agencies violate those principles grossly and with impunity, this makes them into 'a state within the state'. (Poggi 1991, 134)

Of course, there are many ways in which the 'real' state falls short of its ideal representation. For example, citizenship, together with legal enforcement of property rights, can be understood as a *form of closure*, a mechanism for making and managing clear distinctions between citizens and foreigners, including migrants and refugees (Metha 1990; Brubaker 1992; see also Soysal 1994). Marxist and feminist scholars have demonstrated how selective and discriminatory the formally guaranteed protection of its formally equal citizens can be in terms of class, gender and sexuality, even in liberal democratic states (e.g., Jessop 2016). Ethnicity and race are two other major grounds on which state agencies selectively organize, manage and distribute their services and protec-tions. Moreover, there is the history of Western colonial and imperial practices with its violent, racist and far from protective treatment of colonial subjects.

In sum, contrary to how they may seem from books and articles on the mafia and organized crime, states are much less generous, beneficial and benevolent in their everyday performances and in their various historical forms than criminologists, mafia scholars and political scientists claim. What about the 'state in practice' – that is, in its concrete situated operations, and in its relationships with its 'subjects turned citizens'? The ethnography of the state is now an established genre in academic research and discourse – curiously, a genre that has not been particularly appealing to mafia scholars. A good example of what can be read in this kind of studies is in the following excerpt:

> [T]he contemporary state can best be captured ... in the way that it deals with its poor and its delinquents, its immigrants and its detainees, in the manner that it administers sensitive urban neighborhoods and waiting zones at the border, correctional facilities and detention centers, in its use of practices at once opaque and spectacular, deviant, or illegal. (Fassin 2015, 3)

Taken together, ethnographic studies give concrete shape 'to what would otherwise be an abstraction ("the state")' (Gupta 1995, 378). '[T]he state as an institution', write Aradhana Sharma and Akhil Gupta (2006, 11), 'is substantiated in people's lives through the apparently banal practices of bureaucracies', such as waiting in line for a subsidy, attending a court hearing or witnessing police and other state officers break the law (see Auyero and Sobering 2019).

Although a comparison could be made between the being and the working of the (Sicilian) mafia and the Italian state, not only in terms of the latter's formal constitution and official claims, but also in its material constitution and concrete functioning since its inception in 1861 (including atrocities, colonialism, political oppression, fascism, etc.), which would contribute to a better understanding of mafia politics from both the mafia and the state perspective, this is not the path I will follow here. My objective in this concluding chapter is instead to test provisionally the main results of my investigation of the political anatomy of the Sicilian mafia against other historical cases. I will begin with a few studies of established mafias or mafia-like organizations to assess whether and to what extent the political interpretation developed with respect to the Sicilian case can shed light on and be generalized vis-à-vis other 'familiar' cases – cases that show some 'family resemblance' to the Sicilian mafia according to existing scholarship or public debate.

Given the success of the term 'mafia' and the mass media appeal of the Sicilian mafia, there is no shortage of its application to other historical and geographical phenomena. An incomplete list would include: the Archaic Greek polis; the ancient Roman republic (Hopwood 1999); Renaissance Italy; the Florence of the Medicis;[2] the early European state (Tilly 1985); countercultural drug trafficking (Schou 2010); the Hungarian post-communist state (Magyar 2016; Magyar and Vasarhelyi

2017; see also Szelenyi 2019); the Philippine state (Kreuzer 2012); the Albanian organized crime (Arsovska 2015); the Donegal mafia in Northern Ireland (Sacks 1976); Nigerian confraternities/cults and systemic corruption (Ogunbameru 1997; Eguavoen 2008; Ellis 2016; Smith 2006, 2007); Indian Mafia Raj or Goondas Raj (Ghosh 1991; Piliavsky 2015; Piliavsky and Sbriccoli 2016; Michelutti et al. 2018); Brazilian Comando Vermelho and other *favela* gangs (Leeds 1996; Arias and Rodrigues 2006; Pengalese 2008; Ferreira 2019; Fonseca 2020); Jamaican Dons (Sives 2002; Clarke 2006; Johnson and Soeters 2008; Jaffe 2012, 2013; see also Dawson 2016); the Mungiki in Kenya (Anderson 2002; Atieno 2007; Frederiksen 2010) – quite apart from the previously mentioned yakuza, triads, Russian mafia (as well as Georgian, Armenian and other Caucasus-based groups) (see Nordin and Glonti 2006; Slade 2012; Galeotti 2018). Though 'mafia' is a much used (and maybe abused) label in social studies and journalism on organized crime (see, e.g., Kelly 1986; Sterling 1990; Vaksberg 1991; Fijnaut and Paoli 2004; Finckenauer 2007; Glenny 2008; Allum and Gilmour 2011; Harding 2011; Paoli 2014; Varese 2017; dalla Chiesa 2017), not every criminal organization seems to deserve the label. For example, biker gangs such as the outlaw motorcycle clubs (or 'one percent biker clubs'), even those identified as criminal by public authorities and/or banned in certain countries, are rarely, if ever, labelled as 'mafias'.[3] The same can be said for the various 'gangs' around the world, from Los Angeles to Rio de Janeiro (see Hagedorn 2008) – seldom identified as 'mafias' even when their symbols are inspired by their more famous and ancient Sicilian counterpart.

What all these instances have in common is a 'family resemblance' to the Sicilian mafia, a resemblance that is best captured by the idea of mafia politics. In the previous chapters the Sicilian case has offered empirical support to my argument. This chapter gives further substance to the point by collecting evidence across a series of historical and ethnographic cases. It is not really a comparison, or at least not a systematic one: it is more an essay on the etymological meaning of the term, an attempt to support the proposed reading of the mafia as going beyond the Sicilian case. The issue at stake is: to what extent might the claim about the immanent political nature of the Sicilian mafia we have been exploring work for other instances of organized crime or even political life? A full testing of the model would require another book, but some first elements of comparison can be advanced here as indications for further, more in-depth investigations.

Testing the Model: Six Tracks for Future Research

I will limit my exploration to a small sample of cases: the Russian mafi(y) a, Japanese yakuza and the Chinese mafia, especially triads. The reason for this selection is quite simple: they are cases to which the economic theory of the mafia has been applied (respectively, Varese 2001; Hill 2003; Chu 2000).[4] I add to these organized crime exemplars three other cases, drawn from political history and political anthropology: the ancient Greek polis as reinterpreted by historians (see van Wees 1999, 2001); the so-called 'Mafia Raj' in postcolonial India, the focus of recent media coverage and academic research (e.g., Michelutti et al. 2018); and the US Congress, as portrayed by J. McIver Weatherford in *Tribes on the Hill* (1981), where Congressmen acting as Godfather-like politicians account for much of what passes for political life in this influential and highly legitimated *state* body. Two criteria have guided this selection: the availability of authoritative sources of information and, when possible, interpretation and diversity across time and space.

Was there already 'mafia' in ancient Mediterranean civilizations?
According to Hans van Wees, the answer should be 'yes'. In his view, the aristocratic families of early Greece had something in common with the mafia families in Sicily (and later the US): 'they accumulated wealth by violent, deceitful, and otherwise illegitimate means', noting that Solon himself condemned them for stealing indiscriminately from the public (1999, 1). Van Wees bases his analogy between the mafia and the polis ruled by aristocratic families on the fact that both controlled agricultural areas, used force to acquire resources, exploited workers and destabilized communities. In both, power was held by the leading local families, and their oppressive regimes tended to be portrayed in a highly flattering light. Mafiosi often justify their actions as inspired by noble motives, even self-sacrifice for the good of others; indeed, they have not only used their power for purely one-sided exploitation but also provided mediation and conflict resolution in the absence of government action. Some, like Giuseppe Genco Russo, tried to live up to their self-image, becoming widely and genuinely respected figures. And if a mafioso is a hero in his own eyes, and can be a hero even in the eyes of others, could it be that the heroic princes of Homer's *Iliad* and *Odyssey* are *ante litteram* mafiosi? Their power, too, is presented as legitimate because they put their wisdom and lives at the disposal of others, maintaining law and order and defending their communities from external enemies.

If the mafia analogy casts 'a bleak new light on the history of Archaic Greece' by helping 'make sense of the forms of oppression alluded to by ancient sources, and to explain what caused the crises which led to *coup d'état* by tyrants all over Greece, to calls for the redistribution of land in Sparta, and to the reforms of Solon in Athens' (van Wees 1999, 1), for mafia scholars the analogy suggests that what is often seen as criminal conduct has roots in patterns of action and discourse embedded in ancient cultural traditions of political life in the Mediterranean world (see Volkov, 1999).

What may look like an exotic world of honourable warriors and stolen queens may actually consist of deeply embedded cultural structures that give sense and meaning to otherwise 'criminal' practices from the perspective of the underworld. The close links between collective crime and political structures were noted in antiquity by St Augustine in *City of God* (*c.* 426 AD): 'What are states but large bandit bands, and what are bandit bands but small states?' The issue, still latent in much political theory today, was more prominent when state-building was in its fragile infancy. Historians have shown how the earliest polities were communities centred on violent nobles and their followers – acting as godfathers and mafiosi in van Wees's powerful image.

Moreover, the foundational role of gift-giving in Archaic Greece has been well-known since the publication of Moses Finley's *The World of Odysseus* (1978 [1954]). Ian Morris (1986) has investigated the relations between gifts and commodities in ancient Greece, while Paul Veyne (1992 [1976]) has focused on gift-giving by the wealthy to the community as a political practice (see also Zurbach 2010). Marc Domingo Gygax (2013, 45–6) notes that 'there was little ambiguity about the fact that gifts required gifts, and not just any gifts but equivalent gifts, that is gifts that ... represented equivalent acts of generosity and solidarity'. Even in Archaic Greece, gifts could be used for bribery, but not all gifts were bribes, and some were clearly seen as 'good', even sponsored and sanctioned by the polis as a political community because it fostered stability: 'Both the sensation of having been compensated and the impression of being indebted promoted acceptance of the status quo and were important elements in the strategies of domination adopted by the archaic aristocracy. In the archaic polis we thus find the most obvious route to domination through gifts' (2013, 47). How much gift-giving circulated from people in power to the powerless, and how it could be appropriated in projects of social and political mobility, are questions that would arise from an analysis of these archaic societies from the view of mafia politics.

Secret societies, triads, and the mafia in China

What makes the ancient Greek case interesting is its geographical and cultural closeness to the Sicilian one (after all, Sicily was an ancient

Greek colony). But they are also very distant in time. Temporally closer, but much more distant in space, is China.

'Chinese mafia' is an umbrella term widely used in mass media and criminological research (e.g., Chu 2000; Finckenauer 2007; Peng 2017) that covers various phenomena: urban gangs, tongs (Chinese immigrant organizations), drug and human trafficking networks, and triads, regarded as the epitome of Chinese-style mafia. Triads were formed around the seventeenth or eighteenth century from a long tradition of religious secret societies (see Blythe 1969; Chesneaux 1971; Davis 1977; Murray 1994; Ownby 1995) as 'mutual-aid organizations' (Cai 1988, 42). Triads are based on a blood oath – with an organizational model and mission very similar to that of the Sicilian mafia. The sworn bond at the core of this social formation though, as Lee McIsaac (2000) notes, commits them less to brotherhood than to the 'common purpose' (*tong zhi*) or 'shared heart' (*tong xin*) of friends. Indeed, these oaths foster relationships in which junior men share equally in a common relationship of loyalty to a patron, or 'elder brother'; in short, they have political overtones.

These bonds provided leadership opportunities, power and perquisites for the few, and *protection* for the many, especially vulnerable migrants. Codes of conduct were accompanied by elaborate rituals and mythologies, but these bonds were also fragile, easily quashed by a leader's seizure or co-opted for other goals. Thus we have several elements confirming the model: sworn brotherhood, religious ritualism (see ter Haar 1998), a political meaning of the bonds, a political objective.

Triads operate as separate clans based upon kinship and ancestral ties to the founders' birth village; they share a hierarchical structure, but operate independently (Booth, 1999). Historically, triad activity has been concentrated in coastal areas with busy ports and ample opportunities for illicit business activity (Booth, 1999). Today triads are most active in Hong Kong (Lo and Kwok 2014) and, following in Gambetta's footsteps, Chu (2000) has examined how triads there supply protection to businesspeople in legal, illegal and international markets, finding that members sometimes perform two roles – protector and entrepreneur – at the same time, investing protection money in their businesses.

There is a split in the literature between those who focus on secret societies as popular religious and political organizations (Davis 1977; Cai 1984, 1988; Murray 1994; Ownby 1995; Martin 1996; ter Haar 1998), and those who analyse them as organized criminal groups (Lo 1993, 2010; Chu 2000; Chen 2005; Peng 2017; Varese 2017; Catino 2019). The two worlds, however, are one and the same, seen from two different perspectives – with the difference that most research on criminal(ized) triads focuses on Hong Kong, with the implication that much in these sources is mediated by the foreign gaze of a colonizing state. As Diane H. Murray explains, 'over the past century the origins question has been closely intertwined with various political struggles' (1994, 116), and this politicization also influences criminological approaches. As a Chinese sociologist has noted:

> The dominance of Gambetta's theory ... has meant that much of the empirical work produced in other countries ... has focused on testing and reproducing Gambetta's concepts ... The perception of 'global mafia' encouraged existing studies to limit their focus to examining the similarities of the mafia phenomenon in different countries or areas rather than focusing on identifying and explaining differences. This seriously undermines local meanings and understandings of the mafia. (Peng 2017, 10)

Like any other mafia, the triads must be understood within their particular culture, incorporating historical and political analysis. As Mark Granovetter (1985) has argued, economic action is embedded in ongoing systems of social relations, and Peng (2017) has verified this in China, where economic behaviour is embedded in a particular social structural context – a *guanxi* network – rather than dictated by purely economic considerations. According to Peng:

> *Guanxi* is an informal institution which complements ... the formal legal system in China. In fieldwork, *guanxi* ... was spontaneously identified by most interviewees as an important mechanism that protects their rights, facilitates transactions, and guarantees the quality of services. From this perspective, the practice of *guanxi* benefits all society. However, the negative consequences of *guanxi* practice cannot be ignored. Certain kinds of *guanxi* practice are closely associated with corrupt behaviour ... merg[ing] with 'patterns of patron–client relationship' where the *guanxi* principles of reciprocity and *mianzi* (face) violate bureaucratic norms and undermine the rule of law. (2017, 13)

Seen from this perspective, *guanxi* is indeed 'a Chinese version of social capital' (Peng 2017, 13; see also Smart 1993; Lo 2010); seen from another, however, *guanxi* is a Chinese version of gift-giving (Yang 1994; Kipnis 1996; see also Qi 2013). *Guanxi* implies dyadic relationships between individuals in which each can make *unlimited* demands on the other (Pye 1992) and is composed of interpersonal links implying a continued exchange of favours; it differs from friendship and simple interpersonal relationships by including reciprocal obligations to respond to requests for assistance (Luo 2000). This reciprocity is binding and *indefinite in time*. *Guanxi* networks are transferable, reciprocal, intangible and utilitarian (Park and Luo 2001). There is enough, it seems, to explore the *political meaning* of *guanxi*, looking for what this cultural practice does not only to interpersonal networking, but even to secret societies and Chinese style 'organized crime'. What this exploration would presumably find is a strong motive for going 'beyond social capital' (Lo 2010), looking for those political dimensions of triad social life that are implicit, among other features, in their long tradition of supporting nationalist policies.

Sicily as the future of Russia, again

The fall of the Soviet regime opened the way for crime to flourish rapidly. It started with economic liberalization in 1987, as many of those invited to go into private business were those who would later be dubbed 'racketeers' and 'bandits' and who, within a few years, had organized crime and *mafiya* (Vaksberg 1991; Handelman 1995; Galeotti 2018). Various theories have tried to explain this aspect of the post-Soviet transition, but Gambetta's (1993) economic theory of the mafia has come to dominate along with Varese's studies of Russia (1994, 2001), starting from his curiously titled article, 'Is Sicily the future of Russia?'.

Varese argued that the development of property rights in Russia's economic transition was the key to the birth of what is known as the 'Russian mafia'. As in Sicily, the economic transition brought 'a dramatic increase in the number of property owners and in transactions among individuals with property rights'; however, the post-Soviet government failed to establish 'a system of clearly defined property rights, a swift and effective court system, and a credible police that deters crime' (2001, 1). As a result, the Russian mafia emerged to supply private protection for both legal and illegal markets. One important group that emerged, with origins in Soviet prison camps, was the *Vory v zakone*, whose highly selective membership, initiation rituals and symbols (in tattoos) spread throughout the Gulag system, later opening to non-prisoners in the 1980s.

In the 1990s, territorially based groups appeared, with elaborate hierarchical structures and the capacity to deploy violence. Still, the traditions of the *Vory* have not disappeared, since 'their rich apparatus of rituals, rules of interaction, and mythology is being used in the new environment' (Varese, 2001, 177). The *Vory* rituals mark the ascendance of powerful gang leaders to the 'governing body' of the biggest criminal groups. Contrary to the Sicilian mafia, initiation is reserved for leaders rather than ordinary members. It is a marker of quality and commitment and evokes – in the eyes of other criminals – an honourable and distinguished tradition.

In sum, the Russian mafia is not a single crime group. Each group is organized hierarchically and has its own army of enforcers. Some groups have succeeded in forging common trademarks derived from the rich baggage of *Vory v zakone* norms and rules, and the marks of the *Vory* are shared across different crime groups, though each enjoys a high degree of independence – which Varese notes is quite similar to the Sicilian mafia's organization (2001, 188).

Informed by the Sicilian case, as interpreted by Gambetta, this was the model of the Russian mafia developed by Varese. It resonated with the model set forth by Vadim Volkov (1999, 2002) of 'violent entrepreneurship' in both the Russian mafia and its new capitalism. What for Varese (and Gambetta) was just a requisite for the functioning of an industry (of private protection), for Volkov was what makes the Russian underworld an integral part of the 'politics of state formation'.

Looking through the literature, it is apparent that what makes these Russian groups 'mafia' is the legacy of the social institution of the *Vory v zakone* – the so-called 'thieves with a code of honour'. In fact, it is this cultural system from which something like a Russian mafia takes meaning. The model proposed here sees *Vory v zakone* as something like a prison-born 'ruling class' – in Mosca's (1939 [1896]) sense of a 'political class'. Its members are famous for their tattoos and for speaking their own language, for following well-defined rules that regulate interaction among members and between *Vory* and outsiders, and, most importantly, for a ritual-marked entry into the brotherhood. 'Made' – i.e. formally affiliated – members who broke the rules were summoned to a tribunal where their crimes were discussed and, if they were found guilty, a sentence would be passed on behalf of the society as a whole, not of the wronged individual.

While this is in many ways reminiscent of the Sicilian mafia, the organizational structure is more horizontal than vertical, though with a clear progression in rank. Varese sees them as a coalition of criminal leaders, each controlling a sector, but allied with each other; Caroline Humphrey (2002), on the other hand, sees them not as an illegal network, but as a world apart with distinct, fraternity-based groups rather than networks. Her argument is that 'the rackets are not only private suppliers of protection, nor simply ad hoc usurpers of state functions, but culturally distinctive groupings that use what we might call techniques of predation and patronage evolved from historically earlier Soviet contexts' (2002, 101). I would agree that a sociological analysis of these groups requires an acknowledgement of a different, non-Western, definition of 'the state' as well as the 'rule of law' (see also Shelley 1995; Nordin and Glonti 2006).

What Varese undervalues is precisely what makes a case for the conflation of mafia with politics,[5] including the fact that the genealogy of the Russian mafias has deep roots in social and political configurations predating the economic transition. Was Soviet economic planning analogous to the (Sicilian) feudal system? Indeed, a feudal system existed in Russia as well, destroyed not by the 1917 revolution, but by nineteenth-century czarist reforms that abolished slavery and serfdom and made private property available to peasants. Clearly, planning and feudalism are two different regimes of production management, and even of property regulation, as feudalism was a regime of landholding that was both private and public.

An interesting figure to explore in the development of mafias in the ex-Soviet states is the *tolkachi*, employees whose role was to use informal connections to help managers meet or manipulate targets imposed by the central economic plan. The *tolkachi* were premier practitioners of *blat*, identified by Ledeneva (1998) as 'an economy of favours' that, in Soviet vernacular, embraced (1) vertical patterns such as protection and patronage; (2) horizontal, or reciprocal, deals; (3) go-between practices and self-serving brokerage; (4) exchanges of favours and access to resources associated with family, friendship and other relationships; and (5) patterns of sociability such as mutual help and information exchange. By the 1980s, *blat* favours had become so ubiquitous that it was difficult for people to distinguish between them and friendship: friends were meant to help out. *Blat* is, however, just one recent instance of a long-lasting tradition of negotiated reciprocity that Russians invented and adopted for transactions conducted through unofficial channels (Lovell et al. 2000; for variants in other post-Soviet countries, see also Wanner 2005, Werner 2002; Polese 2008). If Sicily had to be the future of Russia, perhaps it was because their popular cultures of politics and survival had long developed along parallel lines.

Yakuza, the Japanese mafia
Believed to be one of the most ancient forms of mafia-like organizations (Kaplan and Dubro 1993 [1986]; Glenny 2008), yakuza is an outlier; members enjoy a semi-public, almost legitimate status, though a (soft) law against them was enacted in 1992 (Gragert 1997; Whiting 1999). This has created some doubt about their status as a truly criminal organization. In my view, this is an important point in reconsidering yakuza as a veritable political institution, together with a stronger sensitivity towards Japanese ethos and culture (for an epistemological argument about studying social life in Japan according to its cultural *emics*, see Hamaguchi 1985).

It is widely held that most modern yakuza groups emerged from two social categories originating in the mid-Edo period: *tekiya*, itinerant peddlers, and *bakuto*, who were involved in gambling. *Tekiya* ranked as one of the lowest social groups and, as they formed organizations of their own, took over certain commercial duties, such as the allocation and security of stalls. Eventually, they were formally recognized and *oyabun* (leaders) were appointed as supervisors and granted near-samurai status. *Bakuto* had even lower social standing, as gambling was illegal, and many ran loansharking businesses and ran their own security. Much of the undesirable image of the yakuza originates from *bakuto*, an effect of the social composition of this category, made up of misfits and delinquents who joined in order to extort customers in local markets by selling fake or shoddy goods. The roots of these early yakuza groups survive today in initiation ceremonies, which incorporate both *tekiya* and *bakuto* rituals, as well as in the popular, if not underclass, social origins of its members (around 70 per cent being *burakumin*, heirs of a sort of untouchable caste; see Amos 2011). Although the modern yakuza has diversified, some gangs still identify with one group or the other – for example, a gang whose primary source of income is illegal gambling may refer to themselves as *bakuto*.

Yakuza adopted the traditional Japanese structure of the *oyabun-kobun*, a family structure-based hierarchy in which a *kobun* (foster child) owes allegiance to an *oyabun* (foster parent) in a ritually formalized relationship. Clearly, this is an area of human affairs where deep personal feelings and instrumental interests intersect, the area where *Bund* emerges. A code of conduct called *jingi* developed, in which loyalty and respect were key elements of a whole way of life and formal greetings capable of establishing yakuza authenticity were learned (Hill 2003). While *jingi* has fallen out of use of late, replaced by business cards and badges, other traditional marks of identification have persisted, in particular tattoos and *yubitsume*, finger amputation as punishment/atonement.

Peter Hill (2003), applying the economic theory of the mafia to Japan, noted that yakuza developed into veritable mafias only after the Second World War, when defeat, crisis of the state and the rise of the black market created new opportunities for traditional criminal groups. Later, the collapse of an economic bubble, as well as inefficient enforcement and dispute resolution mechanisms, created conditions for the establishment of criminal protection associations. Milhaupt and West (2000) argue that inefficient formal legal structures also led to the emergence of groups providing property protection services.

However, I would suggest this reading suffers from a series of weaknesses. First, yakuza's presence as an openly existing and operating, semi-legal organization makes it difficult (even more than the Sicilian mafia) to restrict it to the 'private sphere'. Certainly, the protection offered by yakuza groups is sold as if it were private protection, but there is unquestionably a yakuza *public* sphere, where members not only display their tattoos and amputated fingers and their offices exhibit their names and emblems, but where an in-house news organization circulates stories written and edited by yakuza-journalists (Baradel and Bortolussi, 2020). Above all, it is the nature of the organization's elementary structures of social relations dealing with protection that – like the Sicilian mafia – makes the analogy with the firm forced and misleading.

Its rich symbolic, ritual and mythological repertoire makes the yakuza world a natural laboratory for testing models of power, loyalty, friendship, alliance and betrayal – key ingredients constituting the world of politics. Gift-giving practices also feature prominently for yakuza, linking it to the conceptual frame proposed in Chapter 5 (see, e.g., Raz 1992). There is a broad culture of gift-giving, reciprocity and obligation, which makes what might look like 'corruption' seem normal and go almost unnoticed as there are many ceremonial institutions, known as *girikake* (see Hill 2003, 77–9), where bonds are established, fostered and strengthened through gifts and donations. In the yakuza, gift-giving in the form of massive donations to entire populations is one way it claims its own existence as a public system of assistance and, by implication, protection. For example, yakuza is well known for being one of the most responsive forces on the ground following earthquakes (see Adelstein 2017).

Add to this the fact that the history of the state–yakuza relationship shows an 'unambiguous symbiotic pattern' in which the boundaries between them have often been blurred: as Hill notes, the links between the yakuza and politicians are well-known due to the 'extraordinary degree to which these links were openly displayed … the links were in fact so close as to make it impossible to differentiate between the authorities and gangsters' (2003, 53). It is no surprise, then, that the state figures so prominently in Hill's book – much more than in either Gambetta's or Varese's. As Eiko Maruko Siniawer observes, the intimate historical connection between criminal violence and the state in Japan persisted even as Japan became a modern democracy, to the point that 'it could be suggested that they were not entirely dissimilar entities [....] they had to juggle their acts of illegitimate violence with the need to be endowed with some sense of legitimacy in order to operate. In these respects, states might not be a world away from organized criminal groups' (2012, 635; see also Siniawer 2008).

Is India the future of Sicily?

In South Asia, the Sicilian words 'mafia' and 'mafioso' are increasingly used by media and in everyday vernacular, as well as in academic contexts in the growing literature on Mafia Raj – a new expression replacing *Goonda Raj* (literally, thug rule: see Berenschot 2011). In its South Asian usage, the term 'mafia' usually refers to organized crime in general and has been featured in Bollywood crime film titles (see, e.g.,

Ghosh 1991). Most commonly, though, it refers to businesses seeking to monopolize trades through extra-legal and violent methods, and, still more specifically, to various political protection schemes. It is this intertwining of violence, business and politics that is signified by mafia or Mafia Raj. As Michelutti et al. explain, it became popular in India after 'a government report detailing ... [a] nexus between politicians, the bureaucracy, and mafia organizations ... these organizations had acquired enough political patronage and 'muscle and money power' to 'operate with impunity' and to run 'a parallel government, pushing the state apparatus into irrelevance' (2018, 5).

Mafia Raj has to do with both the legacy of colonialism and the restructuring of the caste system that accompanied the postcolonial democratisation process (Lal 1995; Wagner 2007; Kumar 2014; Schwarz 2010). As Jeffrey Witsoe observed with reference to Bihar, where it is very prominent,

> [I]mportant mafia figures are elected representatives of the state assembly or ... parliament ... elected office and the domain of criminality – popularly referred to with the word mafia – are often embodied in the same individuals ... The official work of a member of the assembly and criminal activities were being conducted simultaneously. (2011, 74)

Michelutti et al. (2018) have described in detail a series of ethnographic portraits of these mafia figures 'who make themselves respected'. By asserting personal mastery and living among common people, they are often imagined as possessing quasi-magical powers and charismatic authority. Contemporary media participate in this process of mytho-poesis, building on the romantic and iconic portrayals of outlaws as figures of popular resistance (Hobsbawm 1959). In South Asia, strongmen are all too often feared and loved, and have long been an integral part of political landscapes. This is hardly 'mafia' as we know it, because things change when wrongdoers, instead of being fugitives, overlap with the state, becoming what mafia scholars have termed 'violent entrepreneurs', individuals who use private (and state) force as a means of social control and economic accumulation.

What exactly 'private' and 'state' mean when 'gangster politicians have increasingly become popular models of authority and public conduct' (Michelutti et al. 2018, 3) is not that easy to assess. Referred to by terms like goonda, dabang, 'mafia don' and 'Godfather', these individuals have become an integral part of everyday social, political and economic life, exerting their power in local fiefdoms built by manipulating capitalist enterprise and electoral politics through systematic corruption and violence (see also Michelutti 2010; Piliavsky and Sbriccoli 2016).

Partha Chatterjee's (2004) Gramscian distinction between an elite-inhabited civil society and a 'political society' can help make sense of this 'criminalization of politics'; political society is where real interactions between most people and state institutions occur, and where a variety of social forms and practices may be found, including illegal networks and mafia, though, as Michelutti et al. (2018) observe, there is no single, well-defined mafia in India but, rather, various mafia-like systems that can differ significantly from the Sicilian mafia.

The mechanism at work seems to be the following: while for subaltern castes violence and corruption are a means for entering into politics, for upper castes they are a means for preserving their domination. For the former, being able to corrupt and be charged with corruption is a sign of power whose legitimacy does not lie in law but in real politics (Witsoe 2011). For both groups, what Michelutti et al. call 'the art of bossing' has become a way of organizing politics. As 'the performance of personal sovereignty', bossing 'requires a capacity for violence and for making money, repeated acts of give and take, figurations and mythologies … these ingredients are put together, joined, mixed, and packaged' to bring 'political-economic authority into existence' (2018, 8). This is a concept that could shed light on other organized crime boss-exemplars whose projects and visions, as well as success in creating authority, are too often forgotten by researchers.

In India there is also an equivalent of *blat* and *guanxi* (Dunlap 2018, 96–9). Here, the age-old practice of facilitating business by exchanging favours is referred to as *jaan-pehchaan*, (see Batjargal 2007). Obviously, while this practice may account for mechanisms of bond creation and loyalty of the gift-giving type, the spread of violence intrinsic to Mafia Raj is only partially attributable to the violent implications of the gift. However, when we recognize that even Mafia Raj belongs to the wider species of politics, violence loses its pathological aspect and the question changes from 'Why violence?' to 'Why so much violence?', and 'Why exactly in these forms?'

What the Indian case signals is the proliferation of mafia-like practices and imagery beyond traditionally defined organized crime and mafias. The notion of Mafia Raj – the 'rule of the mafia' – suggests, however, that something more than organized crime is at stake. There is a strong temptation to claim that in contemporary India we can explore mafia politics in its most visible form. Is India perhaps the future of Sicily?

Looking for the mafia in the US Congress

India is surely exceptional for having criminals in its elective bodies, but every exception has its rule, so long as we are prepared to look for it. It is perhaps surprising that Varese, proponent of the economic theory of the mafia, could write that mafiosi, in some of their duties and practices, resemble politicians like US senators more than they do CEOs (Varese 2011, 191). Readers may recall a quotation from *The Godfather* in which Michael Corleone compares his father to a member of Congress, while Kay insists he must be joking as congressmen work for the nation and not for a family, to which Michael replies that she is naive. In the early 1970s, this parallel might have seemed more of a joke than an illuminating comparison. But history has a way of exceeding our imagination, and since that time many alleged mafiosi have entered governments across the globe.

Pablo Escobar was elected to the Colombian Parliament in 1982. In Georgia, the *vor* Jaba Ioseliani was elected to Parliament in 1992, serving on the Military Council in power at that time, and then became a powerful figure in Eduard Shevardnadze's government. He was later awarded a formal government position to enforce a state of emergency, giving him almost unlimited powers to impose a repressive regime widely criticized by human rights organizations.

In Italy, no one convicted of mafia involvement has been so close to both mafia and state power as Silvio Berlusconi's friend and political aid, Marcello dell'Utri, elected a Deputy in 1996 and Senator from 2001 to 2008. Rumours of his mafia association started in 1994, and in 1996 he was charged with trading favours to Cosa Nostra in exchange for votes. Nonetheless, his political career went ahead, but in 2004 he was sentenced to nine years in prison for collaborating with the mafia and, later, to another twelve years for direct participation in the *trattativa*.

Though close to Cosa Nostra, Dell'Utri was not actually a member. Salvo Lima, son of a mafioso and close associate of Giulio Andreotti, one of Italy's most powerful politicians during the reign of the Christian Democrats, probably was. Lima was killed in 1992, just before the assassination of Falcone and Borsellino, probably because he failed to politically protect Cosa Nostra, a major element of the long-lasting pact between the mafia and Christian Democrats.

Cases of mafiosi entering national institutions as both mafiosi and politicians are rare. In the Sicilian mafia, there is a rule that the mafia and the state must be kept separate, and a similar rule existed for the *Vory v zakone*, though it does not seem to hold true anymore (see Varese 2017; Galeotti 2018). In general, mafiosi are more disposed to infiltrate the local level – where the state is distant and politics can be managed according to local practices.

Given this preference for indirect relationships with the state, it may be somewhat surprising that the final test of my model of mafia politics is the US Congress. Take it as an intellectual exercise to test the model against a case in which organized crime would be excluded almost by definition. For this, I turn to the political anthropology of Weatherford (1981), a reconstruction of how the Congress works utilizing anthropological models used to make sense of politics in primitive, tribal societies.

Identifying the 'clan', a powerful senator or representative's circle of loyal followers, as the elementary political unit of the Congress, Weatherford pinpoints three types of clan-building and career-making strategies: Shamans, Warlords and Godfathers. The latter is an obvious point of departure for us: they are backroom deal-brokers, party officials, tacticians focused on party structure who maintain the balance needed for Congress to function cohesively (Weatherford 1981, 92). The political Godfather participates in every major decision while maintaining a higher level of statesmanship than the feuding Warlords, who, on the other hand, 'choose one piece of organization terrain, slowly dominate it, strengthen it, and gradually extend it outward, increasing the scope of that special area' (1981, 89). In the end, Warlords 'are the real powers of the Congress. Although each controls only a part of the whole organization, they have strategically selected every spot to maximize a particular brand of power ... they ultimately have the clans that stretch furthest' (1981, 91).

While the term 'Godfather' reminds us of the mafia, mafia politics as we have constructed it looks closer to the Warlord strategy. Or rather, the two strategies are complementary and both find exemplars among the rank and file of real mafiosi, in Sicily and elsewhere.

This is not the only insight we can draw from Weatherford's work, however. Indeed, he directly discusses the mafia as a *political* institution, some of whose peculiarities are shared by both Congress and the Supreme Court. Their common clan-like organization is unique 'to institutions that exist above or beyond the law ... The Government and the Mafia are the only major institutions in America that can exempt themselves from ... standards. It is hardly a coincidence that both institutions center on the patron-client relationship derived from and still organized as family units' (1981, 70).

This is indeed politics at its highest level, where the rule of law with all its impersonal controls is at its minimum and a pure logic of power takes over. Clearly, the Warlords and the Godfathers of the US Congress are not real mafiosi – but they are engaged in mafia politics, which shares with the real politics of state institutions all the elements that make politics what it really is, behind the façade of the state as an ideal and formal structure.

From *Mana* to *Mafia*: On the Very Idea of 'Elementary Forms of Political Life'

To conclude, let me return to a great classic in sociology, Durkheim's *The Elementary Forms of Religious Life* (2008 [1912]). Durkheim's intellectual strategy here is well known. Looking for the universal character of religious life (as a way of disclosing an enduring aspect of social life as solidarity), he proposed 'one well-made experiment', a detailed analysis of what appeared to him as the simplest well-known religion: totemism, especially in its Australian variant (though the Native North American variant was also considered as a more developed form). Of course, the very idea of totemism has been disputed and dismissed as 'illusory' by subsequent anthropologists. Lévi-Strauss's (1969 [1949]) detailed criticism of totemism, which he assimilated to 'hysteria', was in many ways devastating. However, if hysteria and totemism have been superseded by developments in the fields of psychology and anthropology, with their symptoms almost magically disappearing, mafia is still with us – with all its symptoms – more than a century and half after emerging as a *sui generis* social reality in the 1860s.

Durkheim's book, however, is more than a book on totemism. Even though it was probably already out of date when it was written, based on empirical evidence that was mostly obsolete (given W. Baldwin Spencer and Francis Gillen's investigations of Australian tribes from 1899 and 1904), the value of Durkheim's theory of religion and society (religion *as* society, indeed) has persisted. Indeed, for many contemporary scholars, it is the most important and influential of Durkheim's works and one of the heights of the sociological imagination. Durkheim never explicitly stated what he meant by 'elementary forms',[6] but he described them at length, making his case through a series of considerations, one of which is useful to us:

> Since all religions are comparable ... they all share certain essential elements. By this we do not mean only the external and visible features they all display ... The discovery of these outward signs is relatively easy, for the observation required does not go beyond the surface of things. But these external resemblances suggest deeper ones. At the basis of all systems of belief and all cults there must be a certain number of fundamental representations and ritual practices that, despite the diversity of forms they assume in the various religions, have the same objective meaning and fulfil the same functions. It is these permanent elements that constitute something eternal and human in religion; they provide the objective content of the idea that is expressed when we speak of *religion* in general. (2008 [1912], 6–7)

But how can we detect these elements? Durkheim is resolute: we must investigate *primitive religions* because

> [they] not only allow us to separate the constituent elements of religion but they also have the great advantage of helping us to explain it. Because the facts are simpler, the connection between the facts are also more apparent. The reasons people give to explain their actions to themselves have not yet been refined and rarefied by informed reflection; they are closer and more related to the motives that have actually caused those actions. (2008 [1912], 9)

And still more enlightening:

> This primary material can therefore be observed with little effort. The inessential, the secondary, the extraneous have not yet concealed the main line of development. Everything is reduced to what is indispensable, to the minimal requirements of religion. But what is indispensable is also fundamental, and therefore crucial for us to know. (2008 [1912], 8)

It is not necessary to agree with Durkheim's (soft) evolutionism. The idea is that there are social forms in which more fundamental things can be looked at more clearly because they are not yet covered by 'the inessential'. This is what we mean here by elementary forms. Instead of looking for their elements in religious life, however, we are concerned with political life (though there is a close relation between mafia and religion). The Catholic Church, with its ceremonies as well as its protection, has contributed to shaping the Sicilian mafia and its cultural legitimacy. This connection is even stronger in some African forms of mafia, Chinese triads and various Latin American mafias. We could even say that mafia has to do with religion *because* it has to do with politics. As a 'total social fact' (Mauss 1990 [1925]; see also Gofman 1998), this is unsurprising. However, it is a major argument of this book that, of all the elements comprising the mafia as a total social fact – including economics – political aspects are the most strategic and central.

Just as Durkheim saw totemism as the most elementary instance of religious life, whose analysis would allow us to grasp the basics of even more complex (and difficult to study) forms, so I suggest we should understand the mafia – what we have learned to call 'mafia' – as an elementary instance of political life. At the same time, it is worth recalling that the Sicilian mafia has been selected as our *Ur-case* only because the word *mafia* began its career in Sicily as the name of both a social (and also moral, legal, economic, political) problem and an intellectual conundrum in the second half of the nineteenth century – thus inscribed in a period of continuous Western and colonial 'discoveries' of other apparently strange and mysterious social realities, all designated with special, indigenous or native words, such as mana (Melanesian), taboo (Polynesian), potlatch (Native North American) and, of course, totem (see Santoro 2019). Indeed, mana and totem crossed paths, as a cursory reading of Durkheim's book shows. As the name for a spiritual substance capable of producing effects, mana fulfilled an important theoretical function in early anthropology as a native concept useful for capturing what makes these exotic institutions work. Thus, mafia is one of a series of native, folk concepts adopted by the cultivated vocabularies of the academic community and public authorities.

Before being an artefact of social scientists – which mafia surely is, as there are models of what it is and how to conceptualize it – mafia is a social artefact, a political artefact to put it more precisely: 'political' because the basics of human organization as a collective endeavour are at stake. Turning again to Wittgenstein, the meaning of a term is in its uses: to understand the meaning of a word, you have to observe how it is used in language games. We could say that the meaning of mafia is less in its supposed contents and more in its social uses – and there is little doubt that the social uses of the word 'mafia' are located primarily in the political sphere. This is where the word first emerged, where it developed into a major social issue in liberal Italy, where Mussolini found it and decided to fight against it, where the Allied forces found it during the invasion of Sicily, where the first governments of the new Republic of Italy cultivated their strategic relations to manage consent in the distant periphery. If there is a field in Bourdieusian terms in which the word 'mafia' has circulated in Italy since its discovery in 1863, it is the political field. The same could be said with respect to the American mafia, from its discovery among Italian immigrants in New Orleans to the Senate Select Committee investigating organized crime in the 1960s.

This elementary political character of the mafia was noticed by its first observers, though never pursued or developed. Alongi called it 'a primitive self-government', an intellectual move that unfortunately he immediately abandoned. Interestingly, Alongi (1977 [1887]; see also 1891, 1904) described a major activity of mafia groups, *abigeato* (cattle rustling), as a kind of 'big-game hunting' – an analogy that evokes famous descriptions of the organized activities through which 'man the hunter' constructed the earliest forms of political organization (Ardrey 1966, 1976; Washburn and Lancaster 1968; see also Wilson 1975).

A point I wish to recall – since the risk of being misunderstood is always high – is that I am not arguing for an equivalence of the mafia and the state. That would misunderstand my argument completely. Arguing for the political nature of the mafia is a different endeavour. The idea of the mafia as 'another state' or 'a state within a state' is an old and persistent one. But it is misleading. Suffice it to say that politics as a human sphere of action is much wider and more encompassing than 'the state' – a point long made by scholars as different as Weber, Gramsci, Schmitt and, more recently, Agamben. The state is just a historical figure of political life, a way in which humans organize their political existence. Other figures have existed and still exist beside and beyond the state, especially if we use the word *state* to identify a historically grounded political institution, and not – as anthropologists sometimes do – as the name for whatever political organization may have superseded, in some evolutionary scheme, the stage of 'what is not yet the state', call it chiefmanship, chiefdom, or the like (e.g., Claessen and Skalnik 1979; Skalnik 2004; Earle 1997). The mafia exists where the idea or ideal, if not the practice, of the state exists. Using the insight advanced by James C. Scott (2010) in his investigation of Zomia (a South Asian region with an extensive culture of opium; see, e.g., McCoy 2003; Chin 2009), we could say that the mafia is 'the art of not being the state', while making use of its resources and forms, and, obviously, changing their meanings. This point can be visualized through a series of Venn diagrams (see Figures 7.1 and 7.2).

An updated map of recognized mafia presence would cover much of the globe. Countries without indigenous mafias, such as Germany, France or Norway, often host mafia groups from other mafia-producing countries. Where the mafia's presence is not acknowledged by law enforcement, it can be recognized by scholars – such as Magyar's analysis of Viktor Orbán's Hungary as a 'Mafia state' (Magyar 2016; Magyar and Vasarhelyi 2017; Szelenyi 2019; see also Harding 2011 for Russia; Chaplin 2013 for an American case). To circulate throughout the world, crossing administrative as well as linguistic and cultural borders, the

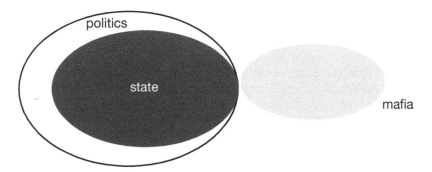

Figure 7.1: The relation between mafia, state and politics, according to mainstream scholarship

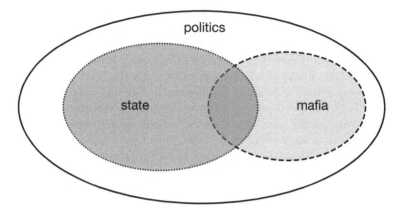

Figure 7.2: The relation between mafia, state and politics, according to this book

term 'mafia' – if we want to save this label – should refer to a set of features that appear as a pattern and recur in different times and places, easily reproduced or generated in different social and political structures. Democratic societies are particularly favourable places for the diffusion and expansion of mafias, especially when they lack the support of a strong civic culture and a deeply ingrained 'rule of law' – which means almost everywhere except where the 'rule of law' as a juridical principle (supported by institutional machinery) was originally envisioned and developed. Democratic elections are a good hunting ground for mafia projects. But in authoritarian states, a mafia-like approach to politics can circulate and find fertile soil to the point that distinguishing mafia from the state is impossible: this would be the case of the so-called 'mafia state' originally described by Naim (2012). But it is not necessary to arrive at this extreme case to have mafia politics. The traditional image of the octopus (a metaphor originally used for capitalism and then for communism) captures crucial aspects of mafias: their flexibility, intelligence and ability to infiltrate different venues with their tentacles. Interestingly, the image of the octopus is the same used by Geertz (1973) to capture the complicated nature of culture; in fact, mafias are culturally embedded political practices and organizations.

Mafias are institutional inventions made up of different cultural 'items' that are basically functionally equivalent. Some of them are genuine inventions (innovations), others are imitations and modifications of known institutions – the Sicilian mafia has been imitated by Russian criminals, and ideas have circulated among the Italian and American mafias. Honour is one of those cultural items that we find with different names in many places. It is the capital of reputation, symbolic capital in Bourdieu's terms. Violence is another of these items because the ways of using physical force to harm others vary across time and place, together with their justifications. Mutual help is another culturally based human instrument. The point is who helps whom, and how. Mafias are ways of providing help among the weak – which means people with fewer resources and less power. Mafias are 'weapons of the weak', in Scott's (1985) terms, which are so effective they can make the weak stronger than their previous masters. Protection is what makes help effective in the last resort: the best way to help someone is to protect them from any source of evil or suffering. Finally, the social bond through which help is given may also vary culturally, but all of these are, in the end, just variations of a basic structural pattern: what social theory calls *Bund*. The model of the gift is capable of capturing most of what is transacted along these bonds, and the gift is one mechanism involved in producing these bonds. This makes the central point of the economic theory of mafia – protection as a commodity – unsatisfying as it assumes what it needs to explain, that is, when the protection inscribed or embedded in the social bonds constitutive of mafias becomes merchandise, its status changes from gift to commodity. My point is that this is not how mafias normally work; it is a transformation of mafias into something different – gangsterism or simply organized crime. Even mafias may corrupt themselves and degenerate into something else.

The mafia is not the most elementary form of politics in human history. It is just the most elementary form existing and acting in the contemporary world inside and within the interstices of the state. It is not a mere surviving remnant but an institutional solution that is always possible and exists potentially everywhere. Perhaps not truly everywhere – some conditions must be satisfied to generate mafia and mafia politics, first of which is the availability of a certain level of resources (including symbolic ones) for which it is worth creating alliances, fighting, risking one's life and, ultimately, even dying – but almost everywhere.

Appendix

'Mafia Studies' as a 'Field'

The genealogical review I have offered in Chapter 2 nowhere near exhausts the research literature on mafia – which is a *huge* literature. The annual average rate of publication of books on mafia(s) in Italy alone has been about forty since the beginning of the millennium, including the bestselling text *Gomorrah*[1] and a host of minor publications that are difficult to locate even in the Italian book market. In fact, like other research programmes or scholarly endeavours, mafia studies comprise something like a *field*, in Bourdieusian terms (see Bourdieu 1996 [1992]), i.e. a social space defined by differences in status, power and capacity to reach an audience. Not all authors, nor all works, share the same amount of visibility and reputation, i.e. symbolic capital. First, we should consider the various different research streams that have contributed, and which are still contributing, to the social science literature on mafia(s): a mix of positivistic and interpretative research, published mainly in Italy and the US, authored by scholars of different nationalities (e.g., German, Dutch, British, Canadian, Chinese, etc.), with various degrees of commitment and even engagement in political life, sometimes personally related through professor/student relationships, co-authorship, friendship and even marriage. There are authors and works that are more central (or, respectively, more peripheral) than others – and considering centrality as a property measured by, for example, the number of citations, you can imagine how to locate authors in a virtual field, at least with respect to the dimension of scientific impact.[2] As we have seen elsewhere, there are schools, approaches and traditions with different levels of prestige and impact – with neoclassical economic theory, in general, being possibly more prestigious than symbolic interactionism, at least in certain influential academic environments and policymaking circles.

Indeed, we could say that, today, there is a canon – a set of frequently referenced texts that is almost compulsory to quote or enlist in bibliographic references of works on mafia. There are signs (not always consistent, to be sure) that today the dominant approach in the field of mafia studies (a field that only in part overlaps with the much larger field of organized crime research) is occupied by exponents and followers of the so-called economic theory of the mafia – with Gambetta's book on the Sicilian mafia working as a manifesto or charter. This does not mean this theory is the dominant or hegemonic one (even if there are signs that this is the case): it only means that you would do better to refer to this theory in order to position yourself and possibly advance in the field.

Table A.1: Most cited social science books on the Sicilian mafia (or US Cosa Nostra)

Title (with year of first English edition)	N. citations ISI	N. citations Scopus	Google Scholar
Gambetta 1993	470	937	2,256
Blok 1974	220	411	1,079
Reuter 1983	206	287	720
Sabetti 1984; 2002		27 (+10 new 2002 edition, with a different title)	60 (+38)
Arlacchi 1983a	145	21	524
Schneider & Schneider 1976	103	196	530
Paoli 2003	81	164	550
Varese 2010	73	163	
Hess 1973/1998 (orig. German edition, 1970)	72	75 (+51, new English edition with different title, 1998)	211 (+117)

Title (with year of first English edition)	N. citations ISI	N. citations Scopus	Google Scholar
Catanzaro 1992	43	8	162
Cressey 1969	91	196	425
Albini 1971		145	517
Smith 1990 [1975]	40	137	352

Sources: ISI Web (consulted 23–26 August 2017); Scopus; Google Scholar (consulted February 2020)

Notes

Preface

1 Other exemplars would include 'machine politics' (e.g., Merton 1949; Scott 1969), 'kinship politics' (e.g., Hammel 2005), 'clan politics' (e.g., Collins 2004; Schatz 2004; Ceccarelli 2007), 'patronal politics' (e.g., Hale 2015), 'warlord politics' (e.g., Reno 1998) or even 'chimpanzee politics' (e.g., de Waal 2007 [1982]).

Chapter 1: Mafia, Politics and Social Theory: An Introduction

1 It is worth noting that the original Italian subtitle of the bestseller *Gomorrah* (Saviano 2007) was *Viaggio nell'impero economico e nel sogno di dominio della camorra*, i.e. A journey into the camorra's economic empire and dream of domination (see Saviano 2006). In other words, the mafia's reality is business, politics is in its fantasies.

2 So ancient that its elements could be traced back to Ancient Greece: see van Wees (1999, 2001).

3 As it is clear, I see no reason to give the label *infrapolitics* to what is in fact 'politics' – for everything except the fact that it is enacted by people not formally in dominant positions.

4 A symmetry that is not different from that advanced by proponents of the Strong Program in the sociology of science in asking for the equal treatment of false beliefs and 'true' (i.e. not yet falsified) theories as research projects, or from ANT scholars (e.g., Bruno Latour, Michel Callon, John Law and others), who claim that human and nonhuman actors embedded in a network should be treated equally and described in the same terms (they call it the principle of *generalized symmetry*). The rationale for this principle is that differences between these actors should not be presupposed, as they are generated in the network of relations. See in general Latour 2005.

5 As Sinisa Malešević has recently observed: 'Although most sociologists recognize that without group solidarity it would be difficult if not

impossible to envisage the existence of social order, this topic still remains under-theorized and under-analysed' (2015, 86). Considering this lack of studies, it is not surprising mafia scholars usually miss the opportunity to address mafia(s) in what is the main point for their members, according to almost all the available witnesses and the charters of mafia and mafia-like groupings – i.e. 'group solidarity.'

6 As a counterpart to, and condition for, secrecy, communication is clearly a central ingredient of mafia life, where everything has meaning and exists through meanings and symbolic forms (Gambetta 2009). It is because of the centrality of communication that deception plays such a role in the mafia and in mafiosi's social life. Curiously, this focus on communication has been pursued not through an emphasis on the category of culture, but against it – possibly because of a narrow and outdated understanding of what culture and cultural analysis are in the social sciences.

7 In this book I reduce to a minimum the use of visual sources. They will figure more prominently in a book in progress on mafia aesthetics.

Chapter 2: The 'Mafia' in 'Mafia Studies': (Re)constructing a Sociological Object

1 In this foreword, Cressey set forth a distinction between 'organized' and 'an organization', insisting that, in Sicily, according to Hess, mafia was organized but had not developed into an organization, as it had in the US. Cressey (1972b) advanced the same distinction in a critical review of Albini (1971).

2 Jeremy Boissevain 'established his name in anthropology as one of the "Bs" – Boissevain, Barth, Bailey, Barnes, Bott – who in the 1960s and 1970s were important in superseding the structural-functionalist paradigm in British social anthropology with an actionist approach. Focusing on choice rather than constraint, on individual agency rather than structure, on manipulation and power-play rather than rules and tradition, and on dyadic relationships and ephemeral groupings rather than corporate groups, these transactionalists were instrumental in bringing the individual back into the scope of social anthropology' (Ginkel and Stengs 2006, 15).

3 Like other villages studied by anthropologists, those studied by mafia scholars are also known by pseudonyms. 'Villamaura' was, indeed, the rural town of Sambuca, in the Province of Agrigento, just a few miles from Contessa Entellina, the village studied by Blok under the name of 'Genuardo'. For the authors' retrospective assessment of their study after thirty years, see Schneider and Schneider (2011).

4 For a very critical review of Sabetti (1984), see Blok (1986, 168): 'We do not hear much about people who disagreed with the illegal regime of self-government. And Sabetti somehow conveys the idea that there were no dissenters, at least not until the 1940s and 1950s when the local mafia of Camporano was deeply involved in regional and national party politics and eventually had become another burden on the villagers.' See also Sabetti's reply, from which I draw just this brief excerpt: 'The misunderstanding

between Blok and me turns upon Blok's failure to recognize that fundamental theoretical problems exist in defining ab initio Sicilian mafia groups
as criminal associations or as creatures of landlords' (1987, 381). For
Sabetti's own assessment of his own study after thirty years, see Sabetti
(2011). For a recent assessment of the field of the anthropology of the mafia
from Blok's perspective, see Blok (2015).

Chapter 3: What is Right with the Economic Theory of the Mafia?

1 An implication of this idea is that most scholars of the mafia – at least,
   the Sicilian mafia and other Italian mafias – have in recent decades
   been *economic* sociologists or economists, when not criminologists (e.g.,
   Arlacchi, dalla Chiesa, Catanzaro, Sciarrone, etc.). In part, this has been
   a consequence of the influence of Marxism and its derivations in this
   research area since the 1950s. Clearly, a circularity is at work here: defined
   as an economic phenomenon, the mafia has appeal for scholars focused on
   the study of economic life, and this has an effect on the way the mafia is
   studied, that is, in the way it is defined and which aspects or dimensions are
   privileged.
2 I emphasize this word because one of the problems with the economic
   theory of the mafia is the selectivity of the sources it has elected as solid
   grounds on which to build. But Franchetti, as we have seen, had at least
   two visions of the mafia: a specific one (*industria di malfattori, industria del
   delitto*) and a more general one (*una maniera di essere di una data Società e
   degli individui che la compongono*): 'a *manner of being* of a certain Society
   and of the individuals which constitute it' (1993 [1877], 117). The general
   usually prevails over the specific.
3 I will come back later to the meaning of the term '*industria*' in Franchetti.
4 See, e.g., Blok (1986), Sabetti (1987), Gambetta (1993), Gambetta and
   Reuter (1995), Schneider and Schneider (2002). For an attempt to read
   these struggles in terms of a politics of value(s) in the social scientific field,
   see Santoro (2019).
5 In this structuralist tradition, we should also include, albeit with some
   caution, those studies focused more on interaction than social structures,
   insofar as they focus more on social forms (e.g., social network analysis)
   than on cultural codes.
6 Interestingly, it is Putnam, with his concept of social capital as civicness,
   whom Varese invokes, considering his research on Italian regions (Putnam
   1993) an exemplar of a 'culturalist' approach to be reversed (Varese 2010).
   Clearly, the concept of culture adopted by Varese (the same could be said
   for many other students of mafia) has little to do with the concept of culture
   used (and even abused) in cultural anthropology and cultural sociology (see,
   e.g., Swidler 1986; Zelizer 1994; Alexander 2003; Santoro and Solaroli
   2016).
7 This point would be worthy of some discussion, indeed. I will limit myself
   to a simple observation. According to the most authoritative dictionary
   of the Italian language (see *Vocabolario della Crusca*, 5th edition, 1865

ad vocem), *industria* is said to mean, first, *diligenza ingegnosa, usata per conseguire chicchessia* and, second, *sagacità, accorgimento ovvero artifizio, destrezza, o anche semplicemente Opera, Cura, posti in conseguire checchessia, ovvero in riuscire a qualche fine o intento desiderato*, also with the specification in *cattivo senso, detto di arti o modi diretti all'utile proprio o al danno altrui*. Finally, the term *industria* could also be used *per Deliberato proposito, Espressa intenzione*. In other words (and in English), the term as it was used in Italy in the second half of the nineteenth century was still distant from the modern meaning of an economic branch or sector of production; rather, it referred to the older meanings of dexterity, care, ingenious diligence and even egoistic pursuit of one's profit – in a truly moral and non-economic sense.

8   It is possible to draw a graphical representation, a diagram – if not a 'nomological theoretical network' (Cronbach and Meehl 1955) – of the model by means of its constructs and their connections. For a simulation model whose structure had been derived partly from ETM (read as a contribution to a model of 'protection rackets'), see Nardin et al. (2016).

9   This segment of the economic theory has to be taken with some caution: 'The property rights theory of mafia emergence remains the most convincing perspective on the origins of mafias. *Yet it has also proved to be a special case.* Not all mafias have developed during times of transition to the market as in Sicily and Japan in the nineteenth century and Russia at the end of the twentieth. Mafias may well emerge within functioning market economies, and for reasons other than to ensure the protection of property rights' (Varese 2010, 194–5; emphasis added).

10 Indeed, Landesco's study remained virtually unknown for a long time, and references to this study are still very rare in the literature on the mafia. It is indeed not referred to in Gambetta (1993), nor in Gambetta and Reuter (1995), or in Varese (2010). On Landesco's study, researched under the supervision of both Robert E. Park and Ernest Burgess, see Yeager (2013).

11 Filippo Sabetti is usually forgotten in writings about ETM; however he is strategically referred to, even quoted, in Varese (2014).

12 I freely paraphrase here from Shortland and Varese (2014).

13 See Shortland and Varese (2014, 742), with references to Lane (1958), Nozick (1974), Tilly (1985), Gambetta (1993), Olson (1993), Varese (2010, 2014), as well as Machiavelli's *The Prince* (1532) and Hobbes's *Leviathan* (1651) as intellectual ancestors.

14 Paoli has insisted on the implicit functionalism of Gambetta's theory as a major fault. Personally, I am not inclined either to underline this aspect of the theory, or to reject functionalism as a defective element of a theory. Functional explanations are a kind of explanation available to scientists, social as well as natural. On this, see Stinchcombe (1968).

15 Clearly inspired by Charles Wright Mills (1959), who famously labelled Lazarsfeld's brand of social research as 'abstract empiricism'. Of course, economism is, by nature, abstract, but, as always, measures can make a difference.

16 But the beginnings of transplantation predate, even by decades, the discovery of mafia presence in places 'not traditionally' home to it, such as Sicily, Calabria and Campania (Naples and the local area) in Italy. On a case of planned transplantation in Apulia, a region of southern Italy originally without mafia presence, see Massari (1998).

17 To be sure, supporters of the theory have made efforts to accommodate the apparently contrary empirical evidence within the original model. One of Varese's (2011) conclusions, for example, is that the supply of protection (by mafia groups) in itself is not sufficient for mafias to become entrenched in new territories, whereas a local 'demand' from sectors of the society is always present in cases of successful 'transplantation'. Building upon Varese, Campana (2011), in an empirical study – based on wiretapped conversations – of a camorra group with branches in Italy, Scotland, and the Netherlands, concludes that these mafia groups act as monopolists in the protection racket in their territory of origin, but that a protection racket is a difficult business to move or expand (in line with Reuter 1983 and Gambetta 1993). Considering the large evidence on mafia spatial movements, it is not easy to understand, however, how this could be consistent with the original tenet that the mafia is *essentially* devoted to the supply of protection.

18 We could also add references to criticisms (together with praises) of the paradigm/school of so-called 'analytical sociology' (Hedstrom 2005; see also Hedstrom and Swedberg 1996, which includes a chapter by Gambetta), which is a still larger box in which it is possible to put both ETM and PT: for exemplars of critical assessments, see Little (2012) and Gross (2009).

19 The connection will become apparent in the following chapter.

20 'Of all the activities that fall within my subject one of the most important is on the borderline of "market arrangements". That is marriage. Aside from everything else that it is, marriage in this country is a voluntary contractual arrangement between people who are free to shop around. The parties most affected are the two who make the contract. Each offers something complementary to the other, and there is expected an economical division of labor. The relationship is asymmetrical in many ways; but so are the contractual relations between people and their nursemaids, housekeepers, business partners, mountaineering guides, tutors, pilots, and income-tax accountants. There is more here than just a remote analogy with long-term bilateral exclusive-service contracts. The legal status is somewhat contractual and becoming more so; and one can imagine secular societies in which marriage would be assimilated to contract law. To refuse on sentimental or religious grounds to acknowledge this is to miss an important characteristic of getting married. But to treat it as just another private long-term reciprocal exclusive-service contract would be to miss even more important characteristics of marriage' (Schelling 2006 [1978], 35). Curiously enough, the same example – Christmas cards – is made by Lévi-Strauss (1969 [1949], ch. 5) in his classic study on systems of marriage and 'elementay forms of kinship.' We will come back to this exemplary case in the next chapter.

21 This makes Sabetti's research, I think, more relevant as a case study than Blok's (1974) which, for all its merits, has the strong limitation of being a case study of a special local case, Contessa Entellina (disguised in the book under the name of Genuardo), which is a town of Albanian roots and culture, where it is still possible to hear conversations in Arbëresh. Curiously, Blok never mentions this feature (a point made also by Sabetti (2002) in the introduction to the second edition of his study). Interestingly, this case could be a strategic one for making a comparison between the Sicilian mafia and what is nowadays known as the Albanian mafia, see Arsovska (2015). Even the Schneiders' site, Sambuca, is in some ways an outlier, as a very rare Sicilian town of solid traditions on the Left.

Chapter 4: The Public Life of Mafiosi

1 On the European genesis of the state, the standard references are Elias (1982 [1969]), Strayer (1970) and Tilly (1975). But see also Poggi (1978), Mann (1986a, 1986b), Tilly (1990) and Bourdieu (2014). For the Weberian theory of the state, see Anter (2014). An interesting issue is the relation between the rise of the mafia in Sicily and the Sicilian origins of a very early experiment in state formation, the Norman and Swabian Kingdom of Sicily (on which, see Marongiu 1964; Strayer 1964). To my knowledge, nobody has yet attempted to solve this historical puzzle.

2 For a subtle historical reading of these fuzzy concepts and their genealogical criss-crossing, see Goodman (1992, 14): 'If, as Habermas argues, the authentic public sphere developed within the private sphere; if the public sphere of the state was private in the sense that it was secretive, while the private sphere had a public face; if the institutions of the public sphere and those of private sociability were the same; then we need to start using these terms in more sensitive ways ... We need to get away from rigidly oppositional thinking that assumes two spheres or two discourses, one public and the other private.' The reference to Habermas is, of course, to his classic *The Structural Transformation of the Public Sphere* (1989 [1962]; see also Habermas 1974, with useful notes by Peter Hohendahl). Note that for Habermas the state and the public sphere do not overlap; rather, they confront one another as opponents. Habermas designates that sphere as 'public' which antiquity understood to be 'private' – i.e. the sphere of nongovernmental opinion-making. For further discussion of the category, see Calhoun (1992).

3 Santi Romano was the foremost representative of the so-called 'Italian school of public law', founded and headed between the nineteenth and twentieth centuries by the jurist and (liberal) politician Vittorio Emanuele Orlando, himself a Sicilian like his favourite pupil. Sociologists, especially Anglo-American ones, may be excused for not being familiar with the name of this important authority on twentieth-century legal thought, whose theoretical masterpiece *L'ordinamento giuridico* (1918) has finally been made available in English as *The Legal Order* (2017).

4 And recall that 'any notion of "public" or "private" makes sense only as

one element in a paired opposition – whether the contrast is being used as an analytical device to address a specific problem or being advanced as a comprehensive model of social structure. To understand what either "public" or "private" means within a given framework, we need to know with what it is being contrasted (explicitly or implicitly) and on what basis the contrast is being drawn' (Weintraub 1997, 4). On the distinction between public and private, see also Gal (2002), who uses semiotics to deconstruct it.

5 Distributive justice is the principle guiding public authority in the distribution of honours and duties. As Bobbio underlines: 'Once again it is necessary to handle all these relationships with care because the coincidence of one with another is never perfect.' Consider the family and international society: the family is a private law institution insofar as it exists within the sphere of the state, but it is at the same time an association of unequals (parents vs. children, husband vs. wife, etc.) and usually (but not always) ruled by distributive justice; international society, which is, on the contrary, an association of equals (formally) and governed by commutative justice, 'is generally attributed to the public sphere, at least *ratione subiecti*, in that the subjects of international society, states, are public entities *par excellence*' (2017 [1989], 9).

6 In the next chapters we will focus on temporality as another contextual feature for making sense of mafia social bonds.

7 This is what Pitrè sustained, famously, even in defence of a Sicilian politician, Raffaele Palizzolo, convicted of being a member of the mafia, indeed one of its *capi*, and in this capacity to have ordered the assassination of the too-honest banker and former mayor of Palermo, Emanuele Notarbartolo. On the trial and this famous court case in general, see Lupo (1993) and, with specific reference to the alleged *capomafia* Raffaele Palizzolo, Marino (2006). A very public man, Notarbartolo was the first of the *cadaveri eccellenti* ('illustrious corpses') of the mafia. Although the murder occurred in 1893, the trial was still open ten years later. The court case was the source of, or catalyst for, a variety of writings, from a journalistic chronicle to a mystery novel and sociological analysis (e.g., Mosca 1980 [1900]). For a more recent, and praised, literary rendition of the whole episode, see Vassalli (1993). See also the memories of the victim's son, originally published in 1949 and recently republished as Notarbartolo (2018).

8 Born in 1896 to a mafia family, he married a cousin with whom he had four sons, the first of whom succeeded him at the time of his death in 1961 (from natural causes). Marriage to a cousin is not that rare in the mafia world and among mafia families, and suggests the potential value of an application to the mafia of the logic behind what Lévi-Strauss (1969 [1949]) called the 'elementary forms of kinship'.

9 The symbolic relevance of this square for the public status and even authority of the mafia has been emphasized by the writer Carlo Levi, author of the praised *Christ Stopped at Eboli* (Italian original in 1945) in his introduction to Pantaleone (1962, 5–13).

10 For a repertory of some relevant historical photos, see the website created by a group of researchers from Tor Vergata University of Rome, available at http://cultiemafie.uniroma2.it/.

11 For an early sociological analysis of an early instance of this model in the US, see Landesco (1968 [1929]), who describes the funeral of mafia boss Big Jim Colosimo with all the ceremony and opulence typically reserved for royalty, with newspapers reporting more than 5,000 mourners as well as extravagant floral arrangements and members of the Chicago Opera Company playing and singing. The list of funeral attendees included judges, aldermen, local politicians, a state representative and a member of Congress, alongside gangsters, gamblers and brothel owners (Landesco 1968 [1929]). Landesco's chapter on gangster funerals reveals one of the most significant aspects of organized crime: its relationship to politics and the legitimate social world. As observed by Papachristos and Smith (2013, 9), 'like a magician revealing a not-so-well-kept secret, the funeral of Colosimo exposed the blatant intermixing of Chicago's official, i.e. public and criminal worlds'.

12 This was the case of Salvatore 'Totò' Riina, one of the biggest bosses of Cosa Nostra in the 1980s, head of the so-called Corleonesi (from Corleone, a rural town near Palermo). While a fugitive in 1974, he married Antonietta Bagarella, an elementary school teacher by profession and the sister of infamous mafioso Leoluca Bagarella; at the time, Riina was a young mafioso in Corleone ready to start his rise to the top of Cosa Nostra through what has been called the second 'mafia war'. He was one of the main people responsible for the assassination of judges Falcone and Borsellino, guilty in his eyes for having brought to trial and convicted hundreds of members of Cosa Nostra in the so-called maxi-trial (1986–92). After twenty-three years living as a fugitive in and around Palermo, he was captured in 1993, inducing a series of indiscriminate bombings of art galleries and churches by his organization. His lack of repentance subjected him to the tough prison regime prescribed by Italian law (Law 416 bis of the penal code) until his death in November 2017.

13 The place of animals in the mafia would be worthy of a detailed analysis that is not possible here. Suffice it to say that animals figure as metaphors for the mafia and mafiosi (the octopus, the spider) and as mafiosi nicknames. I will return to this topic in a study in progress.

14 With the partial exception of the Japanese yakuza, which for a long period enjoyed a certain degree of legality and therefore visibility (Kaplan and Dubro 1993 [1986]; Hill 2003), something rather difficult for Western eyes and minds to understand, which is however to be included in the social 'space of possibilities' (Bourdieu 1998 [1994]).

15 On the Beati Paoli, which is also the title of a historical novel published in 1912 in Palermo by Luigi Natoli (under the pseudonym William Galt), a popular writer of the time and author of other cycles of historical novels in the tradition of the *feuilleton*, see Eco (1978), Renda (1988) and Castiglione (1987), the only contemporary scholar to argue that this sect historically existed and was not a literary creation. The first written evidence about

the sect dates to the eighteenth century and is also a literary text. What we know for sure is that the novel was hugely popular among the lower classes – not only the original publication but also its re-publication after the Second World War. For evidence that mafiosi read the novel, see again what Buscetta says in Arlacchi (1994).

16 Pitrè is here quoting passages of a memoir read at the Regia Accademia di scienze, lettere e arti di Palermo by a Giuseppe Di Menza in 1875. Definitions of *omertà* are present in nearly every text on mafia since at least Franchetti (1993 [1877]). Pitrè's definition had a special impact because of his intellectual reputation and habit of defending the mafia – or rather, the mafioso – as a moral character. Pitrè never recognized the existence of mafia as an organization, even though he had no problem recognizing the existence of aggregations and even collective structures in lower-class forms of criminality.

17 See Udehn (1996, 173): 'Many social norms, or codes, such as manners, or rules of etiquette, are neither instrumental, nor moral. They are followed out of ingrained habit, routine, or unthinking tradition. In the case of most rules, an economic explanation is highly problematic. They are a matter of principle, rather than of utility. What is more, their possible utility seems to depend upon the extent to which they are accepted as valid principles of action.' To assume that a certain class of agent, called 'mafiosi', would be totally alien to matters of principle and must act only according to pure calculus and instrumentality means simply countering the idea that people are puppets governed by interiorized norms by moving to the other extreme. Both of these extreme positions are unsatisfying.

18 Reference to the investigations coordinated by the *questore* Ermanno Sangiorgi at the end of the century, whose outcomes have been collected in the so-called 'Sangiorgi report'; see Santino 2017.

19 Born in Palermo in 1863 to a family of the high bourgeoisie and related to the Pirandello family, he was a lawyer and journalist. Deputy of the Chamber of the Kingdom of Italy (1900–4), he is most famous for having been the civil lawyer in the Bologna trial against the former Deputy Palizzolo.

20 Even in 1989, in a television interview conducted in prison (he was charged with being a member of the mafia and the instigator of an impressive number of murders), Luciano Liggio, allegedly one of the godfathers of Cosa Nostra since the 1980s, also through the activities of his faithful lieutenants Totò Riina and Bernardo Provenzano, still candidly denied knowing anything about the mafia apart from what scholars or journalists write about them, or from judges' sentences.

21 Betrayal is one of the four most common causes of death for a mafioso for strictly mafia reasons, which include: violent competition for high office inside the family; mafia war (violent competition among families); involvements in illegal affairs (including fights with officials of the state); and punishment for betrayal.

Chapter 5: The Mafioso's Gift, or: Making Sense of an 'Offer You Cannot Refuse'

1 See Karsenti (1997). On the genesis of the *Essai*, its personal and intellectual context, and its wide moral and political significance, see the fascinating Mallard (2019). For a coeval study on a similar topic, which was researched and written within the same circle as Durkheim and Mauss and made use of the same sources, but which has been much less influential, see Davy 2018 [1922].

2 On 'foreshadowing' as a permanent temptation in the history of social ideas, see Merton (1949).

3 There is even a journal named after this Maori word, published by a collective of American anthropologists. For a close reading of this section of the *Essai*, with philological additions to Mauss's rendition of the Maori document, see Sahlins (1968; followed up in Sahlins 1972).

4 It is interesting to notice that we find another curious convergence with a previously seen analysis: Gambetta's reading of the protection exchange between a seller (of a horse) and a buyer, as it is mediated, guaranteed in its fairness, by a third person who acts as the protector and who is the mafioso (or camorrista, as in the original source of the vignette). If you recall, there was a puzzling element in the model: the remuneration to the mafioso (the third character) for his service both from the seller as well as – which is more understandable – from the buyer. We find here a possible alternative explanation: the mafioso's *hau* (his mafia spirit) asks to be returned to his owner after the prestation is given. The mafioso gives his valuable possession (his protective *hau*) to the buyer, which enables the transaction with the seller, who has to give it back to the original owner, the mafioso. The cycle is closed, temporarily – with the caveat that the gift in return is not such to make the mafioso in debt. What makes the transaction closer to a commodity exchange is, however, the temporal structure of this system of exchanges: it all happens in synchronic time, with no delay. This is rarely the pattern followed in mafia exchanges. The structural, constitutive relation between time and gift has been emphasized by Pierre Bourdieu (see below), and also by the philosopher Jacques Derrida. I quote the latter, without further comment: 'If there is gift, the given of the gift (that which one gives, that which is given, the gift as given thing or as act of donation) must not come back to the giving (let us not already say to the subject, to the donor). It must not circulate, it must not be exchanged, it must not in any case be exhausted, as a gift, by the process of exchange, by the movement of circulation of the circle in the form of return to the point of departure. If the figure of the circle is essential to economics, the gift must remain uneconomic. Not that it remains foreign to the circle, but it must keep a relation of foreignness to the circle, a relation without relation of familiar foreignness. It is perhaps in this sense that the gift is the impossible' (1992: 7).

5 'We shall describe the phenomena of exchange and contract in those societies that are not, as has been claimed, devoid of economic markets

– since the market is a human phenomenon that, in our view, is not foreign to any known society – but whose system of exchange is different from ours. In these societies we shall see the market as it existed before the institution of traders and before their main invention – money proper. We shall see how it functioned both before the discovery of forms of contract and sale that may be said to be modern (Semitic, Hellenic, Hellenistic and Roman), and also before money, minted and inscribed. We shall see the morality and the organization that operate in such transactions. And we shall note that *this morality and organization still function in our own societies, in unchanging fashion and, so to speak, are hidden, below the surface, and, as we believe that in this we have found one of the human foundations on which our societies are built*, we shall be able to deduce a few moral conclusions concerning certain problems posed by the crisis in our own law and economic organization' (1990 [1925], 5; emphasis added). On the relation between gift and money in ancient Rome, see now Coffee (2017).

6 This unwillingness to acknowledge specificity to gift exchange offers an explanation for the theoretical neglect of the wide evidence about gift circulation in mafia life in the research inspired by economic theory. More difficult is to account for its neglect in studies from different traditions, especially when done by anthropologists. The simplest explanation has to do with the circulation of concepts and models among intellectual traditions: it is a fact that Durkheimian sociology had a very weak impact on mafia studies, and that the two most influential traditions in the anthropological analysis of the mafia – e.g., the Marxist American and the Dutch traditions – are relatively immune to the paradigm of the gift as it has developed in the discipline of anthropology (Sykes, 2005; Liebershon 2011). As I will show, there is good evidence of presents and gifts in existing fieldwork-based studies on the mafia that is worthy of supplementary analysis.

7 It should be added that the agonistic character of the potlatch probably only developed after 1850, as a result of the influx of quantities of goods of considerable value, and also because of the appearance of the *nouveau riche*, etc. We should mention, of course, that we do not reproach Mauss for describing the potlatch under the erroneous label of agonistic gift-giving, given that the research allowing this to be corrected is quite recent and could not have been known to him (see Codere 1950). We can speculate that even in Sicily there was an increase in agonistic gift practices after the demise of feudalism in 1812 and the introduction of elements of market exchange in the regulation of land transfers, with the consequences this change may have had even on the other (goods) markets.

8 The relationship between mafia and the gift was not discussed even during a debate between the sociologist Gambetta and some Italian anthropologists in the pages of the magazine *Ossimori* (see Li Causi and Cassano 1993, followed by comments by Bernardo Bernardi, Luigi Lombardi Satriani and, indeed, Gambetta). Ironically, ethnographic forms of the gift such as kula and potlatch are actually mentioned by Li Causi and Cassano at the beginning of their article, but only to establish a parallel between them

and the mafia as equally legitimate objects of anthropological study. Nor does anthropologist David Moss (2001) ultimately advance what in some ways his article might suggest: namely an extension of the gift paradigm to all mafia phenomenology and not only to its extreme offshoot (leaving the mafia to cooperate with state institutions).

9 Drawing on ethnographic fieldwork conducted in Reggio Calabria, South Italy, Stavroula Pipyrou (2014) explores local mafia, i.e. 'ndrangheta, notions of giving and charity. Indeed, mafia free gifts are conceptualized by the author as 'a form of power that shapes a divine profile for the mafiosi', linking them to 'the religious rhetoric of mafia hierarchy'. What I appreciate in her analysis is that it sees mafia free-gifting as a series of complex nonviolent discourses closely related to religious duty, but working alongside capitalist systems. What I'm not persuaded by is her conclusion that, in principle, these gifts do not bind recipients, even if they are imbued with the potential of a strong relationship. No effort to extend her ethnographic analysis to the theoretical debate on the mafia is apparent. That said, it should be emphasized that this is the only text I have been able to find in the vast literatures on both the gift and the mafia that is focused on the gift aspects of mafia practices.

10 Lévi-Strauss had something precious to say also about the exchange of goods, however: 'In fact, the exchange does not bring a tangible result such as is the case in commercial transactions in our own society ... *Goods are not only economic commodities, but vehicles and instruments for realities of another order, such as power, influence, sympathy, status and emotion; and the skilful game of exchange* ... consists in a complex totality of conscious or unconscious manoeuvres in order to gain security and to guard oneself against risks brought about by alliances and by rivalries (1969 [1949], 54; my emphasis added).

11 See *Palermo, la richiesta del pizzo filmata dall'imprenditore*, in 'Storie italiane', 16 January 2019; available at https://www.youtube.com/watch?v=UP6wzKPdgxE.

Chapter 6: Blood, *Bund* and (Personal) Bonds: The Mafia as an Institutional Type

1 See Boas (1895) and Simmel (1950 [1906]). For an overview, including a chapter on the Sicilian mafia, see MacKenzie (1967). Erickson (1981) is an important reference in recent sociological theory. Recently, the model of the secret society as an organizational type has been taken up by Catino (2019, 24–8).

2 The transcultural diffusion of the set of ten as a principle of social organization did not escape Simmel who, in his classic analysis of the quantitative determination of social groups, traces it back to the importance of the 'number of fingers' as 'the first principle of orientation for ascertaining a large number of units, for making their divisions and groupings clear' (2009 [1908], 22). It may not be a coincidence, therefore, that many of the known

mafia initiation rites involve the use of fingers and hands (they hold the sacred image, and are pierced to make blood flow).

3 On mafia's rules as organizational rules, see the extensive analysis by Catino (2019, ch. 5).

4 This is what clearly distinguishes mafia relationships from patronage.

5 In addition to this, there are many other institutions that contribute to reinforcing this absolute identification and to renewing the pact of brotherhood. For an analysis, see Paoli 2003, 109–16.

6 Moreover, Paoli's references, in addition to Weber's conceptualization, include Otto von Gierke's historical-juridical theory of corporations and historian Henry Sumner Maine's famous passage on the status of the contract in English law. In short, the identification of the mafia as a system of *fratellanze* has many reasons to please, and convince, not only sociologists but also jurists and historians.

7 A substantially shortened version was translated into English by Gregory Stone and published in the collection *Theories of Society*, edited by Talcott Parsons and others. This work has been taken up repeatedly in the critical literature, but has, for the most part, 'remained buried in the footnotes of sociological theory' (Hetherington 1994, 1). It is worth noting that, in his essay, Schmalenbach not only criticizes Tönnies and his classic dichotomy, but also puts forward some significant objections to Weber's theory of sociological categories which had just been made available with the publication of the first edition of *Economy and Society* in 1922.

8 This would also allow us to assess in what sense the mafia can be characterized sociologically as a 'profession' rather than an industry – according to a research hypothesis I advanced years ago (see Santoro 1995), which was criticized by Paoli (2003, 71) and, later, taken up and further developed by Italian political scientist Antonio La Spina (2005). For reasons of space I have to postpone this move, but see Santoro (2007) for some reflections.

9 Schmalenbach's ethnographic main source is Heinrich Schurtz's classic study (1902) on men's associations (*Mannerbunde*), usually in the form of ritual secret societies. But the theme had been studied, among others, by Franz Boas, who had made it the subject of a classic work on the social organization and the secret societies among the Kwakiutl; see Boas (1895).

10 This could open up a further line of research, with an analysis of the mafia in terms of a 'sociology of emotions', along the lines of Barbalet (1998; see also Barbalet 2002).

11 According to Paoli: 'Like the adherents of a religious set, the members of Cosa Nostra and the *'ndrangheta* familes feel "morally qualified" (Weber)' (2003, 83).

12 Discord between a world represented as inspired by the values of honour and friendship and the violent and opportunistic practices that express it socially is often found in literature. In this way, a crucial point emerges, namely that, like a secret, friendship is only realized as an institutional principle when it is broken.

13 Recent witness to this 'folk classification' can be found in the transcripts of judges' interrogations of mafiosi, even in situations in which the issue at

stake is exactly the boundaries between friendship with a chief (considered as a 'father') and belonging to the mafia: see Reale 2010, 203.

14 Eating together is a crucial institution of the mafia universe: as is well known and often portrayed in the media, decisions are typically made during shared meals, whether eaten in a restaurant or in the countryside (see Parker 2008). See also Chapter 5 in this book.

15 On the matrimonial policy of the mafia, and in particular on the use of sisters and daughters as bargaining chips to strengthen mafia bonds of *fratellanze*, see Paoli 2003, 88–9.

16 This results from a simple comparison of vocabulary: while in Cosa Nostra the affiliate is presented to third parties with the formula '*è la stessa cosa*', ('this is the same thing'), the families of the *'ndrangheta* say '*questo è un nostro amico*' ('this is a friend of ours'). See Paoli (2003, 78), who reads this second formula as a weaker expression of the concept conveyed by the first. This can only be sustained, however, under a privatistic notion of friendship, typical of bourgeois and liberal culture, as shown by Silver (1989, 1990) among others.

17 The term 'chain' is given by Collins himself. However, the metaphor of the chain of relationships had already been used by Cutrera who, as regards the mafia of the Conca d'Oro orchards, noted that '*in mezzo a tutti questi giardini a contatto l'uno dall'altro vi stanno migliaia di guardiani, i quali fra loro formano delle estese catene d'amici e compari*' ('in the midst of all these orchards, one up against the other, there are thousands of guardians, which form among themselves extensive chains of friends and compari') (1900, 58).

18 On the feud as a constitutive political institution of the European medieval social structure and therefore pre-state – but according to a reading that would offer more than a suggestion of an extensive application of the analysis to post-revolutionary and even post-state situations – I can only refer to Otto Brunner's classic work (2015 [1938]), recently translated into English.

19 There were already traces of this in Adam Smith's theory of moral feelings.

20 It may be of some relevance that mafiosi have to be on the run for a large part of their life. This makes the parallel with nomads of the desert less forced. Indeed, mafiosi are very often nomads, alone or with their natural, blood families. Even when settled, mafia Families know that they always face the possibility of becoming nomadic. Hospitality is one of the fundamental rules and practices in mafia life, as noticed in Chapter 5. For a philosophical analysis, see Derrida 2000 (interestingly, Derrida was born in Algeria).

21 Arlacchi (1983a) does not show any awareness – neither here, nor in subsequent works that address the same theme – of the category of the *Bund*.

22 Original text: '*Per un Tommaso Buscetta che aveva venti-trent'anni, Cosa Nostra era qualche cosa di bellissimo. Era tutto: era lo strumento per far acquistare dignità e orgoglio all'uomo calpestato, alla vittima delle angherie dei ricchi e dei malfattori.*'

23 As is well known, both Georg Simmel and Robert K. Merton were intellectually engaged with this issue.

24 See Hughes (1971) and, for a short but smart discussion of the concept as a thinking tool, Becker (1998).

25 Like all the sociology of the Chicago School – from Albion Small to Robert Park (Simmel's student) to Gregory Stone, who translated Schmalenbach's essay – Hughes was influenced by Simmelian and, generally, Germanic sources.

26 The sociological tradition offers another useful category for describing the mafia from the inside, framing it within a broader class of institutional phenomena that Lewis Coser (1974) called 'greedy institutions'. See Santoro (2007) for a development on this point, together with a first attempt to assess mafia organizations in light of the sociological theory of the professions – something I don't address here only for reasons of space.

27 Raimondo Catanzaro alerted me to the relevance of this source: see Catanzaro and Santoro (2009). However, only I am responsible for any imperfections.

28 Bernstein (1971) distinguishes between two linguistic codes, the restricted or public code – based on simple, often interrupted sentences, the use of simple and repetitive conjunctions, rigid adjectives and adverbs, little use of personal pronouns, symbolism at a low level of generality, etc. – and the elaborated or formal code – diametrically opposed to the first type. The restricted code is typical of the popular classes and essentially linked to oral communication models, while the elaborated code defines the culture of the middle classes and, although on this point Bernstein is not explicit, the language of written communication, at least that which is transmitted through formal education. On this point, see especially Ong (1982).

29 The absence of writing and a subsistence economy are the standard criteria with which even anthropologists define archaic societies: see, for example, Clastres 1988 [1974] – although he has reservations about the second criterion, he has nothing to complain about the first.

30 However, investigators had already been aware of the existence of *pizzini* since 1994 because of the confession and collaboration of Luigi Ilardo, a boss of the Caltanissetta mafia Family, later killed in mysterious circumstances.

31 In fact, it was not the first time that judicial inquiries had brought a system of written communication into the open. In the early 1990s, the mafia informant Antonino Calvaruso, boss Leoluca Bagarella's driver, had, for example, reported that among his duties was delivering short written messages sealed with adhesive tape, called '*palummedde*' (little doves) in slang, to other men of honour in order to fix appointments or give information about events (e.g., murders) that could not be transmitted by telephone for security reasons. But in that case, it was a matter of very short messages on paper to be destroyed immediately after reading (see Dino 2002, 149). The '*pizzini*' used by Provenzano were something different, with far more profound implications.

32 The quotation is from the document '*Fermo di indiziati di delitto*'

('Arrest of suspects of crime') of the Palermo Prosecutor's Office – Anti-Mafia District Directorate (p. 39), downloadable from the website www.bernardoprovenzano.net.

33 See source in note 32, p. 40.

34 On this issue, see Catanzaro and Santoro (2009), which is an indispensable complement to this chapter. On the *pizzini* and their role in both the religious and political strategy of Bernardo Provenzano, see especially Puccio-Den (2011).

35 For the meaning of an ethnography of writing, see Basso (1974). On the potentialities of an ethnography of silence, see Puccio-Den (2019) as well as the comments on the latter by Santoro (2019).

36 From *pizzu*, beak. As is known, in mafia jargon (and, more generally, in the Sicilian dialect), requests for money made in exchange for protection, real or presumed, are called '*pizzi*': from the point of view of the state and its representatives (and of those who identify with them), it is nothing but a form of extortion, but from the point of view of the mafia, it can instead be conceived (ideologically, and even cognitively) as a legitimately requested tribute in exchange for the service of establishing and maintaining order.

37 Here, it is worth noting that the original testimonies collected by Arlacchi have been edited for publication. What we read in the autobiographies of Antonino Calderone and Tommaso Buscetta that Arlacchi edited (1993; 1994) is therefore not their language, but an edited transcription of conversations: oral (and subcultural) language was subsequently transformed into written language, and into correct Italian (unfortunately, not according to any explicit criteria).

38 Dated 1 October 1997, the *pizzino* was acquired as part of Criminal Procedure n.1687/96 R.G.N.R. DDA upon Maniscalco's arrest, which took place on the following 10 October. *Pizzini* like these can be found on the web at www.bernardoprovenzano.net. See also the work by the editors of the same site, Palazzolo and Prestipino (2007), for an abundant collection of *pizzini* and their attempt at a 'stylistic' reading.

39 With its insistence on the indexical character of everyday life, the current of sociological analysis known as ethnomethodology (Garfinkel 1967) would have much to offer to the study of the mafia on this front.

40 On the notion of a vocabulary of European politics, see the studies by Otto Brunner (2015 [1938]) and Reinhart Koselleck (2000), and in general the whole tradition of the so-called *Begriffsgeschichte* (history of concepts). But see also, for its ancient, archaic roots, Benveniste (2016 [1969]).

41 See McLean (2007) for a study of writing strategies from Renaissance patronage letters in Florence that highlights the underlying political and cultural frames, and Brunner (2015 [1938]) for classic research into the political culture of the landed nobility in Old Regime Austria. On the place of friendship in the politics of the Middle Age, see Althoff (1999) and Haseldine (2013), and on antiquity see Konstan (1997).

42 I derive this concept from Friedland and Alford (1991, 248), who define it as 'a set of material practices and symbolic constructions' upon which, depending on its specific characteristics, a given institutional order – such

as capitalism, the family or the bureaucratic state – is based. Thus, to give some examples, the institutional logic of capitalism would be 'accumulation and the commodification of human activity', while that of the state is the 'rationalization and the regulation of human activity by legal and bureaucratic hierarchies', and that of the family is 'community and the motivation of human activity by unconditional loyalty to its members.' These institutional logics are 'interdependent yet also contradictory' (1991, 256), and it is the scholar's task to detect these relations, without favouring one at the expense of the other. What institutional logics are at work in the case of the mafia – and how their interdependencies and contradictions are structured and have changed over time – is a question that would be worth investigating.

43 The scholar who most insisted on the role of mediation in the mafia and among mafiosi is undoubtedly Blok (1974). But see also Schneider and Schneider (1976; 2011), who speak of 'mediation capitalism', and Pizzorno (1987).

44 On the religious dimension of mafia life, see at least Dino (2008) and Puccio-Den (2011). See also Cavadi (2009) for an attempt to discuss the implicit theology of mafia culture.

Chapter 7: Mafias as an Elementary Form of Politics

1 The *trattativa stato–mafia* ('state–mafia pact') was a purported negotiation between Italian officials and Cosa Nostra after the 1992–3 attacks that killed judges Falcone and Borsellino, among others, and destroyed buildings near the Uffizi Gallery in Florence (killing five). The supposed cornerstone of the deal was an end of the 'massacre season' in return for a revision of the maxi-trial of 1984–6 and the retraction of the 'hard prison regime' introduced by Italian penal code article 41-bis in 1982. The negotiation hypothesis has long been the subject of investigations and reports (see, e.g., Fiandaca and Lupo 2014; Caselli and Lo Forte 2020; see also dalla Chiesa 2010a; Dino 2012). While the exact mode of this negotiation is controversial, the fact that some negotiation occurred at all is widely accepted.

2 For this highly mediatized case, see Loong (2011). See also, for a sociological reconstruction of the political and cultural life in Renaissance Florence, Padgett and Ansell (1993) and McLean (2007). For a very distant – but functionally close – historical case, see Coser (1964).

3 For extensive, ethnographic studies of these criminal subcultures, see Wolf (1991) and Joans (2001). In Russia, the Night Wolves motorcycle gang, has been accused of violent crimes but enjoys the patronage of the Kremlin (see Galeotti 2018).

4 For reasons of space I have omitted a fourth case, Latin American narcotrafficking organizations. For a sample of relevant literature, see Kaplan (1992), Richani (2010), Bunker (2011, 2013), Duncan (2013), Campbell (2014), Krakowski and Zubiria (2019), Trejo and Ley (2021).

5 A clue to this political nature of Russian mafia appears in what looks like a Russian-style *trattativa* between state and mafia. Prominent Russians from

both sides of the law have advocated a deal between criminal groups and the state (see Varese 2001, 181).

6 Expression destined to succeed: see Lévi-Strauss (1987 [1950]); Homans (1961); Kuper (1970); on 'an elementary form of government', see Sahlins (2008).

Appendix

1 As of mid-2012, the book had already sold 2.5 million copies in Italy and more than 3 million across the globe.

2 What about the authors of literature on mafia as recorded in ISI Web of Science? Out of the 849 identified records (in August 2017), eighteen are anonymous. The most recurrent author is Federico Varese (Oxford-based), with thirteen records, followed by Marco Centorrino, an economist from Messina, with seven. Felia Allum, a British historian who has worked on camorra and more general topics in organized crime research, features five records. Several well-known scholars of mafia studies, such as Peter Schneider, Diego Gambetta, and the historian John Dickie – author of a new millennium bestseller on the subject (2004) – have only four records. As you can infer from these data, the field of mafia studies is very dispersed, with only a small core set of recurrent authors and a mass of single record authors.

References

Abbott, A. 1999. *Department and Discipline*. Chicago: Chicago University Press.

Abbott, A. 2001. *Time Matters*. Chicago: University of Chicago Press.

Abbott, A. 2004. *Methods of Discovery*. New York: Norton.

Abrams, P. 1988. 'Notes on the difficulty of studying the state (1977)', *Journal of Historical Sociology*, 1: 58–89.

Abulafia, D. 1977. *The Two Italies. Economic Relations between the Norman Kingdom of Sicily and the Northern Communes*. New York: Cambridge University Press.

Abulafia, D., ed. 1987. *Italy, Sicily and the Mediterranean, 1100–1400*, Aldershot.

Abu-Lughod, J.L. 1989. *Before European Hegemony. The World System*, AD *1250–1350*. Oxford: Oxford University Press.

Adelstein, J. 2017. *Tokyo Vice: An American Reporter on the Police Beat in Japan*. New York: Random House.

Agamben, G. 1998. *Homo Sacer: Sovereign Power and Bare Life*. Stanford: Stanford University Press.

Ahmed, A. 2003. *The Epistemology of Ibn Khaldūn*. London: Routledge.

Akerlof, G. 1970. '*The market for* lemons: Quality uncertainty and *the market* mechanism', *The Quarterly Journal of Economics*, 84(3): 488–500.

Akers, R.L. and Matsueda, R.L. 1989. 'Donald R. Cressey: An intellectual portrait of a criminologist', *Sociological Inquiry*, 59: 423–438.

Alatas, S.F. 2006a. *Alternative Discourses in Asian Social Science. Responses to Eurocentrism*. London: Sage.

Alatas, S.F. 2006b. 'A Khaldunian exemplar for a historical sociology for the south', *Current Sociology*, 54: 397–411.

Alatas, S.F. 2014. *Applying Ibn Khaldūn. The Recovery of a Lost Tradition in Sociology*. London: Routledge.

Albert, H. 2012 [1963], 'Model platonism: Neoclassical economic thought in critical light', *Journal of Institutional Economics*, 8(3): 295–323.

Albini, J. 1971. *The American Mafia: Genesis of a Legend*, New York: Appleton-Century-Crofts.

Albini, J.L. 1978. 'Witches, mafia, mental illness and social reality: A study in the power of mythical belief', *International Journal of Criminology and Penology*, 6: 285–294.

Albini, J.L. and McIllwain, J.S. 2012. *Deconstructing Organized Crime: An Historical and Theoretical Study*. Jefferson-London: McFarland.

Alexander, B. 1997. 'The rational racketeer: Pasta protection in depression era Chicago', *Journal of Law & Economics*, 40(1): 175–202.

Alexander, J.C. 2003. *The Meanings of Social Life. A Cultural Sociology*. Oxford: Oxford University Press.

Alexander, J.C. 2006. *The Civil Sphere*. Oxford: Oxford University Press.

Alexander, J.C. 2013. *The Dark Side of Modernity*. Cambridge: Polity.

Alexander, J.C. and Smith, P. 2001. 'The strong program in cultural sociology', in J. Turner, ed., *Handbook of Sociological Theory*, pp. 135–150. New York: Kluwer.

Alexander, J.C., Jacobs, R. and Smith, P., eds. 2011. *Oxford Handbook of Cultural Sociology*. Oxford: Oxford University Press.

Alfani, G. and Gourdon, V. eds. 2012. *Spiritual Kinship in Europe, 1500–1900*. London: Palgrave.

Alinei, M. 2007. 'Origini pastorali e italiche della *camorra*, della *mafia* e della *'ndrangheta*: Un esperimento di Archeologia Etimologica.' *Quaderni di Semantica*, a.XXVIII(2): 247–286.

Allum, F. and Gilmour, S., eds. 2011. *Routledge Handbook of Transnational Organized Crime*. London: Routledge.

Almond, G.A. 1988. 'The return to the state', *American Political Science Review*, 82(3): 853–874.

Alongi G. 1891. *Studi di patologia sociale. I. L'abigeato in Sicilia*. Marsala: Giliberti.

Alongi, G. 1904. *La mafia: fattori, manifestazioni, rimedi*. Milan-Palermo: Remo Sandron.

Alongi, G. 1977 [1887]. *La maffia*. Palermo: Sellerio.

Althoff, G. 1999. 'Friendship and political order', in J. Haseldine, ed., *Friendship in Medieval Europe*, pp. 91–105. Stroud: Sutton Publishing.

Amadae, S.M. 2003. *Rationalizing Capitalist Democracy: The Cold War Origins of Rational Choice Liberalism*. Chicago: University of Chicago Press.

Amos, T.P. 2011. *Embodying Difference: The Making of Burakumin in Modern Japan*. Honolulu: University of Hawaii Press.

Anderson, A.G. 1979. *The Business of Organized Crime: A Cosa Nostra Family*. Stanford: Stanford University Press.

Anderson, B. 1983. *Imagined Communities*. London: Verso.

Anderson, D. 2002. 'Vigilantes, violence and the politics of public order in Kenya', *African Affairs*, 101(405): 531–555.

Anderson, J.E. and Bandiera, O. 2005. 'Private enforcement and social efficiency', *Journal of Development Economics*, 77(2): 341–366.

Anderson, R.T. 1965. 'From mafia to cosa nostra', *American Journal of Sociology*, 71(3): 302–310.

Anspach, M.R. 2001. 'Violence deceived: Changing reciprocities from vengeance to gift exchange', in C. Gerschlager, ed., *Expanding the Economic Concept of Exchange*, pp. 213–224. Boston: Kluwer.

Anspach, M.R. 2002. *À charge de revanche. Figures élémentaires de la réciprocité*. Paris: Le Seuil.

Anter, A. 2014. *Max Weber's Theory of the Modern State. Origins, Structure and Significance*. London: Palgrave.

Appadurai, A. 1981. 'Gastro-politics in Hindu South Asia', *American Ethnologist*, 8: 494–511.

Appadurai, A. 1986. 'Introduction: Commodities and the politics of value', in A. Appadurai, ed., *The Social Life of Things*, pp. 3–63. New York: Cambridge University Press.

Ardrey, R. 1966. *The Territorial Imperative*. New York: Atheneum.

Ardrey, R. 1976. *The Hunting Hypothesis*. New York: Atheneum.

Arias, E. and Rodrigues, C.D. (2006). 'The myth of personal security: Criminal gangs, dispute resolution, and identity in Rio de Janeiro's favelas', *Latin American Politics and Society*, 48(4): 53–81.

Arlacchi, P. 1983a. *La mafia imprenditrice*. Bologna: Il Mulino. English trans., *Mafia Business: The Mafia Ethic and the Spirit of Capitalism*. London: Verso, 1984.

Arlacchi, P. 1983b [1980]. *Mafia, Peasants and Great Estates: Society in Traditional Calabria*. Cambridge: Cambridge University Press.

Arlacchi, P. 1993. *Men of Dishonor: Inside the Sicilian Mafia: An Account of Antonino Calderone*. London: William Morrow & Co. [*Gli uomini del disonore: la mafia siciliana nella vita del grande pentito Antonino Calderone*. Milan: Mondadori, 1992].

Arlacchi, P. 1994. *Addio cosa nostra: La vita di Tommaso Buscetta*. Milan: Rizzoli.

Armstrong, G. and Rosbrook-Thompson, J. 2016. 'Faith, space and selfhood in East London youth gang culture', *Urbanities*, 6(2): 18–38.

Aron, R. 1950 [1935]. *La sociologie allemande contemporaine*, 2nd edn. Paris: Presses Universitaires de France.

Arsovska, J. 2015. *Decoding Albanian Organized Crime: Culture, Politics, and Globalization*. Oakland: University of California Press.

Atieno, A. 2007. 'Mungiki, "Neo-Mau Mau" and the prospects for democracy in Kenya', *Review of African Political Economy*, 34(113): 526–531.

Auyero, J. and Sobering, K. 2019. *The Ambivalent State: Police–Criminal Collusion at the Urban Margins*. Oxford: Oxford University Press.

Bachmann-Medick, D. 2016. *Cultural Turns. New Orientations in the Study of Culture*. Berlin: de Gruyter.

Bailey, F.G., ed. 1971. *Gifts and Poison: The Politics of Reputation*. Oxford: Blackwell.

Bailey, F.G. 2001 [1969]. *Stratagems and Spoils. A Social Anthropology of Politics*, 2nd edn. Boulder: Westview.

Ballina, S. 2011. 'Crime–terror continuum revisited: A model for the study of hybrid criminal organisations', *Journal of Policing, Intelligence and Counter Terrorism*, 6(2): 121–136.

Bandiera, O. 2003. 'Land reform, the market for protection, and the origins of the Sicilian Mafia: Theory and evidence', *Journal of Law, Economics and Organization*, 19(1): 218–244.

Baradel, M. and Bortolussi, J. 2020. 'Under a setting sun: The spatial displacement of the yakuza and their longing for visibility', *Trends in Organized Crime*, November: 1–18.

Barbalet, J. 1998. *Emotion, Social Theory, and Social Structure: A Macrosociological Approach*. Cambridge: Cambridge University Press.

Barbalet, J., ed. 2002. *Emotions and Sociology*. London: Wiley-Blackwell.

Barnes, H. and Becker, H. 1938. *Social Thought from Lore to Science*. Boston: D.C. Heath and Company.

Barth, F. 1969. *Political Leadership among Swat Pathans*. London: Athlone Press.

Basso, K. 1974. 'The ethnography of writing', in R. Bauman and J. Sherzer, eds, *Explorations in the Ethnography of Speaking*, pp. 425–432. Cambridge: Cambridge University Press.

Bataille, G. 2001 [1949]. *The Accursed Share: An Essay on General Economy*. New York: Zone Books.

Batjargal, B. 2007. 'Comparative social capital: Networks of entrepreneurs and venture capitalists in China and Russia', *Management and Organization Review*, 3: 397–419.

Bayart, J.-F., Ellis, S. and Hibou, B. 1999. *The Criminalization of the State in Africa*. Bloomington: Indiana University Press.

Becker, H.S. 1998. *Tricks of the Trade*. Chicago: University of Chicago Press.

Belk, R.W. 1979. 'Gift-giving behavior', in J.E. Sheth, ed., *Research in Marketing*, vol. 2, Greenwich: JAI Press.

Bell, D. 1953. 'Crime as an American way of life', *Antioch Review*, 13(2): 131–154.

Benigno, F. 2007. 'Integration and conflict in Spanish Sicily', in T. Dandelet and J. Marino, eds, *Spain in Italy. Politics, Society, and Religion 1500–1700*, pp. 21–44. Leiden: Brill.

Benigno, F. 2011. 'Il ritorno dei Thugs: Ancora su trasformazioni discorsive e identità sociali', *Storica*, 51: 97–120.

Benigno, F. 2015. *La mala seta. Alle origini di mafia e camorra, 1859–1878*. Turin: Einaudi.

Benson, R. and Neveu, E., eds. 2005. *Bourdieu and the Journalistic Field*. Cambridge: Polity.

Benveniste, E. 2016 [1969]. *Dictionary of Indo-European Concepts and Society*. London: HAU Books.

Ben-Yehoyada, N. 2018. 'Where do we go when we follow the money? The political-economic construction of antimafia investigators in western Sicily', *History and Anthropology*, 29(3): 359–375.

Bercovitch, E. 1994. 'The agent in the gift: Hidden exchange in Inner New Guinea', *Cultural Anthropology*, 9: 498–536.

Berenschot, W. (2011) 'On the usefulness of *goonda*s in Indian politics: "Moneypower" and "musclepower" in a Gujarati locality', *South Asia: Journal of South Asian Studies* 34(2), 255–275.

Berezin, M. 1997. 'Politics and culture', *Annual Review of Sociology*, 23(1): 361–383.

Bernstein, B. 1971. *Class, Code, and Control*. London: Routledge.

Betancourt, D. and García, M.L. 1994. *Contrabandista, marimberos y mafiosos. Historia de la mafia colombiana (1965–1992)*. Bogotá: Tercer Mundo Editores.

Block, A. 1983. *East Side, West Side. Organizing Crime in New York, 1930–1950*. New Brunswick: Transaction Books.

Blok, A. 1974. *The Mafia of a Sicilian Village, 1860–1960*. New York: Harper & Row.

Blok, A. 1986. 'Review of Filippo Sabetti's *Political Authority in a Sicilian Village*', *American Ethnologist*, 13(1): 168–169.

Blok, A. 2001. *Honour and Violence*. Cambridge: Polity.

Blok, A. 2002. 'Mafia and blood symbolism,' in F.K. Salter, ed., *Risky Transactions Trust, Kinship and Ethnicity*. New York: Berghahn Books.

Blok, A. 2015. 'Anthropology of mafia,' in J. Wright, ed., *International Encyclopedia of the Social and Behavioral Sciences*, 2nd edn, pp. 422–428. Oxford: Elsevier.

Blythe, W. 1969. *The Impact of Chinese Secret Societies in Malaya. A Historical Study*. Oxford: Oxford University Press.

Boas, F. (with G. Hunt). 1895. 'The social organization and the secret societies of the Kwakiutl Indians', in *The Report of the United States National Museum for the year ending June 30, 1895*, pp. 309–738. Washington: Government Printing Office.

Bobbio, N. 2017 [1989]. *Democracy and Dictatorship: The Nature and Limits of State Power*. Chichester: Wiley.

Boissevain, J. 1974. *Friends of Friends: Networks, Manipulators and Coalitions*. Oxford: Basil Blackwell.

Boltanski, L. 2014. *Mysteries and Conspiracies: Detective Stories, Spy Novels and the Making of Modern Societies*. Cambridge: Polity.

Boltanski, L. and Thevenot, L. 1991. *De la justification. Les économies de la grandeur*. Paris: Gallimard.

Bonanno, B. 1999. *Bound by Honor: A Mafioso's Story*. New York: St. Martin Press.

Bonanno, J. 1983. *A Man of Honor. The Autobiography of Joseph Bonanno*. London: Simon and Schuster.

Booth, M. 1999. *The Dragon Syndicates: The Global Phenomenon of the Triads*. London: Doubleday.

Boudon, R. 2002. 'Sociology that really matters', *European Sociological Review*, 8(3): 371–378.

Bourdieu, P. 1977. *Outline of a Theory of Practice*. Cambridge: Cambridge University Press.

Bourdieu, P. 1980. *Le Sens pratique*. Paris: Minuit.

Bourdieu P. 1993 [1982]. *Language and Symbolic Power*. Cambridge: Harvard University Press.

Bourdieu, P. 1996 [1992]. *The Rules of Art: Genesis and Structure of the Literary Field*. Cambridge: Polity.

Bourdieu, P. 1996. 'The work of time', in A. Komter, ed., *The Gift. An Interdisciplinary Perspective*, pp. 135–148. Amsterdam: Amsterdam University Press.

Bourdieu, P. 1997. 'Marginalia: Some additional notes on the gift', in A. Schrift, ed., *The Logic of the Gift. Toward an Ethic of Generosity*, pp. 231–245. London: Routledge.

Bourdieu, P. 1998 [1994]. *Practical Reason: On the Theory of Action*. Stanford: Stanford University Press.

Bourdieu, P. 2001 [1997]. *Pascalian Meditations*, Cambridge: Polity.

Bourdieu, P. 2010 [1979]. *Distinction: A Social Critique of the Judgement of Taste*. London: Routledge.

Bourdieu, P. 2014. *On the State*. Cambridge: Polity.

Bourdieu, P. 2017. *Anthropologie économique*. Paris: Seuil.

Bourdieu, P. and Wacquant, L.J. 1992. *Invitation to Reflexive Sociology*. Chicago: University of Chicago Press.

Bourgois, P. 2001. 'The power of violence in war and peace: Post-Cold War lessons from El Salvador', *Ethnography*, 2(1): 5–34

Bracken, Ch. 1997. *The Potlatch Papers: A Colonial Case History*. Chicago: University of Chicago Press.

Bresc, H. and Bresc-Bautier, G., eds. 1993. *Palerme, 1070–1492. Mosaïque de peuples, nation rebelle: La naissance violente de l'identité sicilienne*. Paris: Autrement.

Briquet, J.-L. and Favarel-Garrigues, G., eds. 2010. *Organized Crime and States*. New York: Palgrave Macmillan.

Britt, K. 2007. 'Roger II of Sicily: Rex, Basileus, and Khalif? Identity, politics, and propaganda in the Cappella Palatina', *Mediterranean Studies*, 16: 21–45.

Brubaker, R. 1992. *Citizenship and Nationhood in France and Germany*. Cambridge: Harvard University Press.

Brunner, O. 2015 [1938]. *Land and Lordship. Structures of Governance in Medieval Austria*. Philadelphia: University of Pennsylvania Press.

Buchanan, J. and Tullock, G. 1962. *The Calculus of Consent: Logical Foundations of Constitutional Democracy*. Ann Arbor: Michigan University Press.

Bunker R. 2011. 'The Mexican cartel debate: As viewed through five divergent fields of security studies', *Small Wars Journal*, 2 November. http://smallwars-journal.com/jrnl/art/the-mexican-cartel-debate.

Bunker, R.J. 2013. 'Introduction: The Mexican cartels – organized crime vs. criminal insurgency,' *Trends in Organized Crime*, 16: 129–137.

Burawoy, M. 2005. 'Provincializing the social sciences', in G. Steinmetz, ed., *The Politics of Method in the Human Sciences: Positivism and its Epistemological Others*, pp. 508–525. Durham: Duke University Press.

Buttitta, I.E. 1999. *Le fiamme dei santi: Usi rituali del fuoco nelle feste siciliane*. Rome: Meltemi.

Cai, S. 1984. 'On the origin of the Gelaohui', *Modern China*, 10(4): 481–508.

Cai, S. 1988. 'An overview of the secret societies of China during the Late Qing Period', *Cina*, 21: 39–47.

Caillé, A. 2001. 'The double inconceivability of the pure gift', *Angelaki*, 6(2): 23–39.

Caillé, A. 2019. *Extensions du domaine du don: Demander, donner, recevoir, rendre*. Arles: Actes Sud.

Caillé, A. 2020. *The Gift Paradigm. A Short Introduction to the Anti-Utilitarian Movement in the Social Sciences*. Cambridge: Prickly Paradigm Press.

Calhoun, C. ed. 1992. *Habermas and the Public Sphere*. Cambridge: MIT Press.

Calise, M. 1988. 'Le categorie del politico nella criminalità organizzata', in F. Barbagallo, ed., *Camorra e criminalità organizzata in Campania*. Naples: Liguori.

Calvi, F. 1984. *La vita quotidiana della mafia dal 1950 ad oggi*. Milan: Rizzoli.

Camerer, C.F. 1988. 'Gifts as economic signals and social symbols', *American Journal of Sociology*, 94: S180–S214.

Campana, P. 2011. 'Eavesdropping on the mob: The functional diversification of Mafia activities across territories', *European Journal of Criminology*, 8: 213–228.

Campana, P. and Varese, F. 2013. 'Cooperation in criminal organizations: Kinship and violence as credible commitments', *Rationality and Society*, 25: 263–289.

Campana, P. and Varese, F. 2018. 'Organized crime in the United Kingdom: Illegal governance of markets and communities', *British Journal of Criminology*, 58(6): 1381–1400.

Campbell, H. 2014. 'Narco-propaganda in the Mexican "drug war": An anthropological perspective', *Latin American Perspectives*, 41(2): 60–77.

Capuana, G. 1898. *L'isola del sole*. Catania: Giannotta.

Carneiro, R.L. 1981. 'The chiefdom: Precursor of the state', in G.D. Jones, and R.R. Kautz, eds, *The Transition to Statehood in the New World*, pp. 37–79. Cambridge: Cambridge University Press.

Carrier, J.G. 1990. 'Reconciling commodities and personal relations in industrial society', *Theory and Society*, 19: 579–598.

Carrier, J.G. 1991. 'Gifts, commodities, and social relations: A Maussian view of exchange', *Sociological Forum*, 6: 119–136.

Carrier, J.G. 1995. *Gifts and Commodities: Exchange and Western Capitalism since 1700*. London: Routledge.

Caselli, G.C. and Lo Forte, G. 2020. *Lo stato illegale. Mafia e politica da Portella della Ginestra a oggi*. Roma-Bari: Laterza.

Cassano, F. 2001. 'Southern thought', *Thesis Eleven*, 67: 1–10.

Castagna, E. 2010. *Sangue e onore in digitale*. Soveria Mannelli: Rubbettino.

Castells, M. 2000. *End of Millennium. The Information Age: Economy, Society and Culture*, vol. 3. Oxford: Blackwell.

Castiglione, F.P. 1987. *Indagine sui Beati Paoli*. Palermo: Sellerio.

Catanzaro, R. 1984. 'La mafia come fenomeno di ibridazione sociale. Proposta di un modello', *Italia contemporanea*, 156: 7–41.

Catanzaro, R. 1992 [1988]. *Men of Respect: A Social History of the Sicilian Mafia*. New York: The Free Press.

Catanzaro, R. 1993. 'Recenti studi sulla mafia', *Polis*, 7: 323–337.

Catanzaro, R. and Santoro, M. 2009. 'Pizzo e pizzini: Cultura e organizzazione nello studio della mafia', in R. Catanzaro and G. Sciortino, eds, *La fatica di cambiare*. Bologna: Il Mulino.

Catino, M. 2019. *Mafia Organizations*. Cambridge: Cambridge University Press.

Cavadi, A. 2009. *Il Dio dei mafiosi*. Milan: San Paolo Edizioni.

Ceccarelli, A. 2007. 'Clans, politics and organized crime in Central Asia', *Trends in Organized Crime*, 10(3): 19–36.

Ceruso, V. 2007. *Le sagrestie di Cosa Nostra. Inchiesta su preti e mafiosi*. Rome: Newton Compton.

Chakrabarty, D. 2000. *Provincializing Europe. Postcolonial Thought and Historical Difference*. Princeton: Princeton University Press.

Chambliss, W.J. 1978. *On the Take: From Petty Crooks to Presidents*. Bloomington: Indiana University Press.

Chambliss, W.J. 1989. 'State-organized crime', *Criminology*, 27: 183–208.

Chambliss, W.J., Michalowski, R. and Kramer, R., eds. 2010. *State Crime in the Global Age*. Cullompton: Willan.

Chaplin, A. 2013. *Chávez's Legacy: The Transformation from Democracy to a Mafia State*. University Press of America.

Chatterjee, P. 2004. *The Politics of the Governed: Reflections on Popular Politics in Most of the World*. New York: Columbia University Press.

Chen, A. 2005. 'Secret societies and organized crime in contemporary China', *Modern Asian Studies*, 39(1): 77–107.

Chesneaux, J. 1971. *Secret Societies in China in the Nineteenth and Twentieth Centuries*. London: Heinemann.

Chin, L.-L. 2009. *The Golden Triangle. Inside South East Asia's Drug Trade*. Ithaca: Cornell University Press.

Chu, Y.K. 2000. *The Triads as Business*. London: Routledge.

Chwe, M.S.-Y. 2001 *Rational Ritual. Culture, Coordination, and Common Knowledge*. Princeton: Princeton University Press.

Claessen, H.J.M. and Skalnik, P., eds. 1979. *The Early State*. The Hague: Mouton.

Claessen, H.J.M. and Skalnik, P., eds. 1981. *The Study of the State*. The Hague: Mouton.

Clarke, C. 2006. 'Politics, violence and drugs in Kingston, Jamaica', *Bulletin of Latin American Research*, 25(3): 420–440.

Clastres, P. 1988 [1974]. *Society Against the State. Essays in Political Anthropology*. London: Zone Books.

Clawson, M.A. 1989. *Constructing Brotherhood: Class, Gender, and Fraternalism*. Princeton: Princeton University Press.

Cockayne, J. 2016. *Hidden Power. The Strategic Logic of Organized Crime*. London: Hurst & Co.

Codere, H. 1950. *Fighting with Property: A Study of Kwakiutl Potlatching and Warfare, 1792–1939*. New York: Monographs of the American Ethnological Society, 28.

Coffee, N. 2017. *Gift and Gain: How Money Transformed Ancient Rome*. Oxford: Oxford University Press.

Cohen, A. 1981. *The Politics of Elite Culture*. Berkeley: University of California Press.

Cohen, S. 1996. 'Crime and politics: Can you spot the difference?' *British Journal of Sociology*, 47(1): 1–21.

Colajanni, N. 1890. *Ire e spropositi di Cesare Lombroso*. Catania: Tropea.

Colajanni, N. 1895. *Gli avvenimenti in Sicilia e le loro cause*. Palermo: Sandron 1894

Colajanni, N. 1900. *Nel regno della mafia, dai Borboni ai Sabaudi*. Rome: Rivista Popolare.

Cole, D. and Chaikin, I. 1990. *An Iron Hand Upon the People: The Law Against the Potlatch on the Northwest Coast*. Seattle: University of Washington Press.

Collins, H.M. 2010. *Tacit and Explicit Knowledge. Chicago:* University of Chicago Press.

Collins, K. 2003. 'The political role of clans in Central Asia', *Comparative Politics*, 35: 171–19.

Collins, K. 2004. 'The logic of clan politics: Evidence from the Central Asian trajectories', *World Politics*, 56(2): 224–261.

Collins, R. 2008. *On Violence*. Princeton: Princeton University Press.

Collins, R. 2011. 'Patrimonial alliances and failures of state penetration: A historical dynamic of crime, corruption, gangs, and mafias', *Annals of the American Academy of Political and Social Science*, 636: 16–31.

Colomy, P. 1988. 'Donald R. Cressey: A personal and intellectual remembrance', *Crime & Delinquency*, 34(3): 242–262.

Comaroff, J. and Comaroff, J.L. 2012. *Theory from the South: or, How Euro-America is Evolving toward Africa*. Boulder: Paradigm.

Comaroff, J. and Comaroff, J.L. 2016. *The Truth about Crime: Sovereignty, Knowledge and Social Order*. Chicago: University of Chicago Press.

Connell, R.W. 2007. *Southern Theory: The Global Dynamics of Knowledge in Social Science*. Cambridge: Polity.

Conti, R. 1877. *Risposta allo orrendo libello di Leopoldo Franchetti, intitolato la Sicilia nel 1876. Condizioni politiche e amministrative*. Catania: Pastore.

Cornell, V.J. 2005. 'Ibn Battuta's opportunism. The networks and loyalties of a medieval Muslim scholar', in M. Cooke and N.B. Lawrence, eds, *Muslim Networks from Hajj to Hip Hop*. Chapel Hill: University of North Carolina Press.

Corriveau, L. 2012. 'Game theory and the kula', *Rationality and Society*, 24(1): 106–128.

Coser, L.A. 1964. 'The political functions of eunuchism', *American Sociological Review*, 29(6): 880–885.

Coser, L.A. 1974. *Greedy Institutions: Patterns of Undivided Commitment*. New York: Free Press.

Crawford, F.M. 1901. *The Rulers of the South. Sicily, Calabria, Malta*, 2 vols. New York: Macmillan.

Cressey, D. 1969. *Theft of the Nation: The Structure and Operations of Organized Crime in America*. New York: Harper & Row.

Cressey, D. 1972a. *Criminal Organization: Its Elementary Forms*. New York: Harper & Row.

Cressey, D. 1972b. 'Review of Joseph L. Albini's *The American Mafia*', *American Journal of Sociology*, 78(3): 744–746.

Crisantino, A. 2000. *Della segreta e operosa associazione. Una setta all'origine della mafia*. Palermo: Sellerio.

Cronbach, L.J. and Meehl, P.C. 1955. 'Construct validity in psychological tests', *Psychological Bulletin*, 52: 281–302.

Cutrera, A. 1900. *La mafia e i mafiosi: origini e manifestazioni. Studio di sociologia criminale.* Palermo: Reber.

Dainotto, R. M. 2015. *The Mafia: A Cultural History.* Islington: Reaktion Books.

dalla Chiesa, N. 1976. *Il potere mafioso. Economia e ideologia.* Milan: Mazzotta.

dalla Chiesa, N. 2010a. *La convergenza. Mafia e politica nella seconda repubblica.* Milan: Melampo.

dalla Chiesa, N. 2010b. 'Mafia, la letteratura dimezzata. Ovvero l'effetto G', *Polis*, XXIV(3): 421–440.

dalla Chiesa, N., ed. 2017. *Mafia globale. Le organizzazioni criminali nel mondo.* Milan: Laurana.

dalla Chiesa, N. and Cabras, F. 2019. *Rosso Mafia.* Milan: Bompiani.

dalla Chiesa, N. and Panzarasa, M. 2011. *Buccinasco. La 'ndrangheta al nord.* Turin: Einaudi.

Dalli, C. 2008. 'Bridging Europe and Africa: Norman Sicily's other kingdom', in J. Carvalho, ed., *Bridging the Gaps: Sources, Methodology and Approaches to Religion in History*, pp. 77–93. Pisa: Pisa University Press.

Das, V. and Poole, D., eds. 2004. *Anthropology in the Margins of the State.* Santa Fe: School of American Research Press.

Davis, F. 1977. *Primitive Revolutionaries of China: A Study of Secret Societies* of the Late Nineteenth Century. London: Routledge & Kegan Paul.

Davy, G. 2018 [1922]. *La Foi jurée. Étude sociologique du problème du contrat: la formation du lien contractuel.* Paris: PUF.

Dawson, A. 2016. 'Political violence in consolidated democracies: The development and institutionalization of partisan violence in late colonial Jamaica (1938–62)', *Social Science History*, 40(2): 185–218.

De Blasio, A. 1897. *Usi e costumi dei camorristi.* Napoli, Gambella.

De Mauro, T. 1963. *Storia linguistica dell'Italia unita.* Bari: Laterza.

Derrida, J. 1988. 'The politics of friendship', *Journal of Philosophy*, 85: 632–644.

Derrida, J. 1992. *Given Time: 1. Counterfeit Money.* Chicago: University of Chicago Press.

Derrida, J. 2000. *Of Hospitality.* Stanford: Stanford University Press.

Dewey, J. 1954 [1927]. *The Public and Its Problems.* New York: Holt.

Dickie, J. 2004. *Cosa Nostra. A History of the Sicilian Mafia.* New York: Palgrave Macmillan.

Digeser, P.E. 2008. 'Friendship between states', *British Journal of Political Science*, 39: 323–344.

DiMaggio, P. 1977. 'Market structure, the creative process, and popular culture: Toward an organizational reinterpretation of mass culture theory', *Journal of Popular Culture*, 11(2): 436–452.

DiMaggio, P. 1994. 'Culture and economy', in N. Smelser and R. Swedberg, eds, *Handbook of Economic Sociology*, pp. 27-57. New York: Russell Sage.

DiMaggio, P. 1997. 'Culture and cognition', *Annual Review of sociology*, 24, 263–287.

DiMaggio, P. and Powell, W. 1983. 'The iron cage revisited: Institutional isomorphism and collective rationality in organizational fields', *American Sociological Review*, 48(2): 147–160.

Dino, A. 2002. *Mutazioni. Etnografia del mondo di Cosa nostra*. Palermo: La Zisa.

Dino, A. 2007. 'Symbolic domination and active power: Female roles in criminal organizations', in G. Fiandaca, ed., *Women and the Mafia*, pp. 67–86. New York: Springer.

Dino, A. 2008. *La mafia devota*. Roma-Bari: Laterza.

Dino, A. 2012. *Gli ultimi padrini. Indagine sul governo di Cosa Nostra*. Rome-Bari: Laterza.

Dino, A. 2016. *A colloquio con Spatuzza*. Bologna: Il Mulino.

Dixit, A. 2006. 'Thomas Schelling's contributions to game theory', *Scandinavian Journal of Economics*, 108(2): 213–229.

Dolci, D. 1964 [1960]. *Waste: An Eye-witness Report on Some Aspects of Waste in Western Sicily*. New York: Monthly Review Press.

Douglas, M. 1986. *How Institutions Think*. New York: Syracuse University Press.

Duggan, C. 1989. *Fascism and the Mafia*. New Haven: Yale University Press.

Duncan, G. 2013. 'Una lectura política de Pablo Escobar', *Co-Herencia*, 10(19): 235–262.

Duneier, M. 1999. *Slim's Table: Race, Respectability, and Masculinity*. Chicago: University of Chicago Press.

Dunlap, D. 2018. 'Jaan-pehchaan (India)', in A. Ledeneva, ed., *The Global Encyclopedia of Informality*, vol. 1, pp. 96–99. London: UCL Press.

Durkheim, É. 2008 [1912]. *The Elementary Forms of Religious Life*. Oxford: Oxford University Press.

Earle, T. 1997. *How Chiefs Come to Power. The Political Economy in Prehistory*. Stanford: Stanford University Press.

Eco, U. 1978. *Il superuomo di massa*. Milan: Bompiani.

Edberg, M.C. 2004. *El Narcotraficante: Narcocorridos and the Construction of a Cultural Persona on the US–Mexican Border*. Austin: University of Texas Press.

Eguavoen, I. 2008. 'Killer cults on campus: Secrets, security and services among Nigerian students', *Sociologus*, 58(1): 1–25.

Elder-Vass, D. 2015. 'Free gifts and positional gifts: Beyond exchangism', *European Journal of Social Theory*, 18: 451–468.

Elder-Vass, D. 2019. 'Defining the gift', *Journal of Institutional Economics* 1: 1–11.

Elias, N. 1982 [1969]. *The Civilizing Process*, vol. 2: *State Formation and Civilization*. Oxford: Basil Blackwell.

Ellis, S. 2016. *This Present Darkness: A History of Nigerian Organized Crime*. New York: Oxford University Press.

Elster, J., ed. 1986. *Rational Choice*. Blackwell.

Elster, J. 2007. *Explaining Social Behavior: More Nuts and Bolts for the Social Sciences*, Cambridge: Cambridge University Press.

Erickson, B.H. 1981. 'Secret societies and social structure', *Social Forces*, 60(1): 188–210.

Evans, P., Rueschemeyer, D. and Skocpol, T., eds. 2010 [1985]. *Bringing the State Back In*. Cambridge: Cambridge University Press.

Falcone, G. and Padovani, M. 1993 [1992]. *Men of Honour: The Truth about the Mafia*. London: Warner.

Fassin, D. et al. 2015. *At the Heart of the State: The Moral World of Institutions*. London: Pluto Press.

Fentress, J. 2000. *Rebels and Mafiosi: Death in a Sicilian Landscape*. Ithaca: Cornell University Press.

Ferreira, M.A.S.V. 2019. 'Brazilian criminal organizations as transnational violent non-state actors: A case study of the Primeiro Comando da Capital (PCC)', *Trends in Organized Crime*, 22: 148–165.

Ferris, E. 2011. *The Politics of Protection: The Limits of Humanitarian Action*. Washington: Brookings Institution Press.

Fiandaca, G., ed. 2017. *Women and the Mafia. Female Roles in Organized Crime Structures*. New York: Springer.

Fiandaca, G. and Lupo, S. 2014. *La mafia non ha vinto. Il labirinto della trattativa*. Roma-Bari: Laterza.

Fijnaut, C. and Paoli, L., eds. 2004. *Organised Crime in Europe: Concepts, Patterns and Policies in the European Union and Beyond*. Dordrecht: Kluwer.

Finckenauer, J.O. 2007. *Mafia and Organized Crime: A Beginner's Guide*. Oxford: Oneworld Publications.

Finley, M.I. 1978 [1954]. *The World of Odysseus*, 3rd edn. London: Chatto & Windus.

Fonseca, G. 2020. 'The use of terrorist tools by criminal organizations: The case of the Brazilian Primeiro Comando da Capital (PCC)', *Perspectives on Terrorism*, 14(4): 64–82.

Foucault, M. 1980. 'Truth and power', in C. Gordon, ed., *Power/Knowledge: Selected Interviews and Other Writings 1972–1977*. New York: Pantheon, 109–133.

Foucault, M. 1988. 'Technologies of the self', in L.H. Martin, H. Gutman and P. H. Hutton, eds., *Technologies of the Self. A Seminar with Michael Foucault*, pp. 16–49. Amherst: University of Massachusetts Press.

Franchetti, L. 1993 [1877]. *Condizioni politiche e amministrative della Sicilia*. Rome: Donzelli.

Frederiksen, B.F. 2010. 'Mungiki, vernacular organization, and political society in Kenya', *Development and Change*, 41(6): 1065–1089.

Freund, J. 1965. *L'Essence du politique*. Paris: Sirey.

Frickel, S. and Gross, N. 2005. 'A general theory of scientific/intellectual movements', *American Sociological Review*, 70(2): 204–232.

Friedland, R. and Alford, R.R. 1991. 'Bringing society back in: Symbols, practices, and institutional contradictions', in W.W. Powell and P.J. DiMaggio, eds, *The New Institutionalism in Organizational Analysis*, pp. 232–263. Chicago: University of Chicago Press.

Frye, T. 2002. 'Private protection in Russia and Poland', *American Journal of Political Science*, 46: 572–584.

Gal, S. 2002. 'A semiotics of the public/private distinction', *Differences*, 13(1): 77–95.

Galeotti, M. 2018. *The Vory: Russia's Super Mafia*. New Haven: Yale University Press.

Gallie, W. 1956. 'Essentially contested concepts', *Proceedings of the Aristotelian Society*, 56: 167–198.

Gambetta, D. 1987. 'Fragments of an economic theory of the mafia', *European Journal of Sociology* 29(1): 127–145.

Gambetta, D. 1993. *The Sicilian Mafia. The Business of Private Protection*. Cambridge: Harvard University Press.

Gambetta, D. 2009. *Codes of the Underworld. How Criminals Communicate*. Princeton: Princeton University Press.

Gambetta, D. 2011. '"The Sicilian Mafia". Twenty years after publication', *Sociologica*. https://www.rivisteweb.it/doi/10.2383/35869.

Gambetta, D. and Reuter, P. 1995. 'Conspiracy among the many: The mafia in legitimate industries', in N.G. Fielding, A. Clarke and R. Witt, eds, *The Economic Dimensions of Crime*. London: Palgrave Macmillan.

Garfinkel, H. 1967. *Studies in Ethnomethodology*. Englewood Cliffs: Prentice Hall

Gavini, D. 2017. 'Mafia and funerals. Representations, stereotypes and identity: The US case', in T. Calò and L. Ceci, eds, *L'immaginario devoto tra mafie e antimafia 1. Riti, culti e santi*, Rome: Viella.

Geertz, C. 1963. 'The integrative revolution: Primordial loyalties and civil sentiments in the new states', in C. Geertz, ed., *Old Societies and New States: The Quest for Modernity in Asia and Africa*, pp. 105–157. New York: Free Press of Glencoe.

Geertz, C. 1973. *The Interpretation of Cultures*. New York: Basic Books.

Geschiere, P. 2002. 'On witch-doctors and spin-doctors: The role of "experts" in African and American politics', in B. Meyer and P. Pels, eds, *Magic and Modernity*. Stanford: Stanford University Press.

Ghosh, S. 1991. *The Indian Mafia*. New Delhi: Ashish Publishing House.

Ginkel, R. and Stengs, I. 2006. 'An outsider looking in: Jeremy Boissevain', *ETNOFOOR*, XIX(1): 15–26.

Ginzburg, C. 1979. 'Clues: Roots of a scientific paradigm', *Theory and Society*, 7(3): 273–288.

Ginzburg, C. 1986. *Spie. Radici di un paradigma indiziario*. Turin: Einaudi.

Giordano, C. 2012. 'The anthropology of Mediterranean societies', in U. Kockel, M.N. Craith and J. Frykman, eds, *A Companion to the Anthropology of Europe*. Oxford: Blackwell.

Glaeser, A. 2011. *Political Epistemics. The Secret Police, the Opposition, and the End of East German Socialism*. Chicago: University of Chicago Press.

Glenny, M. 2008. *McMafia. A Journey Through the Global Criminal Underworld*. New York: Vintage.

Godbout, J.T. and Caillé, A.1998. *The World of the Gift*. Montreal: McGill-Queen's University Press.

Godelier, M. 1999. *The Enigma of the Gift*. Cambridge: Polity.

Goffman, E. 1961. *Asylums: Essays on the Social Situations of Mental Patients and Other Inmates*. New York: Doubleday.

Goffman, E. 1969. *Strategic Interaction*. Philadelphia: University of Pennsylvania Press.

Gofman A. 1998. 'A vague but suggestive concept: The "total social fact"', in W. James and N.J. Allen, eds, *Marcel Mauss: A Centenary Tribute*. Oxford, Berghahn.

Goodman, D. 1992. 'Public sphere and private life: Toward a synthesis of current historiographical approaches to the old regime', *History and Theory*, 31(1): 1–20.

Goody, J. 1986. *The Logic of Writing and the Organization of Society*. Cambridge: Cambridge University Press.

Goody, J. and Watt, I. 1963. 'The consequences of literacy', *Comparative Studies in Society and History*, 5(3): 304–345.

Gould, R.V. 2003. *Collision of Will. How Ambiguity about Social Rank Breeds Conflict*. Chicago: University of Chicago Press.

Gower Chapman, C. 1971. *Milocca: A Sicilian Village*. London: Schenkman.

Graeber, D. 2004. *Fragments of an Anarchist Anthropology*. Cambridge: Prickly Paradigm Press.

Gragert, B.A. 1997. 'Yakuza: The warlords of Japanese organized crime', *Annual Survey of International & Comparative Law*, 4(1): 147–151.

Gramsci, A. 1971. *Selections from the Prison Notebooks*. New York: International Publishers.

Granovetter, M. 1985. 'Economic action and social structure: The problem of embeddedness', *American Journal of Sociology*, 91(3): 487.

Green, D.P. and Shapiro, I. 1994. *The Pathologies of Rational Choice Theory. A Critique of Applications in Political Science*. New Haven: Yale University Press.

Gregory, C.A. 1980. 'Gifts to Men and Gifts to God: Gift Exchange and Capital Accumulation in Contemporary Papua', *Man*, 15(4): 626–652.

Gregory, C.A. 2015 [1982]. *Gifts and Commodities*, 2nd edn. London: HAU Books.

Greif, A. 2006. *Institutions and the Path to the Modern Economy: Lessons from Medieval Trade*. Cambridge: Cambridge University Press.

Gross, N. 2009. 'A pragmatist theory of social mechanisms', *American Sociological Review*, 74: 358–379.

Guha, R. 1999 [1983]. *Elementary Aspects of Peasant Insurgency in Colonial India*. Durham: Duke University Press.

Gupta, A. 1995. 'Blurred boundaries: The discourse of corruption, the culture of politics, and the imagined state', *American Ethnologist*, 22(2): 375–402.

Gygax, M.D. 2013. 'Gift-giving and power relationships in Greek social praxis and public discourse', in M.L. Satlow, ed., *The Gift in Antiquity*, pp. 45–60. Oxford: Oxford University Press.

Habermas, J. 1974. 'The public sphere: An encyclopedia article (1964)', *New German Critique*, 1(3): 49–55.

Habermas, J. 1989 [1962]. *The Structural Transformation of the Public Sphere. An Inquiry into a Category of Bourgeois Society*. Cambridge: MIT Press.

Hagedorn, J.M. (2008). *A World of Gangs: Armed Young Men and Gangsta Culture*. Minneapolis: University of Minnesota Press.

Haidar, L. 2019. 'The emergence of the Mafia in post-war Syria: The terror–crime continuum', *Studies in Conflict & Terrorism*. https://doi.org/10.1080/1057610X.2019.1678869.

Hale, H.E. 2015. *Patronal Politics: Eurasian Regime Dynamics in Comparative Perspective* Cambridge: Cambridge University Press.

Hamaguchi, E. 1985. 'A contextual model of the Japanese: Toward a methodological innovation in Japan studies', *Journal of Japanese Studies*, 11(2): 289–321.

Hammel, E.A. 2005. 'Kinship-based politics and the optimal size of kin groups', *PNAS*, 102(33): 11951–11956.

Handelman, S. 1995. *Comrade Criminal: Russia's New Mafiya*. New Haven: Yale University Press.

Harding, L. 2011. *Mafia State: How One Reporter Became an Enemy of the Brutal New Russia*. London: Guardian Books.

Haseldine, J. 2013. 'Friendship networks in Medieval Europe: New models of a political relationship', *AMITY: The Journal of Friendship Studies*, 1: 69–88.

Hawkins, G. 1969. 'God and the mafia', *The Public Interest*, 14: 24–51.

Hayden, B. 2018. *The Power of Ritual in Prehistory: Secret Societies and Origins of Social Complexity*. Cambridge: Cambridge University Press.

Hedstrom, P. 2005. *Dissecting the Social: On the Principles of Analytic Sociology*. Cambridge: Cambridge University Press.

Hedstrom, P. and Swedberg, R., eds. 1996. *Social Mechanisms. An Analytical Approach to Social Theory*. Cambridge: Cambridge University Press.

Herdt, G.H. 2003. *Secrecy and Cultural Reality: Utopian Ideologies of the New Guinea Men's House*. Ann Arbor: University of Michigan Press.

Herrmann, G.M. 1997. 'Gift or commodity: What changes hands in the US garage sale?' *American Ethnologist*, 24(4): 910–930.

Herzfeld, M. 1987. *Anthropology through the Looking-Glass: Critical Ethnography in the Margins of Europe*. Cambridge: Cambridge University Press.

Hess, H. 1970. *Mafia. Zentrale Herrschaft und lokale Gegenmacht*. Tübingen: Mohr. English trans., *Mafia and Mafiosi. The Structure of Power*. Lexington: Heath Lexington Books, 1973; new edn, *Mafia & Mafiosi. Origin, Power and Myth*. New York: NYU Press, 1998.

Hess, H. 1977. *Prefazione*, in G. Alongi, *La maffia*. Palermo: Sellerio.

Hess, H. 2011. 'Approaching and explaining the Mafia phenomenon. Attempts of a sociologist', *Sociologica*. https://www.rivisteweb.it/doi/10.2383/35870.

Hetherington, K. 1994. 'The contemporary significance of Schmalenbach's concept of the *bund*', *Sociological Review*, 42(1): 1–25.

Heyman, J. Mc. 1999. *States and Illegal Practices*. Oxford: Berg.

Hill, P.B.E. 2003. *The Japanese Mafia. Yakuza, Law, and the State*. Oxford: Oxford University Press.

Hintze, O. 1980. *Stato e società*. Bologna: Zanichelli.

Hobsbawm, E.J. 1959. *Primitive Rebels: Studies in Archaic Forms of Social*

Movement in the 19th and 20th Centuries. Manchester: Manchester University Press.

Hobsbawm, E.J. 1969. *Bandits*. New York: Delacorte Press.

Hobsbawm, E.J. 1973. 'Peasants and politics', *Journal of Peasant Studies*, 1(1): 3–22.

Homans G.C. 1961. *Social Behavior: Its Elementary Forms*. New York: Harcourt, Brace & World.

Hopwood, K., ed. 1999. *Organised Crime in Antiquity*. London: Duckworth.

Hughes, E.C. 1971. *The Sociological Eye. Collected Essays*. New York: Transaction.

Humphrey, C. 2002. The Unmaking of Soviet Life: Everyday Economies after Socialism. Ithaca: Cornell University Press.

Hyde, L. 1983. *The Gift: Imagination and the Erotic Life of Property*. New York: Random House.

Ianni, F.A.J. 1972. *A Family Business. Kinship and Social Control in Organized Crime*. New York: Russell Sage Foundation.

Ianni, F.A.J. 1975. *Black Mafia. Ethnic Succession in Organized Crime*. New York: Pocket Books.

Ikegami, E. 1997. *The Taming of the Samurai*. Cambridge: Harvard University Press.

Inglis, D. and Almila, A.-M., eds. 2016. *The SAGE Handbook of Cultural Sociology*. London: SAGE.

Jackson, B. 2012. 'Bonds of brotherhood: Emotional and social support among college black men', *Annals of the American Academy of Political and Social Science*, 642: 61–71.

Jaffe, R. 2012. 'The popular culture of illegality: Crime and the politics of aesthetics in urban Jamaica', *Anthropological Quarterly*, 85(1): 79–102.

Jaffe, R. 2013. 'The hybrid state: Crime and citizenship in urban Jamaica', *American Ethnologist*, 40(4): 734–748.

Jamieson, E. 1999. *The Antimafia: Italy's Fight Against Organized Crime*. London: Macmillan.

Jessop, B. 2016. *The State: Past, Present, Future*. Cambridge: Polity.

Joans, B. 2001. *Bike Lust: Harleys, Women and American Society*. Madison: University of Wisconsin Press.

Johnson, H.N. and Soeters, J.L. 2008. 'Jamaican dons, Italian godfathers and the chances of a "reversible destiny"', *Political Studies* 56(1): 166–191.

Johnson, P.C. 2002. *Secrets, Gossip, and Gods: The Transformation of Brazilian Candomble*. Oxford: Oxford University Press.

Jussen, B. 2000. *Spiritual Kinship and Social Practice: Godparenthood and Adoption in the Early Middle Ages*. Newark: University of Delaware Press.

Kaplan, D.E. and Dubro, A. 1993 [1986]. *Yakuza: The Explosive Account of Japan's Criminal Underworld*. Reading: Addison-Wesley.

Kaplan, M. 1992. *Narcotraffico: gli aspetti sociopolitici*.Torino: Edizioni Gruppo Abele.

Karsenti, B. 1997. *L'Homme total. Sociologie, anthropologie et philosophie chez Marcel Mauss*. Paris: PUF.

Kelly, D. 2003. *The State of the Political: Conceptions of Politics and the State in the Thought of Max Weber, Carl Schmitt and Franz Neumann*. Oxford: Oxford University Press.

Kelly, R., ed. 1986. *Organized Crime: An International Perspective*. Totowa: Rowan & Littlefield.

Khaldūn, I. 1967. *The Muqaddimah: An Introduction to History*, trans. Franz Rosenthal, ed. N.J. Dawood. New York: Princeton.

Kinna, R. 1995. 'Kropotkin's theory of mutual aid in historical context', *International Review of Social History*, 40(2): 259–283.

Kipnis, A. 1996. 'The language of gifts: Managing *guanxi* in a North China village', *Modern China*, 22(3): 285–314.

Konstan, D. 1997. *Friendship in the Classical World*. Cambridge: Cambridge University Press.

Kopytoff, I. 1986. 'The cultural biography of things: Commodification as process', in A. Appadurai, ed., *The Social Life of Things*, pp. 64–91. New York: Cambridge University Press.

Koselleck, R. 2000. *Critique and Crisis: Enlightenment and the Pathogenesis of Modern Society*. Cambridge: MIT Press.

Krakowski, K. and Zubiria, G. 2019. 'Accounting for turbulence in the Colombian underworld', *Trends in Organized Crime*, 22(2): 166–186.

Kreuzer, P. 2012. *Mafia-style Domination in the Philippines: Comparing Provinces*. Frankfurt: Peace Research Institute.

Kropotkin, P. 1902. *Mutual Aid: A Factor of Evolution*. London: Freedom Press.

Ku, A.S. 1998. 'Boundary politics in the public sphere: Openness, secrecy, and leak', *Sociological Theory*, 16(2): 172–192.

Kumar, A. 2014. *Criminalisation of Politics: Caste, Land and the State*. Delhi: Rawat Publications.

Kuper, A. 1970. *Kalahari Village Politics. An African Democracy*. Cambridge: Cambridge University Press.

Laidlaw, J. 2000. 'A free gift makes no friends', *Journal of the Royal Anthropological Institute*, 6(4): 617–634.

La Spina, A. 2005. *Mafia, legalità debole e sviluppo del Mezzogiorno*. Bologna: il Mulino.

Lal, V. 1995 [1915]. 'Criminality and colonial anthropology', in M.P.R. Naidu, *The History of Railway Thieves, with Illustrations and Hints on Detection*, pp. i–xxvii. Gurgaon, Haryana: Vintage Press.

Landa, J. 1983. 'The enigma of the kula ring: Gift-exchanges and primitive law and order', *International Review of Law and Economics*, 3: 137–160.

Landes, J.B. 1988. *Women and the Public Sphere in the Age of the French Revolution*. Ithaca: Cornell University Press.

Landesco, J. 1968 [1929]. *Organized Crime in Chicago*. Chicago: University of Chicago Press.

Lane, F.C. 1958. 'Economic consequences of organized violence', *Journal of Economic History*, 18(4): 401–417.

Latour, B. 2005. *Reassembling the Social: An Introduction to Actor-Network Theory*. Oxford: Oxford University Press.

Leach, E.R. 1954. *Political Systems of Highland Burma*. London: Bell.

Ledeneva, A.V. 1998. *Russia's Economy of Favours: 'Blat', Networking and Informal Exchange.* Cambridge: Cambridge University Press.

Lee, J. 2011. 'Kula and relation capital: Rational reinterpretation of primitive gift institution', *Rationality and Society*, 23(4): 475–512.

Leeds, E. 1996. 'Cocaine and parallel polities on the Brazilian urban periphery: Constraints on local level democratization', *Latin American Research Review*, 31(3): 47–48.

Leeson, P. 2009. *The Invisible Hook: The Hidden Economics of Pirates.* Princeton: Princeton University Press.

Lemert, C. 1997. *Social Things.* New York: Norton.

Lepenies, W. 1988. *Between Literature and Science. The Rise of Sociology.* Cambridge: Cambridge University Press.

Lestingi, F. 1884. 'L'associazione della Fratellanza nella provincia di Girgenti', *Archivio di Psichiatria, Antropologia Criminale e Scienze Penali*: 452-463.

Levine, D.N. 1995. *Visions of the Sociological Tradition.* Chicago: University of Chicago Press.

Lévi-Strauss, C. 1969 [1949]. *The Elementary Structures of Kinship.* Boston: Beacon Press.

Lévi-Strauss, C. 1987 [1950]. *Introduction to the Work of Marcel Mauss.* London: Routledge.

Li Causi, L. and Cassano, M. 1993. 'Antropologia, mafia e scienze sociali. Riflessioni dall'esterno', *Ossimori*, 3: 10–24

Lichbach, M.I. 1997. 'Social theory and comparative politics', in M.I. Lichbach and A.S Zuckerman, eds, *Comparative Politics: Rationality, Culture, and Structure*, pp. 239–276. Cambridge: Cambridge University Press.

Lichbach, M.I. 2003. *Is Rational Choice Theory All of Social Science?* Ann Arbor: University of Michigan Press.

Liebersohn, H. 2011. *The Return of the Gift: European History of a Global Idea.* New York: Cambridge University Press.

Liebow, E. 1967. *Tally's Corner. A Study of Negro Streetcorner Men.* Boston: Little, Brown & Co.

Little, D. 2012. 'Analytical sociology and the rest of sociology', *Sociologica*, VI(1): 1–46.

Little, K. 1965. 'The political function of the Poro', *Africa: Journal of the International African Institute*, 35(4): 349–365.

Llewellyn, K.N. and Hoebel, E.A. 1941. *The Cheyenne Way. Conflict and Case Law in Primitive Jurisprudence.* Norman: University of Oklahoma Press.

Lo, T.W. 1993. *Corruption and Politics in Hong Kong and China.* Buckingham: Open University Press.

Lo, T.W. 2010. 'Beyond social capital: Triad organized crime in HK and China', *British Journal of Criminology*, 50(5): 851–872.

Lo, T.W. and Kwok, S.I. 2014. 'Triads and tongs', in G. Bruinsma and D. Weisburd, eds, *Encyclopedia of Criminology and Criminal Justice.* New York: Springer.

Lo Monaco, C. 1990. 'A proposito dell'etimologia di mafia e mafioso', *Lingua Nostra*, 51: 1–8.

Lo Verso, G. 1998. *La mafia dentro. Psicologia e Psicopatologia di un fondamentalismo*. Milan: FrancoAngeli.

Lodato, S. 1999. *Ho ucciso Giovanni Falcone. La vita di Giovanni Brusca*. Milan: Mondadori.

Lombardo, R. 2013. *Organized Crime in Chicago: Beyond the Mafia*. Champaign: University of Illinois Press.

Lombroso, C. 1863. *Tre mesi in Calabria*, Torino: UTET.

Loong, C. 2011. 'Reel Medici mobsters? *The Medici: Godfathers of the Renaissance* reassessed'. http://www.screeningthepast.com/issue-26-special-issue-early-europe/reel-medici-mobsters-the-medici-godfathers-of-the-renaissance%C2%A0reassessed/.

Lovell, S., Ledeneva, A. and Rogachevskii, A., eds. 2000. *Bribery and* Blat *in Russia: Negotiating Reciprocity from the Early Modern Period to the 1990s*. London: Palgrave.

Ludden, D. 2001. *Reading Subaltern Studies: Critical History, Contested Meaning and the Globalisation of South Asia*. Delhi: Permanent Black.

Lund, C. 2006. 'Twilight institutions: Public authority and local politics in Africa', *Development and Change*, 37: 685–705.

Luo, Y. 2000. *Guanxi and Business*, 2nd edn. Singapore: World Scientific Publishing.

Lupo, S. 1993. *Storia della mafia. Dalle origini ai nostri giorni*. Rome: Donzelli.

Lupo, S. 2008. *Quando la mafia trovò l'America. Storia di un intreccio intercontinentale, 1888–2008*. Turin: Einaudi.

Lupo, S. 2009. *History of the Mafia*. New York: Columbia University Press.

Maas, P. 1968. *The Valachi Papers*. New York: Putnam.

Mack Smith, D. 1968. *A History of Sicily: Medieval Sicily 800–1713*. London: Chatto & Windus.

MacKenzie, N. 1967. *Secret Societies*. New York: Holt, Rhinehart and Winston.

MacKinnon, C. 1989. *Toward a Feminist Theory of the State*. Cambridge: Harvard University Press.

Maestripieri, D. 2007. *Machiavellian Intelligence. How Rhesus Macaques and Humans Have Conquered the World*. Chicago: University of Chicago Press.

Maffesoli, M. 1996. *The Time of the Tribes: The Decline of Individualism in Mass Society*. London: Sage.

Magyar, B. 2016. *Post-Communist Mafia State: The Case of Hungary*. Budapest: Central European University Press.

Magyar, B. and Vasarhelyi, J., eds. 2017. *Twenty-Five Sides of a Post-Communist Mafia State*. Budapest: Central European University Press.

Mair, L. 1970 [1963]. *Primitive Government*. Harmondsworth: Penguin Books.

Malešević, S. 2015. 'Where does group solidarity come from? Gellner and Ibn Khaldūn revisited', *Thesis Eleven*, 126(1): 85–99.

Malinowski, B. 1922. *Argonauts of the Western Pacific*. London: Routledge.

Mallard, G. 2019. *Gift Exchange: The Transnational History of a Political Idea*. Cambridge: Cambridge University Press.

Maltby, R. 2001. 'The spectacle of criminality', in J.D. Slocum, ed., *Violence and American cinema*. New York: Routledge.

Mann, M. 1986a. *The Sources of Social Power. Vol. I: A History of Power from the Beginning to* AD *1760.* Cambridge: Cambridge University Press.

Mann, M. 1986b. 'The autonomous power of the state: Its origins, mechanisms and results', in J.A. Hall, ed., *States in History*, pp.109–137. Oxford: Basil Blackwell.

Marchesano, G. 1902. *Processo contro Raffaele Palizzolo e Ci: Arringa.* Palermo: Tipografia Calogero Sciarrino.

Marchionatti, R. and Cedrini, M. 2016. *Economics as Social Science: Economics imperialism and the Challenge of Interdisciplinarity.* London: Routledge.

Marino, G.C. 1964. *L'opposizione mafiosa.* Palermo: Flaccovio.

Marino, G.C. 1979. *Storia del separatismo siciliano.* Rome: Editori Riuniti.

Marino, G.C. 1986. *L'opposizione mafiosa. Mafia politica stato liberale.* Palermo: Flaccovio.

Marino, G.C. 2006. *I padrini.* Rome: Newton Compton.

Marongiu, A. 1964. 'A model state in the Middle Ages: The Norman and Swabian Kingdom of Sicily', *Comparative Studies in Society and History*, 6(3): 307–320.

Martin, B. 1996. *The Shanghai Green Gang: Politics and Organized Crime, 1919–1937.* Los Angeles: University of California Press.

Martin, J.L. 2003. 'What is field theory?' *American Journal of Sociology*, 109(1): 1–49.

Martin, J.L. and Forest G. 2015. 'Was Bourdieu a field theorist?', in M. Hilgers and E. Mangez, eds, *Bourdieu's Theory of Social Fields*, pp. 39–61. London: Routledge.

Marx, K. 1860. 'Sicily and the Sicilians', *New York Daily Tribune*, 17 May.

Massari, M. 1998. *La Sacra Corona Unita: potere e segreto.* Roma-Bari: Laterza.

Massari, M. and Martone, V., eds. 2018. *Mafia Violence: Political, Symbolic, and Economic Forms of Violence in Camorra Clans.* London, Routledge.

Masters, R.D. 1989. *The Nature of Politics.* New Haven: Yale University Press.

Matza, D. 1969. *Becoming Deviant.* Englewood Cliffs: Prentice-Hall.

Mauss, M. 1973 [1935]. 'Techniques of the body', *Economy and Society*, 2(1): 70–88.

Mauss, M. 1975a [1921]. 'Una antica forma di contratto presso i Traci', in M. Granet and M. Mauss, *Il linguaggio dei sentimenti*, pp. 57–66. Milan: Adelphi.

Mauss, M. 1975b [1924]. 'Gift-gift', in M. Granet and M. Mauss, *Il linguaggio dei sentimenti*, pp. 67–72. Milan: Adelphi.

Mauss, M. 1990 [1925]. *The Gift: The Form and Reason for Exchange in Archaic Societies*, trans. W.D. Hall, with a foreword by M. Douglas. New York: Norton.

Mayaram, S. 2003. *Against History, Against State. Counter-perspectives from the Margins.* New York: Columbia University Press.

Mbembe, A. 2003. 'Necropolitics', *Public Culture*, 15(1): 11–40.

McCoy, A.W. 2003. *The Politics of Heroin: CIA Complicity in the Global Drug Trade, Afghanistan, Southeast Asia, Central America, Columbia*, 2nd rev. edn. Chicago: Lawrence Hill Books.

McIsaac, L. 2000. '"Righteous fraternities" and honorable men: Sworn brotherhoods in wartime Chongqing', *American Historical Review*, 105(5): 1641–1655.

McLean, P.D. 2007. *The Art of the Network. Strategic Interaction and Patronage in Renaissance Florence*. Durham: Duke University Press:

Mehta, U. 1990. 'Liberal strategies of exclusion', *Politics and Society*, 18(4): 427–454.

Meier, C. 1990. *The Greek Discovery of Politics*. Cambridge: Harvard University Press.

Merlino, S. 1894. 'Camorra, Maffia and brigandage', *Political Science Quarterly*, 9(3): 466–485.

Merton, R.K. 1949. *Social Theory and Social Structure*. New York: Free Press.

Merton, R.K. 1976. *Sociological Ambivalence and Other Essays*. New York: Free Press

Merton, R.K., Reader, G.G. and Kendall, P., eds. 1957. *The Student Physician: Introductory Studies in the Sociology of Medical Education*. Cambridge: Harvard University Press.

Messina Denaro, M. 2008. *Lettere a Svetonio*. Viterbo: Stampa Alternativa.

Metha, U.S. 1990. 'Liberal strategies of exclusion', *Politics and Society*, 18(4): 427–454.

Meyer, J.W, Boli, J., Thomas, G.M. and Ramirez, F.O. 1997. 'World society and the nation-state', *American Journal of Sociology* 103(1): 144–181.

Michelutti, L. 2010. 'Wrestling with (body) politics: Understanding "goonda" political styles in North India', in P. Price and A.E. Ruud, eds, *Power and Influence in South Asia: Bosses, Lords, and Captains*. London: Routledge.

Michelutti, L. 2018. 'Mafia Raj', in A. Ledeneva, ed., *The Global Encyclopedia of Informality*. London: UCL Press.

Michelutti, L., Hoque, A., Martin, N., Picherit, D., Rollier, P., Ruud, A. and Still, C. 2018. *Mafia Raj: The Rule of Bosses in South Asia*. Stanford: Stanford University Press.

Migdal, J.S. 1988. *Strong Societies and Weak States. State–Society Relations and State Capabilities in the Third World*. Princeton: Princeton University Press.

Migdal, J.S. 2001. *State-in-Society: Studying How States and Societies Transform and Constitute One Another*. New York: Cambridge University Press.

Miglio, G. 2011. *Lezioni di politica. 2. Scienza della politica*. Bologna: il Mulino.

Milhaupt, C.J. and West, M.D. 2000. 'The dark side of private ordering: An institutional and empirical analysis of organized crime', *University of Chicago Law Review*, 67: 41–98.

Mills, C.W. 1940. 'Situated actions and vocabularies of motive', *American Sociological Review*, 5(6): 904–913.

Mills, C.W. 1959. *The Sociological Imagination*. Oxford: Oxford University Press.

Mitchell, T. 1988. *Colonizing Egypt*. Chicago: University of Chicago Press.

Mitchell, T. 1991. 'The limits of the state: Beyond statist approaches and their critics', *American Political Science Review*, 85(1): 77–96.

Moe, N. 2002. *The View from Vesuvius: Italian Culture and the Southern Question*. Berkeley: University of California Press.

Monnier, M. 2010 [1862]. *Notizie storiche documentate sul brigantaggio.* Whitefish: Kessinger Publishing.

Morreale, E. 2020. *La mafia immaginaria. Settant'anni di Cosa Nostra al cinema 1949–2019.* Rome: Donzelli.

Morris, I. 1986. 'Gift and commodity in Ancient Greece', *Man*, 21: 1–17.

Mortati, C. 1973. 'Brevi note sul rapporto fra costituzione e politica nel pensiero di Carl Schmitt', *Quaderni Fiorentini per la Storia del Pensiero Giuridico*, 2(1): 511–532.

Mosca, G. 1933. 'Mafia', in *Encyclopedia of the Social Sciences*, vol. 10, p. 36. New York: Macmillan. Italian trans. in G. Mosca, *Uomini e cose di Sicilia.* Palermo: Sellerio.

Mosca, G. 1939 [1896]. *The Ruling Class.* New York: McGraw-Hill.

Mosca, G. 1980 [1900]. 'Che cosa è la mafia', in G. Mosca, *Uomini e cose di Sicilia.* Palermo: Sellerio.

Moss, D. 2001. 'The gift of repentance: A Maussian perspective on twenty years of pentimento in Italy', *European Journal of Sociology*, 42: 297–331.

Mouffe, C. 2005. *On the Political.* London: Routledge.

Mullins, N. 1973. *Theories and Theory Groups in Contemporary American Sociology.* New York: Harper & Row.

Murray, D.H., in collaboration with Qin Baoqi. 1994. *The Origins of the Tiandihui: The Chinese Triads in Legend and History.* Stanford: Stanford University Press.

Naim, M. 2012. 'Mafia states: Organized crime takes office', *Foreign Affairs*, 91(3): 100–111.

Nardin, L.G. et al. 2016. 'Simulating protection rackets: A case study of the Sicilian Mafia', *Autonomous Agents and Multi-Agent Systems*, 30: 1117–1147.

Negt, O. and Kluge, A. 1993. *Public Sphere and Experience: Toward an Analysis of the Bourgeois and Proletarian Public Sphere.* Minneapolis: University of Minnesota Press.

Nelken, D. 1995. 'Review of Gambetta, *The Sicilian Mafia. The Industry of Private Protection*', *British Journal of Criminology*, 35(2): 287–289.

Niceforo, A. 1899. *L'Italia barbara contemporanea.* Palermo: Reber.

Nicotri, G. 1934. *Storia della Sicilia nelle rivoluzioni e rivolte.* New York: Italian Publishers.

Nordin, V.D. and Glonti, G. 2006. 'Thieves of the law and the rule of law in Georgia', *Caucasian Review of International Affairs*, 1(1): 49–64.

Nordstrom, C. 2007. *Global Outlaws. Crime, Money, and Power in the Contemporary World.* Berkeley: University of California Press.

Notarbartolo, L. 2018. *Mio padre Emanuele Notarbartolo.* Palermo: Sellerio.

Novacco, D. 1959. 'Considerazioni sulla fortuna del termine "mafia"', *Belfagor*, 14(2), 206–212.

Nozick, R. 1974. *Anarchy, State, and Utopia.* New York: Basic Books.

Nozick, R. 1994. 'Invisible-hand explanations', *American Economic Review*, 84: 314–318.

Offer, A. 1997. 'Between the gift and the market: The economy of regard', *Economic History Review*, 3(3): 450–476.

Ogunbameru, O.A., ed. 1997. *Readings on Campus Secret Cults*. Ile-Ife: Kuntel Publishing House.

Olson, M. 1993. 'Dictatorship, democracy and development', *American Political Science Review*, 87: 567–576.

Olson, M. 2000. *Power and Prosperity*. New York: Basic Books.

Ong, W.J. 1982. *Orality and Literacy*. New York: Methuen.

Ostrom, V. and Ostrom, E. 1971. 'Public choice: A different approach to the study of public administration', *Public Administration Review*, 31: 203–216.

Ownby, D. 1995. 'The heaven and earth society as popular religion', *Journal of Asian Studies*, 54(4): 1023–1046.

Ownby, D. 1996. *Brotherhoods and Secret Societies in Early and Mid-Qing China: The Formation of a Tradition*. Stanford: Stanford University Press.

Ownby, D. and Heidhues, M.S., eds. 1993. *'Secret Societies' Reconsidered: Perspectives on the Social History of Modern South China and Southeast Asia*. New York: Sharpe.

Padgett, J. and Ansell, C. 1993. 'Robust action and the rise of the Medici, 1400–1434'. *American Journal of Sociology*, 98(6), 1259–1319.

Palazzolo, S. and Prestipino, M. 2007. *Il Codice Provenzano*. Rome-Bari: Laterza.

Palumbo, B. 2020. *Piegare i santi. Inchini rituali e pratiche mafiose*. Casale Monferrato: Marietti.

Pantaleone, M. 1962. *Mafia e politica 1943–1962*, with a preface by Carlo Levi. Turin: Einaudi.

Paoli, L. 2002. 'The paradoxes of organized crime', *Crime, Law & Social Change*, 37: 51–97.

Paoli, L. 2003. *Mafia Brotherhoods. Organized Crime, Italian Style*. Oxford: Oxford University Press.

Paoli, L., ed. 2014. *The Oxford Handbook of Organized Crime*. New York: Oxford University Press.

Papachristos, A.V. and Smith C. 2013. 'The embedded and multiplex nature of Al Capone', in C. Morselli, ed., *Crime and Networks*. New York: Routledge.

Park, S.H. and Luo, Y. 2001. 'Guanxi and organizational dynamics: Organizational networking in Chinese firms', *Strategic Management Journal*, 22(5), 455–477.

Parker, M. 2008. 'Eating with the Mafia: Belonging and violence', *Human Relations*, 61(7): 989–1006.

Parry, J. 1986. 'The gift, the Indian gift and the "Indian gift"', *Man*, 21(3): 453–473.

Pasquino, P. 1986. 'Considerazioni intorno al criterio del politico in Carl Schmitt', *Il Mulino*, 4: 673–688.

Patel, S., ed. 2010. *The ISA Handbook of Diverse Sociological Traditions*. London: Sage.

Patella, P. 2002. *La parola mafia*. Florence: Olschki.

Pateman, C. 1989. 'Feminist critiques of the public/private dichotomy', in C. Pateman, *The Disorder of Women*. Stanford: Stanford University Press.

Peng, W. 2017. *The Chinese Mafia: Organized Crime, Corruption, and Extra-legal Protection*. Oxford: Oxford University Press.

Pengalese, B. 2008. 'The bastard child of the dictatorship: The Comando Vermelho and the Birth of "Narco-Culture" in Rio de Janeiro', *Luso-Brazilian Review*, 45(1): 118–145.

Peristiany, J.G., ed. 1965. *Honour and Shame: The Values of Mediterranean Society*. London: Weidenfeld and Nicolson.

Peristiany, J.G. and Pitt-Rivers, J., eds. 1992. *Honor and Grace in Anthropology*. Cambridge: Cambridge University Press.

Pezzino, P. 1990. *Una certa reciprocità di favori. Mafia e modernizzazione violenta nella Sicilia post–unitaria*. Milan: Angeli.

Piccillo, G. 1970. 'Simboli e metafore nei gerghi della mafia', *Abruzzo. Rivista dell'Istituto di studi abruzzesi*, 8: 93–104.

Pileggi, N. 1985. *Wise Guy*. New York: Pocket Books.

Piliavsky, A. 2015. 'Patronage and community in a society of thieves', *Contributions to Indian Sociology*, 49(2): 135–161.

Piliavsky, A. and Sbriccoli, T. 2016. 'The ethics of efficacy in North India's goonda raj (rule of toughs),' *Journal of the Royal Anthropological Institute*, 22: 373–391.

Pine, J. 2012. *The Art of Making Do in Naples*. Minneapolis: University of Minnesota Press.

Pipyrou, S. 2014. 'Altruism and sacrifice: Mafia free gift-giving in South Italy', *Anthropological Forum: A Journal of Social Anthropology and Comparative Sociology*, 24(4): 412–426.

Piterberg, G., Ruiz, T.F. and Symcox, G., eds. 2010. *Braudel Revisited: The Mediterranean World, 1600–1800*. Toronto: University of Toronto Press.

Pitrè, G. 1880. *Proverbi siciliani raccolti e confrontati con quelli degli altri dialetti d'Italia*. Palermo: Lauriel.

Pitrè, G. 1889. *Usi e costumi credenze e pregiudizi del popolo siciliano*. Palermo: Lauriel.

Pitrè, G. 2008. *La mafia e l'omertà*. Palermo: Biesse.

Pitt-Rivers, J. 1968. 'The stranger, the guest and the hostile host: Introduction to the study of the laws of hospitality', in J.G. Peristiany, ed., *Contributions to Mediterranean Sociology*. Paris, Mouton.

Pitt-Rivers, J. 1977. 'The law of hospitality', in J. Pitt-Rivers, *The Fate of Shechem or the Politics of Sex: Essays in the Anthropology of the Mediterranean*. Cambridge: Cambridge University Press.

Pizzorno, A. 1986. 'Politics unbound', in C. Maier, ed., *Changing Boundaries of the Political: Essays on the Evolving Balance between the State and Society, Public and Private in Europe*, pp. 27–62. Cambridge: Cambridge University Press.

Pizzorno, A. 1987. 'I mafiosi come classe media violenta', *Polis*, 1(1): 195–204.

Pizzorno, A. 1993. *Le radici della politica assoluta e altri saggi*. Milan: Feltrinelli.

Plastino, G. 2012. *Cosa Nostra Social Club. Mafia, malavita e musica in Italia*. Milan: il Saggiatore.

Plummer, K. 2000. *Documents of Life 2*. London: Sage.

Poggi, G. 1978. *The Development of the Modern State*. Stanford: Stanford University Press.

Poggi, G. 1991. *The State. Its Nature, Development and Prospects.* Stanford: Stanford University Press.

Polanyi, M. 1958. *Personal Knowledge: Towards a Post-Critical Philosophy.* Chicago: University of Chicago Press.

Polanyi, M. 1966. *The Tactic Dimension.* Garden City: Doubleday.

Polese, A. 2008. '"If I receive it, it is a gift; if I demand it, then it is a bribe": On the Local meaning of economic transactions in post-Soviet Ukraine', *Anthropology in Action*, 15(3): 47–60.

Pontieri, E. 1943. *Il tramonto del baronaggio siciliano.* Florence: Sansoni.

Pontieri, E. 1945. *Il riformismo borbonico del Sette e dell'Ottocento.* Rome: Perella.

Popper, K. 2002 [1963]. *Conjectures and Refutation: The Growth of Scientific Knowledge*, 3rd edn. London: Routledge.

Posner, R.A. 1979. 'The Homeric version of the minimal state', *Ethics*, 90(1): 27–46.

Pottenger, M. 2014. 'Moving beyond the rational choice debate via social capital: The study of illegal private protection', *Australian Journal of Political Science*, 49: 267–81.

Puccio-Den, D. 2011. '"Dieu vous bénisse et vous protège!" La correspondance secrète du chef de la mafia sicilienne Bernardo Provenzano (1993–2006)', *Revue de l'Histoire des Religions*, 228(2): 307–326.

Puccio-Den, D. 2019. 'Mafiacraft: How to do things with silence', *HAU: Journal of Ethnographic Theory*, 9(3): 599–618.

Putnam, R.D. 1993. *Making Democracy Work: Civic Traditions in Modern Italy.* Princeton: Princeton University Press.

Puzo, M. 1969. *The Godfather.* London: Heinemann.

Puzo, M. 1972. *The Godfather Papers and Other Confessions.* New York: Putnam.

Pye, L. 1992. *Chinese Negotiating Style: Commercial Approaches and Cultural Principles.* New York: Quorum.

Pyyhtinen, O. 2014. *The Gift and Its Paradoxes: Beyond Mauss.* London: Routledge.

Qi, X. 2013. 'Guanxi, social capital theory and beyond: Toward a globalized social science', *British Journal of Sociology*, 64(2): 308–324.

Raith, W. 1992. *Parasiten und Patrone: Siziliens Mafia greift nach der Macht.* Frankfurt: Fischer.

Rakopoulos, T. 2017. 'Façade egalitarianism? Mafia and cooperative in Sicily'. *PoLAR*, 40: 104–121.

Rancière, J. 1998. *Disagreement: Politics and Philosophy.* Minneapolis: Minnesota University Press.

Ravveduto, M. 2019. *Lo spettacolo della mafia. Storia di un immaginario tra realtà e finzione.* Soveria Mannelli: Rubbettino.

Raz, J. 1992. 'Self-presentation and performance in the yakuza way of life: Fieldwork with a Japanese underworld group', in R. Goodman and K. Refsing, eds, *Ideology and Practice in Modern Japan*, pp. 210–233. London: Routledge.

Reale C., ed. 2010. *Io accuso. Tutti i verbali di Gaspare Spatuzza.* Palermo: I Libri di S.

Reclus, E. 1891. *Primitive Folk. Studies in Comparative Ethnology*. London: Walter Scott.

Recupero, A. 1987. 'Ceti medi e "homines novi". Alle origini della mafia', *Polis* 1(2): 307–328

Reed-Danahay, D. 1995. 'The Kabyle and the French: Occidentalism in Bourdieu's *Theory of Practice*', in J. Carrier, ed., *Occidentalism: Images of the West*, pp. 61–84. Oxford: Clarendon Press.

Renda, F. 1988. *I Beati Paoli. Storia, letteratura e leggenda*. Palermo: Sellerio.

Renga, D. 2019 [2011]. *Mafia Movies: A Reader*, 2nd edn. Toronto: University of Toronto Press.

Reno, W. 1998. *Warlord Politics and African States*. London: Lynne Rienner.

Reno, W. 2011. *Warfare in Independent Africa: New Approaches to African History*. Cambridge: Cambridge University Press.

Reuter, P. 1983. *Disorganized Crime: Illegal Markets and the Mafia*. Cambridge: MIT Press.

Richani, N. 2010. 'Fragmentation of sovereignty and violent non-state actors in Colombia', in Klejda Mulaj, ed., *Violent Non-State Actors in World Politics*. New York: Columbia University Press.

Ringel, G. 1979. 'The Kawkiutl potlatch: History, economics, and symbols', *Ethnohistory*, 26(4): 347–362.

Ritter, H. 1948. 'Irrational solidarity groups: A socio-psychological study in connection with Ibn Khaldūn', *Oriens,* 1(1): 1–44.

Romano, S. 1918. *L'ordinamento giuridico*. Pisa: Enrico Spoerri. English trans., *The Legal Order*, ed. and trans. M. Croce. New York: Routledge, 2017.

Rosen, L. 2002. 'Constructing institutions in a political culture of personalism', in L. Rosen, *The Culture of Islam: Changing Aspects of Contemporary Muslim Life*, pp. 56–72. Chicago: University of Chicago Press.

Rosen, L. 2005. 'Theorizing from within: Ibn Khaldūn and his political culture', *Contemporary Sociology*, 34(6): 596–599.

Rossi, N. 2014. 'Breaking the nexus: Conceptualising "illicit sovereigns"', *Global Crime*, 15(3–4): 299–319.

Rudolph, S.H. 2005. 'The imperialism of categories: Situating knowledge in a globalizing world', *Asian Studies*, 3(1): 5–14.

Rudolph, L.I. and Jacobsen, J.K., eds. 2006. *Experiencing the State*. New Delhi: Oxford University Press.

Rudolph, L.I. and Rudolph, S.H., 2010. 'Federalism as state formation in India: A theory of shared and negotiated sovereignty', *International Political Science Review*, 31(5): 1–21.

Ruff, I. 1974. 'Can there be a sociology of literature?' *British Journal of Sociology*, 25(3): 367–372.

Ruggie, J.G. 1993. 'Territoriality and beyond: Problematizing modernity in international relations', *International Organization*, 47(1): 139–174.

Runciman, W.G. 1982. 'Origins of states: The case of Archaic Greece', *Comparative Studies in Society and History*, 24(3): 351–377.

Sabetti, F. 1984. *Political Authority in a Sicilian Village*. New Brunswick: Rutgers University Press.

Sabetti, F. 1987. 'Village politics in Sicily: A response to Peter Schneider', *Journal of Peasant Studies*, 14(4): 549–554.

Sabetti, F. 2002. *Village Politics and the Mafia in Sicily*. Montreal: McGill-Queen's University Press.

Sabetti, F. 2011. 'Stationary bandits. Lessons from the practice of research in Sicily', in *Sociologica*, 2. https://www.rivisteweb.it/doi/10.2383/35871.

Sacks, P.M. 1976. *The Donegal Mafia: An Irish Political Machine*. New Haven: Yale University Press.

Sahlins, M. 1968. 'Philosophie politique de l'*Essai sur le don*', *L'Homme*, 8(4): 5–17.

Sahlins, M. 1972. *Stone Age Economics*. Chicago: Aldine.

Sahlins, M. 2008. 'The stranger-king or, elementary forms of the politics of life', *Indonesia and the Malay World*, 36(105): 177–199.

Said, E. 1978. *Orientalism*. New York: Pantheon Books.

Santino, U. 1994. *La mafia come soggetto politico*. Palermo: Centro Siciliano di Documentazione Peppino Impastato.

Santino, U. 1995. *La mafia interpretata*. Soveria Mannelli: Rubbettino.

Santino, U. 2009. *Storia del movimento antimafia*. Roma: Editori Riuniti.

Santino, U. 2015. *Per una storia delle idee di mafia*, in M. Santoro, ed., *Riconoscere le mafie*, pp. 37–72. Bologna: il Mulino.

Santino, U. 2017. *La mafia dimenticata*. Milan: Melampo.

Santoro, M. 1995. 'La mafia e la protezione. Tre quesiti e una proposta', *Polis*, 9(2): 285–299.

Santoro, M. 1998. 'Mafia cultura e politica', *Rassegna italiana di sociologia*, 4: 441–476.

Santoro, M. 2000. 'Oltre lo stato, dentro la mafia. Note per l'analisi culturale di una istituzione politica', *Teoria politica*, XVI(2): 97–117; repr. in M. Santoro, *La voce del padrino. Mafia, cultura e politica*. Verona: Ombrecorte, 2007.

Santoro, M. 2007. *La voce del padrino. Mafia, cultura e politica*. Verona: Ombrecorte.

Santoro, M. 2010. 'Effetto mafia', *Polis*, XXIV(3): 441–456.

Santoro, M. 2011. 'Introduction. The mafia and the sociological imagination', in *Sociologica*, 2. https://www.rivisteweb.it/doi/10.2383/35868.

Santoro, M. 2013. 'Empire for the poor: Colonial dreams and the quest for an Italian sociology, 1870–1950', in G. Steinmetz, ed., *Sociology and Empire: The Imperial Entanglements of a Discipline*, pp. 106–165. Durham: Duke University Press.

Santoro, M. 2019. 'Mafiacraft, witchcraft, statecraft, or the politics of mafia knowledge and the knowledge of mafia politics', *HAU: Journal of Ethnographic Theory*, 9(3): 631–637.

Santoro, M. and Solaroli, M. 2016. 'Contesting culture: Bourdieu and the strong program in cultural sociology', in *Routledge International Handbook of the Sociology of Art and Culture*, pp. 49–76. New York, Routledge.

Santoro, M. and Solaroli, M. 2017. 'Forme di capitale mafioso e risonanza culturale. Studio di un caso regionale e proposta di una strategia concettuale', *POLIS*, XXXI: 375–408.

Santoro, M., Gallelli, A. and Grüning, B. 2018. 'Bourdieu's international circulation: An exercise in intellectual mapping', in *The Oxford Handbook of Pierre Bourdieu*, pp. 21–67. New York, Oxford University Press.

Sassatelli, R. 2007. *Consumer Culture*. London: Sage.

Saviano, R. 2006. *Gomorra. Viaggio nell'impero economico e nel sogno di dominio della camorra*. Milan: Mondadori.

Saviano, R. 2007. *Gomorrah. A Personal Journey into the Violent International Empire of Naples' Organized Crime System*. New York: Farrar, Straus & Giroux.

Schatz, E. 2004. *Modern Clan Politics: The Power of 'Blood' in Kazakhstan and Beyond*. Seattle: University of Washington.

Schelling, T.C. 1960. *The Strategy of Conflict*. Cambridge: Harvard University Press.

Schelling, T.C. 1967. 'Economics and the criminal enterprise', *The Public Interest*, 7: 61–78.

Schelling, T.C. 1971. 'What is the business of organized crime?', *Journal of Public Law*, 20: 71–84.

Schelling, T.C. 1984. *Choice and Consequence*. Cambridge: Harvard University Press.

Schelling, T.C. 2006 [1978]. *Micromotives and Macrobehavior*. New York: Norton.

Scheper-Hughes, N. and Bourgois, P. 2003. 'Introduction: Making sense of violence', in N. Scheper-Hughes and P. Bourgois, eds, *Violence in War and Peace: An Anthology*, pp. 1–31. Oxford: Blackwell.

Scherma, G. 1896. *Delle maestranze in Sicilia contributo allo studio della questione operaia: Con documenti inediti*. Palermo: Reber.

Schmalenbach, H. 1961. 'The sociological category of communion', in T. Parsons, E. Shils, K. D. Naegele, and J. Pitt, eds, *Theories of Society*, vol. 1, New York: The Free Press.

Schmalenbach, H. 1977 [1922]. 'Communion: A sociological category', in H. Schmalenbach, *On Society and Experience*, pp. 64–125. Chicago: University of Chicago Press.

Schmitt, C. 1996 [1932]. *The Concept of the Political*. Chicago: University of Chicago Press.

Schneider, D.M. 1977. 'Kinship, nationality and religion in American culture. Toward a definition of kinship', in J.L. Dolgin, D.S. Kemnitzer and D.M. Schneider, eds., *Symbolic Anthropology*. New York: Columbia University Press.

Schneider, J., ed. 1998. *Italy's 'Southern Question': Orientalism in One Country*. Oxford: Berg.

Schneider, J. 2008. 'The Mafia', in W.A. Darity, Jr., ed., *International Encyclopedia of the Social Sciences*, 2nd edn., pp. 550–554. Detroit: Macmillan Reference USA.

Schneider, J. and Schneider, P. 1976. *Culture and Political Economy in Western Sicily*. New York: Academic Press.

Schneider, J. and Schneider, P. 1984. 'Mafia burlesque: The profane mass as a peace-making ritual', in E. Wolf, ed., *Religion, Power, and Protest in Local Communities*, pp. 117–136. Berlin: Mouton.

Schneider, J. and Schneider, P. 2002. 'The Mafia and al-Qaeda: Violent and secretive organizations in comparative and historical perspective', *American Anthropologist*, 104(3): 776–782.

Schneider, J. and Schneider, P. 2003. *Reversible Destiny. Mafia, Antimafia, and the Struggle for Palermo*. Berkeley: University of California Press.

Schneider, J. and Schneider, P. 2004. 'Mafias', in R. Nugent and J. Vincent, eds., *A Companion to Political Anthropology*. Oxford: Blackwell.

Schneider, J. and Schneider, P. 2006. 'Sicily: Reflections on forty years of change', *Journal of Modern Italian Studies*, 11: 61–83.

Schneider, J. and Schneider, P. 2011 'The mafia and capitalism. An emerging paradigm', in *Sociologica*, 2. https://www.rivisteweb.it/doi/10.2383/35873.

Schou, N. 2010. *Orange Sunshine: The Brotherhood of Eternal Love and Its Quest to Spread Peace, Love, and Acid to the World*. New York: Thomas Dunne Books.

Schumpeter, J.A. 1981. *Capitalism, Socialism and Democracy*. London: Allen & Unwin.

Schurtz, H. 1902. *Altersklassen und Männerbünde. Eine Darstellung der Gesellschaft*. Berlin: Reimer.

Schwarz, H. 2010. *Constructing the Criminal Tribe in Colonial India: Acting Like a Thief*. Oxford: Backwell.

Sciarrone, R. 2009 [1998]. *Mafie vecchie, mafie nuove*. Rome: Donzelli.

Sciarrone, R., ed. 2014. *Mafie al nord*. Rome: Donzelli.

Sciarrone, R. 2018. 'Forms of capital and mafia violence', in M. Massari and V. Martone, eds, *Mafia Violence: Political, Symbolic, and Economic Forms of Violence in Camorra Clans*, pp. 72–89. London: Routledge.

Sciascia, L. 1961. *Il giorno della civetta*. Torino: Einaudi. English trans., *The Day of the Owl*. New York: NYRB Classics, 2003.

Sciascia, L. 1979. *Dalle parti degli infedeli*. Palermo: Sellerio.

Scott, J.C. 1969. 'Corruption, machine politics, and political change', *American Political Science Review*, 63(4): 1142–1158.

Scott, J.C. 1985. *Weapons of the Weak. Everyday Forms of Peasant Resistance*. New Haven: Yale University Press.

Scott, J.C. 1990. *Domination and the Arts of Resistance. Hidden Transcripts*. New Haven: Yale University Press.

Scott, J.C. 1998. *Seeing like a State. How Certain Schemes to Improve the Human Condition Have Failed*. New Haven: Yale University Press.

Scott, J.C. 2010. *The Art of Not Being Governed. An Anarchist History of Upland Southeast Asia*. New Haven: Yale University Press.

Scott, J.C. 2012. *Two Cheers for Anarchism: Six Easy Pieces on Autonomy, Dignity, and Meaningful Work and Play*. Princeton: Princeton University Press.

Sent, E.-M. 2007. 'Some like it cold: Thomas Schelling as a Cold Warrior', *Journal of Economic Methodology*, 14(4): 455–471.

Service, E.R. 1962. *Primitive Social Organization. An Evolutionary Perspective*. New York: Random House.

Sewell, W.H. 1980. *Work and Revolution in France: The Language of Labor from the Old Regime to 1848*, Cambridge: Cambridge University Press.

Sewell, W.H. 2005. *Logics of History*. Chicago: University of Chicago Press.

Shanin, T. 1971. 'Peasantry as a political factor', in T. Shanin, ed., *Peasants and Peasant Societies*, pp. 238–630. Harmondsworth: Penguin.

Sharma, A. and Gupta, A., eds. 2006. *The Anthropology of the State: A Reader*. Oxford: Blackwell Publishing.

Shaw, M. 2015. Drug trafficking in Guinea-Bissau, 1998–2014: The evolution of an elite protection network. *Journal of Modern African Studies*, 53(3): 339–364.

Shaw, M. and Mangan, F. 2014. *Illicit Trafficking and Libya's Transition: Profits and Losses*. Washington: US Institute of Peace Press.

Shelley, L. 1995. 'Post-Soviet organized crime and the rule of law', *Journal of Marshall Law Review*, 28: 827–829.

Shils, E. 1957. 'Primordial, personal, sacred and civil ties', *British Journal of Sociology*, 8: 130–145.

Shortland, A. and Varese, F. 2014. 'The protector's choice: An application of protection theory to Somali piracy', *British Journal of Criminology*, 54(5): 741–764.

Shortland, A. and Varese, F. 2016. 'State-building, informal governance and organised crime: The case of Somali piracy', *Political Studies*, 64(4): 811–831.

Shryock, A. 2012. 'Breaking hospitality apart: Bad hosts, bad guests, and the problem of sovereignty', *Journal of the Royal Anthropological Institute*, 18 (June): S20–S33.

Shryock, A. and Howell, S. 2001. 'Ever a guest in our house: The Emir Abdullah, Shaykh Majid al-Adwan, and the practice of Jordanian house politics, as remembered by Umm Sultan, the widow of Majid', *International Journal of Middle East Studies*, 33(2): 247–269.

Siebert, R. 1996. *Secrets of Life and Death: Women and the Mafia*. London: Verso.

Sigurdsson, J. 2017. *Viking Friendship: The Social Bond in Iceland and Norway, c. 900–1300*. Ithaca: Cornell University Press.

Silber, I. 2009. 'Bourdieu's gift to gift's theory: An unacknowledged trajectory', *Sociological Theory*, 27: 173–190.

Silver, A. 1989. 'Friendship and trust as moral ideals: An historical approach', *European Journal of Sociology*, 30: 274–297.

Silver, A. 1990. 'Friendship in commercial society: Eighteenth-century social theory and modern sociology', *American Journal of Sociology*, 95(6): 1474–1504.

Simmel, G. 1950 [1906]. 'The sociology of secrecy and of secret societies', in *The Sociology of Georg Simmel*, ed. and trans. K.H. Wolff. New York: The Free Press.

Simmel, G. 2009 [1908]. *Sociology: Inquiries into the Construction of Social Forms*, vol. 1. Leiden: Brill.

Simon, F. 2021. 'The economist and the secret agent. Strategies to introduce the British model of society into Sicily of 1812', *European Journal of the History of Economic Thought*. https://doi.org/10.1080/09672567.2020.1849338.

Siniawer, E.M. 2008. *Ruffians, Yakuza, Nationalists: The Violent Politics of Modern Japan, 1860–1960*. Ithaca: Cornell University Press.

Siniawer, E.M. 2012. 'Befitting bedfellows: Yakuza and the state in modern Japan', *Journal of Social History*, 45(3), 623–641.

Sives, A. 2002. 'Changing patrons, from politician to drug don: Clientelism in downtown Kingston, Jamaica', *Latin American Perspectives*, 29(5): 66–89.

Skalnik, P. 2004. 'Chiefdom. A universal political formation?' *Focaal*, 43: 77–98.

Skaperdas, S. 2001. 'The political economy of organized crime: Providing protection when the state does not', *Economics of Governance*, 2(3): 173–202.

Skaperdas, S. and Syropoulos, C. 1995. 'Gangs as primitive states', in G. Fiorentini and S. Peltzman, eds, *The Economics of Organised Crime*, pp. 61–81. Cambridge: Cambridge University Press.

Skarbek, D. 2011. 'Governance and prison gangs', *American Political Science Review*, 105(4): 702–716.

Skarbek, D. 2014. *The Social Order of the Underworld: How Prison Gangs Govern the American Penal System*. Oxford: Oxford University Press.

Slade, G. 2012. 'No country for made men: The decline of the mafia in post-Soviet Georgia', *Law & Society Review*, 46(3): 623–649.

Slomp, G. 2007. 'Carl Schmitt on friendship: Polemics and diagnostics', *Critical Review of International Social and Political Philosophy*, 10(2): 199–213.

Smart, A. 1993. 'Gifts, bribes, and *guanxi*: A reconsideration of Bourdieu's social capital', *Cultural Anthropology*, 8: 388–408.

Smith, C. 2011. *What Is a Person? Rethinking Humanity, Social Life, and the Moral Good from the Person Up*. Chicago: University of Chicago Press.

Smith, D.C. 1990 [1975]. *The Mafia Mystique*. New York: University Press of America.

Smith, D.J. 2006. 'Violent vigilantism and the state in Nigeria. The case of the Bakassi Boys', in E.G. Bay and D.L. Donham, eds, *States of Violence. Politics, Youth, and Memory in Contemporary Africa*, pp. 127–147. Charlottesville: University of Virginia Press.

Smith, D.J. 2007. *A Culture of Corruption. Everyday Deception and Popular Discontent in Nigeria*. Princeton: Princeton University Press.

Smith, P., ed. 1998. *The New American Cultural Sociology*. Oxford: Blackwell.

Smith, P. 2001. *Cultural Theory. An Introduction*. Oxford: Blackwell.

Smith, P. 2005. *Why War? The Cultural Logic of Iraq, The Gulf War, and Suez*. Chicago: University of Chicago Press.

Sneed, P. 2007. 'Bandidos de Cristo: Representations of the power of criminal factions in Rio's Proibidão funk', *Latin American Music Review/Revista De Música Latinoamericana*, 28(2): 220–241.

Sondern, F. 1959. *Brotherhood of Evil: The Mafia*. London: Victor Gollancz.

Soysal, Y.N. 1994. *Limits of Citizenship: Migrants and Postnational Membership in Europe*. Chicago: University of Chicago Press.

Spruyt, H. 1994. *The Sovereign State and Its Competitors*. Princeton: Princeton University Press.

Spruyt, H. 2002. 'The origins, development, and possible decline of the modern state', *Annual Review of Political Science*, 5: 127–149.

Stajano, C. 1986. *Mafia: l'atto d'accusa dei giudici di Palermo*. Rome: Editori Riuniti.

Stark, D. 2013. *The sense of dissonance*, Princeton: Princeton University Press.

Starr, P. 1988. 'The meaning of privatization', *Yale Law & Policy Review*, 6(1): 6–41.

Steinmetz, G. ed. 1999. *State/Culture*. Durham: Duke University Press.

Sterling, C. 1990. *Octopus. The Long Reach of the International Sicilian Mafia*. New York: Norton.

Stewart, P. and Strathern, A. 2004. *Witchcraft, Sorcery, Rumors, and Gossip*. Cambridge: Cambridge University Press.

Stinchcombe, A.S. 1959. 'Bureaucratic and craft administration of production: A comparative study', *Administrative Science Quarterly*, 4(2): 168–187.

Stinchcombe, A.S. 1968. *Constructing Social Theories*. New York: Harcourt, Brace & World.

Stirrat, R.L. 1989. 'Money, men and women', in J. Parry and M. Bloch, eds, *Money and the Morality of Exchange*, pp. 94–117. New York: Cambridge University Press.

Strayer, J.R. 1964. 'A model state in the Middle Ages: The Norman and Swabian Kingdom of Sicily: Comment', *Comparative Studies in Society and History*, 6(3): 321–324.

Strayer, J.R. 1970. *On the Medieval Origins of the Modern State*. Princeton: Princeton University Press.

Sundberg, M. 2019. 'Brotherhood as a social relationship', in G. Ahrne and N. Brunsson, eds, *Organization Outside Organization: The Abundance of Partial Organization in Social Life*. Cambridge: Cambridge University Press.

Swartz, M.J., ed. 1969. *Local-level Politics: Social and Cultural Perspectives*. London: University of London Press.

Swartz, M.J., Turner, V.W. and Tuden, A. 1966. 'Introduction', in M.J. Swartz, V.W. Turner and A. Tuden, eds, *Political Anthropology*, pp. 1–41. Chicago: Aldine Atherton.

Swidler, A. 1986. 'Culture in action: Symbols and strategies', *American Sociological Review*, 51(2): 273–286.

Sykes, K. 2005. *Arguing with Anthropology: An Introduction to Critical Theories of the Gift*. London: Routledge.

Szelenyi, I. 2019. 'Paternal domination and the mafia state under post-communism', *Theory and Society*, 48: 639–644.

Takayama, H. 2019. *Sicily and the Mediterranean in the Middle Ages*. New York: Routledge.

Tamassia, G. 1886. *L'affratellamento*. Turin: Bocca.

Tarrow, S. 2006. 'From Villamaura to Palermo: Two songs of the Mafia', *Journal of Modern Italian Studies*, 11(1): 16-21.

Taussig, M. 1980. *The Devil and Commodity Fetishism in South America*. Chapel Hill: University of North Carolina Press.

Taussig, M. 1999. *Defacement: Pubic Secrecy and the Labor of the Negative*. Stanford: Stanford University Press.

Taylor, M. 1982. *Community, Anarchy and Liberty*. Cambridge: Cambridge University Press.

ter Haar, B.J. 1998. *Ritual and Mythology of the Chinese Triads*. Leiden: Brill.

Testart, A. 1998. 'Uncertainties of the "obligation to reciprocate": A critique of Mauss', in W. James and N.J. Allen, eds, *Marcel Mauss: A Centenary Tribute*, pp. 97–110. New York: Berghahn Books.

Thomas, N. 1991. *Entangled Objects: Exchange, Material Culture, and Colonialism in the Pacific*. Cambridge: Harvard University Press.

Thomas, T., Malik, A. and Wellman, R.E., eds. 2017. *New Directions in Spiritual Kinship. Sacred Ties across the Abrahamic Religions*. New York: Palgrave.

Thompson, E.P. 1975. *Whigs and Hunters: The Origin of the Black Act*. London: Allen Lane.

Thompson, J.B. 1995. *Media and Modernity: A Social Theory of the Media*. Cambridge: Polity.

Thompson, J.E. 1994. *Mercenaries, Pirates, and Sovereigns*. Princeton: Princeton University Press.

Thrasher, F. 1927. *The Gang: A Study on 1,313 Gangs in Chicago*. Chicago: Chicago University Press.

Tilly, C. 1974. 'Forward', in A. Blok, *The Mafia of a Sicilian Village, 1860–1960*. New York: Harper & Row.

Tilly, C., ed. 1975. *The Formation of National States in Western Europe*. Princeton: Princeton University Press.

Tilly, C. 1978. *From Mobilization to Revolution*. Reading: Addison-Wesley.

Tilly, C. 1985. 'War-making and state-making as organized crime', in P. Evans, D. Rueschemeyer and T. Skocpol, eds, *Bringing the State Back In*, pp. 169–191. Cambridge: Cambridge University

Tilly, C. 1990. *Coercion, Capital and European States, AD 990–1990*. Oxford: Blackwell.

Tilly, C. 1995. 'Contentious repertoires in Great Britain, 1758–1834', in M. Traugott, ed., *Repertoires and Cycles of Collective Action*, pp. 43–56. Durham: Duke University Press.

Titmuss, R. 1997 [1970]. *The Gift Relationship*. New York: The New Press.

Traugott, M. ed., 1995. *Repertoires and Cycles of Collective Action*. Durham: Duke University Press.

Trejo, G. and Ley, S. 2021. 'High-profile criminal violence: Why drug cartels murder government officials and party candidates in Mexico', *British Journal of Political Science*, 51(1): 203–229.

Turner, V. 1969. *The Ritual Process: Structure and Anti-Structure*. New York: Aldine de Gruyter.

Turner, V. 1974. *Dramas, Fields, and Metaphors: Symbolic Action in Human Society*. Ithaca: Cornell University Press.

Tzvetkova, M. 2008. 'Aspects of the evolution of extra-legal protection in Bulgaria (1989–1999)', *Trends in Organized Crime*, 11: 326–351.

Uberoi, J.P.S. 1962. *Politics of the Kula Ring: An Analysis of the Findings of Bronislaw Malinowski*. Manchester: Manchester University Press.

Udehn, L. 1996. *The Limits of Public Choice: A Sociological Critique of the Economic Theory of Politics*. New York: Routledge.

Vaksberg, A. 1991. *The Soviet Mafia*. New York: St Martin's Press.

Vaishnav, M. 2017. *When Crime Pays: Money and Muscle in Indian Politics*. New Haven: Yale University Press.

Valeri, V. 1994. 'Buying women but not selling them: Gift and commodity exchange in Huaulu alliance', *Man*, 29(1): 1–26.

van der Pijl, K. 2007. 'The conquest of the oceans: Ethnogenesis of the West', in K. van der Pijl, *Nomads, Empires, States: Modes of Foreign Relations and Political Economy*, vol. I, pp. 110–163. London: Pluto Press.

van Wees, H. 1999. 'The mafia of early Greece: Violent exploitation in the seventh and sixth centuries BC', in K. Hopwood, ed., *Organised Crime in Antiquity*. London: Duckworth.

van Wees, H. 2001. 'Megara's Mafiosi: Timocracy and violence in Theognis', in R. Brock and S. Hodkinson, eds, *Alternatives to Athens: Varieties of Political Organization and Community in Ancient Greece*, pp. 52–67. Oxford: Oxford University Press.

Varese, F. 1994. 'Is Sicily the future of Russia? Private protection and the rise of the Russian Mafia', *European Journal of Sociology*, 35(2): 224–258.

Varese, F. 2001. *The Russian Mafia*. Oxford: Oxford University Press.

Varese, F. 2006. 'The secret history of Japanese cinema: The Yakuza movies', *Global Crime*, 7: 105–124.

Varese, F. 2010. 'What is organized crime?' in F. Varese, ed., *Organized Crime: Critical Concepts in Criminology*, vol. 1, pp. 1–33, London: Routledge.

Varese, F. 2011. *Mafia on the Move. How Organized Crime Conquers New Territories*. Princeton: Princeton University Press.

Varese, F. 2014. 'Protection and extortion', in L. Paoli, ed., *The Oxford Handbook of Organized Crime*, pp. 343–58. Oxford: Oxford University Press.

Varese, F. 2017. *Mafia Life. Love, Death and Money at the Heart of Organised Crime*. London, Profile Books.

Vassalli, S. 1993. *Il cigno*. Turin: Einaudi.

Veblen, T. 1994 [1899]. *The Theory of the Leisure Class*. New York: Dover.

Veyne, P. 1992 [1976]. *Bread and Circuses: Historical Sociology and Political Pluralism*. London, Penguin Books.

Vierkandt, A., ed. 1931. *Handwörterbuch der Soziologie*. Stuttgart: F. Enke.

Vinci, A. 2013. *Gaspare Mutolo. La mafia non lascia tempo*. Milan: Rizzoli.

Volkov, V. 1999. 'Violent entrepreneurship in post-communist Russia', *Europe-Asia Studies,* 51(5): 741–754.

Volkov, V. 2002. *Violent Entrepreneurs. The Use of Force in the Making of Russian Capitalism*. Ithaca: Cornell University Press.

de Waal, F. 2007 [1982]. *Chimpanzee Politics: Power and Sex among Apes*. Baltimore: Johns Hopkins University Press.

Wacquant, L.J.D. 1993. 'On the tracks of symbolic power: Prefatory notes to Bourdieu's 'State Nobility', *Theory, Culture & Society*, 10(3): 1–17.

Wagner, K.A. 2007. *Thuggee: Banditry and the British in Early Nineteenth-Century India*. Houndmills: Palgrave Macmillan.

Wallerstein, I. 1974. *The Modern World-System*, vol. 1. London: Academic Press.

Wang, P. 2011. 'The Chinese mafia: Private protection in a socialist market economy', *Global Crime*, 12(4): 290–311.

Wang, P. 2017. *The Chinese Mafia: Organized Crime, Corruption, and Extra-legal Protection*. Oxford: Oxford University Press.

Wanner, C. 2005. 'Money, morality and new forms of exchange in post-socialist Ukraine', *Ethnos*, 70(4): 515–537.

Washburn, S.L. and Lancaster, C.S. 1968. 'The evolution of hunting', in R.B. Lee and I. DeVore, eds., *Man the Hunter*. London: Routledge.

Watts, M.J. 2016. 'The mafia of a Sicilian village, 1860–1960: A study of violent peasant entrepreneurs, by Anton Blok', *Journal of Peasant Studies*, 43(1): 67–91.

Weatherford, J.M. 1981. *Tribes on the Hill*. South Hadley: Bergin & Garvey.

Weber, M. 1978 [1922]. *Economy and Society. An Outline of Interpretive Sociology*, 3 vols, ed. G. Roth and C. Wittich. Berkeley: University of California Press.

Webster, H. 1908. *Primitive Secret Societies. A Study in Early Politics and Religion*. London: Macmillan.

Weintraub J. 1997. 'The theory and politics of the public/private distinction', in J. Weintraub and K. Kumar, eds, *Public and Private in Thought and Practice*, pp. 1–42. Chicago: University of Chicago Press.

Werner, C.A. 2002. 'Gifts, bribes and development in post-Soviet Kazakhstan', in J.H. Cohen and N. Dannhaeuser, eds, *Economic Development: An Anthropological Approach*, pp. 183–208. Walnut Creek: Altamira Press.

White, S.D. 2009. 'Protection, warranty, and vengeance in *La Chanson de Roland*', in T.B. Lambert and D. Rollason, eds, *Peace and Protection in the Middle Ages*, pp. 155–167. Centre for Medieval and Renaissance Studies, Durham University.

Whiting, R. 1999. *Tokyo Underworld. The Fast Times and Hard Life of an American Gangster in Japan*. New York: Knopf Doubleday.

Whyte, W.F. 1943. *Street Corner Society: The Social Structure of an Italian Slum*. Chicago: University of Chicago Press.

Whyte, W.F. 1955 [1943]. *Street Corner Society. The Social Structure of an Italian Slum*. Chicago: University of Chicago Press.

Wilson, E. 2009. 'Deconstructing the shadows', in E. Wilson, ed., *Government of the Shadows: Parapolitics and Criminal Sovereignty*. London: Pluto Press.

Wilson, E.O. 1975. *Sociobiology: The New Synthesis*. Cambridge: Belknap Press of Harvard University Press.

Wilson, D. 2015. *The Politics of Protection Rackets in Post-New Order Indonesia: Coercive Capital, Authority and Street Politics*. London: Routledge.

Wimmer, A. and Glick Schiller, N. 2002. 'Methodological nationalism and beyond: Nation-state building, migration and the social sciences', *Global Networks*, 2: 301–334.

Witsoe, J. 2011. 'Corruption as power: Caste and the political imagination of the postcolonial state', *American Ethnologist*, 38: 73–85.

Wittgenstein, L. (1958). *The Blue and Brown Books*, ed. R. Rhees, Oxford: Blackwell.

Wolf, D.R. 1991. *The Rebels: A Brotherhood of Outlaw Bikers*. Toronto: University of Toronto Press.

Wolfgang, M.E. and Ferracuti, F. 1967. *The Subculture of Violence*. London: Tavistock Publications.

Yang, M.M. 1994. *Gifts, Favors, and Banquets: The Art of Social Relationships in China*. Ithaca: Cornell University Press.

Yeager, M.G. 2013. 'On the importance of being John Landesco', *Trends in Organized Crime*, 18: 143–56.

Zagari, A. 2008 [1992]. *Ammazzare stanca*. Milan: Aliberti.

Zelizer, V.A. 1994. *The Social Meaning of Money*. New York: Basic Books.

Zinoviev, A. 1979. *The Yawning Heights*. New York: Random House.

Zitara, N. 2010. *L'Unità d'Italia: Nascita di una colonia*. Milan: Jaca Book.

Zitara, N. 2011. *L'invenzione del mezzogiorno. Una storia finanziaria*. Milan: Jaca Book.

Zurbach, J. 2010. 'La "société homérique" et le don', *Gaia: Revue Interdisciplinaire sur la Grèce Archaïque*, 13: 57–79.

Name Index

Subject Index

෭ඁ